Selling War and Peace

By analysing Anglosphere foreign policy debates during the Syrian Civil War from 2011 to 2019, this book provides a significant contribution to the literature in three fields. First, it analyses the entirety of the Syrian Civil War in an innovative four-phase chronology, as the conflict evolved from calls for democracy, through chemical weapons concerns, to the rise of ISIL and the onset of a Great Power proxy war. Second, the book maps and theorises Anglosphere foreign policy, charting the history and future of the US–UK–Australian military alliance during a key period of political uncertainty, defined by Donald Trump's presidency and the UK's Brexit negotiations. Third, the book develops a post-constructivist framework for the analysis of transnational political debates that determine war and peace in Syria and beyond. This framework emphasises the hard nature of soft power and the coercion of political opponents through forceful words.

JACK HOLLAND is Associate Professor in International Security at the University of Leeds. He is the author of *Selling the War on Terror: Foreign Policy Discourses after 9/11* (2012) and *Fictional Television and American Politics: From 9/11 to Donald Trump* (2019) and co-author of *Security: A Critical Introduction* (2014). He is also co-editor of *Obama's Foreign Policy: Ending the War on Terror* (2013) and *The Obama Doctrine: A Legacy of Continuity in Foreign Policy?* (2016). Alongside these books, he has published in journals such as the *European Journal of International Relations*, *International Political Sociology* and *Review of International Studies*.

Selling War and Peace

Syria and the Anglosphere

JACK HOLLAND
University of Leeds

CAMBRIDGE
UNIVERSITY PRESS

CAMBRIDGE
UNIVERSITY PRESS

University Printing House, Cambridge CB2 8BS, United Kingdom

One Liberty Plaza, 20th Floor, New York, NY 10006, USA

477 Williamstown Road, Port Melbourne, VIC 3207, Australia

314–321, 3rd Floor, Plot 3, Splendor Forum, Jasola District Centre,
New Delhi – 110025, India

79 Anson Road, #06–04/06, Singapore 079906

Cambridge University Press is part of the University of Cambridge.

It furthers the University's mission by disseminating knowledge in the pursuit of
education, learning, and research at the highest international levels of excellence.

www.cambridge.org
Information on this title: www.cambridge.org/9781108489249
DOI: 10.1017/9781108774314

First published 2020

Printed in the United Kingdom by TJ International Ltd. Padstow Cornwall

A catalogue record for this publication is available from the British Library.

Library of Congress Cataloging-in-Publication Data
Names: Holland, Jack, 1984– author.
Title: Selling war and peace : Syria and the Anglosphere / Jack Holland.
Description: Cambridge, United Kingdom ; New York, NY : Cambridge University Press,
    2020. | Includes bibliographical references and index.
Identifiers: LCCN 2019042010 (print) | LCCN 2019042011 (ebook) |
    ISBN 9781108489249 (hardback) | ISBN 9781108702171 (paperback) |
    ISBN 9781108774314 (epub)
Subjects: LCSH: United States–Foreign relations–Syria. | Syria–Foreign relations–
    United States. | Great Britain–Foreign relations–Syria. | Syria–Foreign relations–Great
    Britain. | Australia–Foreign relations–Syria. | Syria–Foreign relations–Australia. |
    Syria–Foreign relations–21st century. | Syria–History–Civil War, 2011-
Classification: LCC E183.8.S95 H65 2020 (print) | LCC E183.8.S95 (ebook) |
    DDC 327.7305691–dc23
LC record available at https://lccn.loc.gov/2019042010
LC ebook record available at https://lccn.loc.gov/2019042011

ISBN 978-1-108-48924-9 Hardback

Summary of Contents

Contents

Tables

Acknowledgements

During the course of writing this book, I started a new job, bought a house, got married and became a father! My wife, Linda, above all others, deserves a great deal of gratitude for supporting my writing efforts. Likewise, friends and family have helped make the last three years particularly memorable. And Leo's arrival has topped everything.

Along the way, several people have been great sounding boards, pushing me to refine my thinking. Friends, whether near the frontlines in Syria or in a pub in Leeds, have helped to motivate me to keep writing. This book emerges (phoenix like, perhaps) out of the ashes of one of the UK's top small Politics departments. And it has been completed, in part, thanks to the vibrancy of one of the country's largest. Friends and colleagues at Surrey and Leeds have, at times, been inspirational. In particular, I am grateful to Jason Ralph for involving me in his own research project on Syria and UK foreign policy. A great many others have offered help and feedback, including: Chris Browning, Gordon Clubb, Laura Considine, Ben Fermor, Tim Legrand, Xavier Mathieu, Eglantine Staunton, Srdjan Vucetic and Kalina Zhekova. Thank you all for your time in the ever more frenetic landscape of higher education.

Of course, the ideas and errors contained within this book remain my own. But it is important to acknowledge that all research – even when only one name features on the cover – is the product of a broader research community, comprised of engaged and committed experts. As we face a new era, in which the Anglosphere appears set to become more important than ever, the collective and critical endeavours of such experts will be vital. Their insights are imperative as part of a collective effort to confront and remedy the world's wrongs. I wrote this book, mainly and simply, because atrocities in Syria have been too terrible to ignore.

Abbreviations

ISIL	Islamic State of Iraq and the Levant
ISIS	Islamic State of Iraq and Syria (or Islamic State of Iraq and al-Sham)
KRG	Kurdish Regional Government
LGBT	Lesbian, gay, bisexual and transgender
MENA	Middle East and North Africa
NATO	North Atlantic Treaty Organization
NGO	Non-governmental organisation
NSC	National Security Council (US)
OPCW	Organisation for the Prohibition of Chemical Weapons
P2	Russia and China
P3	USA, United Kingdom and France
P5	The five permanent members of the UN Security Council
PKK	Kurdish Workers' Party
R2P	Responsibility to Protect
RAF	Royal Air Force (UK)
SDI	Strategic Defense Initiative (US)
SIF	Syrian Islamic Front
SNC	Syrian National Council
UK	United Kingdom
UN	United Nations
UNICEF	United Nations International Children's Emergency Fund
UNSC	United Nations Security Council
UNSCR	United Nations Security Council Resolution
US	United States
USA	United States of America
USAF	United States Air Force
USD	US dollar
WMD	Weapons of mass destruction
YPG	People's Protection Units (a Kurdish militia in Syria)

ISIL	Islamic State of Iraq and the Levant
ISIS	Islamic State of Iraq and Syria (or Islamic State of Iraq and al-Sham)
KRG	Kurdish Regional Government
LGBT	Lesbian, gay, bisexual and transgender
MENA	Middle East and North Africa
NATO	North Atlantic Treaty Organization
NGO	Non-governmental organisation
NSC	National Security Council (US)
OPCW	Organisation for the Prohibition of Chemical Weapons
P2	Russia and China
P3	USA, United Kingdom and France
P5	The five permanent members of the UN Security Council
PKK	Kurdish Workers' Party
R2P	Responsibility to Protect
RAF	Royal Air Force (UK)
DI	Strategic Defense Initiative (US)
SIF	Syrian Islamic Front
SNC	Syrian National Council
UK	United Kingdom
UN	United Nations
UNICEF	United Nations International Children's Emergency Fund
UNSC	United Nations Security Council
UNSCR	United Nations Security Council Resolution
US	United States
USA	United States of America
USAF	United States Air Force
USD	US dollar
WMD	Weapons of mass destruction
YPG	People's Protection Units (a Kurdish militia in Syria)

Introduction

One Syrian in twenty has been killed or wounded; one in five is a refugee; one in two has been displaced; the average life expectancy in Syria has dropped twenty years.

US Secretary of State John Kerry[1]

Why Syria?

In October 2014, Islamic State released a video showing Mohammed Emwazi, the notorious 'Jihadi John', beheading Alan Henning with a knife. Emwazi grew up in North Kensington in West London and was described by various acquaintances as shy, football mad, a model employee and an IT genius. He first travelled to Syria in 2012, having been radicalised over the previous three years. Henning was a taxi driver from Salford in Greater Manchester, who was on his third convoy, bringing humanitarian aid to Syria. The video showed one Briton killing another, in the most horrific manner, set against the backdrop of the Syrian Desert and British foreign policy. The video explained that the execution was in response to the fact a 'seven-hour long debate in the British Parliament has culminated in a landslide approval of UK strikes on Islamic State positions in Iraq'. Emwazi insisted that Henning's 'blood is on the hands of the British parliament'.[2]

One year later, on a Wednesday morning in September 2015, a three-year-old Syrian boy named Aylan (since revised to Alan) Kurdi washed up on a beach in Bodrum, Turkey. His father, Abdullah, had paid people smugglers €4,000 for the chance to take his family on the

[1] J. Kerry, 'Remarks at the United Nations Security Council meeting', 18 December 2015, www.state.gov/secretary/remarks/2015/12/250800.htm. The number of killed and injured Syrians has since risen to more than one in ten.
[2] Unlike earlier IS videos, which revelled in the detail of executions, these videos did not show the beheading itself, just its aftermath.

1

voyage to the Greek island of Kos. That voyage would be made in a five metre-long rubber dinghy, which the smugglers abandoned when the seas became rough. It soon overturned. Abdullah clung onto his wife and children for as long as he could, but 'one by one they were washed away by waves'.[3] Abdullah and his family were fleeing the siege of Kobani, in northern Syria, near the Turkish border. ISIL had slowly captured the city, before being repelled by a combination of Kurdish forces, the Free Syrian Army and Coalition airstrikes. Over the course of the previous year, the citizens of Kobani had suffered chemical weapons attacks,[4] as well as widespread torture, mutilation and rape.[5]

Two months after that Wednesday morning, on a Friday evening in Paris, Moroccan architect Mohamed Amine Benmbarek was dining with his new wife on the terrace of Le Carillon Café. A black Seat car pulled up and a man stepped out, coolly gunning down both.[6] Once done, the gunman crossed the road and shot at people inside Le Petit Cambodge restaurant. A few streets away, Café Bonne Biere and restaurant La Belle Equipe were next. Eight minutes later, a man took a seat in the Comptoir Voltaire Cafe and placed an order, shortly before blowing himself up. Across town, footballers Bacary Sagna and Patrice Evra hesitated at the Stade de France, as the sound of exploding suicide vests interrupted the match against Germany. And, at the same time, in the 11th arrondissement, the bodies of young

[3] A. Withnall, 'Aylan Kurdi's story', *The Independent*, 22 September 2015, www.independent.co.uk/news/world/europe/aylan-kurdi-s-story-how-a-small-syrian-child-came-to-be-washed-up-on-a-beach-in-turkey-10484588.html

[4] Widespread reports noted that ISIL used chemical weapons during the siege. See, for example, E. Graham-Harrison, 'Kurds fear Isis use of chemical weapon in Kobani', *The Guardian*, 24 October 2014, www.theguardian.com/world/2014/oct/24/kurds-fear-isis-chemical-weapon-kobani; andJ. Lederman, 'War with Isis: US investigating chemical weapons attacks against Kurds in Iraq', *The Independent*, 15 August 2015, www.independent.co.uk/news/world/middle-east/war-with-isis-us-investigating-chemical-weapons-attacks-against-kurds-in-iraq-10456619.html

[5] C. James, 'Tales of torture, mutilation and rape as Isis targets key town of Kobani', *The Guardian*, 4 October 2014, www.theguardian.com/world/2014/oct/04/turkey-troops-isis-siege-kobani-refugees-rape-and-murder

[6] Widowed, his wife survived three gunshot wounds. For details of events, see, amongst many others, E. Steafel, 'Paris terror attack: everything we know on Saturday afternoon', *The Telegraph*, 21 November 2015, www.telegraph.co.uk/news/worldnews/europe/france/11995246/Paris-shooting-What-we-know-so-far.html

music fans were piling up in the Bataclan theatre, as three gunmen shot from the balcony.

It is not easy to make sense of Syria, which is why this book begins with three brief and relatively familiar stories – on radicalisation, refugees and terrorism – before turning to consider the situation on the ground.[7] It is likely that these are stories you have already heard. They are terrible and tragic and difficult to hear let alone imagine. But they are only the most obvious manifestations of the carnage wrought by the Syrian Civil War. And they are only obvious because of perceived proximity and media coverage. Topics such as radicalisation, refugees and terrorism receive disproportionate airtime compared with bloody, complex and enduring civil wars. For every Alan Henning, for every Alan Kurdi and Abdullah and for every Mohamed Benmbarek, there are near countless others. But counting is important, even if we can become numb to numbers difficult to comprehend.[8]

While Alan Henning was a new victim, the act and its perpetrator were already familiar to Anglosphere audiences. Henning's murder followed that of fellow Brit David Haines and Americans Steven Sotloff and James Foley. One hundred and thirty people died in the Paris Attacks of Friday 13 November 2015, with some 350 injured. Eighty of those deaths and 200 injuries were from the Bataclan alone. The actions of a security guard at the Stade de France, denying would-be bombers access to the stadium, surely saved many others, including potentially President François Hollande.[9] Alan Kurdi's death, too, was one of many. In 2015 alone, refugees made approximately half a

---

[7] It is also part of an important process of academic storytelling, touched on by Annick Wibben. See A. Wibben, 'How stories matter: thoughts on contextuality, temporality, reflexivity & certainty', *Duck of Minerva*, 29 December 2015, http://duckofminerva.com/2015/12/how-stories-matter.html#more-28374

[8] M. Breen-Smyth, 'When the past is present: the casualty, the body and its politics', inaugural lecture at the University of Surrey, 8 March 2012.

[9] That said, it is vital to contextualise the death toll. Even in 2015 – the worst year for political violence on French soil since World War II – French people were 4.5 times more likely to be the victim of ordinary homicide than terrorism. And, shockingly, French people were seventy times more likely to commit suicide than be killed in a terrorist act. In the two years after the financial crash of 2008, an *additional* 600 suicides were recorded that were directly attributable to the economic fallout across France. Yet suicide, mental health, job creation, re-skilling and resilience training are rarely spoken about with the same urgency as counter-terrorism, despite their far greater consequences. Data on causes of death are available from the World Health Organization.

million voyages across the Mediterranean Sea by boat.[10] Over 3,000 drowned attempting the crossing. This means that more refugees drowned in one year than perished in the events of 11 September 2001. And, in 2016, things got much worse.[11] But these figures remain fixated on events that 'we' have seen by virtue of 'our' televisions and newspapers. The most shockingly appalling data emerge from the battlefields that were once flourishing Syrian streets.

The Syrian conflict has created an estimated eight million internally displaced persons and nearly five million international refugees, which together amount to more than half of the total Syrian population. The majority of these refugees have found temporary sanctuary in neighbouring countries, such as Turkey, Jordan and Lebanon.[12] Worse still, the conflict has generated almost half a million Syrian casualties and around thirteen million people within Syria in urgent need of humanitarian assistance. In November 2015, US Secretary of State John Kerry noted that the crisis had been no less than 'four and a half years of non-stop horror. One Syrian in twenty has been wounded or killed. One in five is a refugee. One in two has been displaced. The average life expectancy dropped by 20 years'.[13] And these statistics continued to worsen, with one estimate, only three months later, reporting that 11.5 per cent of the Syrian population had been killed or wounded in the civil war.[14] The vast majority of these deaths were caused not by ISIL

---

[10] It is important to specify why this takes place. European governments fine airlines for any passengers who do not have the right to remain in their destination country. Syrians pay far more than the price of a plane ticket to risk their lives in dangerous overcrowded boats. They frequently have money, passports and often possess desired skills, but their only route to Europe involves the risk of drowning at sea. However, as Somali poet Warsan Shire has noted, for fleeing refugees, 'the water is safer than the land'.

[11] N. Squires, 'More than 2,500 refugees and migrants have died trying to cross the Mediterranean to Europe so far this year, UN reveals', *The Telegraph*, 31 May 2016, www.telegraph.co.uk/news/2016/05/31/more-than-2500-refugees-and-migrants-have-died-trying-to-cross-t

[12] Over two million Syrian refugees are in Turkey, over one million in Lebanon and 600,000 in Jordan. See, for example, UNHCR, 'Syria regional refugee response', Inter-agency information sharing portal, http://data.unhcr.org/syrianrefugees/regional.php

[13] J. Kerry, 'Remarks on the US strategy in Syria', The White House, 12 November 2015, www.state.gov/secretary/remarks/2015/11/249454.htm

[14] The report was by the Syrian Center for Policy Research. See I. Black, 'Report on Syria conflict finds 11.5% of population killed or injured', *The Guardian*, 11 February 2016, www.theguardian.com/world/2016/feb/11/report-on-syria-conflict-finds-115-of-population-killed-or-injured

but by forces loyal to Bashar al-Assad. For every Syrian that ISIL killed, Assad's forces killed seven.[15]

Amnesty International has documented some of the 'unthinkable atrocities' of Assad's government forces, which began with a 'brutal crackdown on peaceful protesters' and escalated to include 'unrelenting aerial bombardment of civilian neighbourhoods', including the use of infamously inaccurate barrel bombs, which alone killed 12,000 Syrian civilians between 2012 and 2015.[16] Survivors of barrel bomb attacks reported seeing 'children without heads, body parts everywhere' – a vision of 'hell'.[17] Amnesty argue that 'reprehensible and continual strikes on residential areas point to a policy of deliberately and systematically targeting civilians in attacks that constitute war crimes and crimes against humanity'. While rebels have been guilty of using improvised 'hell cannons'[18] that often kill civilians, 'government forces have been responsible for the large majority of violations and crimes... By relentlessly and deliberately targeting civilians, the Syrian government appears to have adopted a callous policy of collective punishment against the civilian population'.[19]

Yet, emboldened by UNSC inaction,[20] Assad retains his suitors, meaning that two interwoven and international conflicts have

[15] H. Naylor, 'Islamic State has killed many Syrians, but Assad's forces have killed more', *Washington Post*, 5 September 2015, www.washingtonpost.com/world/ islamic-state-has-killed-many-syrians-but-assads-forces-have-killed-even-more/ 2015/09/05/b8150d0c-4d85-11e5-80c2-106ea7fb80d4_story.html

[16] Amnesty International, 'Syria: "Death everywhere" – war crimes and human rights abuses in Aleppo, Syria', 5 May 2015, www.amnesty.org/en/documents/ mde24/1370/2015/en

[17] K. Shaheen, 'Syria war: "unthinkable atrocities" documented in report on Aleppo', *The Guardian*, 5 May 2015, www.theguardian.com/world/2015/may/ 05/syria-forces-war-crime-barrel-bombs-aleppo-amnesty-report

[18] 'A towed, projectile launcher' that can 'launch a plethora of improvised explosive projectiles, but its main ammunition of choice (or of necessity?) is a highly modified propane gas cylinder, complete with stabilizing fins and filled with a crude explosive mixture', with a range of around one mile. See T. Rogerway, 'Meet the hell cannon, the Free Syrian Army's homemade howitzer', *Foxtrot Alpha*, 29 August 2014, http://foxtrotalpha.jalopnik.com/ meet-the-hell-cannon-the-free-syrian-armys-homemade-ho-1628114916

[19] Ibid.

[20] J. G. Ralph, 'What should be done? Pragmatic constructivist ethics and the responsibility to protect', *International Organization*, 72 (2018), 173–203; see also J. Holland, 'By insisting Assad must go, the West has prolonged the Syrian conflict', *The Independent*, 14 April 2017, www.independent.co.uk/news/world/ politics/by-insisting-assad-must-go-the-west-has-prolonged-the-syrian-conflict- a7681671.html; and Amnesty International, 'Syria: "Death everywhere"'.

effectively been fought in the decimated cities of Syria. The first conflict is a US-led war on ISIL, designed to reduce the terror threat to the region and Western states. Despite widespread human rights abuses and the use of chemical weapons by Assad's forces, it was not until the rise of Islamic State in the summer of 2014 that US-led military intervention commenced. By September 2015, British, French, Canadian and Australian forces joined the United States in bombing ISIL.[21] The second conflict is a Great Power proxy war, with the USA and its allies backing rebel forces in opposition to Russia's support for the embattled Assad.[22] Russian forces, backed by Iran and Hezbollah, have repeatedly struck rebel and opposition forces fighting Bashar al-Assad.[23] The war(s) in Syria then pivot around two principal groups: ISIL and Assad's government forces. While the former find few supporters,[24] the latter divides the world's great powers in echoes of the Cold War. Any political solution to the crisis hinges on the question of Assad's return to power – a desired outcome for Russia but a particularly unwelcome prospect for the USA, UK and Australia.

Summarising the crisis in Syria is difficult. The Syrian Civil War began within the context of the regional Arab Uprisings in the spring of 2011. It has divided the UN Security Council and wider international community, brought NATO head to head with Russia and developed into a complex, multifaceted proxy war due to divided international support for government and rebel forces. From Europe, North America and Australasia, Syria has drawn hundreds of fighters sufficiently

---

[21] British assistance was initially limited to surveillance and support on the Syrian side of the border, with one airstrike conducted under the auspices of self-defence, targeting the notorious British ISIL recruit 'Jihadi John'. Nevertheless, RAF pilots routinely flew with American counterparts as embedded forces and British bombing was frequent in Northern Iraq. On 2 December 2015, the British parliament voted in favour of extending airstrikes to Syria. Australia, in contrast, temporarily suspended bombing in response to Russia's entry into the conflict at the end of 2015. New Prime Minister Justin Trudeau ended Canadian airstrikes in November 2015.

[22] In October 2015, Putin invited Assad to Moscow for his first diplomatic visit since the conflict began in 2011.

[23] Russia falsely claimed to target ISIL exclusively. The congestion of Syrian airspace was made apparent and matters were further complicated in November 2015 when Turkish forces shot down a Russian warplane for crossing into Turkish airspace, resulting in the deaths of one of the pilots and a rescuing Russian marine.

[24] Although they certainly receive limited Sunni support, with funding from wealthy donors in Gulf States and particularly Saudi Arabia.

radicalised to abandon western lives in favour of the battlefields perceived to be at the heart of the global jihad. And, in 2015, the flow of displaced Syrian refugees into neighbouring countries and across Europe reached its zenith, as haunting images of drowned children were plastered across televisions and newspapers. These are good reasons for studying this particular conflict, but they are ones of a Eurocentric nature; an even better reason is that the conflict is decimating the men, women and children of Syria.[25]

Why the Old Anglosphere Coalition?

This book analyses the foreign policy of three of the world's most important and reliably interventionist states: the USA, UK and Australia. Two of these states, through their wars and influence, have done more to shape the modern world than any other. Together, this 'old Anglosphere coalition' remains arguably the principal guarantor of global security. Their policies and divisions frequently guide and shape the response of the wider international community to the world's major crises. And Syria has been no exception. These states collectively possess the majority of the world's means to deliver military-premised solutions to such crises. In pure, crude military terms, the USA accounts for almost half of global military expenditure, while British and Australian force projection capabilities ensure the continuation of arguably disproportionate influences on world politics and international security. At present, rightly or wrongly, no other informal grouping of states comes close to the influence and importance of this English-speaking coalition in determining the landscape of international security.[26]

---

[25] Other cases could be selected but lack the qualities that make this particular case study the most urgent and pressing in the world today. Sadly, Syria stands out for a number of reasons: the relative difficulty of military intervention, the complexity of the situation on the ground, and the high death toll and number of displaced persons. For this book, however, important reasons for study also include the conflict's prolonged duration, in conjunction with the sustained focus of the international community. Studying Syria alone is a necessary feature of this monograph in order to develop a sufficiently detailed analysis. The project analyses three states and four time periods within this single case study in order to produce the level of analytical detail necessitated by this important and tragic subject.

[26] Formal groupings, such as NATO, the UN Security Council, and even increasingly the European Union, play considerable roles. However, within NATO and the UNSC (the world's two foremost formalised security actors), the

Alongside a history of shared military interventions, these three states possess intertwined colonial histories, perceptions of shared culture and a common tongue. These close cultural ties help to cement an incredible and consequential propensity for coalition warfare. In America and Australia, British-inspired systems of governance create similar political foundations for the preservation and promotion of shared values. American appeals to freedom, British appeals to democracy and Australian appeals to shared values all mine a similar theme and a mutual understanding of the broadly liberal underpinnings that are perceived to be worth fighting for. It is infrequently acknowledged that many of these underpinnings were in fact the seed of Albion; they developed in Britain and were brought to America and Australia in the beliefs of early migrants.[27] Consider, for example, two well-known US foreign policy traditions: the Jacksonian impulse to respond viscerally to attack and the Wilsonian desire to spread democracy. Both find cultural and colonial roots in the United Kingdom; they are formative British exports.[28] Coalition warfare for these nations feels natural because the ideas and impulses sustaining it are more than just similar: they are shared. This is a point that their political leaders understand quite well and rarely tire of repeating; emphasising reliability as an ally is a seemingly natural imperative for Anglosphere political elites.

In 2008, five years into the war in Iraq and three years before the Arab Uprisings would send shockwaves throughout the Middle East, former Australian Defence Minister Joel Fitzgibbon reminded the Brookings Institute in Washington DC that Australia is the only US ally to always and invariably participate in US-led coalition warfare.[29]

USA and UK frequently act in concert to shape and steer policy, notwithstanding P2 vetoes. Moreover, during the Syrian Civil War, the USA and UK have also worked closely with Australia within the UNSC.

[27] See D. Fischer, *Albion's Seed: Four British Folkways in America* (Oxford: Oxford University Press, 1989); and W. R. Mead, *Special Providence: American Foreign Policy and How It Changed the World* (New York/London: Routledge, 2002).

[28] The Jacksonian tradition developed following the flight of the Scots-Irish, first from the Borders area of Britain to Ulster, in a series of migration waves from 1717 to 1775. The Wilsonian tradition was borne of the exodus of English Puritans to Massachusetts between 1629 and 1641. Fischer, *Albion's Seed*; Mead, *Special Providence*.

[29] J. Fitzgibbon, 'Shaping peace and security in the Asia-Pacific region: the new Australian government's defence and security priorities', Lowy Institute for International Policy, Brookings Institute, Washington DC, 15 July 2008.

Fitzgibbon, like every Australian prime, foreign and defence minister for forty years, was reminding the United States that they have no greater and more reliable ally; Australia is always there to fight in shared battles with this great and powerful nation. The defence minister, like nearly all contemporary Australian political leaders, was keen to stress that Australians went to war alongside Americans as comrades in arms – as mates – prepared to fight and die together for mutual values. It is hard to overstate the importance of this narrative for Australian foreign policy and Anglosphere cooperation. It suggests that, on the beaches of Gallipoli in 1915, 'mateship' – and with it the Australian national identity – was forged in the fires of mutual military sacrifice.[30] A century on, it was possible to commemorate the ANZAC legend's centenary by purchasing celebratory clothing, mouse mats and beer coolers, as the power of the narrative to bind together Australians with each other and with culturally similar great and powerful friends remained as strong and pervasive as ever.

As an Australian, Joel Fitzgibbon was keen to have a dig at the United Kingdom and its so-called special relationship, reminding his audience that, unlike Britain, Australia has never been at war with USA.[31] Fortunately for the UK, the United States is a relatively young country, rendering the 1814 decision to burn Washington and the White House as an event now buried in quite distant political history.[32] By 1859, British and American troops were already fighting side by side in the Second Opium War, but, as with Australia, it was the joint experience of the First and Second World Wars that really cemented Anglo-American solidarity – reinforcing the notion that the

---

[30] J. Holland, 'Howard's "War on Terror": a conceivable, communicable and coercive foreign policy discourse', *Australian Journal of Political Science*, 45 (2010), 643–61; J. Holland and M. McDonald, 'Australian identity, interventionism and the "War on Terror"' in A. Siniver (ed.), *International Terrorism Post 9/11: Comparative Dynamics and Responses* (Abingdon/New York: Routledge, 2010). See also N. Dyrenfurth, 'Battlers, refugees and the republic: John Howard's language of citizenship', *Journal of Australian Studies*, 28 (2005), 183–96; N. Dyrenfurth, 'John Howard's hegemony of values: the politics of mateship in the Howard decade', *Australian Journal of Political Science*, 42 (2007), 211–30; M. McDonald and M. Merefield, '"Lest we forget": the politics of memory and Australian military intervention', *International Political Sociology*, 4 (2010), 287–302.

[31] See also J. Holland, *Selling the War on Terror: Foreign Policy Discourses after 9/11* (Abingdon/New York: Routledge, 2012).

[32] See Mead, *Special Providence*, on Americans' foreign policy amnesia.

'special relationship' exists at three interwoven levels: the personal, ideational and material. First, the personal relationships of political leaders have been crucial to its furtherance. In particular, three of Britain's greatest leaders – Churchill, Thatcher and Blair – went to great lengths to cement the UK's position as America's staunchest ally.[33] Second, the special relationship is sustained as a fundamental ideal, premised on a sense of shared identity and even fraternal intimacy. This was certainly true for Churchill, as he envisaged, wrote and spoke of the close familial bonds of the English-speaking nations.[34] Third, these ties have given rise to an unprecedented level of material cooperation between great powers. Military bases, nuclear technology, diplomatic efforts and intelligence collection are all, to a significant extent, shared for mutual benefit.

Despite a preponderance of hard power options, relative material capability alone fails to account for the persistent and repeated behaviour of these three states, which has manifested most obviously and consequentially in a century of repeated coalition warfare. Why would the United States risk destabilising a system atop of which it sits without equal or significant challenge? Interventions are costly, and the pursuit of international justice – the promotion of democracy or defence of human rights – risks arguably more fundamental components of international order: sovereignty and the norm of conflict avoidance. Prioritising the latter and promoting stability while Americans continue to grow rich and fat at the apex of a global liberal hegemony would seem to be a rational policy outcome for the greatest superpower the world has ever known. And yet America frequently dismisses the warnings of John Quincy Adams, going abroad in search of monsters to destroy. Understanding the US proclivity for war requires an exploration of American culture, values and tradition. It is inspired by ideals, ideology and identity. And contrary to those who speak of 'bandwagoning', insurance policies and sheltering beneath the eagle's wing, the same is equally true of Australia and the UK.

The mutual proclivity to participate in international interventions in an 'old Anglosphere coalition' is remarkably strong, enduring and

---

[33] In one memorable instance, dubbed the 'Colgate Summit', Prime Minister Tony Blair even remarked that he and President George W. Bush used the same toothpaste.

[34] Churchill, born to an American mother, felt these ties at a personal as well as national level.

consequential. Shortly after the turn of the twenty-first century, the old Anglosphere coalition fought side by side on the front lines of the 'War on Terror'. They comprised three of the four states participating in the initial stages of the 2003 war in Iraq,[35] having two years earlier spearheaded intervention in Afghanistan.[36] These actions were simply the latest in a long and predictable history of coalition wars, which seemed to reach something of an apogee with John Howard's presence in Washington DC on 9/11 and Tony Blair's standing ovation in Congress nine days later, as Bush drawled, 'Thank you for coming, friend'.[37] One hundred years on from the founding alliance of The Great War, the old Anglosphere coalition continues to lead the fight against global terrorism, committing to airstrikes against Islamic State despite the damaging legacy of recent wars in the Middle East. Clearly, fully imbricated within each other's cultures, these three warrior states 'constitute a logical triumvirate for comparison'.[38] As recent French requests demonstrate, it is to these English-speaking nations – and particularly the USA and UK – that other great nations turn when seeking assistance for military interventions abroad.[39]

Why Language?

You could be sat reading this in Liverpool, or Brisbane, or San Francisco – three sizeable cities near the coast, with more than 22,000 miles between them, which helped to launch, connect and develop the Anglosphere. It is, of course, language that remains arguably the most important factor binding the Anglosphere together and overcoming the physical separation of distance. This is more salient now, in an era of instant global communication, than ever previously.

---

[35] The Polish contribution, at fewer than 200 troops, was ten times smaller than that of Australia, which in turn was over twenty times smaller than that of the UK, which in turn was about one fifth that of the USA. See Holland, *Selling the War on Terror*.

[36] Officially at least, Australia committed troops shortly after the war began.

[37] D. A. Debats, T. McDonald and M. Williams, 'Mr Howard goes to Washington: September 11, the Australian–American relationship and attributes of leadership', *Australian Journal of Political Science*, 42 (2007), 231–51.

[38] Holland, *Selling the War on Terror*.

[39] French Defence Minister Jean-Yves Le Drian wrote an unusual appeal for RAF assistance in *The Guardian*. See J.-Y. Le Drian, 'Britain, France needs you in this fight against ISIL', *The Guardian*, 26 November 2015, www.theguardian.com/commentisfree/2015/nov/26/britain-france-fight-isis

Along with Canada and New Zealand, the USA, UK and Australia comprise an 'old Anglosphere', in which the first language is English. This factor, as Churchill noted, bound together these 'great democracies' into the future, building on their mutually intertwined colonial histories.[40] However, language does far more even than the already impressive task of uniting these distant great nations through a common tongue: it helps to write the world they inhabit and establish their role within it.[41]

It is the productivity of language that makes it so powerful and its study imperative. This is far from a radical claim. It amounts, quite simply, to the fact that language helps to create our world by filling it with meaning. When teaching the theory of social constructivism to my students, I begin by placing a chair in the middle of the room and asking what it is.[42] The reply comes hesitantly but inquisitively, confirming that it is indeed a chair. Next, I turn the chair on its side, repeating the question, which elicits the same answer. But, I ask, 'What if this were not a lecture theatre? What if we were in the Tate, or the Museum of Modern Art in New York?' Answers, at this stage, start to spread along a spectrum, from the realist die-hards to the postmodern true believers: 'It is still a chair', 'No, it is art!', 'It's both!'. Finally, I pick the chair up, lift it over my head in as menacing a manner as is possible for a university lecturer and walk slowly towards the students. 'Imagine I am an angry sports fan and my team

---

[40] Churchill famously wrote a four-part history of the English-speaking peoples. See, for example, W. Churchill, *A History of the English-Speaking Peoples: A One-Volume Abridgement* (New York: Skyhorse Publishing, 2011).

[41] D. Gregory, *The Colonial Present: Afghanistan, Palestine, Iraq* (Malden, MA/ Oxford/Carlton, Vic.: Blackwell Publishing, 2004); Foucault and Gregory cite Jorge Luis Borges' taxonomy, see M. Foucault, *The Order of Things: An Archaeology of the Human Sciences* (London/New York: Routledge, 2001 [1966]).

[42] Seminal constructivist analyses include: R. Doty, 'Foreign policy as social construction: a post-positivist analysis of US counterinsurgency policy in the Philippines', *International Studies Quarterly*, 37 (1993), 297–320; K. Fierke, 'Multiple identities, interfacing games: the social construction of Western action in Bosnia', *European Journal of International Relations*, 2 (1996), 467–97; J. Weldes, 'Making state action possible: the United States and the discursive construction of "the Cuban problem", 1960–1994', *Millennium: Journal of International Studies*, 25 (1996), 361–98; A. Wendt, 'Anarchy is what states make of it: the social construction of power politics', *International Organisation*, 46 (1992), 391–425; and A. Wendt, *Social Theory of International Politics* (Cambridge: Cambridge University Press, 1999).

has just lost. What is it now?' Many students immediately see it as 'a weapon'. 'Is it still a chair?' Whether the thing I am holding aloft is a chair, or a weapon, or both depends on the series of other things it relates to, such as a table, an artist, or a riot. It relies upon the context of the situation (a lecture theatre, a museum, or a football stadium) and the mutual understandings that accompany cultural commonalities (is it something to sit on, contemplate and admire, or throw?), as well as the associated linguistic categories that structure our thinking. These categories, in relation to one another, not only label the thing but moreover help to give it meaning, bringing it into being as that which we so intuitively know it to be. For social constructivists, this is not to suggest that the chair has no material properties or that they do not matter – if I throw the chair at you, it will hurt – but rather that it is the interaction of these physical characteristics with the ideas, expressed in language, which give it meaning as a chair, a piece of artwork, a weapon, or something else.[43]

As with chairs, language is used to structure, categorise and construct international relations. The actors and events of world politics – its array of states, leaders and terrorist groups – are given meaning and identity through language. We can see this in the three brief and familiar stories set out at the start of this introduction. Whether, in Paris, Mohamed Benmbarek was caught up in an 'act of war' or a 'criminal act' depends on political choices and the consequences of the language that is used to frame and fix meaning to the act. Likewise, whether Alan Kurdi and Abdullah helped to comprise a movement of people best understood as a refugee crisis, a migrant crisis, a broader security threat, or an economic opportunity for Europe, depends on the discourses that fill such events with meaning. And whether Mohammed Emwazi was a 'beautiful man', radicalised through a combination of harassment by British intelligence services and exposure to a dangerous ideology, or an evil terrorist fully deserving of his November 2015 death by US Hellfire missile, is contingent upon the narratives that construct his identity.[44]

---

[43] If this example seems silly to you because the object in question is so *obviously* a chair, it might help to think about cultures in which chairs are historically less ubiquitous (e.g. Han Chinese culture, or Japan and Korea).

[44] This example builds on the fierce debate that followed a press conference by UK NGO 'Cage', which had been in contact with Emwazi, as he complained of harassment by British intelligence agencies.

We see this process of the discursive construction of world politics play out clearly if complexly in Syria. It is a process that determines the fate of the Syrian state and its people, as well as the policies of the old Anglosphere coalition. Perhaps the most immediately illuminating example to consider is the construction of the identity of Bashar al-Assad, who has been framed within American, British and Australian foreign policy since 2011 as a bloodthirsty tyrant. This discourse has meant that any negotiation or solution that sees Assad remaining in power has long been viewed as more than simply politically unpalatable: it remains utterly unthinkable. And yet Russian intervention on behalf of Assad, coupled to the rise of ISIL, altered the political stakes and inspired a partial momentary reconsideration of these powerful dominant narratives. At an even broader level, what it is that the Syrian crisis *is* remains up for grabs. At its various stages the conflict has been framed through different lenses – human rights, chemical weapons, international terrorism and proxy war – to different political effects and possibilities. It is these lenses and their respective chronological phases that structure the empirical analysis of the book, in its exploration of the battle to produce and control the dominant discourses filling the crisis in Syria with meaning, which have ultimately helped to determine the fate of Anglosphere foreign policy and the Syrian people.

The Structure and Argument of the Book

In order to explore the Syrian crisis and the response of the old Anglosphere coalition, the book is structured in two parts. In the first half, the book: outlines the nature of the crisis in Syria; assesses the composition of the old Anglosphere coalition; and sets out a framework for the analysis of coalition foreign policy discourse. The first chapter outlines the background to the Syrian crisis, including how the conflict has evolved, how its constituent parts entangle and the range of actors involved in its prosecution and potential resolution. This chapter focuses on the situation *within* Syria. The case is made for the study of the Syrian Civil War in four overlapping but broadly chronological phases, each (heuristically) characterised by a different feature of the conflict. In the second chapter, the book outlines the case for the study of the 'old Anglosphere coalition', tracing the historical and contemporary contexts of American, British and Australian foreign policy.

In this chapter, as well as tracing its roots and binds, I develop the argument that the Anglosphere is the world's foremost military alliance, bound together by language, culture and history, as well as being perpetually co-constituted through participation in wars often understood through racialised narratives. In the third chapter, the book turns to consider how we might analyse Anglosphere policy towards Syria, in light of the importance and intertwinement of language and politics. In this chapter, I argue that the Anglosphere functions as a transnational political community, within and across which an international discursive war of position takes place, enabling, shaping and constraining policy options. Within this conceptualisation, I argue that war and peace are, in significant part, determined by Anglosphere discursive contestation.

The second half of the book traces the discursive war of position played out across the Anglosphere during the Syrian crisis and civil war. This analysis is structured in four phases. Chapter 4 analyses the period from 2011 to 2012, as Assad's government responded to protests calling for democracy and the country descended into civil war. In this chapter, I trace the formation, evolution and clash of two competing discourses – a teleological (liberal) 'Arab Spring' discourse and a (realist) reminder to 'Remember Iraq'. I argue that these discourses shaped the parameters of the politically possible in the early stages of the Syrian crisis, with the avoidance of war resulting from the tempering effect that the latter had on the former. Building on this, Chapter 5 considers Obama's entanglement in his own 'red line' on chemical weapons through 2012 and 2013. In this chapter, I argue that proponents of a (realist) 'Syria is not Libya' discourse actively sought to incorporate the teleology of the (liberal) Arab Spring discourse – focused on Assad's inevitable downfall – within a case for war's continued avoidance. Like Chapter 5's focus on the use of chemical weapons, Chapter 6 explores another potentially 'game-changing' event: the rise of Islamic State in 2014 and the subsequent re-framing of the crisis through the language of counter-terrorism. In this chapter, I argue that discourses of (counter-)terrorism successfully reframed the Syrian crisis, resonating with supporters and coercing doubters across the Anglosphere to an extent necessary to sell and prosecute military intervention. Chapter 7 turns to consider the emergence of proxy warfare in 2015, with the intervention of Russia in support of Assad. In this chapter, I argue that Russia's intervention rejuvenated a discourse of (realist) caution, chipping away at any remaining (liberal) optimism and encouraging a(n exclusive and damaging) focus on Syria as the latest front in the War on Terror. That focus was reinforced by the unexpected election of US President Donald Trump, notwithstanding his unpredictable foreign policy and the return of chemical weapons concerns, as Syria's four phases bled together.

Throughout, then, a single argument focuses the book: the outcome of the Syrian Civil War has hinged upon the selling of war and peace within the single transnational space of the world's foremost military alliance, the old Anglosphere coalition. This book is an exploration and analysis of that discursive battle – a contest of ideas, upon which Syria's fate continues to depend.

1 | *The Syrian Civil War*

The flutter of a butterfly's wing can ultimately cause a typhoon.[1]

Introduction

On 17 December 2010, in the small central Tunisian town of Sidi Bouzid, Mohamed Bouazizi set up his wheelbarrow cart of fruit and vegetables, as he did every day. His stall was mobile for good reason. Like the majority of street vendors, Mohamed sold his produce illegally, in lieu of a licence. It did not take long for the police to arrive. Usually, at this point, Mohamed and the other vendors would hurriedly pack up their carts and move on, in an endless game of cat and mouse. But, on that day, for some reason, Mohamed stayed put. Reports of what happened next vary.[2] What is clear is that the street seller's cart and produce were confiscated and impounded, despite his efforts to retrieve them from the governor. Two hours later, Mohamed doused himself in petrol, before setting himself on fire. The severity of his burns would eventually prove too much; he died of his injuries in hospital eighteen days later.

This act of self-immolation was reported across the Arab world, including on pan-Arab television station Al Jazeera and in Arabic newspapers, such as *Al-Ahram*. This 'flutter of a butterfly's wing' was about to cause a typhoon. Mohamed's death inspired protests in Tunisia and across the region, leading to a series of linked revolutions in 2011 and 2012 that would topple six governments in four states. First, despite a panicked visit to Mohamed Bouazizi's hospital bedside,

---

[1] This quote appears at the start of the movie *The Butterfly Effect* (2004), and has since been widely recirculated within popular discussions of Chaos Theory to denote the idea that a minor instability within an ordered system can multiply exponentially, causing chaos. American meteorologist Edward Lorenz coined the term.

[2] Accusations of being slapped by a female police officer, for example, ultimately were not upheld in court and have been denied by some of those present.

came the overthrow of Tunisian president Zine al-Abidine Ben Ali, who had ruled since 1987. Next up was Hosni Mubarak in Egypt – in power since 1981. Egypt's longest-serving president for almost 200 years was forced to step down and found guilty of corruption as well as failing to halt the actions of security forces towards protestors. Third was Libya, where 'Mad Dog' Colonel Muammar Gaddafi had ruled since 1969. Amidst the context of civil war, he met a bloody and public fate, flushed by coalition airstrikes from his storm drain hiding place into the hands of Libyan rebels. Prior to his burial in the Libyan Desert, Gaddafi's body was displayed to the public in an industrial freezer near Misrata, in order to assure the people of his gruesome demise. Fourth was Yemen, where Ali Abdullah Saleh had ruled since unification in 1990, as well as in the north for twelve years before that. Other states underwent important transitions but fell short of regime change. In turn, Jordan, Oman, Bahrain, Kuwait, Morocco and Lebanon all witnessed significant protests, leading to changes in governance, if not government. From the Western Sahara to the Gulf of Oman, Mohamed Bouazizi's death sent shockwaves across the Middle East and North Africa (MENA). Damascus did not escape them.

It did not take long for events to reach and inspire Syrians. The country 'stands in the middle of the most volatile conflicts in [the] region', giving Damascus a 'pivotal role' in most of the Middle East's 'flashpoint issues'.[3] Three weeks after Bouazizi's death, small protests broke out in Old Damascus, following accusations of police brutality. Tensions simmered throughout February, coming to the boil in mid-March, triggered once again by police beatings and interrogations, this time in Dera'a in Syria's south-west. Protests erupted in opposition to the Ba'athist regime, led by Bashar al-Assad. From 1971 to the turn of the millennium, Bashar's father Hafez al-Assad ruled Syria.[4] A cult of personality enabled Hafez to institute modernising reforms while significantly concentrating power in the presidency and dividing up the apparatus of state along sectarian lines. In 1982, aided by his brother Rifaat, Hafez infamously responded to a potential Sunni insurgency in Hama with an overwhelming display of force, in which tens of thousands of civilians perished – a scenario that would be recreated thirty

---

[3] NPR staff and wires, 'Syria "Great Friday" protest turns bloody', 22 April 2011, www.npr.org/2011/04/22/135628118/syrian-forces-protesters-face-off-on-great-friday

[4] The Ba'ath Party had been in power since 1963.

years later, under the rule of his son.[5] Bashar al-Assad came to power in 2000, following his father's death.[6] The Damascus Spring met his ascension with calls for reform, organised through political fora. Despite initial concessions, debate was ultimately shut down through force.[7] Eleven years later, Bashar would face a new wave of protests as part of the Arab Spring, in response to which he would once again mobilise the government's military might; a move that would lead to the disintegration of the state in a protracted and devastating civil war.

Bashar al-Assad's crackdown on the Syrian protests of the Arab Spring commenced the first phase of the Syrian crisis. Syria's civil war has since evolved through four principal phases, which are used to structure this chapter and the analysis of Anglosphere foreign policy in the second half of the book.[8] This chapter's primary focus is the domestic situation in Syria. Its aim is to provide a reminder and guide for the reader in order to assist with the navigation of a complex civil war. It provides an overview and context for the crisis, before turning to consider Anglosphere foreign policy during these four phases. The first of these phases began in the spring of 2011, with the Arab Uprisings and government response and lasted until the end of 2012. This period represents the onset of the Syrian conflict and its development as a civil war, fought between government and opposition forces. The defining theme of this period for international onlookers was concern for human rights, amidst calls for democracy. The second phase of the Syrian crisis and civil war began in August 2012 and lasted until the end of 2013. This period was distinct due to increasing concerns about chemical weapon usage, in particular following reports of sarin gas being used in Ghouta. The third phase of the crisis began at the start of 2014 and lasted until August 2015. This period is noteworthy for the dramatic rise of Islamic State (IS). The fourth phase of the crisis began in September 2015, dominated by the onset of explicit proxy war as Russian airstrikes targeted opposition and rebel forces. This period

---

[5] Reports vary between 10,000 and 40,000.

[6] Bashar was not his father's first choice successor. He was not even his second choice. Bashar's uncle, Rifaat, was exiled following a failed attempt to seize power. And Bashar learned of his brother's death, in a car crash in Damascus, while studying in London, where he had lived for nearly two years.

[7] Prisoner release, for example, was an early concession.

[8] For an alternative four-part chronology, see K. B. Kanat, *A Tale of Four Augusts: Obama's Syria Policy* (Ankara: SETA Publications, 2015).

was also remarkable because of threefold European concerns (linked to the events listed at the start of this book), pertaining to an unprecedented refugee crisis, fears of domestic radicalisation and foreign terrorism. These phases are not discrete, but rather overlap, with each additional stage of the crisis increasing the complexity of involved parties with myriad concerns. Calls for democracy and human rights were not supplanted by chemical weapons concerns or the rise of ISIL (Islamic State of Iraq and the Levant). As the Anglosphere reacted to proxy war in 2015, calls for democracy – sparked four years previously – remained unextinguished, helping to structure competing Anglosphere discourses of war and peace.

Democracy and Human Rights, 2011–

In March 2011, *Vogue* magazine ran a feature article on Asma al-Assad, titled 'A rose in the desert'.[9] The British-born wife of the Syrian president was described, in gushing terms, as 'glamorous, young and very chic – the freshest and most magnetic of first ladies'. The article described the 'wildly democratic principles' in the Assad household, as the Syrian First Lady attempted to empower her children. It also noted that her husband Bashar al-Assad was attracted to study eye surgery (in London, where they met) because 'there is very little blood'. Syria was described as 'a secular country where women earn as much as men and the Muslim veil is forbidden in universities, a place without bombings, unrest, or kidnappings'.[10]

Alongside Asma al-Assad's fashion sense, Syria made international headlines in March 2011 for other reasons. The waves of popular protest sweeping the MENA region reached Damascus. Having begun slowly in January and February – protests after police beat a shopkeeper, a riot at a football match and calls for resistance on social media – March was the month that Syria's attempted revolution caught light. The spark of ignition, as in Egypt, was otherwise inconspicuous enough. It would turn out to be the single match that would go on to burn down an entire country. Not so much out of political activism as 'boredom' and 'teenage rebellion', fifteen schoolchildren –

---

[9] J. Buck, 'Asma al-Assad: a rose in the desert', *Vogue*, March 2011, http:// gawker.com/asma-al-assad-a-rose-in-the-desert-1265002284
[10] Ibid.

friends and cousins – wrote graffiti on the wall of a local school in Dera'a, in south-west Syria. Slogans included the pan-regional rallying cry, 'The people want the fall of the regime,' as well as the more targeted, 'It's your turn, doctor' – directed at, what *Vogue* had noted to be, Syria's squeamish ophthalmologist president.[11]

In the context of the regional Arab Uprisings, the Syrian government was nervous. The boys were arrested and interrogated over three days, sparking protests in Dera'a, during which security forces shot and killed four people.[12] When the boys returned home, family members report that they were 'unrecognisable', with torture techniques including the removal of fingernails in children as young as thirteen.[13] In conjunction with their arrests, thirteen political prisoners, supported by 'dozens of Kurdish prisoners', had gone on hunger strike in protest. Two days later, rioters burned local Syrian Ba'ath Party offices, with security forces killing seven and wounding several of the crowd.[14] On 15 March, Syria witnessed a 'Day of Rage' and the broadening out of protests to Damascus and Aleppo. 'Small but significant', *The Washington Post* noted that the pro-democracy movement had begun 'in earnest'.[15] In an historical echo of Hafez and Rifaat, the regime's response was swift and decisive. Led by Bashar al-Assad's brother Maher, the elite 4th Armoured Division took control of the Omari

---

[11] The boys were influenced by events in Egypt and Syria, where the slogan had become the rallying cry of the Arab Uprisings. See J. Bowen, *The Arab Uprisings: The People Want the Fall of the Regime* (London: Simon & Schuster, 2012); Buck, 'Asma al-Assad'; and L. Sinjab, 'Middle East unrest: silence broken in Syria', *BBC News*, 19 March 2011, www.bbc.co.uk/news/world-middle-east-12794882. The teenager who actually wrote the graffiti avoided arrest, going on to fight for rebel forces, before being killed in 2013. His cousin, falsely arrested, admitted the act under interrogation, returning home 'unrecognisable'. He fled to Jordan. See K. Fahim and H. Saad, 'A faceless teenage refugee who helped ignite Syria's war', *New York Times*, 8 February 2013, www.nytimes.com/2013/02/09/world/middleeast/a-faceless-teenage-refugee-who-helped-ignite-syrias-war.html?_r=1

[12] Sinjab, 'Middle East unrest'. The term 'security forces' is vague and encompasses the range of official and unofficial militias (Shahiba) fighting on behalf of Assad.

[13] NPR, 'Syria "Great Friday" protest turns bloody'.

[14] J. Holliday, 'The struggle for Syria in 2011: an operational and regional analysis', Institute for the Study of War, December 2011, www.understandingwar.org/sites/default/files/Struggle_For_Syria.pdf

[15] E. Flock, 'Syria revolution: a revolt brews against Bashar al-Assad's regime', *Washington Post*, 15 March 2011, www.washingtonpost.com/blogs/blogpost/post/syria-revolution-revolt-against-bashar-al–assads-regime/2011/03/15/ABrwNEX_blog.html

Mosque, which was at the heart of the protest movement, with approximately fifteen further casualties during a two-day assault. The decisive action quelled protests in Dera'a and enabled government withdrawal. This apparent success would become a template for the government response to the uprising in the coming weeks.[16] Indeed, it was a pattern that was repeated in Dera'a in May, following further protests throughout April. Withdrawal of government tanks and armed vehicles on the second occasion would last for seven months, as once again force was seen to restore stability.

On the same day that troops withdrew from the Omari Mosque in Dera'a (25 March) 'protests erupted across the country' at a scale that 'took the Assad regime by surprise'. Protests broke out in 'six of twelve provincial capitals', including to a limited extent in Damascus. However, government attention turned foremost to Latakia, where security forces met protests, checkpoints were established and unarmed protestors were again shot at.[17] As well as the apparent lessons of Dera'a and Assad's general nervousness in the context of having witnessed regional turmoil, the reason for the strong response in Latakia relates to Syria's ethnic, cultural and religious divisions. Bashar al-Assad is an Alawite; a member of a religious sect derived from Shia Islam.[18] A minority in Syria, where Sunni Muslims comprised almost two thirds of the population at the start of 2011, the Alawites' homeland is Syria's north-west coastal highlands, overlooking the Mediterranean.[19] In 2011, this group dominated the government and the upper ranks of the military.[20] British Broadcasting Corporation (BBC) Middle East correspondent Jeremy Bowen describes walking through District 86 of Damascus – an Alawite area of the capital – in late 2011 and witnessing a combination of fabricated and genuine support for the regime amongst people who both feared the personal consequences Assad's

[16] However, ten further protestors were killed as forces withdrew. See Holliday, 'The struggle for Syria'.
[17] Ibid.
[18] Although many Alawis are secularists. See Bowen, *The Arab Uprisings*, p. 195.
[19] Alawites accounted for roughly 10 per cent of the Syrian population in 2010–2011.
[20] Sunni Muslims dominated more junior ranks. As civil war broke out, the largest military fissure broke out along fault lines demarcated by seniority, associated with religious divisions. While the majority of Syria's 300,000 conscripts were Sunni, as much as 70 per cent of the army's professional ranks was made up of Alawites.

potential downfall and felt compelled to support him.[21] In March in Latakia – Alawites' and Assad's heartland – government security forces responded to protests with deadly force. An increasingly familiar pattern was followed, with pro-government supporters bussed in, checkpoints established and unarmed protestors shot.[22] Over the coming weeks and months, government forces repeatedly intervened in Latakia and the region, recreating and ramping up the model of early clearance efforts. The net outcome was an outflow of Sunni residents, replaced by Alawis relocating from other regions.[23]

After Latakia came Homs.[24] The 'March clashes in Dera'a sparked unrest, but it was the April escalation in Homs that fanned the flames'.[25] The reason for the intensity of fighting relates to Homs' geography and demography. First, Homs occupies a highly strategic location on Syria's main route from north to south (the M5 motorway), as well as lying at a vital point of access to the Mediterranean Sea (the M1 motorway connects Homs and Latakia). Almost as crucially, Homs also lies at a vital oil pipeline intersection. Second, the population of Homs shifted in line with the demographic changes of the 1960s and 1970s, as Alawites moved from the highlands to the central plain, in line with their increasing prominence in Syrian society. These reasons were not lost on Assad's government and security forces, which responded to protestors with their violent dispersal and the infamous cudgel of the riot police.[26] Protestors were shot from rooftops and military-aged males were arrested.[27] One protestor described the government bullets as falling on protestors 'like rain'.[28] In Homs, the effect was the opposite of Dera'a and violence escalated on both sides.

---

[21] Bowen contrasts the genuine support of the large number of Alawis carrying rolled up posters of Assad with the put-on rallies of Muammar Gaddafi. Bowen, *The Arab Uprisings*, p. 198.

[22] Holliday, 'The struggle for Syria', p. 19.

[23] Holliday's excellent account of the situation in late 2011 takes a useful regional approach to explaining the complex and fluid situation on the ground at the time. Ibid.

[24] Because of the complexity of events, I have opted to focus on Latakia and Homs here. Many other towns, cities and villages were obviously impacted. Baliyas and Hama, in particular, endured similar fates to Latakia and Homs, respectively.

[25] Holliday, 'The struggle for Syria', p. 19.   [26] Ibid.   [27] Ibid.

[28] See BBC News, 'Syria protests: Assad to lift state of emergency', 21 April 2011, www.bbc.co.uk/news/world-middle-east-13134322

On 22 April, one day after the lifting of the hated State of Emergency,[29] came 'the Great Friday': a series of countrywide protests following Friday prayers, which resulted in approximately 100 deaths, including by sniper fire.[30] NPR and Amnesty International reported Syrians dragging corpses through the streets to be piled inside buildings.[31] Following arrests, Bowen notes that security forces made no attempts to conceal the results of their interrogations.[32] To illustrate the point, he reports the arrest of a 'chubby thirteen-year-old boy called Hamza al-Khatib' in the village of Jizah near Dera'a, at the end of April. Along with bullet wounds and burns, likely made by electric torture devices and whips, he was returned to his family in May with a broken neck and having had his penis cut off.[33] The intended effect was deterrence through the display of spectacular violence inflicted on a young teenage boy. Just as government violence backfired in Homs, fuelling protests, so too did the mutilation of Hamza, whose broken body was seen by thousands on YouTube. Within days, tens of thousands had joined a social media page declaring, 'We are all Hamza al-Khatib'.[34]

By the start of May, Assad's security forces were stretched, conducting simultaneous clearances in Dera'a, Latakia, Homs and Damascus. Following the 'bloody crackdown', Assad declared that government forces had gained the upper hand and would soon restore order.[35] However, from this point, it was clear to many observers inside and outside of Syria that change was coming, with or without Assad, regardless of the outcome of any short-term crackdown.[36] The following month of June saw the first significant armed resistance, in Jisr al-Shughour in Idlib Province, near the Turkish border.[37] Across three days, 120 members of the security forces were killed, as buildings

---

[29] Syria's emergency law had been in place since 1963. It effectively suspended most constitutional protections. See BBC News, 'Syria protests'.
[30] NPR, 'Syria "Great Friday" protest turns bloody'.   [31] Ibid.
[32] Bowen, *The Arab Uprisings*, p. 214.   [33] Ibid.   [34] Ibid., p. 215.
[35] M. Weaver, 'Syria, Libya and Middle East unrest – Monday 9 May 2011', *The Guardian*, 9 May 2011, www.theguardian.com/world/middle-east-live/2011/may/09/syria-libya-middle-east-unrest-live
[36] B. Whitaker, 'Syria will change – with or without Assad', *The Guardian*, 9 May 2011, www.theguardian.com/commentisfree/2011/may/09/syria-assad-uprising
[37] Holliday, 'The struggle for Syria'.

were seized in response to government forces opening fire on a funeral.[38] When met by an inevitable government response, the fighting and fears of a massacre led tens of thousands of Syrians to flee over the Turkish border. The Syrian crisis had morphed from countywide protests to an informal and improvised armed uprising.

Six weeks later, in July, a small group of defected Syrian Army commanders established the first *organised* armed resistance, the Free Syrian Army (FSA). Defectors from government and security forces were mainly Sunni, but not exclusively so. Reasons for defection varied from support for rebel causes to the threat of execution for refusing orders to shoot protestors. By the end of the year, defections would number up to 10,000 and by the end of the following year, that number had reached approximately 100,000.[39] By the autumn of 2011, observers estimated that the FSA numbered 20,000 fighters in and around Homs alone.[40] What began as a call for democratic change in response to government crackdowns had descended first into an armed uprising and then into full-blown civil war. Syria, however, would not witness the pace of change seen in Tunisia, Egypt, Libya or Yemen, despite the initial fervour surrounding the rebel cause and appeals for democratic transition.

The FSA would continue to increase in personnel, organisation, funding and weaponry over 2011 and into 2012. Homs became a temporary refuge for Syrian Army defectors, but was under siege – a siege beginning in 2011 that would last for three years. In 2012, apart from a short and only partially observed UN-brokered ceasefire in May, Homs was the site of fierce fighting between government and rebel forces. The central Syrian town, home to 1.5 million people, would become synonymous with the crisis in Syria, as the media distributed before and after images of a city that appeared almost entirely destroyed by conflict. By December 2012, Assad's forces had

---

[38] J. Muir, 'Analysis', in 'Syria vows "decisive" response in Jisr al-Shughour', *BBC News*, 7 June 2011, www.bbc.co.uk/news/world-middle-east-13677200

[39] N. Bakri, 'Defectors claim attack that killed Syria soldiers', *New York Times*, 26 October 2011, www.nytimes.com/2011/10/27/world/middleeast/army-defectors-in-syria-take-credit-for-deadly-attack.html; BBC News, 'Guide to the Syrian rebels', 13 December 2013, www.bbc.co.uk/news/world-middle-east-24403003

[40] Team Observers, 'Who is the Free Syrian Army?', *France 24*, 8 October 2012, http://observers.france24.com/en/20120810-syria-free-syrian-army-structure-funding-ideology-methods-fight-against-assad-regime

retaken much of Homs, following wave after wave of government offensives and extensive shelling, but the city was in ruins and its people scattered. It would not be until May 2014 that an interim truce would be reached, with rebel forces retreating to the country-side and residents returning to discover homes destroyed and to collect personal items, such as guitars and photograph albums.[41] A more wholesale truce and rebel withdrawal was agreed in December 2015, with opposition fighters relocating to rebel-held areas of Idlib Province.[42]

Alongside the ongoing Siege of Homs, July 2012 saw fighting break out in Syria's two largest cities, Damascus and Aleppo, which Homs connects. In the south, in Damascus, rebel forces infiltrated the city from the surrounding countryside. However, the Battle of Damascus – or Operation Damascus Volcano – did not last long. Damascus is a government stronghold, with dense security forces, as well as support for Assad. Within two weeks, rebel forces were repelled, having inflicted only a minor casualty toll. Despite fears of a looming battle, Damascus has remained relatively free of the scale and intensity of conflict seen in other Syrian cities, although the crisis is visible through price fluctuations, shortages, beggars, closed factories, checkpoints and traffic jams.[43] While Damascus suburbs have seen conflict, Old and central Damascus have escaped relatively unscathed. This relative level of security has enabled the capital to reportedly remain home to the Assad family throughout the crisis.[44] In contrast, in the north, Aleppo has suffered a far worse fate.

Aleppo is Syria's largest city, economic hub and a UNESCO World Heritage Site. Protests began later there than in the rest of the country, starting in February 2012 and ramping up in scale and intensity in the summer months. During the second half of 2012, opposition forces

[41] A. Lucas, 'Syrians make emotional return to Homs', *The Star*, 9 May 2014, www.thestar.com/news/world/2014/05/09/syrians_make_emotional_return_to_homs.html

[42] BBC News, 'Syria crisis: rebels leave Homs', 9 December 2015, www.bbc.co.uk/news/world-middle-east-35048404

[43] E. Black, 'Damascus, the city where everything's for sale but no one's buying', *The Guardian*, 26 April 2013, www.theguardian.com/world/2013/apr/26/damascus-economic-dead-zone

[44] The Economist, 'The Assad family: where are they now?', 21 February 2013, www.economist.com/blogs/pomegranate/2013/02/assad-family

took control and cut government supply lines. The next three years saw repeated offensives met with counter-offensives, as both sides attempted to wrest control of the city. At the start of 2016, five years into the war, Aleppo remained locked in stalemate. Maps of the city's conflict resembled a drain, as both sides swirled in symmetry in a clockwise direction around the central business district.[45] But by late 2016, Assad's forces, backed by Russian airpower, were slowly grinding out victory in the city, at colossal human cost. By early 2017, the last stalwart residents of rebel-held Eastern Aleppo had been killed, dispersed or evacuated.

In its Introduction, this book drew upon an Amnesty International report, which spoke of 'unimaginable atrocities' in Syria. The location of those atrocities was Aleppo. Amnesty International interviewed 100 residents and aid workers, painting a damning picture of the actions of both the regime and the rebel groups.[46] These actions, the report makes clear, are in clear violation of UN Security Council Resolution 2139; in some cases, the actions of Assad's security forces have amounted to crimes against humanity. In Aleppo, civilians 'have been bombarded in their homes, hospitals, schools, public markets and places of worship in [government] air attacks', the majority of which 'have involved the use of "barrel bombs"'. Barrel bombs are 'large, improvised explosive devices, which are delivered from helicopters and consist of oil barrels, fuel tanks or gas cylinders that have been packed with explosives, fuel and metal fragments to increase their lethal effect'.[47] They are so indiscriminate that their use alone is usually seen to constitute a war crime. In one fifteen-month period alone, barrel bombs killed thirty-five rebel fighters and more than 3,000 civilians, meaning that nearly 99 per cent of the weapon's victims were the ordinary men, women and children of Aleppo.[48] For them, tragically, barrel bombs have not garnered international attention in the way that other weapons have.[49]

---

[45] Ibid.   [46] Amnesty International, 'Syria: "Death everywhere"'.
[47] Ibid., p. 6.
[48] The BBC reported research from the Violations Documentation Center. See BBC News, 'Syria conflict: Aleppo civilians suffer "unthinkable atrocities"', 5 May 2015, www.bbc.co.uk/news/world-middle-east-32581007
[49] Although, tragically, in late 2016, Aleppo witnessed the relatively new tactic of filling barrel bombs with chlorine gas, combining two sources of death for Syria's population.

Chemical Weapons, 2012–

Syria first acquired chemical weapons from Egypt during the 1973 Arab–Israeli War. Their procurement was likely intended as a deterrent.[50] Syria's chemical weapons programme accelerated in the 1980s, motivated by fears of Israeli military, and especially aerial, superiority in the early part of that decade.[51] In lieu of nuclear weapons, Syria's chemical weapons programme can be viewed as an attempt to develop a mutual mass-destruction capacity, as part of a process of balancing Israeli capabilities.[52] However, relatively few concrete details of Syria's chemical weapons programme were known before civil war broke out, with limited details emerging from British, American and Israeli intelligence, or reports from defectors.[53] Although uncertainty remained regarding the types and amounts of Syrian chemical weapons stockpiles, their possession by the Assad regime's security forces was unambiguous, as was Syria's deliberate failure to become a signatory to the Chemical Weapons Convention in the 1990s. As civil war broke out in 2011 and developed ferociously through 2012, concerns arose regarding their potential use, human rights violations and desires to retain the international norm of rendering unconventional weapons illegitimate.

These fears were building inside and outside of Syria in the summer of 2012, with numerous commentators noting the concerning possibility that chemical weapons could be used in the conflict. It was, however, inevitably the President of the United States who, in August 2012, brought these concerns to global attention by flagging up the potential

---

[50] M. Diab, 'Syria's chemical and biological weapons: assessing capabilities and motivations', *The Nonproliferation Review*, Fall 1997, http://cns.miis.edu/npr/pdfs/diab51.pdf

[51] In particular, Israel's actions in 1982.

[52] Ibid. This stance was reiterated in mid-2012 by a Syrian Foreign Affairs spokesman, Jihad Makdissi, who argued that 'No chemical or biological weapons will ever be used and I repeat, will never be used, during the crisis in Syria no matter what the developments inside Syria... All of these types of weapons are in storage and under security and the direct supervision of the Syrian armed forces and will never be used unless Syria is exposed to external aggression.' Associated Press, 'Syria says it will use chemical weapons if attacked', *USA Today*, 23 July 2012, http://usatoday30.usatoday.com/news/world/story/2012-07-23/Syria-violence-rebels/56425402/1

[53] Diab, 'Syria's chemical and biological weapons'. Diab, for example, was a former Syrian diplomat at the start of the 1980s who had moved to London.

for military consequences in the case of their use. During a White House press conference, Obama answered a journalist's question with an apparently unplanned[54] but hugely impactful response: 'a red line for us is we start seeing a whole bunch of chemical weapons moving around or being utilised'.[55] That, he added, 'would change my calculus'.[56] That would change my equation'. The following day, White House Spokesperson Josh Earnest clarified the president's remarks, reiterating that chemical weapons use would be a 'grave mistake', for which Assad would be 'held accountable' for failing to live 'up to... international obligations'.[57] It would not take long for Obama's 'red line' to be tested and crossed.

In December 2012, disturbing, if fragmentary, reports emerged from Homs, reinforced by amateur YouTube footage.[58] A leaked State Department cable, signed by the US Consul General in Istanbul following an investigation, soon corroborated the sketchy initial information. The cable noted that the gathered evidence made for 'a compelling case that Agent 15 was used in Homs on Dec. 23'.[59] Its use caused an estimated seven deaths, with scores injured.[60] Agent 15 is a poisonous gas – a 'CX-level incapacitating agent' at 'the less harmful end of the spectrum of chemical warfare agents'[61] – the use of which is controlled by the CWC.[62] The spring brought a series of transgressions. First, in March, chemical weapons usage was reported in suburbs of Aleppo and Damascus, with government and rebel forces both accusing each other of carrying out the attacks. Conflicting

---

[54] P. Baker et al., 'Off-the-cuff Obama line put U.S. in bind on Syria', *New York Times*, 4 May 2013, www.nytimes.com/2013/05/05/world/middleeast/obamas-vow-on-chemical-weapons-puts-him-in-tough-spot.html; G. Kessler, 'President Obama and the "red line" on Syria's chemical weapons', *Washington Post*, 6 September 2013, www.washingtonpost.com/news/fact-checker/wp/2013/09/06/president-obama-and-the-red-line-on-syrias-chemical-weapons

[55] B. Obama, 'Remarks by the President to the White House press corps', James S. Brady Press Briefing Room, 20 August 2012, www.whitehouse.gov/the-press-office/2012/08/20/remarks-president-white-house-press-corps

[56] Ibid.   [57] Ibid.

[58] Al Jazeera, 'Gas used in Homs leaves seven people dead and scores affected, activists say', 24 December 2012, http://blogs.aljazeera.com/topic/syria/gas-used-homs-leaves-seven-people-dead-and-scores-affected-activists-say

[59] J. Rogin, 'Exclusive: secret State Department cable: chemical weapons used in Syria', *Foreign Policy*, 15 January 2013, https://foreignpolicy.com/2013/01/15/exclusive-secret-state-department-cable-chemical-weapons-used-in-syria

[60] Al Jazeera, 'Gas used'.   [61] Ibid.

[62] Rogin, 'Exclusive: secret State Department cable'.

reports suggested chlorine or sarin gas might have been used. A UN investigation confirmed the resulting nineteen civilian and one military deaths were caused by 'organophosphorus intoxication' from unspecified chemical weapons.[63] Second, in April, a small-scale chemical weapons attack on civilians was reported in Sanaqueb, east of Idlib, killing one person. A UN-supervised autopsy found traces of sarin in the victim's organs.[64] Unusually, both the Syrian government and the Obama administration requested a UN-led investigation into the March incident in Aleppo, which took place in the suburb of Khan al-Assal. While the UN investigatory team were on the ground in Damascus, however, events took a further and significant turn for the worse for the people of Syria.

On 21 August 2013, the deadliest chemical weapons attack since the Iran–Iraq War was carried out in Ghouta, in the eastern suburbs of Damascus.[65] Casualty figures vary dramatically, with estimates ranging from a few hundred to almost 2,000, but are likely to have been between 1,200 and 1,400.[66] Once again, YouTube videos quickly emerged, backing up claims of a chemical weapons attack, amidst shelling and rockets. The UN investigatory team, already in Damascus, established the explosion of surface-to-surface rockets, capable of carrying a chemical payload.[67] The environment and bodies of victims and survivors provided evidence of the use of sarin.[68] The nerve agent does not directly kill, instead affecting the nervous system in dramatic ways that can lead to death.[69] By blocking enzymes, the usual actions of the nervous system are left to continue unabated, without the usual feedback loops to switch them off. A victim's eyes and nose will run, they will froth at the mouth, vomit, urinate and defecate, while muscles spasm uncontrollably. The process starts within seconds. Convulsions,

[63] United Nations Mission to Investigate Allegations of the Use of Chemical Weapons in the Syrian Arab Republic, 'Final report', https://unoda-web.s3.amazonaws.com/wp-content/uploads/2013/12/report.pdf
[64] Ibid.
[65] The Week, 'Syria gas attack: death toll at 1,400 worst since Halabja', 22 August 2013, www.theweek.co.uk/world-news/syria-uprising/54759/syria-gas-attack-death-toll-1400-worst-halabja
[66] See, for example, S.B. 'If this isn't a red line, what is?', *The Economist*, 21 August 2013, www.economist.com/blogs/pomegranate/2013/08/syria-s-war
[67] UN, 'Final report', p. 19.   [68] Ibid.
[69] J. Hamblin, 'What does sarin do to people?', *The Atlantic*, 6 May 2013, www.theatlantic.com/health/archive/2013/05/what-does-sarin-do-to-people/275577

paralysis and a particularly undignified and unpleasant death can occur within between one and ten minutes.[70] That was the fate of over 1,000 civilians in Ghouta – while a UN chemical weapons team was located a few miles down the road.

At this moment, the Anglosphere was close to taking military action against Assad. Its avoidance hinged upon the calculus of one man, the leader of the free world. Obama recalls taking a walk around the White House gardens as the clamour for airstrikes reached a deafening crescendo.[71] Dissenters were hard to find.[72] Yet Obama – a president who ran his campaign for office on the promise of ending a dumb war in the Middle East – was uneasy. This was, after all, a president schooled in the Jeffersonian tradition of managing America's exposure to global risk through the avoidance of unnecessary cost.[73] The president opted to buy some time, flipping the decision to Congress,[74] giving the Republican-majority House the opportunity to debate intervention, just as the British parliament had. In the UK, parliamentarians had unexpectedly voted against airstrikes – a surprising outcome, which impacted Obama's decision to pause in the rush to war. The stakes were high. As *The New York Times* provocatively put it, Congress now had the chance to 'stand by' Obama or give the green light to Assad 'murdering children with unconventional weapons'.[75] As it transpired, the fractured British political landscape ultimately meant that, while there was a US debate, there was ultimately no vote, letting lawmakers off the hook.

At this stage, Obama cut an isolated figure, as he stood firm against the tide of establishment thinking – as he put it, 'the blob'. An escape route emerged in an unlikely place, as Secretary of State John Kerry pontificated in reply to a reporter's question in the UK. Hypothesising, Kerry suggested war could be avoided if Assad complied and handed

---

[70] Ibid.

[71] J. Goldberg, 'The Obama doctrine', *The Atlantic*, April 2016, www.theatlantic.com/magazine/archive/2016/04/the-obama-doctrine/471525

[72] Ibid.

[73] J. Holland, 'Obama as modern Jeffersonian' in M. Bentley and J. Holland (eds.), *The Obama Doctrine: A Foreign Policy Legacy of Continuity?* (Abingdon/New York: Routledge, 2016).

[74] P. Baker and J. Weisman, 'Obama seeks approval by Congress for strike in Syria', *New York Times*, 31 August 2013, www.nytimes.com/2013/09/01/world/middleeast/syria.html

[75] Ibid.

over all of Syria's chemical weapons stockpiles.[76] Russian Foreign
Secretary Sergei Lavrov took him at his word. And Obama welcomed
the Russian-led effort to hammer out an agreement and plan to put
Syria's chemical weapons beyond use.[77] When American additions
were made, the Russian-initiated plan comprised four principal components, which promised to identify, destroy and remove all chemical
weapons capacity. Enforced by a UNSCR and the OPCW, this would
lead to full CWC membership. This apparent solution began in October 2013 and was a sufficient effort to prevent Anglosphere airstrikes
at the time. But that situation would not last long.

Islamic State, 2014–

At the end of 2013 and start of 2014, the term 'Islamic State' was not
common in the international press. More frequently, the emerging
group was referred to as 'Al Qaeda-affiliated'. In January 2014,
editor David Remnick interviewed President Barack Obama for a
profile in *The New Yorker*. Asked about the group that had, three
days previously, seized control of the city of Fallujah in the geographical heart of Iraq, Obama replied, 'I think the analogy we use around
here sometimes and I think is accurate, is if a JV team puts on Lakers'
uniforms, that doesn't make them Kobe Bryant'.[78] One week into
what would become an unexpectedly and devastatingly successful
military campaign for ISIL, the President of the United States saw

[76] J. Kerry, 'Remarks with UK Foreign Secretary William Hague', at the Foreign
and Commonwealth Office, London, 9 September 2013, US Department of
State, www.state.gov/secretary/remarks/2013/09/213956.htm; see also
H. Alexander, 'Syria: if Bashar al-Assad hands over chemical weapons we will
not attack, says John Kerry', *The Telegraph*, 9 September 2013, www.telegraph
.co.uk/news/worldnews/middleeast/syria/10295638/Syria-If-Bashar-al-Assad-
hands-over-chemical-weapons-we-will-not-attack-says-John-Kerry.html

[77] P. Foster, 'Syria crisis: Obama entertaining Russian-led peace-for-weapons plan
reflects weak domestic position', *The Telegraph*, 10 September 2013,
www.telegraph.co.uk/news/worldnews/barackobama/10297820/Syria-crisis-
Obama-entertaining-Russian-led-peace-for-weapons-plan-reflects-weak-
domestic-position.html; and M. Gordon and S. Myers, 'Obama calls Russia
offer on Syria possible "breakthrough"', *New York Times*, 9 September 2013,
www.nytimes.com/2013/09/10/world/middleeast/kerry-says-syria-should-hand-
over-all-chemical-arms.html?pagewanted=all

[78] S. Contorno, 'What Obama said about Islamic State', *Politifact*, 7 September
2014, www.politifact.com/truth-o-meter/statements/2014/sep/07/barack-
obama/what-obama-said-about-islamic-state-jv-team

the group as akin to an amateur Junior Varsity team. By the end of June, ISIL would control 70 per cent of Iraq's Anbar province, including the strategic city of Ramadi, located on the Euphrates and the main road to Syria. Outside of Anbar, they would also control the much larger city of Mosul in the north, home to almost two million Iraqis. In six months, ISIL would take control of 25–30 per cent of populated Iraqi territory and rule lands home to an estimated eight million people.[79] President Obama was not the only one caught out by the dramatic rise of ISIL. After all, they began their startlingly successful campaign to seize Iraqi territory at the end of December 2013 – a year in which the principal focus of the Obama administration had been the prevention of chemical weapons usage. Remarkably quickly, the crisis and civil war in Syria would develop a very different feel, focus and framing; 2014 would be a very different year for Syria and international onlookers.

Despite appearing to come from nowhere, ISIL's existence can be explained with reference to two dominant narratives on their emergence – religious and political. The first narrative ties the group's identity and beliefs to the long arc of extremist Islamist philosophy and the struggle for its territorial realisation – the history of jihad and its underlying ideas. Within this narrative, ISIL are located on a narrative trajectory that encompasses actors such as Al Qaeda and the Wahhabis, but remain distinct from them due to recognition of the heterogeneity of (Salafi) jihadism in the contemporary world.[80] The focus of this narrative, then, is the tracing of ISIL's 'intellectual genealogy', in order to understand the group's roots, beliefs, motivations and aspirations.[81] Despite the claims of some western leaders that ISIL is un-Islamic, the group's belief system explicitly emerges out

[79] K. Gilsinan, 'How ISIS territory has changed since the U.S. bombing campaign began', *The Atlantic*, 11 September 2015, www.theatlantic.com/international/archive/2015/09/isis-territory-map-us-campaign/404776; see also United Nations, 'In ISIL-controlled territory, 8 million civilians living in "state of fear" – UN expert', *UN News*, 31 July 2015, www.un.org/apps/news/story.asp?NewsID=51542#.VmwwM4SwEbA

[80] G. Wood, 'What ISIS really wants', *The Atlantic*, March 2015, www.theatlantic.com/magazine/archive/2015/03/what-isis-really-wants/384980

[81] Ibid. This lengthy article also received significant commentary and criticism. See, for example, J. Jenkins, 'What The Atlantic left out about ISIS according to their own expert', *Think Progress*, 20 February 2015, http://thinkprogress.org/world/2015/02/20/3625446/atlantic-left-isis-conversation-bernard-haykel

of a particularly extreme variant of Sunni Islam and a near-literal reading of the Koran. This reading underpins desires to return Islam to its purest form, as ISIL's supporters perceive it to have been thirteen centuries ago. It is a reading sufficiently extreme to disqualify Islam's other variants: Shia Muslims are seen to be apostates, alongside non-Muslims.[82] Within this narrative explanation of ISIL, it is possible to join the intellectual dots through the history of Islamic theology. Connecting thinkers and writers influential for Salafi jihadists is also useful for distinguishing the theological bases of groups such as Al Qaeda and ISIL, with the former arguably more influenced by the writings of Sayyid Qutb, whereas the latter appear more proximal to the beliefs of Muhammed al-Wahhab. ISIL share with the Wahhabis of the eighteenth century the label of Islam's strictest and most sustained attempt to enforce a pure form of Sharia law.

In the second narrative, ISIL's emergence is traced out of the political and security vacuum left in Iraq following the American-led intervention of 2003. Under the leadership of Jordanian militant Abu Musab al-Zarqawi, the 'Group for Monotheism and Jihad' formed in 1999. In 2004, al-Zarqawi pledged allegiance to Osama bin Laden and the group became widely known as Al Qaeda in Iraq (AQI). By 2006, AQI controlled significant portions of Sunni Iraq, before a series of substantial defeats at the hands of coalition and local forces as part of a resistance dubbed the Anbar Awakening, in which US bombs killed Zarqawi. Four months after Zarqawi's death, under the leadership of Abu Ayyub Al-Masri, AQI announced the formation of Islamic State in Iraq (ISI) and developed early plans for operations in Syria, centred on the economics and infrastructure of oil production. Iraqis who had lost their jobs and pensions in the post-2003 de-Ba'athification process occupy the majority of ISI's leadership positions. The group's leader, since 2010, was Abu Bakr al-Baghdadi, who had previously been held by US Forces at Camp Bucca.[83] Under the leadership of al-Baghdadi, as the instability of civil war spread across Syria in August 2011, ISI commenced activities in Syria, in direct contravention of the orders of

---

[82] Shia Islam is seen to be an innovation, therefore insufficiently acknowledging of the perfection of Islam in its original form: an apostasy. Wood, 'What ISIS really wants'.

[83] He was assessed as low risk and released, but the prison provided him with excellent networking opportunities and a chance to establish himself as a religious expert and leader.

Al Qaeda leader Ayman al-Zawahiri (who had replaced Osama bin Laden in May 2011). In May 2013, in a move that led al-Zawahiri to cut all ties to the group, ISI rebranded as ISIS/ISIL (ad-Dawlah al-Islāmiyah fī 'l-'Irāq wa-sh-Shām) following a merger with an Al Qaeda-affiliated group in Syria, the Nusra Front.[84]

These two narratives come together and coalesce in space and time around the territory of the Caliphate and the anticipated teleology of the apocalypse. Having led ISIL to a stunning series of military victories in the Iraqi Anbar Province in the first six months of 2014,[85] al-Baghdadi was named as caliph of a new worldwide caliphate at the end of June. Unlike Al Qaeda and affiliated groups, ISIL controlled significant territory in which it could establish Sharia law, and from which it could gain perceived legitimacy. The self-pronounced Islamic State enacts *all* of Sharia, the majority of which they see to have been denied and withheld by most Islamic governments; crucifixion, amputation and stoning are pursued alongside the enactment of elements of perceived social justice. Allied to this physical occupation of land, ISIL distinguishes itself from Al Qaeda in its focus on longer-term and relatively unworldly concerns. Rather than preoccupation with the expulsion of foreigners from holy lands, ISIL is awaiting the End Times. The coming apocalypse, ISIL believes, is scripted in the Koran. At Dabiq, in northern Syria, this teleological vision anticipates a great and final war between Christian, Western forces and defenders of Islam. The strategically unimportant town, comprising mainly farmland, gives its name to ISIL's propaganda magazine. And the eschatology centred on Dabiq frames ISIL's messages in beheading videos directed at western audiences. When Mohammed Emwazi (Jihadi John) beheaded US journalist James Foley in August 2014, he said, 'Here we are, burying the first American crusader in Dabiq, eagerly waiting for the remainder of your armies to arrive'.[86]

These videos were designed to elicit maximum shock, horror and revulsion from western audiences. But the levels of violence they depicted were by no means isolated to incidents of western-targeted propaganda. The previous month, Australians were shocked to witness

---

[84] J. Turner, 'Strategic differences: Al Qaeda's split with the Islamic State of Iraq and al-Sham', *Small Wars & Insurgencies*, 26 (2015), 208–25.

[85] The Iraqi Army was frequently reported to flee as ISIL approached, abandoning posts, weapons and populations.

[86] Wood, 'What ISIS really wants'.

images of a seven-year-old boy, who had been taken to Syria from Sydney along with his four siblings and mother. Khaled Sharrouf's son was pictured holding the severed head of a Syrian soldier, at his father's urging. Sharrouf went on to feature, as executioner, in ISIL beheading videos. Between August and November 2014, Americans James Foley, Steven Sotloff and Peter Kassig, along with Britons David Haines and Alan Henning, were all beheaded in videos produced to instil fear in western audiences and elicit a response from western political leaders. In December, approximately 100 ISIL fighters, deserting from Raqqa, met the same grizzly fate. It is likely that the images of Sharrouf's son also surfaced from the ISIL stronghold of Raqqa, in central Syria; the town became an ISIL safe haven under a particularly bloody rule. In 2014, Raqqa was dubbed the 'bride of the revolution' as the first city to fall to ISIL. With its quarter of a million residents now under al-Baghdadi's command, Raqqa, in eastern Syria, became ISIL's de facto capital. In order to announce their arrival and control, ISIL displayed the decapitated heads of Syrian Army soldiers on spikes and railings.

These spectacular displays of violence were not isolated to Raqqa or even Syria. Most notoriously, following the successful Anbar campaign and declaration of a global caliphate, ISIL launched their second Northern Iraq offensive. In August 2014, ISIL seized the town of Sinjar, near the Syrian border in northern Iraq, precipitating genocide.[87] Sinjar is home to Iraq's Yazidis – a community of non-Muslims with their own culture and faith derived from ancient Meso-potamian religions. ISIL see the Yazidis as devil worshippers and treated them accordingly. Along with 100,000 Iraqi Christians, 200,000 Yazidis were driven from their homes in the second ISIL offensive.[88] Despite fleeing to the Sinjar Mountain, tens of thousands were trapped behind ISIL lines as the Kurdish Peshmerga withdrew. Near Sinjar, Yazidi children were lined up, with older ones killed and younger ones – later dubbed 'Caliphate cubs' – sent to camps for

[87] H. Johnson, 'U.S. Holocaust Museum: the Islamic State's war On Yazidis is genocide', *Foreign Policy*, 12 November 2015, http://foreignpolicy.com/2015/11/12/u-s-holocaust-museum-the-islamic-states-war-on-yazidis-is-genocide

[88] R. Spencer, 'Isil carried out massacres and mass sexual enslavement of Yazidis, UN confirms', *The Telegraph*, 14 October 2014, www.telegraph.co.uk/news/worldnews/islamic-state/11160906/Isil-carried-out-massacres-and-mass-sexual-enslavement-of-Yazidis-UN-confirms.html

training and indoctrination.[89] Five thousand Yazidi men were killed and up to 7,000 Yazidi women enslaved. Captured women and children were treated as the spoils of war, with hundreds of women and young girls sent to markets in Mosul where they were bought and sold into sexual slavery.[90] ISIL fighters were recorded eagerly discussing the purchase of women. Eighteen months later, many remained enslaved and those who escaped struggled to speak out, having experienced considerable trauma.[91] One captured, sold and enslaved Yazidi named Aniya recalled that her 'owner' used to rape her while her daughter was outside the room, despite both of their screams.[92] According to reports by organisations such as the United Nations and the US Holocaust Museum in New York, ISIL's treatment of the Yazidis amounted to mass rape, sexual enslavement and genocide.[93]

ISIL's treatment of the Yazidis and their advance towards the Kurdish city of Erbil inspired a significant reappraisal of US foreign policy. On 7 August 2014, at the request of the Iraqi government, Obama authorised US airstrikes in Iraq. Appearing on television, he told the Yazidi people that 'America is coming to help', reassuring sceptical citizens that 'boots on the ground' was not an option and that he believed there was no American military solution in the region. Over the following week, US airstrikes contributed to the escape of some 40,000 Yazidis, trapped without food and water on Sinjar Mountain. They were assisted by Kurdish fighters' efforts to recapture towns lost to ISIL, halting and partially reversing their advance toward Erbil.[94] In response, Mohammed Emwazi executed

---

[89] L. Whyte, 'Caliphate cubs of Isis: "The children with armpit hair were killed. I became a boy soldier"', *International Business Times*, 15 December 2015, www.ibtimes.co.uk/caliphate-cubs-isis-children-armpit-hair-were-killed-i-became-boy-soldier-1533264

[90] The Guardian, 'UN: Islamic State may have committed genocide against Yazidis in Iraq', 19 March 2015, www.theguardian.com/world/2015/mar/19/un-islamic-state-genocide-yazidis-iraq-human-rights-war-crimes

[91] P. Wood, 'Islamic State: Yazidi women tell of sex-slavery trauma', *BBC News*, 22 December 2014, www.bbc.co.uk/news/world-middle-east-30573385; B. Stoter, 'After mass rape by the Islamic State, Yazidi women still struggle to break the silence', *Al-Monitor*, 9 September 2015, www.al-monitor.com/pulse/originals/2015/09/yazidi-women-rape-slave-islamic-state.html

[92] Stoter, 'After mass rape'.   [93] Johnson, 'US Holocaust Museum'.

[94] H. Cooper and M. Shear, 'Militants' siege on mountain in Iraq is over, Pentagon says', *New York Times*, 13 August 2014, www.nytimes.com/2014/08/14/world/middleeast/iraq-yazidi-refugees.html?_r=1

James Foley – ISIL's first killing of an American citizen. The video and
Emwazi's distinctive London accent ensured that 'Jihadi John' would
become the face of ISIL for western audiences. Two weeks later, on
2 September, Emwazi made good on his promise to execute Steven
Sotloff.[95] One week after that, on 10 September, Obama outlined
a four-part strategy to 'degrade and destroy' ISIL, which included
plans for US airstrikes inside Syria, with or without congressional
approval.[96]

On 22 September, Syrian Twitter user Abdulkader Hariri tweeted
that 'the sky is full of drones': the United States was bombing Raqqa.[97]
Thirty minutes later, Obama confirmed America's first airstrikes inside
Syria. Over the coming months, US airstrikes would injure ISIL leader
al-Baghdadi and kill ISIL's second-in-command Abu Sayyaf. They
would also contribute to the freeing of Tikrit and help to end the
four-month siege of Kobani (from which Alan Kurdi's family were
fleeing).[98] Despite this impact, through the second half of 2014, ISIL's
influence spread to a number of countries, including Algeria (where a
French tourist was beheaded) and Libya, where significant military
advances were made. As well as Libya and Algeria, al-Baghdadi

---

[95] It is worth noting that video analysis raised doubts about the authenticity of the
execution. While Foley and Sotloff were certainly killed, it is possible that their
murder took place off camera, with Emwazi presented as a 'front man' for media
purposes. See, for example, B. Gardner, 'Foley murder video "may have been
staged"', *The Telegraph*, 25 August 2014, www.telegraph.co.uk/news/
worldnews/middleeast/iraq/11054488/Foley-murder-video-may-have-been-
staged.html. At the start of 2016, a new British jihadist was featured in an ISIL
propaganda video, as the apparent successor to Emwazi. He was accompanied
in the video by a four-year-old British boy, dubbed the 'Junior Jihadi', who had
been taken by his mother – a 'jihadi bride' – to Syria.

[96] B. Obama, 'Statement by the President on ISIL', The White House, 10 September
2014, www.whitehouse.gov/the-press-office/2014/09/10/statement-president-
isil-1

[97] J. Saul, 'Syria air strike: Twitter user Abdulkader Hariri live tweets US Islamic
State attack "before Pentagon breaks news"', *The Independent*, 23 September
2014, www.independent.co.uk/news/world/middle-east/twitter-user-live-tweets-
attack-before-pentagon-breaks-news-9749973.html

[98] However, they would contribute to numerous and uncounted civilian deaths
(estimated at around 500 within twelve months) as well as generating divisions
within the US government, leading to the November resignation of Defense
Secretary Chuck Hagel. S. Ackerman and D. Roberts, 'Chuck Hagel forced to
step down as US defense secretary', *The Guardian*, 24 November 2014,
www.theguardian.com/us-news/2014/nov/24/chuck-hagel-step-down-us-
defence-secretary

claimed the successful extension of the caliphate into parts of Saudi Arabia, Yemen and Egypt. And, in retaliation for airstrikes, ISIL called for home-grown acts of terrorism in the West.

In the second half of 2014, facing US airstrikes and in conjunction with their continued spectacular displays of violence, ISIL set about establishing the infrastructure of a state, fixing telecommunications and setting taxes.[99] Most significant for their capabilities and finances were ISIL's social media campaign and oil infrastructure. The former was a sophisticated affair, making use of an estimated 50,000 pro-ISIL Twitter accounts.[100] Recruits are guided on social media strategy, using handbooks and software designed to maximise marketing impact.[101] The latter – centred on control of several of Syria's oil wells – was run so successfully that even ISIL's enemies were forced to trade with them.[102] As one Syrian rebel commander noted, when buying oil from ISIL, 'It's a situation that makes you laugh and cry';[103] 'Oil is the black gold that funds Isis' black flag – it fuels its war machine, provides electricity and gives the fanatical jihadis critical leverage against their neighbours.'[104] ISIL's oil infrastructure employed skilled engineers, technicians and managers, paying them high salaries, in order to produce up to 40,000 barrels of oil every day. Oil production was controlled at the top of the organisation's hierarchy. It was run seriously and effectively and was very difficult to disrupt.

By the start of 2015, Islamic State was doing its utmost to replicate the functions of a state, while implementing a full vision of Sharia law based on a literal reading of the Koran. Crucifixions, amputations, beheadings and enslavement continued unabated. Following the

---

[99] M. Karouny, 'Life under Isis: for residents of Raqqa is this really a caliphate worse than death?', *The Independent*, 5 September 2014, www.independent.co.uk/news/world/middle-east/life-under-isis-for-residents-of-raqqa-is-this-really-a-caliphate-worse-than-death-9715799.html

[100] J. Berger and J. Morgan, 'The ISIS Twitter Census', *Brooking Institute*, March 2015, www.brookings.edu/~/media/research/files/papers/2015/03/isis-twitter-census-berger-morgan/isis_twitter_census_berger_morgan.pdf

[101] M. Chastain, 'ISIS propaganda manual reveals social media strategy', *Breitbart*, 28 October 2015, www.breitbart.com/national-security/2015/10/28/isis-propaganda-manual-reveals-social-media-strategy

[102] E. Solomon, 'Isis Inc: how oil fuels the jihadi terrorists', *Financial Times*, 14 October 2015, www.ft.com/cms/s/2/b8234932-719b-11e5-ad6d-f4ed76f0900a.html#axzz3uPxjJcxg

[103] Ibid.   [104] Ibid.

beheadings of Alan Henning and Peter Kassig, Japanese nationals Haruna Yakawa and Kenji Goto were executed in January 2015. The following month, ISIL executed a Jordanian pilot, Moaz al-Kasasbeh, who had been held captive for two months, following the crash of his F16 near Raqqa. This execution was particularly gruesome as a carefully edited, high-quality video emerged showing the pilot being burned alive inside a cage.[105] The video was reportedly shown on big screens to large crowds, including young children.[106] At the same time, reports began to emerge of ISIL killing gay men by throwing them off buildings in front of large crowds.[107] In June, a video emerged showing a group of hostages being split into three, before some were executed using a rocket-propelled grenade, others were drowned in a cage and the rest were beheaded using electrical charges.[108] In addition to the bloodshed, ISIL were accused of 'cultural genocide', with the destruction of several sites of historical significance, including parts of the ancient archaeological city of Palmyra, where the retired chief archaeologist Khalid al-Assad was beheaded.[109]

The year 2015 also saw the rapid international extension of ISIL activity and influence. In Libya, twenty-one Egyptian Christians and thirty Ethiopian Christians were killed; the majority were beheaded by the shore of the Mediterranean. In Afghanistan, thirty-five people were killed in a suicide bombing.[110] In Yemen, 137 people were killed by

---

[105] A. Marszal, 'Jordanian pilot "burned alive" in new Isil video', *The Telegraph*, 3 February 2015, www.telegraph.co.uk/news/worldnews/islamic-state/11387756/Jordanian-pilot-burned-alive-in-new-Isil-video.html

[106] A. Marszal, 'Isil "broadcast video of pilot burning on giant public screen to young children"', *The Telegraph*, 4 February 2015, www.telegraph.co.uk/news/worldnews/islamic-state/11390609/Isil-broadcast-video-of-pilot-burning-on-giant-public-screen-to-young-children.html

[107] Others have been stoned, or beheaded. These atrocities led to LGBT rights being discussed at the United Nations Security Council for the first time. S. Power, @AmbassadorPower, 24 August 2015, https://twitter.com/AmbassadorPower/status/635873001913851904?ref_src=twsrc%5Etfw

[108] D. Romero, 'Isis timeline: A year under the so-called Islamic State', *The Independent*, 28 June 2015, www.independent.co.uk/news/world/middle-east/isis-timeline-a-year-under-the-so-called-islamic-state-10342197.html

[109] L. Porter, 'Destruction of Middle East's heritage is "cultural genocide"', *The Telegraph*, 23 July 2015, www.telegraph.co.uk/travel/destinations/middleeast/11756540/Destruction-of-Middle-Easts-heritage-is-cultural-genocide.html

[110] N. Kumar, 'ISIS claims suicide bombing in Afghanistan that killed 35', *Time*, 18 April 2015, http://time.com/3827434/isis-suicide-bombing-afghanistan

suicide bombings in mosques.[111] In Texas, two people were killed at a competition to draw the Prophet Mohammed. In Nigeria, Boko Harem pledged allegiance to ISIL and al-Baghdadi. In Tunisia, thirty-eight tourists, thirty of whom were British, were shot at a beach resort in Sousse.[112] In Saudi Arabia, two suicide bombers at Shi'ite mosques killed twenty-four people. In Kuwait, twenty-five people were killed in a similar attack. In France, a man was beheaded at a chemical plant.[113] In Turkey, thirty-two people were killed at a cultural centre in Suruc by a suicide bomber. In Egypt, 224 people were killed in the bombing of Russian Metrojet Flight 9268 from Sharm el-Sheikh. In California, fourteen people were killed and twenty-two injured in a shooting in San Bernadino.[114] These combined efforts, allied with a remarkable propaganda campaign, drew tens of thousands of foreign fighters to ISIL ranks, mainly from Saudi Arabia, Tunisia and other nearby states, but also from numerous Western states, particularly the UK, France, Australia, the Low Countries/Benelux and Scandinavia.

Proxy War, 2015–

As two of the most significant and deadly parties involved in the Syrian Civil War, ISIL and Assad's forces have dominated international headlines. However, they are two groups amongst very many others, which – through their multifaceted aspirations and interactions – create a barrier to understanding and resolving the crisis. The plethora of competing factions in Syria reflects the complexity of the civil war. During the civil war's fourth phase, as many as eighteen distinct opposition groups were represented on the ground in Aleppo alone. A *simplified* BBC guide to the diversity of the rebel groupings listed

---

[111] H. Almasmari and J. Hannah, 'Yemen: bombs kill 137 at mosques; ISIS purportedly lays claim', *CNN*, 21 March 2015, http://edition.cnn.com/2015/03/20/middleeast/yemen-violence

[112] Although ISIL claimed responsibility, the Tunisian government blamed the attacks on Al Qaeda in the Islamic Maghreb (AQIM).

[113] Conflicting reports have emerged linking and de-linking this attack to ISIL. However, it came in conjunction with a shooting on a train to Paris and the earlier Al Qaeda-linked Charlie Hebdo attacks, as well as the later Paris attacks and an additional shooting at a police station on the Charlie Hebdo anniversary.

[114] LA Times, 'San Bernadino shooting updates', 9 December 2015, www.latimes.com/local/lanow/la-me-ln-san-bernardino-shooting-live-updates-htmlstory.html

twenty-one named organisations and affiliates.[115] This is not entirely an accidental occurrence. At the start of the conflict in 2011, Bashar al-Assad released from prison a large number of people who would go on to become leaders within Islamic State and Islamist rebel groups.[116] It appears that this was an attempt first to tinge rebel forces with extremism, making international support less palatable, and second to create tensions and division within opposition camps. It worked, with CIA and Pentagon attempts to bolster, arm and train rebel forces failing and US airstrikes focusing on Islamic State, rather than Assad. This strategy fuelled the rise of a veritable smorgasbord of actors, the complexity of which remains overwhelming to lay and expert observers alike.[117] Here, the diversity of rebel, Kurdish, regional and international forces is discussed in turn, in order to unravel some of this complexity and complement earlier discussions of government forces, the FSA and ISIL.

In late 2013, prior to ISIL's rise to fame through their devastating Anbar Campaign, Syrian opposition and rebel forces split in two, leaving the Free Syrian Army and the newly created Islamic Front. The principal immediate reasons for the creation of the new Islamic Front were concerns regarding the FSA's potential participation in peace talks in Geneva and an under-representation of forces on the ground in the National Coalition exile opposition. The split came following discussions with the FSA leadership and after the United States had agreed to fund and train the FSA.[118] Through Chief Commander of the Supreme Military Council Salim Idriss – a Syrian Army defector and multilingual German-educated professor – the USA had agreed to supply significant levels of military aid, despite the FSA

[115] BBC, 'Guide to the Syrian rebels'.
[116] R. Salloum, 'From jail to jihad: former prisoners fight in Syrian insurgency', *Der Spiegel*, 10 October 2013, www.spiegel.de/international/world/former-prisoners-fight-in-syrian-insurgency-a-927158.html
[117] As Assad likely calculated, some of these actors diverted attention from the atrocities of the regime, even the use of barrel bombs and chemical weapons.
[118] The FSA itself was never a homogenous group. Instead, it was made up of a variety of actors and ad hoc coalitions. These included the Free Men of Syria, the Northern Storm Brigade and Ahrar Souriya. See BBC, 'Guide to the Syrian rebels' and E. O'Bagy, 'The Free Syrian Army', *Institute for the Study of War*, March 2013, www.understandingwar.org/sites/default/files/The-Free-Syrian-Army-24MAR.pdf

leader's own admission that rebel forces were chronically divided and unruly.[119] Although specific elements were subsequently cut,[120] this policy was continued from 2013 through to late 2015. This was despite FSA desertions, as brutal conditions, divided alliances and other imperatives decimated FSA numbers, with Russian Foreign Minister Sergey Lavrov suggesting they had become 'a phantom' by late 2015.[121] By this stage, it was Islamic Front, rather than the FSA, which dominated opposition forces, making a mockery of British claims that 70,000 moderate fighters could be supported on the ground through Western airstrikes.[122]

At the time of the announcement of their formation in November 2013, the Islamic Front comprised seven distinct named groups.[123] Fourteen months later, the most important of those groups were Ahrar Ash-Sham (Islamic Movement of Free Men of the Levant), Jaysh al-Islam (Army of Islam) and Ansar al-Sham (Supporters of the Levant). The former, Ahrar Ash-Sham, dominated the Islamic Front's predecessor organisation, the Syrian Islamic Front, which formed at the end of 2012 and dissolved with the formation of the new Islamic Front alliance.[124] Behind the FSA, in 2013, Ahrar Ash-Sham was the largest united opposition force, albeit itself comprised of multiple factions and brigades. The creation of Islamic Front brought together approximately 45,000 Islamist and Salafi fighters, united in defeating Assad and creating an Islamic state (albeit opposed to ISIL and broadly opposed to Al Qaeda-affiliated groups). Frequently, alliances of convenience have formed with other groups and been fought through a range of temporary command centres – joint operations rooms – where

---

[119] BBC News, 'US says it will give military aid to Syria rebels', 14 June 2013, www.bbc.co.uk/news/world-us-canada-22899289

[120] Specifically, efforts to train and equip rebels, which had cost the USA over $500 million, despite yielding only a handful of local troops.

[121] A. Entous, 'U.S., allies to boost aid to Syria rebels', *Wall Street Journal*, 4 November 2015, www.wsj.com/articles/u-s-allies-to-boost-aid-to-syria-rebels-1446682624

[122] Numerous commentators and Members of Parliament (MPs) ridiculed the British prime minister's claim in December 2015, suggesting it was akin to Tony Blair's infamous forty-five minute claim on the threat of Iraqi WMD to the UK.

[123] A. Lund, 'Say hello to the Islamic Front', *Carnegie*, 22 November 2013, http://carnegieendowment.org/syriaincrisis/?fa=53679

[124] A. Lund, 'The non-state militant landscape in Syria', *Combating Terrorism Center*, West Point, 27 August 2013, https://ctc.usma.edu/the-non-state-militant-landscape-in-syria

localised campaigns are coordinated against mutual enemies. For example, rebel groups and the FSA have cooperated with al-Nusra – Al Qaeda in Syria – in order to fight government forces.[125] Significant rebel successes have been achieved through such coordinated efforts. At the time of its formation, the Islamic Front also included a small number of Islamist Kurdish fighters, 'adding a touch of ethnic diversity to the new [otherwise Sunni] alliance'.[126] However, the vast majority of Kurdish fighters were fighting (initially) defensive battles elsewhere.

In Iraq, the Kurdish Peshmerga – loyal to and fighting for the Kurdish Regional Government in Erbil in the north of the country – met ISIL's Anbar Campaign, limiting advances and winning back key towns. Turkish PKK (Kurdistan Workers' Party) fighters assisted these efforts, helping, amongst others, the escape of the stranded Yazidis. In 2015, the Peshmerga received training from the USA as part of Operation Inherent Resolve, with multiple countries trying to supply arms, despite the Iraqi government in Baghdad intercepting many. Three years previously, in mid-2012 in the north of Syria, People's Protection Units (YPG) – Kurdish fighters, together with Syriac and Christian groups, loyal to the Kurdish Supreme Committee – engaged Assad's forces in a stand-off that resulted in the Syrian Army withdrawing, following negotiations. From 2013, the YPG fought with the aim of repelling first Islamist and then (from 2014) ISIL advances into Kurdish regions and communities. Like Islamic Front groups and ISIL, the Kurds have attracted numerous international fighters, including a perhaps surprising mix of former US troops and Han Chinese, as well as the former Australian politician and trade unionist Matthew Gardiner.[127] From 2015, US airstrikes were increasingly coordinated with YPG efforts on the ground, in a relatively effective alliance, with Arab fighters slowly being 'glued on' to Kurdish forces.[128]

---

[125] Following the rise of ISIL and Al Qaeda's split from them, al-Nusra have, at times, attempted to present themselves as a moderate alternative.

[126] Lund, 'Say hello to the Islamic Front'.

[127] However, the numbers of foreign fighters recruited by Kurdish forces is dwarfed by the lure of ISIL for attracting international focus. On Gardiner, see X. LaCanna, 'NT political figure Matthew Gardiner breaks silence on Kurdish groups', *ABC News*, 28 April 2015, www.abc.net.au/news/2015-04-28/nt-political-figure-matthew-gardiner-breaks-silence/6428608

[128] A. Lund, 'Syria's Kurds at the center of America's anti-jihadi strategy', *Carnegie Center*, 2 December 2015, http://carnegieendowment.org/syriaincrisis/?fa=62158

While Bashar al-Assad had narrowly avoided facing US military force in 2012 and 2013, the rise of ISIL in 2014 was a game changer for the Obama administration's stance on Syria. The USA commenced an air campaign in September 2014, having previously limited US involvement on the Syrian side of the border to the supplying of arms and training of rebel and opposition groups. The United States' Operation Inherent Resolve was accompanied by airstrikes conducted by Canada (Operation Impact), France (Operation Chammal), Australia (Operation Okra), the UK (Operation Shader) and Jordan.[129] France, too, was an early military participant (from September 2014), with French airstrikes supporting the US-led mission in Syria. These efforts were significantly ramped up following the attacks in Paris in November 2015, with numerous bombings of ISIL positions in Raqqa. Canadian airstrikes in Iraq also began in September 2014, before their extension over the border to Syria in April 2015, following a parliamentary vote at the end of the previous month; in October 2015, newly elected Canadian Prime Minister Justin Trudeau halted Canadian airstrikes. Australian airstrikes in Iraq also began in September 2014, extending to Syria one year later, in September 2015. Britain joined airstrikes in Iraq in September 2014, following the request of the Iraqi Government, extending these efforts to Syria in December 2015, after a second (and this time supportive) parliamentary vote. Although the USA was responsible for 80 per cent of the coalition's airstrikes, French, British and Australian efforts were significant, both militarily and in terms of furthering the perceived legitimacy of an increasingly multilateral operation. The addition, extension or intensification of British, French and Australian airstrikes, in the second half of 2015, constituted one half of the transition of the Syrian crisis from a domestic civil war with international sponsors to an explicit proxy war with external military intervention.

The most dramatic and consequential military intervention of 2015, however, was not the entry of additional coalition partners into the equation. Rather, late 2015 was most notable for the commencement of Russian airstrikes in Syria. While coalition forces struck almost exclusively ISIL (and occasionally Al Qaeda-affiliated) positions, Russian strikes were frequently at odds with President Vladimir Putin's

---

[129] Jordan's intervention resulted in the burning alive of pilot Moaz al-Kasasbeh (see above).

anti-terrorist rhetoric.[130] Instead of an effort to 'destroy and degrade' ISIL,[131] which unified the US-led coalition, Russian airstrikes can be understood as supporting Assad, following his request to Putin and on whose behalf they were begun. This meant that Russian airstrikes, flown from an Assad stronghold near Latakia, were perfectly in lock step with the strategy of the Syrian government. In and around Aleppo, across Idlib and east of Homs – against different groups – Russian airstrikes made moderately effective progress in the Assad regime's cause.[132] And, sadly, like Assad's forces, Russian airstrikes frequently caused significant non-combatant fatalities.[133]

Russia, of course, is not Assad's only international sponsor.[134] The Middle East and Gulf Region is divided by the Syrian crisis and civil war. Iran and Hezbollah joined Russia in supporting the Syrian government. The Assad regime, and his father's before it, has been a key and consistent strategic ally for Iran. Iran has therefore 'conducted an extensive, expensive and integrated effort to keep President Bashar al-Assad in power as long as possible'.[135] Funding, supplies and training are part of this strategy, at a cost of billions of dollars annually.[136] As of late 2015, this involvement was increasing.[137] Allied with Iran, Lebanese Hezbollah have also pursued 'a more direct combat role in Syria as the Assad regime began losing control over Syrian territory in

---

[130] One observer noted that Moscow's claims demonstrated 'a sanctimonious pigheadedness unseen since Baghdad Bob'. A. Lund, 'Ten most important developments in Syria in 2015', *Syria Comment*, 3 January 2016, www.joshualandis.com/blog/ten-most-important-developments-syria-2015

[131] AFP, '"More than 90%" of Russian airstrikes in Syria have not targeted Isis, US says', *The Guardian*, 7 October 2015, www.theguardian.com/world/2015/oct/07/russia-airstrikes-syria-not-targetting-isis

[132] A. Lund, 'Assessing the Russian intervention in Syria', *Carnegie*, 7 December 2015, http://carnegieendowment.org/syriaincrisis/?fa=62207

[133] J. Malsin, 'Russian airstrikes in Syria seem to be hurting civilians more than ISIS', *Time*, 30 November 2015, http://time.com/4129222/russia-airstrikes-syria-civilian-casualties-isis

[134] China's position of non-interference has arguably also indirectly supported Assad, preventing the isolation of Russia in the UN Security Council.

[135] W. Fulton, J. Holliday and S. Wyer, 'Iranian strategy in Syria', Institute for the Study of War, May 2013, www.understandingwar.org/sites/default/files/IranianStrategyinSyria-1MAY.pdf

[136] BBC News, 'Syria crisis: where key countries stand', 30 October 2015, www.bbc.co.uk/news/world-middle-east-23849587

[137] H. Bastni, 'Iran quietly deepens involvement in Syria's war', *BBC News*, 20 October 2015, www.bbc.co.uk/news/world-middle-east-34572756

2012'.[138] In response, Israel has occasionally struck Hezbollah positions inside Syria. Shi'a militants from across the region – Lebanon, Iraq and Iran in particular – have been drawn to fight on behalf of Assad.

In contrast, Turkey and Saudi Arabia were early and vocal critics of the Assad regime in 2011 and 2012.[139] However, concerns that Assad's demise facilitated ISIL's rise and success caused President Erdogan to soften his stance towards the Syrian government in 2015.[140] This was coupled to a re-calculation of ISIL's potential role in degrading Kurdish forces in Turkey and the wider region. Turkey has also been critical of Western support for Kurdish YPG forces and, in November 2015, risked bringing NATO and Russia head to head with the downing of a Russian fighter jet that had reportedly twice crossed into Turkish airspace.[141] Saudi Arabia, on the other hand, although partially distracted by conflict in Yemen, has maintained a hard-line stance against Assad, funding and supplying arms to Sunni Islamist opposition forces.[142]

Standing at the crossroads of the Middle East's fractured ethnic, religious and geopolitical landscape, the crisis and civil war in Syria has split the region and its various international sponsors, all the way up to the UN Security Council. Although cooperation in specific areas has been achieved – for example, coordinated US–Russian airstrikes against ISIL in areas such as Palmyra – Syria has helped to initiate the onset of a contemporary bipolarity reminiscent of the Cold War. This division has repeatedly scuppered efforts at negotiation and peace talks. In short, then, the crisis in Syria has divided the country, the region and the world. This division has come, first and foremost, at the expense of the Syrian people, although its implications reach much further.

[138] Fulton et al., 'Iranian strategy in Syria'.

[139] C. Phillips, 'Into the quagmire: Turkey's frustrated Syria policy', *Chatham House*, December 2012, www.chathamhouse.org/sites/files/chathamhouse/public/Research/Middle%20East/1212bp_phillips.pdf

[140] S. Sharma, 'What made Turkey change its Syria policy?', *Middle East Eye*, 1 October 2015, www.middleeasteye.net/news/what-made-turkey-change-its-syria-policy-519642437

[141] One pilot was killed, the other made it to the safety of a government base inside Syria. One member of a Russian special forces team attempting the pilots' recovery was also killed.

[142] John McCain's endorsement of the policy extended to him proclaiming, 'Thank God for Saudi Arabia!'

Conclusion

Over Christmas 2015, it was possible to walk through Hamburg in northern Germany and witness a large group of teenagers and young men huddled in the unusually mild winter outside the Apple Store on the banks of the Binnenalster, the city's small central lake. Previously, it would have been reasonable to assume, perhaps, that these were young Germans of Turkish descent. They were, of course, Syrian refugees, making use of the free and reliable wireless internet access the shop offered through its glass frontage, even when closed. Across town in the main train station, volunteers in high-visibility jackets guided and advised new arrivals – mainly families with a few bags and suitcases. In 2015, Germany welcomed over one million refugees. In part this was an economic opportunity for a country faced with an ageing and stag-nating population. For Angela Merkel, her government and many Germans, it was a moral imperative, based on a desire to remember and redress the wrongs of the past, whether the horrors of World War II or the impact of impassable borders during the Cold War.[143] This response was unique within Europe. By late 2015, however, Merkel was forced to accept a compromise, reversing her previous position and accepting the need for quotas, in order to avoid a plan for fencing off parts of the German border. In the New Year, Denmark and Sweden – previously principal destinations for refugees – reversed years of com-mitment to the free movement of people within the Schengen area, reinstituting border controls. And Germany reeled as it became apparent that a series of assaults on women across several towns was apparently coordinated by groups of refugees, suspected to be from North Africa.

In the United States, following the shooting of thirty-six people in California and fifty in Orlando,[144] calls for tough anti-terrorist and

---

[143] *Time* named Merkel person of the year for 2015, recalling her experience as an East Berliner during the Cold War in explaining her response to the refugee crisis. K. Vick, 'Chancellor of the Free World', *Time*, December 2015, http://time.com/time-person-of-the-year-2015-angela-merkel. See also M. Amman, et al., 'Quiet capitulation: Merkel slowly changes tune on refugee issue', *Der Spiegel*, 20 November 2015, www.spiegel.de/international/germany/angela-merkel-changes-her-stance-on-refugee-limits-a-1063773.html

[144] The first incident took place in San Bernardino, west of Los Angeles, where thirty-six people were shot and fourteen killed by two shooters accused of being radicalised and influenced by Islamic State. In June 2016, in Orlando, a lone-wolf gunman, radicalised by Islamic State propaganda, opened fire in a

anti-immigration policies were increasingly vocal. Most notably, Republican Party nominee for president Donald Trump espoused a series of anti-Muslim policies. These included a national database of Muslim Americans, with their 'granting' of special identity cards and a temporary ban on foreign Muslims entering the USA. These statements were alarming, coming from a potential presidential candidate polling twice as well as his nearest party competitor. They were more concerning still in the event of his unexpected Electoral College victory in November 2016. As is discussed in Chapter 7, it did not take long, following his inauguration, for America's 45th president to make good on his election promise, signing an Executive Order instigating a temporary ban on refugees and the extreme vetting of anyone arriving in the USA with links, however tenuous, to seven majority-Muslim states. While the Order's constitutionality met legal challenges, halting its operation, its rapid and widespread initial impact endured through the fear its passing and carrying out had generated. And, America's president would learn from his mistakes, signing a second Order that took into account the successful legal challenges of the first.

Five years after a group of teenage boys had scrawled graffiti on the wall of a local school, inadvertently instigating Syria's demise, the victims of the country's collapse, alongside those who just happened to hold particular religious beliefs, were facing discrimination across the Western world. If the first two phases of the Syrian Crisis had largely exhausted Western onlookers, the third and fourth phases of the crisis had regained the attention of the public and politicians alike, to both positive and negative effect. The rise of ISIL at the start of 2014 and the commencement of Russian airstrikes in September 2015 re-framed the Syrian crisis as a new global war on terrorism and the onset of a new Cold War. Together, the fears instilled by ISIL; the prospects of Great Power conflict in Syria; terrorism in America, Northern Africa and Europe; and the onset of a refugee crisis without precedent since World War II have exacerbated and engrained despair, disdain and discrimination. Moreover, in the past five years, these

---

nightclub, killing fifty people. Across the Atlantic, in Leytonstone, London, a lone man wielding a knife was arrested for attempted murder in response to British airstrikes in Syria. An onlooker's remark that 'You ain't no Muslim, Bruv' resonated widely, circulating virally on social media. Elsewhere, numerous reports emerged of foiled plots in France (e.g. in Orleans), as well as the United States.

issues have increasingly cross-contaminated each other, spinning an ever-more complex web, from which escape is difficult.

From 2016, the Syrian Civil War's four principal phases (more clearly and more evidently than ever previously) bled into each other. No longer is it commonplace for Anglosphere leaders to describe the conflict in terms almost exclusive to human rights, chemical weapons, ISIL or the dangers of Russian intervention. Now, all four co-exist and intertwine to the extent that their imbricated complexity represents for the Anglosphere a Gordian knot apparently too messy and tightly bound to cut through or disentangle. The co-existence of all four features simultaneously has been potentially debilitating for Anglosphere foreign policy, as public (and elite) confusion as to what the Syrian Civil War *is* threatens to inspire disengagement with the crux of the conflict, centring on Assad. Since attempting to isolate any given component, with the exception of ISIL, appears to risk unsettling another, calls have inevitably arisen that, since there are no good options, it is better to do nothing. These calls have been both reinforced and undermined by recent developments within the domestic political landscape of the Anglosphere.

The election of Donald Trump followed the equally surprising British referendum on membership of the European Union. Both have threatened to turn common sense political affairs on their head, whilst leading to the possibility of a resurgent ethno-nationalism at the heart of Anglosphere foreign policy. Despite Brexit, the chaos and complexity of the situation in the Syrian Civil War has not been matched by the tumult evident in the domestic political landscapes of Anglosphere partners, but uncertainty and the epistemological entry costs of engaging with the Syrian Civil War are significant. Within that immediate reality, in the chapters that follow, this book explores the response of three of the most important states – and the most important international coalition – to have intervened militarily in Syria: the old Anglosphere coalition, comprising the United States, United Kingdom and Australia. Joined by France, the fate of Syria hinged on the role played by this coalition, as it confronted Assad, chemical weapons fears, ISIL and Russia. Perhaps that should not be the case. But the nature of these three states – their culture, traditions and identities – means that it was always likely that it would end up this way. That is a remarkable thing and it is explored in the following chapter.

2 | *The Anglosphere*

> If the population of the English-speaking commonwealth be added to that of the United States... there will be no quivering, precarious balance of power to offer its temptation to ambition or adventure. On the contrary, there will be an overwhelming assurance of security.
>
> Winston Churchill[1]

> The English-speaking nations have made an enormous contribution... to the defense of liberty in the last two hundred years... a contribution, I would argue, in excess of any other grouping of countries.
>
> John Howard[2]

Introduction

Talk of an Anglosphere is a case of old wine in new bottles: although the label is relatively new, the contents are of a considerably more mature vintage. In his novel, *The Diamond Age*, Neal Stephenson first coined the term 'Anglosphere' in the mid 1990s, using it exactly once across 450 pages.[3] As a literary device and challenge to his readers to re-think Westphalian international order, Stephenson's noun was new, but the idea drew on other influential writers, thinkers and politicians. Whether in the form of George Orwell's 'Oceania', Samuel Huntington's 'Western civilisation', or Winston Churchill's 'English-speaking nations', the

---

[1] In 1946, Winston Churchill delivered this line during his infamous 'Iron Curtain' speech, cited in S. Vucetic, *The Anglosphere: A Genealogy of a Racialized Identity in International Relations* (Stanford: Stanford University Press, 2011).

[2] J. Howard, 'The Anglosphere and the advance of freedom', Heritage Lectures 1176, Heritage Foundation, speech given 28 September 2010, published 3 January 2011, p. 6.

[3] N. Stephenson, *The Diamond Age: Or, A Young Lady's Illustrated Primer* (New York: Random House, 1995). And see S. Vucetic, 'The logics of culture in the Anglosphere' in J. Batora and A. Mokra (eds.), *Culture and External Relations: Europe and Beyond* (Farnham: Ashgate, 2011), p. 47.

notion of an Anglosphere predates its naming.[4] A glaring contemporary neologism,[5] in its simplest formulation, the term Anglosphere is used to denote 'the countries where English is the main native language, considered collectively'.[6] If only things were so simple. A term such as the Anglosphere is 'impossible': a 'quintessentially contested' category.[7] Yet, the idea that this 'impossible' term denotes has been at the heart of prosecutions and understandings of world politics for a century and a quarter. This idea, perhaps more than any other, has shaped international order in the modern world.

Alongside 'English-speaking peoples', the term 'Anglosphere' refers to older phenomena, such as 'Anglo-Saxondom', 'Anglo-America' and 'Greater Britain'.[8] The academic discipline of International Relations has attributed 'little or no theoretical status to these terms', despite the fact 'they have long defined' patterns of inclusion and exclusion for

---

[4] Orwell's tripartite division of Earth meant that his Oceania encompassed South America, as well as those countries more usually included in understandings of the Anglosphere. It did, however, divide the UK from his imagined Eurasia. Huntington's Western civilisation includes North America, the UK, Australasia and South Africa. Perhaps Winston Churchill did more than any other for the cause of tracing and popularising the notion of an alliance of the English-speaking nations and their peoples, across his four-volume history. S. P. Huntington, *The Clash of Civilizations: And the Remaking of World Order* (New York: Simon & Schuster, 1996); G. Orwell, *Nineteen Eighty-Four* (London: Penguin, 2004 [1949]); W. Churchill, *A History of the English-Speaking Peoples: A One-Volume Abridgement* (New York: Skyhorse Publishing, 2011). Similar connections can be made to Walter Lippmann's 'Atlantic community': S. Vucetic, 'A racialized peace? How Britain and the US made their relationship special', *Foreign Policy Analysis*, 7 (2011), pp. 403–21, 416.

[5] See S. Vucetic, 'Bound to follow? The Anglosphere and US-led coalitions of the willing, 1950–2001', *European Journal of International Relations*, 17 (2011), 27–49.

[6] Oxford English Dictionary, 'Anglosphere', www.oxforddictionaries.com/definition/english/anglosphere (accessed 3 November 2019).

[7] J. O'Hagan, *Conceptions of the West in International Relations Thought: From Oswald Spengler to Edward Said* (Basingstoke: Macmillan, 2002), cited in Vucetic, 'Bound to follow?', p. 6.

[8] Vucetic, 'Bound to follow?'; Sir John Seeley's *The Expansion of England* was also popular and influential. See C. Browning and B. Tonra, 'Beyond the West and towards the Anglosphere?' in C. Browning and M. Lehti (eds.), *The Struggle for the West: A Divided and Contested Legacy* (Abingdon: Routledge, 2010), FN 3 and the version, C. Browning and B. Tonra, 'Beyond the West and towards the Anglosphere?', pp. 1–21, www.academia.edu/341929/Beyond_the_West_and_Towards_the_Anglosphere

'millions and, indeed, billions of people'.[9] The idea of Greater Britain, for example, has had an enduring influence, 'informing calls for a "union of democracies"' in the 1930s and helping to inspire the Anglosphere's resurgence in the 2000s.[10] In between, its ideas have resonated with and informed the language of some of Britain's greatest and longest reigning leaders. As Margaret Thatcher put it:

The relationship between our nations is founded not just on a shared language, but also on shared history, on shared values and upon shared ideals. Together we have withstood the forces of evil and tyranny in whatever form we found them. In the words of Winston Churchill, we have 'discharged our common duty to the human race'. And if freedom is to flourish, we must continue with our task.[11]

It is certainly true that in 'times of crisis', the Anglosphere has tended to fall 'back into the habit of working together'.[12] It is more than this, however: the Anglosphere goes far beyond global crisis management; it is about the proactive creation of modern world order, often in its own image and nearly always towards its own benefit. In these repeated acts of internationalism, interventionism and imperialism, the Anglosphere has been the vehicle through which the mantle of global leadership has been passed and continuity achieved, in a remarkably smooth process of hegemonic transition. This conceptualisation of the Anglosphere enabled Thatcher and Churchill to agree with Harold Macmillan: 'These Americans represent the new Roman Empire and we Britons, like the Greeks of old, must teach them how to make it go'.[13]

[9] Vucetic, 'A racialized peace?', p. 416.
[10] D. Deudney, 'Greater Britain or greater synthesis: Seeley, Mackinder, and Wells on Britain in the global industrial era', *Review of International Studies*, 27 (2001), 187–208; and D. Bell, *The Idea of Greater Britain: Empire and the Future of World Order, 1860–1900* (Princeton: Princeton University Press, 2007), pp. 271–2; both cited in Vucetic, 'A racialized peace', p. 416.
[11] These are Margaret Thatcher's words from a speech in 2001, cited by John Howard at a speech in her honour. Howard, 'The Anglosphere'.
[12] R. Ponnuru, 'The empire of freedom: where the United States belongs: the Anglosphere', *National Review*, 55 (2003), 4–6; cited in Vucetic, 'Bound to follow?', p. 2.
[13] Macmillan's words are cited from 1943 in J. Heer, 'Operation Anglosphere: today's most ardent American imperialists weren't born in the USA', *Boston Globe Ideas*, 23 March 2003, www.jeetheer.com/politics/anglosphere.htm. See also C. Hitchens, *Blood, Class and Empire: The Enduring Anglo-American Relationship* (London: Atlantic Books, 2004), who makes use of this analogy in the title of his first chapter.

This transition and the 'outbreak of peace', as Britain waned and America grew,[14] is one of the most consequential occurrences of the modern world. And the Anglosphere's perseverance, despite challenges and adversity, is remarkable. Walter Russell Mead has termed it 'the biggest geopolitical story in modern times: the birth, rise, triumph, defense and continuing growth of Anglo-American power despite continuing and always renewed opposition and conflict'.[15] From the rise of the British Empire to the era of unrivalled and unprecedented American primacy, 'the Anglo nations – singly or in concert – have taken a special responsibility for the world order'.[16] Today, they account for 7 per cent of the global population but a staggering one third of global gross domestic product, as well as predictably but impressively recording well over half of all global military expenditure. The apparent triumph and coordinated foreign policies 'of the Anglo-Saxons' have achieved no less than the creation of a 'maritime-capitalist order that now encompasses the whole world'.[17]

What then binds these nations together, creating the most consequential, powerful and dispersed alliance in history? The extant literature finds 'defining features' in the 'values and institutions associated with the historical experience of England/Britain as well as the English language'.[18] Ethnicity and religion are often downplayed,[19] despite their formative importance. This pattern of selective emphasis, while likely well meant, deliberately follows lines of acceptable enquiry and political correctness. It is, understandably, mirrored in contemporary political statements. For John Howard, the defining feature of Anglosphere bonds and cooperation is:

... a very long and very rich heritage of the defense of freedom: in a world in which the values of openness and freedom are under constant assault, the fidelity of the Anglospheric nations to openness, to a robust parliamentary system of government – and in the case of the United States, certainly of a

---

[14] Alongside the subsequent adoption of a perceived mentoring role.

[15] W. R. Mead, *God and Gold: Britain, America, and the Making of the Modern World* (New York: Alfred Knopf, 2007).

[16] L. M. Mead, 'Why Anglos lead', *The National Interest*, 82 (2006), 1–8.

[17] O. Harries, 'Anglo-Saxon attitudes: the making of the modern world', *Foreign Affairs*, 87 (2008), 170–4.

[18] Vucetic, 'Bound to follow?', p. 6.

[19] Ibid., see also J. Bennett, 'The emerging Anglosphere', *Orbis*, 46 (2002), 111–26.

different brand but no less robust, no less open and no less committed to freedom – the fidelity of those nations to the rule of law, the willingness of those nations to apply the rule of law not only to the behavior of others but also to their own behavior and of course the remarkable facility of the English language.[20]

This chapter explores several of these entangled bonds of fidelity, investigating downplayed and formative racialised narratives alongside the role played by language, identity, culture, elites and institutions. It also explores the often-overlooked importance of war and war's consequences for mutual familiarity and revisited alliance politics because, 'when push comes to shove, the English-speaking peoples tend to flock together'; this flocking is symbiotic, re-creating the notion that Anglosphere members are birds of a feather.[21] That sense of familial kinship has been central to the prosecution of the War on Terror, despite the legacy of the 2003 war in Iraq. It remains vital in responding to today's most significant crisis: the civil war in Syria. It is, certainly, a process of transnational storytelling – as national (hi)stories interlock. But it is a story that is sufficiently widespread and deeply resonant to be something that is *felt* and lived by very many people in the Anglosphere.

The Old Anglosphere Coalition

The Anglosphere is more than a group of states united by a common tongue. These states repeatedly fight together: they are a coalition. Here, I argue that three states – the USA, UK and Australia – constitute its core: the 'old Anglosphere coalition'. Vucetic has shown that, statistically, controlling for other variables, 'English-speaking states/nations tend to be more willing to help the US wage its wars than states selected at random. Particularly willing to fight America's wars, it seems, are core Anglosphere states – Australia, Britain, Canada and New Zealand.'[22] Of course, the Anglosphere could be defined more broadly than the five countries Vucetic names or the three I have identified. Bennett, for example, considers the variable geometry of the Anglosphere, with the US–UK core followed up (in a fading gradation of

---

[20] Howard, 'The Anglosphere', p. 4.
[21] Vucetic, 'Bound to follow?', p. 2. Vucetic notes this critically, as part of a critique of the idea, targeted at exactly those political elites who might exploit the notion for instrumental gain.
[22] Vucetic, 'Bound to follow?', p. 17.

genuine membership) by Australia, Canada, Ireland and New Zealand, and then (a more peripheral membership of) others, such as the English-speaking Caribbean and India, before finally old Islamic colonies of the United Kingdom in the final class of admission.[23]

The crux of the Anglosphere remains the US–UK relationship, so frequently described as 'special'. While this label is usually referenced to indicate the cultural ties and institutional manifestations of the bilateral relationship, it should also be read as indicating a situation *unique* to global politics: 'cooperation between Britain and the US differs in magnitude, frequency and durability from any other major power dyad in the international system'.[24] This unique level of connection and synchronicity has endured through various crises, challenging both the international system generally and the bilateral relationship specifically. In fact, throughout 'the entire post-1945 period no major international security policy divergence between Britain and the US managed to upset the overall cooperation pattern – think of Iran or Suez during the Cold War or, in the European unification era, the Amsterdam Treaty or Saint Malo Initiative'.[25] And yet, as we have already seen, there is one country that claims even closer union with the world's hegemon. John Howard put this 'remarkable association' succinctly, when he reminded Americans that Australia, not the UK, is 'the only country that has participated side by side with the United States in every conflict of any degree in which the United States has been involved since we first fought together at the Battle of Hamel on the Fourth of July in 1918'.[26]

How was this rendered so? Clearly, the UK has a long imperial history, but how did it manage to transfer a taste for liberal internationalism and then liberal imperialism, despite the rest of the Anglosphere being once-colonised and now post-colonial nations?[27] It is in this fading gradation of post-colonial identity, coupled to brute

---

[23] J. Bennett, *The Anglosphere Challenge: Why the English-Speaking Nations Will Lead the Way in the Twenty-First Century* (Plymouth: Rowman & Littlefield, 2007). See, for discussion, W. R. Mead, 'Review: the United States; the Anglosphere challenge: why the English-speaking nations will lead the way in the twenty-first century', *Foreign Affairs*, 84 (2005), 158; and Browning and Tonra, 'Beyond the West'.

[24] Vucetic, 'A racialized peace?', p. 403.   [25] Vucetic, 'Bound to follow?', p. 14.

[26] Australia, unlike the UK, fought alongside the USA in Vietnam. Howard, 'The Anglosphere', p. 11.

[27] And, in the USA, even a hard-Wilsonian ease with the notion of Empire.

material capability, that we can find clues as to the formation of a hard core – the UK, USA and Australia – at the centre of the Anglosphere. All three countries have gained regional or global hegemonic status in their own right and all have pursued colonial policies. Canada and New Zealand, to a greater extent, have been the victims (as well as the victors) of the liberal imperialism of, first, the UK and, second, the USA and Australia, generating a very different historical trajectory and degree of comfort with imperial wars. While, in identity terms, both are (and particularly *were*) acutely aware of their perceived natural home allied to their more powerful neighbours and the British mother-land, their simultaneous inferiority to those neighbours has led to a heightened criticality, made possible by the (perhaps taken for granted) geopolitical security afforded by virtue of having large, powerful and culturally similar liberal imperialist neighbours.

At the edge of the Anglosphere core, the unusually borne out two-step process of Anglo-Saxon colonial and post-colonial relations experienced by Canada and New Zealand has dampened the militarism and imperialism that remains evident within the old Anglosphere coalition states. This plays out in a greater selectivity of war, despite strong and enduring perceptions of an Anglosphere community. Browning has traced, for example, Canada's transition from 'seeing itself in the 1920s as the lynchpin nation, destined to bring the US and UK together in an Anglo-Saxon brotherhood for international peace' to instead placing 'themselves as advocates and practical supporters of the UN and its multilateral institutions'.[28] Likewise, Vucetic maps out Canada's decision to avoid entanglement in the 2003 US-led intervention in Iraq.[29] He identifies Canada's liberal discourse, opposed to a North American 'elephant other', as vital to Canadian self-understandings of its identity as a unique part of the English-speaking west.[30] While the decision to stay out of Iraq was, certainly, very unusual, it was not an anomaly but rather an outcome of an identity formed in part through relations with its imperial, superpower neighbour, as well as internal

---

[28] D. G. Haglund, 'Canada and the Anglosphere: in, out, or different?' *Options Politiques*, 1 February 2005, https://policyoptions.irpp.org/fr/magazines/canada-in-the-world/canada-and-the-anglosphere-in-out-or-indifferent; see also Browning and Tonra, 'Beyond the West'.

[29] S. Vucetic, 'Why did Canada sit out of the Iraq war? One constructivist analysis', *Canadian Foreign Policy Journal*, 13 (2006), 133–53.

[30] Ibid.

political developments. As Rod Lyon has noted, 'The group falls naturally into three geographic pairs and in each pairing, there's one extroverted strategic player (the USA, Britain and Australia) and another less extroverted one (Canada, Ireland, New Zealand)'.[31] The USA, UK and Australia, in Lyon's terms, are the 'extroverted', militaristic core of the Anglosphere. And, I argue, this results from the specific mix of mutual and divergent colonial experiences within the Anglosphere.

Added to Canada and New Zealand, Irish and Indian experiences of British colonialism included what the UK understood to be the necessity of despotism.[32] Partially as a consequence of this, in conjunction with their own unique cultural contexts, neither Ireland nor India possesses the 'orientation towards a civilising mission' that other Anglosphere members 'tend to' exhibit.[33] This civilising mission suggests that perhaps we are approaching the issue backwards. Instead of assessing what individual Anglosphere members lack, we should focus on what the USA, UK and Australia share; for example, their mutual colonial experiences, a civilising zeal and what Belich has termed the 'settlerism' of the old 'Anglo-wests'.[34] These mutual, violent civilising experiences were crucial to the formation of history's most consequential coalition. A combination of perceived religious virtue and bloody racialised conflict was at the heart of the Anglosphere from the outset.

'A Blood of the Body'?[35]

In summer of 1768, Captain James Cook received orders from the British Admiralty to show 'civility and regard' to any Australian 'natives' he might encounter on his voyage to the great southern landmass.[36] 'In Botany Bay in 1770, Cook immediately clashed with

---

[31] R. Lyon, 'Editors' picks for 2016: "An introverted Anglosphere?"', *The Strategist*, Australian Strategic Policy Institute, 29 December 2016, www.aspistrategist.org.au/editors-picks-2016-introverted-anglosphere

[32] Bell, *The Idea of Greater Britain*.

[33] Browning and Tonra, 'Beyond the West', p. 13.

[34] Belich in Vucetic, *The Anglosphere*, chapter 61.

[35] This term, like 'blood of the mind' below, comes from Madhav Das Nalapat. See M. D. Nalapat, 'India & the Anglosphere', *New Criterion*, 29 (2011).

[36] P. Daley, 'It is beyond time for Britain to apologise to Australia's indigenous people', *The Guardian*, 25 January 2016, www.theguardian.com/commentisfree/2016/jan/26/it-is-beyond-time-for-britain-to-apologise-to-australias-indigenous-people

Gweagal Tribesmen, shooting at least one', initiating a by now familiar pattern of British-led genocide. In the following years, the raiding
parties of the new 'settlers' would have instruction to 'bring back the
severed heads of the black trouble-makers',[37] who were seen as 'sub-
human... fly-blown, Stone Age savages'.[38] Australia's foundational
'War of Extermination' was followed by a sixty-year policy of the
forcible removal of children from the homes of Aboriginal and Torres
Strait Islander peoples: genocide by other means. Australia has long
wrestled with the crushing knowledge of these terrible acts. The so-
called history wars saw heated debate on the teaching of the story of
Australian settlement; on one side, a 'black armband' reading of
officially sanctioned acts of evil and, on the other, a 'white blindfold'
colonial amnesia enabling a picture of benign occupation and governance. In 1992, Prime Minister Paul Keating apologised on behalf of
the Australian government and nation to the Stolen Generations in his
Redfern Speech.[39] But subsequent prime ministers have been far more
bullish about Australia's ability to be 'relaxed and comfortable' with
itself.[40] Australia Day remains the usual 'barbecues and slabs and
fetishisation of a flag': 'a flag that, with the Union Jack, symbolises
violence and oppression of indigenous people'.[41] Amidst the patriotic
fervour, however, are calls for introspection. Veteran journalist
Stan Grant noted in his speech on 'the Australian Dream' that an
indigenous Australian child was more likely to be incarcerated than
finish school.[42]

These issues are repeated across the Anglosphere today. In Canada,
Prime Minister Justin Trudeau has launched an enquiry into the murder
of some 1,200 indigenous women in the past three decades. In the
United States, the New York State village of Whitesboro faced national
outrage over its reluctance to change its emblem, depicting its white

---

[37] M. Davey, 'Stan Grant's speech on racism and the Australian Dream goes viral',
The Guardian, 24 January 2016, www.theguardian.com/australia-news/2016/
jan/24/stan-grants-speech-on-racism-and-the-australian-dream-goes-viral

[38] Ibid.

[39] P. Keating, 'Redfern speech (Year for the World's Indigenous People)', ANTaR,
10 December 1992, https://antar.org.au/sites/default/files/paul_keating_speech_
transcript.pdf

[40] For analysis, see R. Flanagan, 'A decade of John Howard has left a country of
timidity, fear and shame', *The Guardian*, 26 November 2007,
www.theguardian.com/commentisfree/2007/nov/26/comment.australia

[41] Daley, 'It is beyond time'.   [42] Davey, 'Stan Grant's speech'.

founder appearing to choke a Native American.[43] In America, of course, the legacy of slavery looms large, with homicide the leading cause of death for black males under the age of thirty-five. In New Zealand, efforts are ongoing to improve the position of the Maori people within society. The model for the physical violence of Anglosphere colonialism, which has subsequently given way to the structural violence of post-colonialism, was the British Empire, particularly its experiences in Ireland and India. Make no mistake: race and war are located at the heart of the Anglosphere, with formative colonial conflicts against the English-speaking nations' various indigenous Others. This claim requires an alternative ontology of International Relations in a number of respects, but, at the same time, constructivist approaches within IR are well placed to make sense of racialised discourses and identities forged through conflict. This is necessary because the Anglosphere was and remains far more than an alliance: it is a security community, bound by a shared identity forged through racialised conflicts and their subsequent retelling in national mythology. To understand the series of exclusions, hierarchies and affiliations that underpin the Anglosphere, it is necessary to explore the foundations of Anglo-American peace at the turn of the twentieth century, where cooperation was 'originally established on the basis of race' thanks to successful elite framings of a single community: an 'Anglo-Saxon brotherhood, the vanguard of a racially defined humankind'.[44]

Going against the theoretical and historiographical grain, Vucetic has made this argument explicitly and persuasively.[45] His analysis returns to the 1890s and the near miss over Venezuela, exploring why peace 'broke out' between the USA and UK. He finds that this was possible due to a framing of racial brotherhood (rather than shared democratic norms or similar political institutions).[46] Crucially, it was not Americanism and Englishness that informed a prevalent discourse of racial hierarchy and superiority at the turn of the twentieth century; rather, it was a discourse of Anglo-Saxons. This discourse 'emphasized the distinctiveness and unity of white, Protestant, English-speaking and "self-governing" gentlemen'. And, 'in Britain, Anglo-Saxonism was

---

[43] Residents and officials initially argued that the image showed a 'friendly wrestling match', but ultimately bowed to public pressure.

[44] Vucetic, 'A racialized peace?', pp. 403–4.

[45] Ibid. See also Vucetic, *The Anglosphere*.

[46] Vucetic, 'A racialized peace?', p. 404.

hegemonic at all levels of discourse, including foreign policy'.[47] 'The grip of Anglo-Saxonism was so powerful' in fact that 'British "race patriotism" ... implied not only a "race alliance" with America but also a "federation of race" ... and, in the boldest move, a political integration with the "cousins" and "brothers" in the US.' This 'reunion' was variably considered the 'United States of Empire', 'Grand Imperial Federation', or simply 'Greater Britain'.[48]

The 'intellectual roots of the Anglosphere' can therefore be traced to this 'emergence of Anglo-Saxonism in the mid-to-late nineteenth century'.[49] This discourse was 'a response to the evolutionary theory of Charles Darwin'; 'Anglo-Saxonism posited the existence of an Anglo-Saxon race distinct from that of other races and in unavoidable competition and conflict with them'.[50] Of course, those inclined to build theories of IR on the basis of social Darwinism rarely see their own race as inferior. For Chamberlain, like many of his countrymen, it was clear that the 'Anglo-Saxon race is infallibly destined to be the predominant force in the history and civilisation of the world'.[51] Rudyard Kipling, in 'The White Man's Burden', encapsulated this sense of assumed racial superiority and its associated responsibilities. While the poem certainly attempted to justify 'imperial rule over inferior races less suited or fit for self-government',[52] it is often forgotten that its subject matter was, specifically, support for 'Theodore Roosevelt's campaign to extend the American sphere of influence into the Philippines' and not 'England's rule over India', which is usually assumed.[53] The kinship of race was clear, as was its extended tasks of world leadership; far more than a call for alliance politics, this was a call for political union, premised on the perception of common Anglo-Saxon roots. This call was not only well received in the UK; it resonated in the

---

[47] Ibid., p. 8.   [48] Ibid., p. 9. See also Bell, *The Idea of Greater Britain*.
[49] Browning and Tonra, 'Beyond the West', p. 2. See also I. Parmar, 'Anglo-American elites in the interwar years: idealism and power in the intellectual roots of Chatham House and the Council on Foreign Relations', *International Relations*, 16 (2002), 53–75.
[50] Browning and Tonra, 'Beyond the West', p. 2.
[51] Cited by A. Gamble, *Between Europe and America: The Future of British Politics* (Houndmills: Palgrave Macmillan, 2003), p. 83; and Browning and Tonra, 'Beyond the West', p. 2.
[52] Parmar, 'Anglo-American elites', p. 61; and Browning and Tonra, 'Beyond the West', p. 2.
[53] Heer, 'Operation Anglosphere'; and Browning and Tonra, 'Beyond the West', p. 3.

USA and Australia, in part thanks to its logical pronouncements on race relations at the frontier.[54] These pronouncements were supported and reinforced through the perception of religious doctrine.

   Religion has made something of a comeback in International Relations. Whether through Huntington's 'Clash of Civilizations' or George W. Bush's frequent recourse to the language of good versus evil, religion has re-entered debates that were previously stripped back to the logical consequence of objective material realities.[55] For the development of the Anglosphere, religion served to bolster Darwinian claims of racial superiority. The Anglosphere's myriad Others were seen to be and spoken of as mired in both a racial and religious inferiority, such that the latter flowed naturally from the former. Christianity and specifically Protestantism were juxtaposed to the multiplicity of 'false' religious orders clung to by lesser races. Whether Muslim hordes or indigenous tribes, the Anglosphere actively wrote barbarism into its Others, in a form whereby belief and the body were intimately – if not inextricably – intertwined. Efforts at religious conversion – the roots of a Wilsonian impulse to promote democracy as well as Christian values – were seen as possible and necessary, but working against the grain that nature had set. Here, we see that the 'blood of the body' was seen to flow into the 'blood of the mind'. However, for Anglosphere elites, the potential for altering the latter contrasted the brute fact of race. That is ironic, given the significance of ideas – including ideas of race – for binding together the English-speaking nations.

'A Blood of the Mind'

Browning and Tonra note the range of foci evident amongst the various authors who have attempted to explain the Anglosphere, its actions and importance.[56] Bennett, for example, focuses mainly on

---

[54] Vucetic, 'A racialized peace?', pp. 410–11. Of course, it was not immediately clear why, once infused with the notion of Manifest Destiny, American expansionism should stop at the water's edge. Racial superiority – drawn from Anglo-Saxon settlers – was seen to extend over natives of North America, the Philippines and beyond.

[55] See, for example, the work of Lee Marsden, e.g. L. Marsden, *For God's Sake: The Christian Right and US Foreign Policy* (London: Zed Books Ltd, 2013).

[56] Browning and Tonra, 'Beyond the West'.

culture, escaping the tainted racialism of past understandings,[57] whereas Vucetic deliberately emphasises that IR has falsely ignored the racial discourse that was central to the Anglosphere's formation.[58] To begin with, it is useful to consider the relationship between the privileging of different drivers of mutual affinity and the theoretical bases of IR. At one end of the theoretical spectrum within IR, realist-premised explanations of the Anglosphere centre on the security calculations inherent within decisions to maximise cooperation. For the UK and USA, for example, Tim Dunne notes that at 'its core, the relationship represents a bargain: Britain pledges its loyalty to the United States in return for influence over the direction of the hegemonic power's foreign policy'.[59] Likewise, Tim Lynch has noted that Australia's repeated decision to fight in America's wars is actually a policy of sheltering under the eagle's wing: a rational calculation for a large, under-populated, strategically vulnerable state, located in a turbulent region.[60] Australian political elites, within this formulation, are seen to be gambling on the USA reciprocating in this arrangement by paying back its accumulated debt as Australia's security guarantor in a time of need.

Both of these arguments carry some weight, but fail to do justice to the nature of Anglosphere binds. Such explanations can also explain ad hoc coalitions of the willing, comprised of states sharing nothing more than temporary allegiances in pursuit of momentarily convergent interests. Both of the British Tims – Dunne and Lynch[61] – know this, of course. As Dunne notes, the 'special relationship is an example of a shared identity (based on shared culture, language and history) that

---

[57] Ibid.
[58] See also A. Winter, 'Race, empire and the British-American "special relationship" in the Obama era' in G. Scott-Smith (ed.), *Obama, US Politics and Transatlantic Relation: Change or Continuity?* (Brussels: Peter Lang, 2012), pp. 229–46.
[59] T. Dunne, 'When the shooting starts: Atlanticism in British security strategy', *International Affairs*, 80 (2004), 893–909.
[60] T. Lynch, Presentation on Australia–US relations, BISA US Foreign Policy Working Group, annual conference, London School of Economics, September 2014.
[61] Both Dunne and Lynch have written extensively on US foreign policy and both have relocated from British academia to Australia, making them well placed to comment on the Anglosphere, albeit from quite contrasting theoretical standpoints.

generated converging interests'.[62] Here, we start to get closer to the ties that bind, but, once again, these perceptions of commonality are filtered through the lens of national interest, complete with its distorting view of an international system comprised of states acting in logical, and even optimal, ways for their own ends. This thinner or conventional constructivism is insufficient in its addition of a new variable – whether culture or identity – into the familiar equations of rationalist foreign policy analysis. It is necessary to move further along the IR theory spectrum and away from the purely rationalist- and interest-premised approaches. In a thicker variant, critical constructivism can help us to understand why it is that states such as the UK and Australia will (*eagerly*) follow the United States into wars, even when such decisions appear to go against the national interest. In fact, the national interest, I argue, has been a secondary consideration at best for British and Australian political elites when it comes to the question of fighting alongside the Anglosphere's principal member and Anglo-Saxon brethren. It is a sense of shared identity and shared values[63] – not shared interests – that drives the old Anglosphere coalition forward, from war to inevitable war. As Vucetic, again, has shown and argued:

From a [critical] constructivist perspective, then, what causes English-speaking states/nations to cooperate is not simply an outside threat, economic interdependence, shared democratic institutions or some combination of these factors; rather, cooperation is a function of the (historically and cross-nationally variable) collective/shared identity. The Anglosphere, in this view, is not simply an alliance or a zone of peace, but a security community or a 'family of nations' ... Characterized by two centuries of peaceful change, the Anglosphere 'core' can be seen as a mature security community par excellence.[64]

It is precisely because 'Anglo-America is a transnational political space and an imagined community'[65] – in the sense that Benedict

---

[62] Dunne, 'When the shooting starts', p. 898.

[63] Dan Hannan, for example, argues that it is the Anglo-Saxon invention and defence of 'freedom' that defines the Anglosphere. D. Hannan, *How We Invented Freedom & Why It Matters* (London: Head of Zeus, 2013).

[64] Vucetic, 'Bound to follow?', p. 4.

[65] A. Gamble, 'The Anglo-American hegemony: from Greater Britain to the Anglosphere', PAIS Graduate Working Papers, University of Warwick, Number 05/06 (2006), 8, www2.warwick.ac.uk/fac/soc/pais/currentstudents/phd/resources/crips/working_papers/2006/working_paper_5_gamble.pdf

Anderson spoke of – that the (now) junior partners of the old Anglo-sphere coalition are compelled to fight as comrades in arms. They are 'bound to follow'[66] in two senses: they are tied together in prevalent political, cultural and racial imaginations, to the extent that their impending cooperation in wartime becomes an inevitability. It is any absence of cooperation that is shocking. For very many Britons, Americans and Australians, the Anglosphere alliance is simply 'the natural order of things' and is 'taken for granted'.[67] The old Anglosphere coalition reflects this perfectly, as the 'pattern of consultation' under-pinning it rests on the 'the common language and culture' of 'sister peoples' such that it has become 'so matter-of-factly intimate' as to have naturalised a highly unusual degree of cooperation, influence, coordination and synchronicity.[68] As Henry Kissinger put it:

There evolved a habit of meeting so regular that autonomous American action somehow came to seem to violate club rule... This was an extraordin-ary relationship because it rested on no legal claim; it was formalized by no document; it was carried forward by succeeding British governments as if no alternative were conceivable. Britain's influence was great precisely because it never insisted on it; the 'special relationship' demonstrated the value of intangibles.[69]

It is these intangibles that are so important and yet have been so readily dismissed in the history of IR theory.[70] Here, I focus on their role and development by considering language, culture, elite networks and institutions in turn, before affording significant space to the most undervalued component of the Anglosphere's foundational ties: the co-constitutive nature of mutual participation in war.

The English-Speaking Peoples

The role played by mutual intelligibility, whether linguistic or cultural, is hugely important. The latter, however, rests on the former. And the importance of that fact continues to increase. The 'key fact, as

---

[66] Vucetic, 'Bound to follow?'   [67] Hitchens, *Blood, Class and Empire.*
[68] Kissinger 1979, 39–40, cited in Vucetic, 'Bound to follow?', p. 16.   [69] Ibid.
[70] Formalised structures are often simply a case of 'brass-hatting' existing informal arrangements. See, on AUSMIN, J. O'Sullivan, 'A British-led Anglosphere in world politics?', *The Telegraph*, 29 December 2007, www.telegraph.co.uk/comment/3645011/A-British-led-Anglosphere-in-world-politics.html

Bismarck noted, is that the North Americans speak English'.[71] Language is the unifier that Churchill deemed sufficiently important to name his four-part history after, labelling the Anglosphere the 'English-speaking peoples'.[72] The British brought the English language to the United States and Australia, replete with idioms and accents that would certainly evolve relative to the idiosyncrasies of their new environment and cultural context but which would enable an ease of dialogue and deep sense of familiarity with the New World and Down Under. Today, the accents and vocabulary of North America and Australasia still bear the hallmarks of British (and Irish) emigration patterns.[73] And, moreover, the importance of this linguistic inheritance is increasing due to the ubiquity of technology enabling instantaneous communication and the consumption of cross-cultural news and entertainment.[74]

While, as John Howard has noted, the ubiquity of English in international discourse is certainly an advantage for the Anglosphere, its principal effect is to facilitate the formation and furtherance of the cultural ties that bind. For Lawrence Mead, 'What makes a country Anglo is that its original settler population came mainly from Britain. So even though a minority of Americans today have British roots, they inherit a political culture initially formed by the British.'[75] David Hackett Fischer has shown how the political culture(s) of the USA grew from 'Albion's seed', with the germination of four distinct British folkways in the USA.[76] These folkways were transported to the USA with the migration of distinct groups – the Ulster Scots, East Anglian puritans, southern cavaliers and midlands workers.[77] Although developing in ways necessary to fulfil their new niches in the cultural ecology of the rich young land, they brought with them and maintained a number of the qualities and beliefs that influenced the development of British political culture.[78] Although barely explored at all, the same is true of Australia, where numerous population waves,

---

[71] Mead, 'Why Anglos lead', p. 7.
[72] The fourth considers Australia, albeit in a fairly superficial manner.
W. Churchill, *A History of the English-Speaking Peoples, Volume 4: The Great Democracies* (New York: Rosetta Books, 2013).
[73] Fischer, *Albion's Seed*.
[74] Bennett, *The Anglosphere Challenge*; and Bennett, 'The emerging Anglosphere'. For commentary, see Mead, 'Review'.
[75] Mead, 'Why Anglos lead', p. 1.   [76] Fischer, *Albion's Seed*.   [77] Ibid.
[78] Ibid. and, see also, Mead, *Special Providence*.

including the Ulster Scots, migrated en masse, helping to build Australian political culture not just in Britain's image but also through migrants who had British ideas and values.[79] The presence of these groups during America and Australia's formative eras ensured that their influence on national political cultures has remained strong, despite the influx of other 'non-Anglo' groups; British values have been embodied in national elites and institutionalised in laws and structures of governance. Moreover, they have been promoted overseas in foreign policies that have extended liberal internationalism into liberal imperialist ventures.[80] In short, we can see the influence of British cultural values in Anglosphere elites, institutions and wars.

On the first of these, Inderjeet Parmar has traced the role played by elite networks in the establishment of the Anglosphere.[81] In particular, he emphasises the formative role of the 'Cliveden Set' (sometimes called 'Milner's Kindergarten'), as well as the (British) Royal Institute for International Affairs (Chatham House) and the (American) Council on Foreign Relations.[82] The impact of these groups was quite remarkable. 'As forces for consensus-building in their respective countries and between them, Chatham House and the Council on Foreign Relations provided critical forums for the more respectable "liberal"

---

[79] Ulster Scot population waves coincided with the need to find a new Anglosphere destination as the American Civil War placed the USA temporarily off limits. Australia was the principal beneficiary. It is possible to trace the careers and influence of prominent Ulster Scots as they rose to positions of authority (e.g. in the police, unions and government). For example, Samuel McCaughey – a prominent and wealthy Ulster Scot sheep farmer, philanthropist and Australian military supporter – helped to fund and promote Australian participation in the Boer War and initiate the development of the Australian Air Force.

[80] Mead extends Fischer's analysis to consider the influence of these four migrant groups on the development of US foreign policy. See Mead, *Special Providence*. Wesley and Warren have come closest to achieving something similar for Australia, albeit without the historical analysis of the influence of migration. M. Wesley and T. Warren, 'Wild colonial ploys: currents of thought in Australian foreign policy making', *Australian Journal of Political Science*, 35 (2000), 9–26; see also O. Harries, 'Punching above our weight?' Boyer Lectures, ABC Radio National, 21 December 2003, www.abc.net.au/rn/boyerlectures/stories/2003/987633.htm

[81] Parmar, 'Anglo-American elites'. The influential 'Cliveden Set' took their name from Nancy Astor's Buckinghamshire residence. The group had its origins in a 'bunch of young men, mostly from New College, Oxford, whom Lord [Alfred] Milner summoned or took with him to rebuild South Africa after the Boer War'. I. Gilmour, 'Termagant', *London Review of Books*, 22 (2000), 12–13.

[82] Parmar, 'Anglo-American elites', p. 53.

elements within the US and the UK to map out a new world order.'[83]
Parmar shows how a powerful mix of scientism, elitism and religi-
osity, as well as the plain racism of Anglo-Saxonism influenced by
social Darwinism, drove these influential think-tanks forward in their
agenda.[84] As ardent and influential liberal internationalists, they
helped to promote and foster the distinctive foreign policy disposition
of the Anglosphere.[85]

The impact of influential elite networks extends well beyond the
Anglosphere's formative period, driving it forward and fostering
the conditions for its further and continued institutionalisation.[86]
Tim Legrand has explored 'the emergence and evolution of inter-
government policy networks across Australia, Canada, Ireland, New
Zealand, the United Kingdom and the United States', finding that
'over the past twenty years, mandarins of some of the most significant
government institutions in these countries have jointly established
distinctive, and highly exclusive, policy learning networks with their
counterparts'.[87] Legrand argues that these 'international institutional
relationships' and 'international policy ideas' have significant
impact 'on domestic institutions', as part of a continuous process of
Anglosphere policy learning.[88] During 'the past 25 years' these 'transgovernmental networks' – comprising 'a cadre of top-level public
servants from the Anglosphere', 'particularly the "core" countries of
Australia, Canada, New Zealand, the United Kingdom and the United
States' – 'have increasingly engaged in systematic and reciprocal
policy learning'.[89] This is an insight that has thus far been notable
by its absence from the IR literature. And it is an insight that helps us
to understand the frequent institutionalisation and 'brass hatting'
of the crucial 'intangibles' identified by Kissinger; previously tacit

---

[83] Ibid., p. 53.   [84] Ibid.   [85] Ibid., pp. 58–62.

[86] Consider, for example, the continued influence and circulation of political ideas
and personnel, such as Bill Clinton's influence on New Labour's development in
the UK (through a mutual 'third way' project), the hiring of British political
advisers such as John McTernan in recent Australian governments, or vice versa
with the influence of Lynton Crosby's 'dog whistle politics'. Crosby was the so-
called Wizard of Oz, renowned for practicing the political dark arts.

[87] T. Legrand, 'Transgovernmental policy networks in the Anglosphere', *Policy
Administration*, 93 (2015), 973–91; see also T. Legrand, 'Learning mandarins:
elite policy transfer networks in the Anglosphere', paper presented at the IPSA
World Congress, Montreal, July 2014, p. 973.

[88] Legrand, 'Transgovernmental policy networks'.   [89] Ibid., p. 979.

agreements are solidified in more formalised, visible and concrete arrangements. In particular, we can see evidence of this institutionalisation in the realm of security and intelligence.

The Anglosphere possesses the most extensive cross-national security cooperation in the world.[90] Growing up in rural East Anglia in the United Kingdom afforded the chance to witness this first hand, as US fighter jets would practice dive-bombing the local church and basketball or ten-pin bowling would take place at RAF bases hosting USAF units and personnel.[91] During the Cold War, popular rumour suggests that, in the case of an impending nuclear strike, the unofficial advice for those in the region was to head outside and ensure a quick demise, given that these airbases would certainly be targeted early on.[92] The UK's current ten US air bases have Australian equivalents, near Alice Springs,[93] and, most recently, near Darwin, where 2,500 US marines rotate, following an agreement between former Prime Minister Julia Gillard and Barack Obama. As well as the physical presence of military personnel in each other's countries, the Anglosphere also cooperates to an unprecedented degree on the battlefield, with embedded forces (including in Syria)[94] and troops taking command from military leaders from other Anglosphere states.[95] Military procurement and contracts are coordinated between Anglosphere states, with similarly high degrees of collaboration in the private sector. And, at the most fundamental level, Anglosphere states are committed to the defence of each other in times of crisis, as the invocation of NATO's Article V and

---

[90] See, for discussion of the institutionalisation of the Anglosphere, R. Conquest, *The Dragons of Expectation: Reality and Delusion in the Course of History* (London: Duckworth, 2006).

[91] RAF Lakenheath, RAF Mildenhall and RAF Feltwell were nearby, although only the former is likely to remain in the medium to long term as the USA continues to reallocate its forces following their Cold War peak. Mildenhall's forces will be redeployed within the UK but primarily to Germany.

[92] Of course, nuclear technology and capacity has been a key component of US–UK cooperation.

[93] Pine Gap.

[94] British pilots were flying with US counterparts in Syria, even following the parliamentary vote against UK intervention. See C. Turner, 'David Cameron "knew British pilots were bombing Syria" – as it happened, July 17, 2015', *The Telegraph*, 17 July 2015, www.telegraph.co.uk/news/uknews/defence/11745689/British-pilots-in-air-strikes-against-Isil-in-Syria-live.html

[95] This was the case in specific theatres during both world wars and, much more recently, in Afghanistan in 2010. BBC News, 'UK troops in Afghanistan to come under US command', 21 May 2010, http://news.bbc.co.uk/1/hi/uk/8697371.stm

the Australia–New Zealand–United States Pact (ANZUS) demonstrated after the events of 11 September 2001. Although written to ensure America's interests were tied to the Pacific, the invocation of the ANZUS treaty – framing 9/11 as an attack on Australia and New Zealand, as well as the United States – while John Howard was in Washington DC served to further cement the notion that the Anglosphere fights as one in the defence and promotion of shared values.[96]

During the War on Terror, Anglosphere intelligence sharing has reached new (and at times troubling) heights. The USA, UK and Australia, as well as Canada and New Zealand, are party to the UKUSA Security Agreement, popularly known as Five Eyes or (by its former code name) Echelon. This arrangement sees an unusual degree of cooperation and information sharing in the area of signals intelligence, which amounts to a combined capacity to intercept global communications. Set up during the Cold War, with the Soviet Union in mind, the War on Terror has transformed intelligence arrangements across the Anglosphere, with members now being asked to spy on each other's citizens so as to avoid breaking domestic laws or falling foul of the US Constitution. Recent revelations about Dragnet and Prism have revealed that the NSA and GCHQ now participate in incredibly large-scale bulk data collection on foreigners and citizens alike. Despite the revelations, spearheaded by Edward Snowden, the alliance remains strong as one of the most comprehensive espionage arrangements of all time.[97] The impact on those such as France, who lie outside of the Five Eyes arrangement,[98] is one of exclusion. As one report put it, new members are simply not welcome, however senior you are, or close to Washington; if outside of the Anglosphere, 'your communications could easily be being shared among the handful of white, English-speaking nations with membership privileges'.[99] This was proven, most recently, by reports that UK and US intelligence had hacked into and watched live footage of attacks by Israeli fighter jets and

---

[96] Holland, *Selling the War on Terror*; Holland, 'Howard's War on Terror'; Holland and McDonald, 'Australian identity'.

[97] John Howard described this as 'the single closest intelligence-sharing arrangement that exists anywhere in the world'. Howard, 'The Anglosphere', p. 6.

[98] Or even the less formal Nine and Fourteen Eyes arrangements.

[99] J. Borgen, 'Merkel spying claim: with allies like these, who needs enemies?', *The Guardian*, 23 October 2013, www.theguardian.com/world/2013/oct/23/merkel-nsa-phone-allies-enemies

unmanned aerial vehicles.[100] The fact such revelations have been possible – with the release of official, if secret, documentation – reflects the 'brass-hatting' of previously more informal arrangements; these arrangements build on and further the cooperation that has been uniquely 'characteristic of English-speaking, common law countries such as, well, Britain, Australia and America'.[101]

Clearly, the Anglosphere coalition regularly exempts itself 'from the rules that have shaped war, peace, alliances, coalitions and other manifestations of international cooperation and conflict in world politics'.[102] And this exemption, as it applies to intelligence, security and conflict, is of global consequence. Here, we both move on from and find answers to Vucetic's evocative question, 'Why do (some) English-speaking states/nations continue to go to war together?'[103] As Coleman puts it, Anglos run the world because of their taste for war.[104] And, in addition, their Anglo identity is reinforced through the pursuit of this global mission in repeated coalition wars – armed conflicts of global significance, which shape international order, including its norms, institutions and economics. As Lawrence Mead argues, the Anglosphere is 'available to deal with chaos and aggression abroad, as other countries usually are not. One or another of the Anglos has led all the major military operations of the last fifteen years'.[105] A combination of the impulse to lead and the resources to do so, Mead argues, enable the repeated projection of force overseas through a combination of habit and a desire for good global governance. He notes that 'Anglo governments combine strong executive leadership with legislative consent. Both features make for effective warfighting overseas.'[106] The 'Anglo countries... approach war more confidently than their potential rivals' in part because armed conflict has been a

---

[100] P. Beaumont, 'Snowden files reveal US and UK spied on feeds from Israeli drones and jets', *The Guardian*, 29 January 2016, www.theguardian.com/world/2016/jan/29/snowden-files-us-uk-spied-feeds-israeli-drones-jets

[101] O'Sullivan, 'A British-led Anglosphere'; and see also Bennett, *The Anglosphere Challenge*.

[102] Vucetic, *The Anglosphere*, p. 3.   [103] Vucetic, 'Bound to follow?', p. 16.

[104] P. Coleman, 'Why Anglos run the world: a taste for war', *Quadrant*, 50 (2006), 88–90.

[105] Mead lists the 'Afghanistan and Iraq conflicts... the 1991 Gulf War, the ensuing no-fly zones over Iraq, military operations in Bosnia in 1995 and Kosovo in 1999 and humanitarian interventions in Somalia, Haiti, Sierra Leone and East Timor'. See Mead, 'Why Anglos lead', p. 1.

[106] Ibid., p. 2.

continuation of domestic political projects – liberal projects applied
internationally and imperially, to protect themselves and world order.
For 'the Anglos', war confirms rather than threatens 'their deepest
values'.[107] Just as the British derived confidence and pride from military victories and conquests (over Spain, France and Germany), so too
are the USA and Australia able 'to look back on World War II and the
Cold War as glorious crusades'.[108]

It is important to make three points about these military victories: they
are sufficiently naturalised so as to be taken entirely for granted; they are
of global significance in shaping international order and global governance; and they are co-constitutive of the Anglosphere and thus mutually
reinforcing of this remarkable coalition's thirst for battle. On the first, 'it
was largely unremarkable for [Australian] Prime Minister Cook to
announce in August 1914 that "when the Empire is at war, Australia
is at war"'.[109] This blunt matter of fact-ness continued throughout the
twentieth century. In 1939, Prime Minister Robert Menzies announced
Australia's entry into World War II as his 'melancholy duty to inform. . .
that in consequence of persistence by Germany in her invasion of
Poland, Great Britain has declared war upon her and that, as a result,
Australia is also at war'.[110] On the second point, Vucetic argues that the
Anglosphere is 'comparable perhaps only to the Nordic security community', despite being 'conceptually comparable to half a dozen post-
colonial networks such as the *Francophonie*, the *Hispanidad* or even the
Danish and Dutch mini- commonwealths. What makes the Anglosphere
unique, at least in the eyes of its proponents, is its centrality to the course
of world history'.[111] Walter Russell Mead, more than any other, elab-
orates on this point across his range of books on this subject and related
ones.[112] As Vucetic summarises, the 'core Anglosphere states/nations
have been constantly winning battles and wars, thus profoundly shaping
a succession of international orders' to the extent that we might talk of
'*An*global governance or *An*globalization'.[113] On the third point, we
must return to critical constructivism in order to understand how and

---

[107] Ibid., p. 5.   [108] Ibid.
[109] D. Kissane, 'Anglosphere united? Examining and explaining 20th century war
      time alliances in the English speaking world', Centre d'Etudes Franco-
      Americain de Management (2010), http://ssrn.com/abstract=1688272
[110] Ibid.   [111] Vucetic, 'Bound to follow?', p. 4.
[112] Mead, *God and Gold*; and also Mead, *Special Providence*, on America's often
      unremarked and relatively low-cost successes.
[113] Vucetic, 'Bound to follow?', p. 4.

why the Anglosphere repeatedly goes to war as one, with military ventures reinforcing a collective desire to fight together.

A range of constructivist scholars in International Relations and beyond have shown that foreign policy is not just something that states *do*; foreign policy is something that states *are*.[114] The identity of the state is written through its foreign policy – and that foreign policy, in turn, is contingent upon its identity. Very often, foreign policy and identity are mutually reinforcing; they operate in a co-constitutive relationship. Few foreign policies are more consequential and defining than those pertaining to military intervention overseas. That is certainly true of the Anglosphere, where American, British and Australian foreign policy has both been enabled by and formed through repeated coalition warfare. We can trace this process in each of the old Anglosphere coalition states with respect to their distinct domestic contexts and particular narratives of national identity, which facilitate and even necessitate ideas and patterns of belonging to a larger Anglo community (see Chapter 3). Most explicitly and easily for our purposes, it is possible to see how Australian national identity underpins and encourages repeated patterns of Anglosphere coalition warfare.

In Australia, the foundational moment of the national identity is very often considered to be a seminal battle of World War I, some fourteen years after federation. The ANZAC legend 'portrays the birth of the Australian nation through [mutual] sacrifice in war',[115] suggesting 'that the Australian national identity was forged through the remarkable courage shown by Australian soldiers in the face of overwhelming odds in a military campaign at Gallipoli in 1915'.[116] Courage, humour and larrikinism are all central to the imagined qualities that the Australian soldiers ('diggers', perceived to have gone from the mines to the trenches) were believed to have demonstrated in the face of repeatedly flawed leadership.[117] Above all else though, it is mateship that is held

---

[114] For example, Doty, 'Foreign policy as social construction'; Weldes, 'Making state action possible'; Fierke, 'Multiple identities'.

[115] Holland, 'Howard's War on Terror'; Holland and McDonald, 'Australian identity'.

[116] M. McDonald and R. Jackson, 'Selling war: the coalition of the willing and the "War on Terror"', paper presented at the International Studies Association Conference, San Francisco, 26–29 March 2008, p. 16.

[117] See J. Holland and K. Wright, 'The double delegitimisation of Julia Gillard: gender, the media and Australian political culture', *Australian Journal of Politics and History*, 63 (2017), 588–602.

up as the defining quality of the ANZAC spirit and the Australian identity it underpins. For many Australians, including former Prime Minister John Howard, 'Australian mateship and national identity [saw] its fiery birth in the ANZAC legend'.[118] According to Australia's most influential national narrative, then, an ideal Australian character is prepared to fight alongside culturally similar, powerful mates – as comrades in arms.[119]

In the United States, the prevalent national identity has formed at the intersection of three trends. First, the USA has defined itself in opposition to the corruptions of the Old World, from which its early settlers fled. This has allowed America to see itself as the defender of, and world's last great hope for, freedom. Second and related, as freedom's global bastion, the USA has embraced a teleological narrative in which it stands at the zenith of a worldwide project to improve the cause of humanity.[120] Third, pioneers and settlers understood the 'discovery', foundation and development of the USA as providentially blessed, thanks to the considerable security of its geography and abundance of its resources, adding a significant religious fervour to the perception of standing on the front lines of a global mission to defend and promote freedom.[121] Within this narrative, divine providence suggests that God approves such a mission.[122] Together, these trends combine to create an intoxicating discourse of American exceptionalism, in which the USA is held up as unique and, yet, world-leading: the nation to which the torch of freedom has been passed, charged with ensuring it continues to burn brightly.[123] In its more vindicationalist variant, this discourse is a powerful, legitimating and inspirational component of American internationalism, interventionism and imperialism.[124]

---

[118] Dyrenfurth, 'John Howard's hegemony of values'.

[119] J. Howard, 'Address to the National Press Club', 11 September 2002.

[120] F. Fukuyama, *The End of History and the Last Man* (London: Penguin, 2012 [1992]).

[121] Mead, *Special Providence*.

[122] See Mead, in particular, on the role and ideas of the Wilsonian tradition of US foreign policy. Mead, *Special Providence*.

[123] Holland, 'Obama as modern Jeffersonian'; T. McCrisken, *American Exceptionalism and the Legacy of Vietnam* (Houndmills: Palgrave Macmillan, 2003). American exceptionalism enables the USA to espouse a 'seemingly paradoxical idea': 'a state being exceptional by virtue of uniquely being built on universal principles'. N. Bouchet, 'The democracy tradition in US foreign policy and the Obama presidency', *International Affairs*, 89 (2013), 31–51.

[124] G. Brands, *What America Owes the World: The Struggle for the Soul of Foreign Policy* (New York: Cambridge University Press, 1998).

In the United Kingdom, the Empire may have been disbanded, but several of the narratives upon which it was built remain influential. As with the wider Anglosphere, British victory in globally consequential wars has been seen to vindicate a militaristic and interventionist British national identity, reinforcing the narratives such policies produce and promote in a virtuous circle of proclaimed global leadership and its apparent enactment. While explicit appeals to racial superiority have thankfully waned, narratives of British leadership on the world stage have remained influential. These narratives comprise multiple perceived qualities and beliefs, focusing on rationality and common sense, as well as the defence and promotion of democracy.[125] As Inderjeet Parmar has shown, at its core there is an intimate relationship between contemporary interventionism and historical pride in the policies of the British Empire.[126] Today's imperial present is built on selective amnesia and nostalgia for a colonial past,[127] in which British action is often re-written as ethical and altruistic, advancing the development and democratic cause of others.[128] Like the ANZAC myth and a belief in American exceptionalism, narratives of British global leadership remain pervasive across the political spectrum.[129] These are hegemonic stories that enable, shape and constrain the range of possible foreign policies that old Anglosphere coalition members can employ. It would be too strong to suggest that they are 'locked in' indefinitely: change is certainly possible, even where agency has limits. But repeated coalition warfare is the expected and default state of affairs, likely to continue into the future; abstention not inclusion is the exception to the rule. Anglosphere war is the normal and consequential condition.

The War on Terror and the Legacy of Iraq

During the War on Terror, these interventionist narratives and the policies they promote reached something of an apogee. The post 9/11

---

[125] J. Holland, 'Blair's war on terror: selling intervention to Middle England', *British Journal of Politics and International Relations*, 14 (2012), 74–95; Holland, *Selling the War on Terror*.

[126] I. Parmar, '"I'm proud of the British Empire": why Tony Blair backs George W. Bush', *The Political Quarterly*, 76 (2005), 218–31.

[127] Gregory, *The Colonial Present*.

[128] See Dan Bulley on options for more wholesale ethical UK foreign policy, through engagement with the work of Jacques Derrida. D. Bulley, 'The politics of ethical foreign policy: a responsibility to protect whom?', *European Journal of International Relations*, 16 (2010), 441–61.

[129] And particularly at its centre. See Holland, 'Blair's war on terror'.

era saw an intensification of Howard's efforts to frame Australian foreign and security policy in terms of values shared with 'great and powerful friends'; a project begun in 1996.[130] Camilleri, amongst others, notes the links between an increasingly narrowed national identity and Australia's past polices – such as White Australia – which were explicitly defined in racial terms. For Camilleri, 'Howard's international conception' in part reflected 'a deeper sense of White Australia's cultural and racial identity': his 'conception of the world mirrors his image of Australia'; when he spoke 'of Australia's "national character", of its "distinct and enduring values" and of "an Australian way"',[131] he was employing a form of dog whistle politics 'to refer to key aspects of the white Anglo-Australian heritage'.[132] 'The narrowing and exclusion at the heart of John Howard's conception of Australian identity was therefore significantly tied to an interpretation of identity that emphasised Australia's white, Anglo-heritage.'[133] And, as McKenna has warned, this narrowing of Australian identity 'gives rise to a military tradition within which those values and ideals are given their most profound expression'.[134]

By framing the policies of the War on Terror as simply the most recent examples of the ANZAC spirit, Howard justified and naturalised Australian participation in the old Anglosphere coalition's post 9/11 wars. For example, on ANZAC Day one year into the 2003 Iraq War, Howard gave a speech to Australian troops at Baghdad Airport, *insisting that their actions and values 'belong to that great and long tradition that was forged on the beaches of Gallipoli in 1915'.*[135] This, then, was part of an ongoing project across an influential decade of political office. Two years previously, referring to the war in

---

[130] R. Lyon and W. Tow, 'The future of the Australian–US security relationship', paper presented at Strategic Studies Institute, December 2003, www.strategicstudiesinstitute.army.mil/pdffiles/00047.pdf; J. Fitzpatrick, 'European settler colonialism and national security ideologies in Australian history' in R. Leaver and D. Cox (eds.), *Middling, Meddling, Muddling: Issues in Australian Foreign Policy* (St Leonards: Allen & Unwin, 1997). See also Holland and McDonald, 'Australian identity'; Holland, 'Howard's War on Terror'.

[131] J. Camilleri, 'A leap into the past – in the name of the "national interest"', *Australian Journal of International Affairs*, 57 (2003), 448–9. Cited by Holland and McDonald, 'Australian identity'.

[132] Holland and McDonald, 'Australian identity'.   [133] Ibid.

[134] McKenna, 'Patriot Act'.

[135] J. Howard, 'Address to troops in Iraq', 25 April 2004.

Afghanistan, Howard had insisted that Australians 'are fighting now for the same values the ANZACs fought for in 1915: courage, valour, mateship, decency [and] a willingness as a nation to do the right thing, whatever the cost'.[136] For Australia, like its allies, the principal conflicts of the War on Terror provided the immediate context for the forthcoming Anglosphere wars in response to the Arab Uprisings across the Middle East and North Africa. Howard, for example, had already promised that Australians 'resolve to work ever closer together to root out evil, we resolve ever more firmly to extend the hand of Australian friendship and mateship... We are Australians and Americans and others together in the campaign against evil'.[137] As the war in Iraq drew to a close, the last Australian troops left 'Operation Riverbank' at the end of November 2013, five weeks before the commencement of ISIL's dramatic Anbar Campaign.[138] Eighteen months later, Tony Abbott would send 330 Australian troops back to Iraq.[139]

In Britain, Tony Blair concurred wholeheartedly with Howard's assertion that the events of 11 September 2001, were 'not just an assault on the United States', but also 'an assault on the way of life that we [the Anglosphere] hold dear in common'.[140] Tim Dunne describes this as the 'resurgent Atlanticist identity' that has shaped 'British security strategy after 9/11'.[141] For Heer, this was more than a pro-Atlantic leaning in UK foreign and security policy: he argues that the most ardent American imperialists at the time of the invasion of Iraq in March 2003 were in fact not American at all, but British.[142] Notwithstanding important debate and contestation,[143] it is certainly

---

[136] Cited in McKenna, 'Patriot Act'.

[137] J. Howard, 'Address to 11 September ecumenical service', St Christopher's Cathedral, Manuka, Canberra, 11 September 2002.

[138] Most Australian troops were withdrawn in 2008, as Kevin Rudd declared 'mission accomplished'. See T. Wright, 'Last Australian soldiers leave Iraq, ending 11-year campaign', *Sydney Morning Herald*, 26 November 2013, www.smh.com.au/federal-politics/political-news/last-australian-soldiers-leave-iraq-ending-11year-campaign-20131126-2y7bz.html

[139] D. Hurst, 'Abbott confirms Australian military deploying to Iraq to help tackle Isis threat', *The Guardian*, 14 April 2015, www.theguardian.com/australia-news/2015/apr/14/abbott-confirms-australian-military-deploying-to-iraq-to-help-tackle-isis-threat

[140] Howard, 'The Anglosphere'.

[141] Dunne, 'When the shooting starts', p. 894.

[142] Heer, 'Operation Anglosphere'.

[143] P. Roe, 'Actor, audience(s) and emergency measures: securitization and the UK's decision to invade Iraq', *Security Dialogue*, 39 (2008), 615–33.

true that the likes of Wolfowitz, Perle and even Max Boot had equivalents in the UK, such as Robert Cooper, eager to re-establish (what they perceived to be) the benefits of imperialism, and even empire, for the Anglosphere and the world. Such seemingly alarming sentiments had been given greater policy relevance and mainstream acceptance by Tony Blair's infamous doctrine of international community – articulated in his 1999 Chicago speech. This speech and the doctrine it gave voice to redefined the notion of the international community; membership was now contingent upon the willingness to take military action in defence of shared western values. Lip service alone was insufficient. Moral multilateralism would no longer cut it in a new era of global terrorism; the international community was reimagined through a lens that crudely redefined the old Anglosphere coalition as comprising only central *interventionist* members, at the expense of those who erred and failed to act.[144]

The outcome of British and Australian eagerness to rush to war alongside the United States was profound but predictable. In Iraq, 'Only Australia and Britain helped the US with significant combat troops, leading some pundits to describe the coalition as "Anglosphere-heavy".'[145] The scale of the US operation and British contribution dwarfed Polish, Danish and Spanish deployments. And Howard was so keen to be seen to play his part that Australian troops were on the ground in Afghanistan before Australians even knew they were going to be fighting a new war.[146] If a desire to be America's 'Deputy Sheriff' helped inspire the decision to contribute early and in a meaningful way, it would soon become a term of derision rather than a badge of honour. In much the same way, one impact of the quagmire in Iraq[147] has been a push to question Britain's apparently uncritical assistance of the USA in times of war and crisis. Labels such as 'airstrip one' returned along with new probing insults for British political elites. A far cry from Winston Churchill being pictured as a British bulldog, Tony Blair was frequently portrayed in the popular press as George W. Bush's 'poodle', at the beck and call of his master, the leader of the free world. In 2004, as Blair faced increasing consternation regarding

---

[144] For discussion, see Holland, 'Blair's war on terror' and Holland, *Selling the War on Terror*.

[145] Vucetic, 'Bound to follow?', p. 2.   [146] Holland, *Selling the War on Terror*.

[147] Which now extends some seventeen years beyond President George W. Bush declaring 'mission accomplished'.

the failure to locate Iraqi WMD amidst ongoing allegations of 'sexing up' the intelligence case supporting the war, Dunne warned that, of 'all "Blair's wars", the decision to join the US mission to disarm Iraq by force will have the most lasting impact. It is not too far-fetched to suggest that it may become a defining moment in UK foreign policy, alongside Munich in 1938 and Suez in 1956'.[148]

Iraq has generated a threefold legacy, inclusive of overriding patterns and currents of Anglosphere behaviour: (i) a heightened sensitivity to the limitations of hard power; and (ii) protracted entanglement in post-Saddam Iraq; amidst (iii) the continued propensity for the Anglosphere to pursue military solutions to developments in the region. It is the latter that this chapter has explored. While it is possible – and necessary – to detail the considerable problems of Blair's war in Iraq,[149] a counterfactual reading of British foreign policy would suggest that, far from being a 'mistake per se', Blair's decision to once again rally to America's side makes perfect sense when considering that 'the idea of Anglo-America has enjoyed such a hold over the British political imagination during the era of imperial decline'.[150] Iraq, for both the UK and Australia, was business as usual – a mutual war, pursued by a common community, occupying a single transnational political space. For the Anglosphere's most ardent theorists and advocates, asking whether it was the *wrong* decision is to, perhaps mistakenly, suppose that within this set up there was much of a choice to make in the first place.[151]

The first point – recognition of the limits of hard power – influenced the foreign policy of Barack Obama above all others. For Obama, a range of factors combined to inspire a foreign policy that prioritised soft power and engagement in order to achieve rebalancing and retrenchment.[152] Strategic reassessment in the wake of economic crisis,

---

[148] Dunne, 'When the shooting starts', p. 893.

[149] See, for example, J. Dumbrell, 'Working with allies: the United States, the United Kingdom and the War on Terror', *Politics and Policy*, 34 (2006), 452–72.

[150] Gamble, 'The Anglo-American hegemony', p. 8.

[151] For me, this is too strong a suggestion, absolving our political leaders of agency and responsibility.

[152] J. Holland, 'Obama's War on Terror: why is change so hard?' in M. Bentley and J. Holland (eds.), *Obama's Foreign Policy: Ending the War on Terror* (Abingdon/New York: Routledge, 2014); and J. Holland and M. Bentley, 'Conceptualising Change and Continuity in US Foreign Policy', Ibid.

aligned with a habitual Jeffersonian prioritisation of domestic issues, encouraged a more cautious foreign policy approach.[153] And, yet, for a president defined by caution and patience in international affairs, Obama repeatedly ended up pursuing foreign policies that appeared decidedly squeamish.[154] Whether acting as 'Assassin in Chief' through US drone strikes,[155] leading from behind with airstrikes in Libya, or authorising the extrajudicial assassination of Osama bin Laden, Obama repeatedly demonstrated that he was prepared to use American force for lethal purposes, notwithstanding his reluctance to go abroad in search of monsters to destroy. Despite these actions, Obama's foreign policy was characterised by an attempt to end (what he infamously termed) his predecessor's 'dumb war' in Iraq, while at the same time refocusing American efforts in Afghanistan and Pakistan. Reluctance, where possible, to put boots on the ground, in the wake of the quagmire in Iraq, elevated American airpower to the default solution when lofty rhetoric fell short of achieving desired outcomes. And the UK and Australia largely fell into line behind these policy, strategy and tactical decisions.

On the second point – the protracted entanglement in post-Saddam Iraq – Ralph and Souter have noted that this has brought a series of military and ethical engagements for the old Anglosphere coalition. Having destabilised the country, these states have inherited a presumed ethical commitment towards its rebuilding.[156] This responsibility stems from a 'reparative obligation'.[157] Having created the context in which extremism and, specifically, ISIL have flourished, the old Anglosphere coalition is ethically committed to Iraq in a way that others (such as

[153] M. Bentley and J. Holland (eds.), *The Obama Doctrine: A Foreign Policy Legacy of Continuity?* (Abingdon/New York: Routledge, 2016).

[154] Holland, 'Obama as modern Jeffersonian'; L. Jarvis and J. Holland, 'We (for) got him: remembering and forgetting in the narration of bin Laden's death', *Millennium Journal of International Studies*, 42 (2014), 425–47; J. Holland and L. Jarvis, '"Night fell on a different world": experiencing, constructing and remembering 9/11', *Critical Studies on Terrorism*, 7 (2014), 184–204; J. Holland and M. Aaronson, 'Dominance through coercion: rhetorical balancing and the tactics of justification in Afghanistan and Libya', *Intervention and Statebuilding*, 8 (2014), 1–20; J. Holland and M. Aaronson, 'Strategic rhetorical balancing and the tactics of justification in Afghanistan, Libya and beyond', *Intervention and Statebuilding*, 10 (2016), 3–24.

[155] C. Fuller, 'Assassin in chief' in *The Obama Doctrine: A Foreign Policy Legacy of Continuity?*

[156] J. Ralph and J. Souter, 'A special responsibility to protect: the UK, Australia and the rise of Islamic State', *International Affairs*, 91 (2015), 709–23.

[157] Ibid., p. 710.

France) are not.[158] This is an obligation understood and articulated by leaders of all three states.[159] It is a significant legacy that has gone much of the way to overriding the reluctance to engage hard power options following the explicit highlighting of their limitations in and after 2003. It has not, however, come at the expense of a second important outcome of the War on Terror: that, once again, has been the reaffirming of an Anglosphere commitment to united warfare in conflicts of significant global consequence. The War on Terror, like old Anglosphere coalition wars of the past, helped to make intervention in Syria a question of when not if; it served to make war's avoidance or delay the exception and its prosecution the expectation. Anglosphere war is a seemingly inevitable constant in international relations: a consequential global norm.

Conclusion

Unlike the significant consensus acknowledging the Anglosphere's empirical existence, its role as a positive global force is fiercely disputed. Like all analysts of international relations, Anglospherists are engaged in political storytelling. At various points, however, their strategic narratives have been troubling, as with notable attempts 'to present a somewhat rosy [historical] picture', 'marked by progress and humanitarianism in which bad behaviour tends to be forgiven, played down or explained away'.[160] Browning and Tonra note that, while escaping the Anglosphere's 'racialist origins in Anglo-Saxonism', it is necessary to interrogate 'the logic of memes over genes', not least as cultural essentialism can result 'in the underestimation of cultural differences within the Anglosphere', whilst overestimating the extent to which Anglosphere values 'are part of a distinct Anglosphere, rather than European/Western tradition'.[161] These are important points that I have addressed in my previous research, which has shown how the USA, UK and Australia sold the War on Terror in different ways to articulate, appeal and acquiesce effectively in distinct domestic contexts.[162] Yet, despite these divergences, there is more that unites than divides.

---

[158] Ibid.   [159] Ibid.   [160] Browning and Tonra, 'Beyond the West', pp. 9–10.
[161] Ibid., p. 16. Harries makes a similar argument directed at Mead, on brushing over the similar educational backgrounds of western and European leaders in *Guns and Gold*. See Harries, 'Anglo-Saxon attitudes'.
[162] Holland, *Selling the War on Terror*; J. Holland, 'Foreign policy and political possibility', *European Journal of International Relations*, 19 (2013), 48–67.

On Browning and Tonra's second point, it is these three countries together – and not a broader West – that *repeatedly and inevitably* line up to fight. Blair's redefinition of the international community may have been troubling politically and normatively, but it pointed to a clear global reality: only a handful of states – with the USA, UK and Australia at the forefront – are prepared to take military action in the defence of values often shared more broadly by western states. This is not a one off or even an isolated era of cooperation: the old Anglosphere coalition has fought together in very nearly every single US-led war of the past century. And many of these wars have shaped world order. Browning and Tonra are correct that Anglosphere narratives play down the role of Greco-Roman ideas and European or western influence. But those ideas and influences play into a warrior culture formed in the United Kingdom and exported to the United States and Australia, the latter connected, umbilically, to the motherland and the former now offering assistance and protection to its weaker parent. If Anglosphere wars inspire UN Security Council resolutions, it is possible that they will be joined by others – recently, for example, France – but that is a secondary question. Old Anglosphere coalition warfare has been constructed as the natural order of things to the extent that it is a near constant of the post-1918, post-1945, post-Cold War and post 9/11 eras – the modern era. It remains so today, following the regional turbulence of the Arab Uprisings. Those who would repudiate the 'link between being an English-speaking state and acting in concert with other English-speaking states'[163] in favour of old-fashioned national interest miss the point that this is, very frequently, not the principal concern of Anglosphere leaders when considering whether to participate in Anglosphere wars; not to do so is, very often, unpalatable or even, quite simply, unthinkable.

Lastly, before we move on to consider the linguistic choices and dynamics of these English-speaking states, it is important to reflect on the normative resurgence the Anglosphere has of late inspired, including its conservative bias. Lloyd notes that 'the Anglosphere idea pushes so many of the right's emotional buttons'.[164] Following Churchill's Herculean undertaking,[165] the Anglosphere has gone on to inspire

---

[163] Kissane, 'Anglosphere united?'.

[164] J. Lloyd, 'The Anglosphere project', *The New Statesman*, 13 March 2000, www.newstatesman.com/node/193400

[165] Perhaps the most famous author on the subject, Churchill's final work on the subject – the fourth volume – was delayed until near his death in his eighties. Its

contemporary conservative historians, some of whom have made quite worrying and problematic arguments. For example, the 'enthusiasm for the old Pax Britannia has been bolstered by the revisionist scholarship of Scottish historian Niall Ferguson'.[166] He 'argues that the British Empire was a progressive force in world history that lay the foundations of our current global economy'.[167] Ferguson is certainly not alone,[168] but conservative affinities for Anglosphere imperialism are not sufficient reason to abandon a term that well encapsulates one of the most striking patterns of behaviour in modern and contemporary world politics. At this moment, the term has greater analytical value than at any time previously, off the back of: (i) several large recent Anglosphere wars, which – whether successes or failures – have served only to reinforce the cultural bonds of war; and (ii) a technological revolution that has accelerated and intensified global communications, heightening the importance of linguistic and cultural fluency.[169] Today, as Syria burns, the Anglosphere continues to grow stronger and more unified.[170] As it does so, we do well to remember the important critique of Anglosphere foreign policy as helping to sustain the conditions necessary in the Middle East for persistent civil war, as well as asymmetric economic exploitation.[171]

topics are noticeably unbalanced, with significant scope afforded to subjects Churchill himself found to be interesting, at the expense of other, seemingly important, issues. In contrast with his admiration for and knowledge of the political history of the United States, Churchill's take on Australia is somewhat rudimentary, with talk of boomerangs and digger debauchery, quelled by British policing.

[166] Heer, 'Operation Anglosphere'.   [167] Ibid.

[168] See, for example, the work of Walter Russell Mead or Conquest, *The Dragons of Expectation.*

[169] Bennett, *The Anglosphere Challenge*; Mead, 'Review'.

[170] The outcome of the British 'Brexit' referendum on the UK's membership of the European Union also served to further increase interest in and calls for an enhanced Anglosphere relationship. Even the election of Donald Trump, whilst causing concern, has not derailed this project, in part due to his brand of ethno-populism.

[171] Many have made this argument, inspired by the work of Edward Said. Most famously, E. Said, *Orientalism* (New York: Vintage, 1994 [1979]).

3 | *Selling War and Peace*

Language is the means of getting an idea from my brain into yours without surgery.

Mark Amidon

Change your language and you change your thoughts.

Karl Albrecht[1]

Introduction

'Political activity does not exist without the use of language.'[2] Aristotle recognised as much, arguing that 'politics and language are intimately linked at a fundamental level'.[3] When he spoke of the Polis – the human inclination to reside in a political community, such as the Anglosphere – he also spoke of humanity's unique abilities for speech and language.[4] As Charteris-Black notes, it 'has always been preferable for the governed to be ruled by the spoken word rather than the whip, the chain or the gun'.[5] Political community simultaneously enables and relies upon this possibility. In both its internal configurations – its laws and values – and in its sense of Self, a political community is an inherently linguistic entity. The laws of the Polis, alongside its proclaimed values and common identity, are forged through the use of language in particular and specific ways, in a crucial but contingent

---

[1] Albrecht is the co-founder of Aldi. See also F. Nietzsche, *Beyond Good and Evil* (New York: Vintage Books, 1966), although it is necessary to read this critically.
[2] P. Chilton, *Analysing Political Discourse: Theory and Practice* (London/New York: Routledge, 2004), p. 6.
[3] Ibid., p. 4.
[4] Chilton notes that Aristotle distinguishes between 'voice', common to all animals in the expression of basic sensations such as pleasure and pain, and 'man's' capacity to converse in the communication of complex ideas. Ibid., pp. 4–5.
[5] J. Charteris-Black, *Politicians and Rhetoric: The Persuasive Power of Metaphor* (Houndmills: Palgrave Macmillan, 2005), p. xi.

and contestable process of meaning-making. It is language that enables the emergence, formation and functioning of the Polis, as well as helping to determine its fate.

Quite simply, language and politics are inseparable; the study of the former remains incomplete in the absence of the latter. Today's Anglosphere Polis may well be several orders of magnitude larger than those envisaged by Aristotle, but it remains a globally consequential coalition, bound by language. Just as at the outset of political life language was essential for the 'socialisation of humans' into coalitions, language's centrality to the composition of the Anglosphere remains fundamental.[6] In fact, today, we see the *increasing* importance of language in an era of instant communication.[7] Communication enables ideas to be intersubjectively shared by Anglosphere citizens, who, despite the separation of distance, become affectively invested in them, as they shape and define the community.[8] As with all groups, language is vital for the signalling of the Anglosphere's boundaries.[9] It is key to the development of a sense of shared identity – built on history, values and even (perceived) race. In short, it is in and through language that the Anglosphere has taken shape as a shared and single transnational political space.

Not famed for his devastating oratory, George W. Bush was the Anglosphere's foremost leader during its most pressing hour of recent decades. Nonetheless, in this moment of crisis and trauma, he frequently gave voice and identity to an imaged transnational political community of 'freedom-loving countries'.[10] In his linguistic 'strategery',[11] the President of the United States performed that most Aristotelian of functions, prioritising issues, identifying good and evil in the world and rallying a coalition.[12] Despite his propensity to mangle his words, several of Bush's turns of phrase have been particularly consequential, amidst what Fred Halliday has so eloquently described as the

---

[6] Ibid.; see also, on the importance of language, gossip and collective stories (or myths) as humans began to live in groups larger than 150 people, Y. Harari, *Sapiens: A Brief History of Humankind* (London: Random House, 2014).
[7] Bennett, *The Anglosphere Challenge*; and Bennett, 'The emerging Anglosphere'.
[8] Ibid., p. 6.   [9] Ibid.   [10] See Holland, *Selling the War on Terror*.
[11] Bush's advisers and speech writers first labelled themselves as this on the campaign trail in 1999 and 2000, due to Bush's frequent linguistic inventiveness. Ibid.
[12] Chilton, *Analysing Political Discourse*, p. 6.

'linguistic harvest of war'.[13] Terms such as 'axis of evil' and 'illegal enemy combatant' are chronicled and dissected in Halliday's 'dictionary' of the War on Terror.[14] Readers can revisit the chronology of the War on Terror through some of its less salubrious phrases; 'from a pre-9/11 "failure of imagination", via a "sexed-up" dossier and exculpatory claims that "freedom is untidy", to ultimate "shoe thrower" acts of resistance'.[15] Words such as these can certainly exalt and explain, at the same time as helping to form political identities, but they can also 'promote fear, hatred and misunderstanding'.[16] Words can 'kill'.[17]

One of the reasons that words 'be studied, challenged and controlled' is in order to 'reveal and resist the role of language in naturalising and/or concealing violence'.[18] For example, it helps to note that when politicians use a term such as 'detention facility' to describe a 'jail', it is akin to describing 'soap' as 'body lotion', or a blatant 'bank rip-off' as an 'arrangement fee'.[19] Likewise (and, again, in Halliday's delightful prose), to speak of 'Grand Strategy' is to invoke a 'pompous term much used in Washington', which gives 'bogus coherence to random bits of aggressive and bellicose fantasy'.[20] As George Orwell urged us to remember, 'political language... is designed to make lies sound truthful and murder respectable and to give an appearance of solidity to pure wind'.[21] Of course, there is far more to language than this. In the space betwixt language and politics occurs a process at once both more complex and more fundamental than simply deception and fabrication. And, thankfully, it is far from all bad. Language's saturation of the world with meaning is a vital part of how we make sense of it. It helps us to understand, navigate and interact with our environment. In this, political language, such as foreign policy, can work for

---

[13] F. Halliday, *Shocked and Awed: How the War on Terror and Jihad Have Changed the English Language* (London: I.B. Tauris, 2010). See also J. Holland, 'Review of Shocked and Awed: How the War on Terror and Jihad Have Changed the English Language. London: I.B. Tauris, 2010', *Critical Studies on Terrorism*, 4 (2011), 293–5.

[14] Halliday, *Shocked and Awed.*   [15] Holland, 'Review of Shocked and Awed'.

[16] Halliday, *Shocked and Awed*, p. xv.   [17] Ibid.   [18] Ibid.

[19] Halliday, *Shocked and Awed*, p. 66. See also Holland, 'Review of Shocked and Awed'.

[20] Halliday, *Shocked and Awed*, p. 296; and Holland, 'Review of Shocked and Awed'. Halliday also discusses such wonderful terms as 'Scottish Guantanamo', 'Colinectomy' and 'pretzel of preposterousness'.

[21] G. Orwell, *Politics and the English Language* (London: Penguin, 2013 [1946]).

the people and against the people. Political narrative can help to create a shared identity, a sense of community, a perception of security or even purpose, helping to make meaning out of a complex world and bind citizens together in common endeavour.[22] Political language can also justify extrajudicial assassination,[23] industrial pollution and political corruption; it can sell wars, encourage apathy and alienate citizens. Language determines who wins and who loses, as well as how and why. Words carry great power – if your voice is heard.

Who gets to speak? Political language, like all language, emerges from the interaction of people and their surroundings. In 1939 in the British House of Commons, Conservative MP Leo Amery lamented Prime Minister Neville Chamberlain's appeasement of Hitler, with a call for Arthur Greenwood to 'speak for England'. The charge, 'speak for England!' has become infamous. It indicates the importance and interwoven nature of politicians, their political context and the construction of the national identity within their oratory. Political elites are charged with articulating the national identity, constrained, as they are, by the contextual terrain within which they operate. The first point to note, then, is that political language generally and foreign policy specifically is dependent upon the motivations and skills of key agents: the political elites institutionally empowered to have their words heard and potentially enacted.

While nearly *all* citizens can and do engage in processes of meaning-making through (explicitly or implicitly political) language, it is our elected politicians and practitioners who demonstrate the most influence over the nature and direction of political language, including foreign policy. They act, however, subject to the same contextual conditions as the rest of us and are inevitably shaped by them. Therefore, second, political language, including foreign policy, is enabled, shaped and constrained by its discursive, cultural and political contexts. This twin realisation – of the importance of the interaction of strategic agents within a facilitating and structuring context – is vital

---

[22] See R. Krebs, *Narrative and the Making of U.S. National Security* (Cambridge: Cambridge University Press, 2015); and J. Mitzen, 'Ontological security in world politics: state identity and the security dilemma', *European Journal of International Relations*, 12 (2006), 341–70.

[23] See C. Fuller, 'The eagle comes home to roost: the historical origins of the CIA's lethal drone program', *Intelligence & National Security*, 30 (2014), 769–92; and, on assassination, Jarvis and Holland, 'We (for)got him'.

and its exploration guides much of this chapter. How is it that political elites create political language, and to what effect? How is it that some foreign policy language wins out, while other discourses are defeated and dismissed? These questions are fundamental to the aim of this book: their exploration can help us to understand the pre-conditions for policies of war and peace in Syria.

In its exploration of these questions, the chapter is structured in four parts. In its first section, the chapter lays out the relationship of language and discourse, stressing the importance but impermanence of meaning production through discursive regularities. Second, the remainder of the chapter turns to consider how it is that some foreign policies prosper, while others lose out. As a first step in this exploration, resonance is theorised as comprising several salient and interrelated features, which help to determine the success or failure of foreign policy language. Third, the chapter turns to consider work at the forefront of constructivism and post-constructivism on representational force, which explores a vital additional and under-explored element of language's power. Here, going beyond an analysis of *seductive* language, the chapter assesses the potential for elites to achieve policy acquiescence through the construction of coercive and ultimately dominant discourses. Such narratives might, for example, draw on strategies of rhetorical entrapment or rhetorical balancing in order to achieve representational force. This insight means that we need to rethink the nature of the power of language, which, contrary to popular misconception, is not so 'soft' after all.[24] Fourth and finally, the chapter assesses how, together, these elements of the relationship of foreign policy and political possibility combine. Together, they shape the discursive battlefield in which a war of position takes place over the language of war and peace. This contest is conceptualised, drawing on the work of Antonio Gramsci, noting that discursive victory or defeat is consequential not only for Anglosphere states, but also for international order generally and the people of Syria specifically. The resolution of the wars of position at the heart of this book determines policies of military intervention and/or its avoidance for the world's

---

[24] J. S. Nye, Jr, *Soft Power: The Means to Success in World Politics* (New York: Public Affairs, 2005). See also J. Mattern, 'Why "soft power" isn't so soft: representational force and the sociolinguistic construction of attraction in world politics', *Millennium Journal of International Studies*, 33 (2005), 583–612.

foremost alliance, including in the contemporary era's principal international crisis.

Language and Politics

Foreign policy is a key component of politics, political life and the political community – helping to constitute the identity and values of that community. That is in part because, like Aristotle's Polis, foreign policy is irrevocably linguistic.[25] Foreign policy is a special linguistic domain in that it gives form to that *beyond* the Polis, defining its *outside* and naming the *foreign*. A prerequisite for establishing policy towards that which lies beyond the boundaries of a political community is to give meaning and character to its various Others. This is a theme that has been elaborated by numerous constructivist and post-structural scholars, amongst them David Campbell and Richard Jackson.[26] Between them, Campbell and Jackson have made a compelling and consequential argument, which I breakdown here into three parts. First, foreign policy – whether dealing with issues of international security, conflicts such as those of the War on Terror, or the nature of terrorist groups – is written into existence.[27] Second, writing the 'policy' of foreign policy is to simultaneously write the 'foreign' of foreign policy; the Other, outside of the Polis, inevitably gains meaning within the language of foreign policy. Third, writing the outside of the Polis unavoidably gives form to its inside; through foreign policy, the identity and values of the political community are socially and discursively produced. Things could not be otherwise; it is simply not possible to opt out of this arrangement. Language's importance – to the political community and to the foreign policy that gives it shape and meaning – is fundamental and enduring.

Campbell's seminal work demonstrates the ways in which foreign policy is a process of writing security – identifying, classifying and prioritising threats and enemies, in opposition to a co-constitutively

---

[25] D. Campbell, *Writing Security: United States Foreign Policy and the Politics of Identity*, Revised Edition (Minneapolis: University of Minnesota Press, 1998).

[26] Ibid.; and R. Jackson, *Writing the War on Terrorism* (Manchester: Manchester University Press, 2005).

[27] Campbell, *Writing Security*; Jackson, *Writing*; T. Barnes and J. Duncan, *Writing Worlds: Discourse, Text and Metaphor in the Representation of Landscape* (Abingdon/New York: Routledge, 1991).

determined sense of Self. For Campbell, it is possible to trace the formation of American identity through the identification, naming and construction of various Others in US foreign policy history. In turn, Native Americans, fascist Germans and communist Russians have all played a formative role for the United States through their framing as diametrically opposed Others, embodying the antithesis of American-ness.[28] While no state possesses a pre-discursive understanding of itself, Campbell shows how, as a 'new' and 'history-less' nation, the USA is the imagined community *par excellence*; clearly and explicitly brought into being as a coherent political community through its narrative scripting in foreign policy.[29] Drawing on mutual philosophical anchorage in the works of Foucault, Derrida and Fairclough, Richard Jackson extends Campbell's analysis to the era of the War on Terror and the more recent Other of American foreign policy: Islamic terrorism.[30] Here, again, the Commander-in-Chief is shown to serve the dual and unavoidable role of articulating a foreign Them and an American Us. Only, this time, Osama bin Laden, Al Qaeda and the Taliban provided the range of evils against which American heroism was readily juxtaposed and (re-)produced.

Barnes and Duncan push this argument further still. For them, it is not just foreign policy, issues of international security and contemporary wars that are 'written', but rather the whole world.[31] It is from this Foucauldian and broadly post-structural ontological position that critical constructivists have taken their cue in recognising that even apparently 'brute' facts rarely are. While it is relatively easy to see that the so-called material reality of a nuclear weapon is still entirely dependent upon subjective readings of whose hands it happens to be in – contrast US policy towards Israeli and Iranian nuclear programmes – it is certainly more difficult but equally necessary to recognise that *everything* – even something as apparently 'natural' as geography – is formed within language, at the intersection of the material and the ideational. Consider: Britain's island status and perennial debates about the UK's position within or outside of Europe; or changing perceptions of the usefulness of Alaska (infamously sold to the USA by Russia for only $7 million); or conflicting images of Australia's immediate Asia-Pacific neighbourhood as an area of economic opportunity or

---

[28] Campbell, *Writing Security*.   [29] Ibid., p. 91.   [30] Jackson, *Writing*.
[31] Barnes and Duncan, *Writing Worlds*.

existential threat. While 'brute' material qualities matter – what former Australian Prime Minister Paul Keating once referred to as the geophysics of the situation – their meaning is formed largely through language. Contrast the strategic and resource importance of Alaska today in contrast to the lament of some at the time of Alaska's purchase, who decried the 'folly' of wasting money on what amounted to an 'icebox' perceived to be good for nothing but a 'polar bear's garden'.[32]

The writing of the world that occurs within and through foreign policy therefore extends beyond the construction of identities; political elites are cartographers, colouring space and place, defining proximal and distant, and giving character to our globe. As geographers have shown, foreign policy is a largely linguistic process, in which the world is divided up into safe areas and wild zones, as maps of amity and enmity are drawn.[33] Foreign policy, then, is a process of mapping with words – a linguistic cartography – in which actors are given meaning and geographic addresses. Our geographical and geopolitical imaginations take shape in a constant (even if, at times, implicit) negotiation between the words of our elected officials and our accumulated knowledge of the world, gained through our experience of a plethora of (popular) cultural sources and earlier times. This is crucial. We can reject, modify or accept the words of our politicians. They well know this and are, usually, intelligent and capable actors. Political elites know that it is not possible to draw *any* map they like, to construct *any* identity they see fit, or to articulate *any* preferred foreign policy. It is not possible to fill the world with simply any old meaning that takes their fancy. Foreign policy is not written on a blank slate.[34] New ideas are certainly possible – elites can act as norm entrepreneurs – but these ideas compete with what an audience already knows to be true. Strategic political elites therefore certainly can and do write a nation's foreign policy in what can be an innovative discursive enterprise. However, foreign policy is culturally embedded in two senses;[35] it is

---

[32] The terms 'Seward's folly' and 'Seward's icebox' were used to describe the purchase. See Library of Congress, 'Have you been to the polar bear's garden?', www.loc.gov/wiseguide/mar05/bear.html

[33] G. Toal, *Critical Geopolitics: The Politics of Writing Global Space* (Minneapolis: University of Minnesota Press, 1996); Gregory, *The Colonial Present*.

[34] Others have suggested the metaphor of a palimpsest.

[35] For further discussion of the cultural mediation of the international, see F. Debrix and C. Weber (eds.), *Rituals of Mediation: International Politics and Social Meaning* (Minneapolis: University of Minnesota Press, 2003).

drawn from and framed for a specific political and cultural context. In these two related steps, foreign policy is enabled, shaped and constrained by its culturally (dis)embedded nature.[36]

What, then, does it mean to suggest that foreign policy is written but is far more complex than simply the use of *any* language? First, it is necessary to consider the role of rhetoric and discourse, as they relate to language. This terminology is important but should not perform the constraining role that has at times been the case in International Relations. Frequently, researchers are categorised on the basis of their preferences for analysing rhetoric, narrative, language *or* discourse. To claim that using one or other ties you to a particular camp is an arbitrary limitation of an odd discipline indeed. *All* are important and must necessarily be brought together in order to facilitate a fuller understanding and analysis of foreign policy, which inevitably involves elements of each.[37] To begin with, let us start with language, defined by the *Oxford English Dictionary* as, 'the method of human communication, either spoken or written, consisting of the use of words in a structured and conventional way'.[38] Within language, rhetoric alludes to the employment of style or oratorical device in order to persuade. Consider, for example, deliberate appeals to metaphor or the use of a pleasant cadence in foreign policy speeches. Rhetoric suggests agency and strategy on the part of the politician, as well as the necessity of striving for certain forms of communication, tied to the specificities of context and audience.[39] Narrative too shares some of these assumptions, as politicians employ a story-like mode of articulation in foreign policy speeches, involving plots and characters, in an effort to connect events and issues through space and time. Consider, for example, the famous British narrative of standing alone, fighting on and ultimately prevailing in World War II. Character, plot and the unfolding of a story through time are, therefore, central features of foreign policy

---

[36] The reason for the including of the bracketed '(dis)' is that foreign policy which fails to account for the cultural landscape will often fail to resonate or be realised. See Krebs, *Narrative*, chapter 3.

[37] For a novel framework showing how rhetoric and narrative might be combined, see Krebs, *Narrative*.

[38] Oxford English Dictionary, 'Language', www.oxforddictionaries.com/definition/english/language (accessed 4 November 2019).

[39] Charteris-Black, *Politicians and Rhetoric*; and A. Crines, 'Rhetoric and the coalition: governing in the national interest?' *Representation*, 49 (2013), 207–18.

narratives and help to distinguish them from the rhetorical devices that may be found within them.[40]

If these two modes – rhetoric and narrative – exist (largely) *within* language, discourse exists at a larger scale. Discourses are certainly linguistic but not exclusively so, encompassing non-linguistic features, such as images, buildings, fashion, landscapes and body language, amongst many other features (some would suggest *all* of the world's features). Discourses form where language stabilises, producing meaning in a relatively systematic way, albeit without ever achieving a total fixity. It is possible to see discourses form, rise, compete and fall – perhaps, along the way, enabling and shaping specific policies. The conditions that allow or prevent their rise, influence and fall are the subject matter for much of the remainder of this chapter. They help to determine whether language might remain as 'just words' or be realised through its stabilisation as a foreign policy discourse – comprised of rhetorical devices and strategic narratives employed by instrumental elites – which both enables and gives meaning to the international actions of the state. For example, in order to establish a discourse of humanitarian intervention, politicians seeking such action might employ strategic narratives tying despotic leaders to unspeakable atrocities against innocent civilians that will continue unabated without intervention. These narratives may be embellished with rhetorical flourishes such as metaphors and analogies – a reign of terror that we must not appease, for example. If a sufficient number of people buy into this language and its central features and tropes are repeated, meaning-making may stabilise around the new discourse, creating the requisite discursive conditions – the conditions of possibility – that enable a military intervention to take place in the name of humanitarianism. Counter-discourses might alternatively attempt to limit the possibility of such activity, or reframe the meaning of an intervention. Consider, for example, attempts to derail the war in Iraq through narratives and discourses centred on the twin issues of oil and imperialism, which gained considerable and increasing traction after 2003. In order to conceptualise discursive contests such as this and establish a framework for the analysis of Anglosphere discursive wars of position over

---

[40] For example, A. Miskimmon, B. O'Loughlin and L. Roselle, *Strategic Narratives: Communication Power and the New World Order* (New York/Abingdon: Routledge, 2013).

Syria, this chapter explores, in turn, how it is that foreign policy discourses might achieve resonance, dominance and hegemony.

Persuading an Audience

Few would disagree with Richard Jackson's argument that 'the act of going to war is so costly as to warrant extraordinary discursive effort to persuade audiences and populations of its necessity, virtue and practicality'.[41] Likewise, Lene Hansen presents a seemingly incontrovertible argument that it 'would be extremely unlikely and politically unsavvy for politicians to articulate foreign policy without any concern for the representations found within the wider public sphere as they attempt to present their policies as legitimate to their constituencies'.[42] Surely, then, between them, Jackson and Hansen have made a succinct but compelling case for the study of strategic framing, audience reception and the importance of resonance within foreign policy? Not quite, not yet. It is still important to ask whether language, resonance and the political legitimacy it implies are really *necessary*.[43] That is because of the electoral and constitutional mandates governing the use of force in the three members of the old Anglosphere coalition. Electoral wins, in combination with the codified and implicit powers of the executive branch of government, enable the following question to be posed: does Anglosphere foreign policy really need linguistic justification?

In order to answer a resounding 'no', one might point to the infamous example of New Labour's early years, when the party had become an election-winning machine in the UK and foreign policy was afforded a relatively minor role in the party's policy platform. Electoral successes came on the back of well-packaged domestic policies[44] and fatigue with the existing government; a combination that helped to inspire the accumulation of exceptional political capital through unprecedented parliamentary majorities in 1997 and 2001. I argue that such a platform was plainly useful *but alone*

[41] Quotation taken from Holland, 'Foreign policy and political possibility', paraphrasing Jackson, *Writing the War on Terrorism*, p. 1.
[42] L. Hansen, *Security as Practice: Discourse Analysis and the Bosnian War* (London: Routledge, 2006), p. 7.
[43] Holland, 'Howard's War on Terror'.
[44] N. Fairclough, *New Labour, New Language?* (London: Routledge, 2000).

insufficient for the prosecution of the War on Terror that followed.[45] Anglosphere leaders possess 'the (legal) capacity to commit troops to intervention... without majority support',[46] but rarely do; legitimacy is actively sought. Blair, for example, 'was acutely aware of the need to craft a compelling foreign policy discourse in order to realise' his foreign policy aims.[47] This pattern was continued during the prime ministership of David Cameron, with two votes put to parliament on the use of force. And it is a pattern that extends beyond Britain, as, across the Anglosphere, 'the use of force is generally perceived to require public justification'.[48]

That is because 'one of the most basic features of [the] democratic politics' of the old Anglosphere coalition 'is that military force is not used without some consideration of the will of the public'.[49] The accountability of elections and public opinion is coupled to the *expectation* of justification; in the Anglosphere, foreign policy legitimation – through the pursuit of resonance – is a democratic norm.[50] This means that the 'will of the public' influences foreign policy through its direct and indirect influence on political decision-making, as well as helping to shape foreign policy's presentation to the public. Bill Clinton, for example, was famed for his sensitivity to public opinion, including on foreign policy issues, amidst a revolution in polling's sophistication.[51] Likewise, Tony Blair was renowned for his confidence in possessing the

---

[45] Holland, 'Blair's War on Terror'.

[46] M. McDonald and M. Merefield, 'How was Howard's war possible? Winning the war of position over Iraq', *Australian Journal of International Affairs*, 64 (2010), 186–204.

[47] Holland, 'Blair's War on Terror'. And his use of force in Operation Desert Fox in 1998 was an exception pertaining to an 'institutionalised securitisation', rather than the norm. See Roe, 'Actor, audience(s) and emergency measures', p. 632.

[48] Holland, 'Blair's War on Terror'.

[49] J. Western, 'The war over Iraq: selling war to the American public', *Security Studies*, 14 (2005), 106–39. See also C. Gelpi, P. Feaver and J. Reifler, *Paying the Human Costs of War: American Public Opinion and Military Casualties in Conflicts* (Princeton: Princeton University Press, 2009); and J. Western, *Selling Intervention and War: The Presidency, the Media and the General Public* (Baltimore: Johns Hopkins University Press, 2005).

[50] See, on the Copenhagen School and securitisation theory's wrestling with questions of resonance, T. Balzacq, 'The three faces of securitization: political agency, audience and context', *European Journal of International Relations*, 11 (2005), 171–201.

[51] Holland, *Selling the War on Terror*.

ability to persuade an audience of his preferred course of action and thus to *move* public opinion towards his chosen course of action.[52] There is evidence to suggest Blair's self-confidence was not misplaced and that political elites in general possess considerable influence over public support for foreign policy, including the use of force.[53]

In the United States, a growing literature on 'elite cues' has shown that 'public exposure to elite discourse is a more important determinant of support for intervention than knowledge of foreign policy events', and, moreover, elite 'cues' and frames 'are especially important in determining support for intervention'.[54] For instance, public support for war is not proportional to the number of 'our boys' returning home in body bags, as might be assumed:[55] rather 'support is more closely tied to the clarity of rationale for intervention and, if framed accordingly, military casualties can even increase support for war'.[56] This realisation offers numerous benefits to political elites and helps to explain their pursuit of resonance. Beyond the simple act of warding off a 'recalcitrant public', which might resist and derail policy,[57] political elites attempt to avoid limitations on their future 'room for

---

[52] Ibid.   [53] Holland, 'Blair's War on Terror'.

[54] See, for example, Gelpi et al., *Paying the Human Costs of War*; W. Boettcher and M. Cobb, 'Don't let them die in vain: casualty frames and public tolerance for escalating commitment in Iraq', *The Journal of Conflict Resolution*, 53 (2009), 677–97; W. Boettcher and M. Cobb, 'Echoes of Vietnam? Casualty framings and public perceptions of success and failure in Iraq', *Journal of Conflict Resolution*, 50 (2006), 831–54; P. Sullivan, 'Sustaining the fight: a cross-sectional time series analysis of public support for ongoing military interventions', *Conflict Management and Peace Science*, 25 (2008), 112–35; A. Berinsky, 'Assuming the costs of war: events, elites and American public support for military conflict', *The Journal of Politics*, 69 (2007), 975–97.

[55] Ibid. and also, R. Johns and G. Davies, 'The impact of military and civilian casualties on British public support for war: an experimental study', presented at the International Studies Association Annual Conference, Montreal, Canada, 16 March 2011.

[56] Contrast J. Mueller, *War, Presidents and Public Opinion* (New York: Wiley, 1973/Grandview Heights, OH: Zip Publishing, 2009) with Boettcher and Cobb, 'Don't let them die in vain'; Sullivan, 'Sustaining the fight'; and Johns and Davies, 'The impact of military and civilian casualties'. On the framing of 'sacrifice', see also T. McCrisken, 'Justifying sacrifice: Barack Obama and the selling of the war in Afghanistan', presented at the British International Studies Association annual conference of the US Foreign Policy Working Group, University of Leeds, 14 September 2010, cited in Holland, 'Blair's War on Terror'.

[57] Krebs, *Narrative*, chapter 3.

political manoeuvre' that might follow perceptions of a foreign policy being unpopular.[58] Politicians in the Anglosphere seek support, therefore, because their policies and their jobs depend on it: in these great democracies, rule hinges on a continued strategy of policy articulation, even after significant victory at the ballot box.[59] In short, Anglosphere foreign policy relies as much on legitimation as it does on landslides and legislation.[60]

Politicians within the great democracies of the old Anglosphere coalition, therefore, are 'engaged in endless strategies of legitimation, in order to present certain actions as legitimate'.[61] In pursuit of this endless requirement, Anglosphere politicians attempt to, first, craft a resonant foreign policy discourse, before turning, second, to more coercive tactics of justification.[62] In this task, they have a range of rhetorical, narrative and discursive devices at their disposal. Here, I explore several of these in turn, grouped into two overarching categories: (i) linguistic appeal, comprising rhetorical and linguistic devices, intertextuality and the hailing/interpellation of national identities; and (ii) cognitive framing, comprising the affective investment of an audience through emotional assemblages and playing to psychological biases. Throughout, we see the strategic exploitation, by instrumental elites, of political and electoral dynamics: a process that helps to bridge the heuristic division of attempts to achieve resonance from

---

[58] I. Danjoux, 'Negotiating security', presented at the International Studies Association annual conference, San Francisco, 26–29 March 2008, p. 1.

[59] R. Krebs and P. Jackson, 'Twisting tongues and twisting arms: the power of political rhetoric', *European Journal of International Relations*, 13 (2007), 35–66; M. Suchman, 'Managing legitimacy: strategic and institutional approaches', *Academy of Management Review*, 20 (2005), 571–610, cited in C. Reus-Smit, 'International crises of legitimacy', *International Politics*, 44 (2007), 157–74; I. Hurd, *After Anarchy: Legitimacy and Power in the United Nations Security Council* (Princeton: Princeton University Press, 2007), p. 30; Reus-Smit, 'International crises', p. 3, cited in Holland, 'Blair's War on Terror'. See also I. Clarke, *Legitimacy in International Society* (Oxford: Oxford University Press, 2007), p. 2.

[60] As Reus-Smit notes, legitimacy shares etymological roots with 'legislate' for good reason: it concerns a 'right to rule' through mutual recognition that government and policy are 'socially sanctioned'. Reus-Smit, 'International crises', p. 3, cited in Holland, 'Blair's War on Terror'. See also Clarke, *Legitimacy*.

[61] Clarke, *Legitimacy*, p. 2.

[62] Holland and Aaronson, 'Dominance through coercion'.

attempts to achieve dominance – the strategic exploitation of political and electoral cleavages links these two crucial analytical moments.

Linguistic Appeal

The first act in the pursuit of resonance is the simplest. *Linguistic appeal*, as the art of seduction, is the purest variant of what Joseph Nye termed soft power and what Walter Russell Mead termed sweet power – the power of attraction.[63] Linguistic appeal works at a range of levels, in a variety of ways, through the use of rhetoric and narrative. Most straightforward is the employment of general and specific *rhetorical appeal*. As students, journalists, lawyers and politicians know, the same idea expressed in persuasive English will resonate more widely and more deeply than the same idea presented in poor prose. Rhetorical devices can carry the day. Rhetoric is defined, simply, as the content of speeches and rhetorical devices might include ethos, pathos and logos – respectively concerning the credibility or authority of the speaker, the imagination or sympathy of the audience, and the logic or reason of an argument.[64] Ultimately, all of these are part and parcel of an effort to persuade an audience of the merits of foreign policy, and they tie in with some of the 'deeper' elements of resonance discussed in this section. Within these overarching rhetorical modes, speakers employ specific rhetorical and oratorical devices. Rhetorical devices might include the use of elegant metaphors,[65] such as 'axis of evil', or alliteration, such as 'decade of disorder'. Oratory pertains to the delivery of rhetoric – its style and manner of presentation – and may include particular uses of cadence, such as the steady rhythm of 'we did not demand, nor did we invite', as well as volume, tone, or intonation. For example, in the UK, media reporting on the second vote on intervention in Syria was dominated by coverage of Hilary Benn's speech, which was revered, in part, for its delivery in 'hushed tones'.[66]

---

[63] Nye, *Soft Power*; and W. R. Mead, *Power, Terror, Peace and War: America's Grand Strategy in a World at Risk* (New York/Toronto: Random House, 2005).

[64] Crines, 'Rhetoric and the coalition'.

[65] See Charteris-Black, *Politicians*; and Chilton, *Analysing Political Discourse*.

[66] N. Gutteridge and D. Maddox, 'Voice of defiance: Hilary Benn's impassioned speech shames Corbyn and moves MPs to tears', *The Express*, 3 December 2015, www.express.co.uk/news/politics/623874/Hilary-Benn-makes-impassioned-speech-convincing-Labour-to-back-strikes

As anyone who has ever listened to a political debate well knows, rhetoric, however elegant and well delivered, is not *universally* seductive; the appeal of language varies with audience. The crucial question is *which* language and *which* rhetoric resonates *with whom*? Political elites employ speechwriters and advisers with this insight in mind, in order to exploit it for their own gain. This could be seen, for example, on the campaign trail in 2004, as George W. Bush tailored his jokes for different regional audiences in a variety of key states.[67] For those audiences least squeamish about human rights transgressions in pursuit of national security, Bush would more readily joke about killing terrorists. The Commander in Chief knew when to play up his appeals in a specific kind of pathos, where his audience placed a low value on the lives of terrorists. In turn, this boosted appeals to a particular form of ethos – portraying him as a powerful, masculine leader. Politicians clearly, then, adapt their language to meet the requirements of a given audience; for example, ramping up or playing down levels of sophistication or flowery prose when an audience implicitly demands it. Consider, for example, the divergent response that Sarah Palin's infamous remark inspired, when she asked, 'How's that hopey-changey stuff workin' out for ya'?' Despite its mocking in liberal circles, the Republican Party's vice presidential candidate knew her target audience well: the line met with roars of approval.

Political elites employ language specifically and strategically for instrumental gain across the Anglosphere. In Australia, Dyrenfurth has repeatedly shown how the language of mateship is strategically deployed, in part due to the simple fact that very many Australians – and in particular mainstream (non-elite) Australians – revere the term.[68] Likewise, Tony Blair and David Cameron have both paid homage to the household god of Middle England – common sense – as the term's relative vacuity is dwarfed by the benefits of its widespread appeal amongst this key demographic.[69] Invoking notions of mateship, or joking about killing terrorists, simply would not have worked in the distinct cultural context of Middle England. And political elites know this. Linguistic appeal, then, works through the

---

[67] Holland, *Selling the War on Terror.*

[68] N. Dyrenfurth, 'John Howard's hegemony of values: the politics of "mateship" in the Howard decade', *Australian Journal of Political Science*, 42 (2007), 211–30.

[69] Holland, 'Blair's War on Terror'.

employment of targeted rhetorical devices to persuade a *specific* audience. And this audience is nearly always selected in relation to the domestic political and electoral landscape. Linguistic appeals are designed to win over those voters most useful to political elites in the pursuit of significant or majority support and approval.

The *strategic exploitation of the electoral landscape* is common to all democracies, but is a particularly acute condition in the old Anglosphere coalition, due to the nature of its political systems. The USA, UK and Australia all 'possess electoral systems that divide the state into regions from which one winner is picked. These constituency- or state-based systems serve to accentuate social, demographic and geographical differences, creating, consolidating and exaggerating divides within the population'.[70] In these states, public opinion lies at the heart of the system of checks and balances ensuring democratic accountability – which, in turn, ensures 'that issues of political legitimacy extend throughout the electoral cycle'.[71] Decreased legitimacy is often politically debilitating, either temporarily or permanently, as it results in political elites no longer being able to claim to 'speak for' the population.[72] As intelligent, instrumental actors, therefore, political elites not only act in a manner designed to maximise the chances of their preferred foreign policy resonating, but also calculate how to articulate foreign policy based on the relative merits of particular appeals vis-à-vis the choices of major competitors, as these pertain to the political and electoral landscape. Politics does not stop at the water's edge.

It is a function of democracy that a politician's audience is domestic. It is a function of domestic electoral politics that a politician's key audience is far narrower than that; electoral considerations drive the instrumental isolation and targeting of key voters, ensuring that some citizens are 'spoken to' at the exclusion of others. Anglosphere political elites, operating in multi-party systems, frequently therefore do not attempt to appeal to the entire electorate, instead opting to target foreign policy at a coalition of voters who together provide a political majority of popular opinion. Electorally consequential segments of society therefore take on heightened importance for the language of foreign policy as a consequence of the contemporary domestic political

---

[70] Holland, *Selling the War on Terror.*   [71] Ibid.
[72] McDonald and Merefield, 'How was Howard's war possible?', pp. 186–7. This was played out in the USA, UK and Australia after mid-2003, as protestors repeated lines such as 'not in my name'.

landscape.[73] This insight encourages us to think beyond, and more specifically than, Barnett's notion of targeted appeals to national audiences through the crafting of a language designed to mesh with the cultural terrain; it encourages us to consider *whose* cultural terrain is targeted.[74] Understanding resonance requires an appreciation of the 'specificity of attempts on the part of political elites to "speak to" key sections of the population as a function of the domestic political and electoral landscape'.[75] And, contra popular perception and, perhaps, a preferential state of affairs, foreign policy does not escape this logic. Political elites 'strategically frame foreign policy discourse to maximise resonance with those sections (target groups) of the population deemed electorally vital'.[76] Despite claims to the contrary, political and electoral strategies lie at the heart of foreign policy.[77]

Terms such as 'mateship' and 'common sense', then, demonstrate general and specific appeal, in a number of ways. First, their rhetorical appeal is evident, appealing respectively to Australian pathos and British logos. Second, however, their allure is more specific, targeting the values and beliefs of the psephologically consequential population groups: mainstream Australia and Middle England. Third, resonance derives not just from an ability to tap into *individually* held beliefs, preferences and biases, but rather from a capacity to mesh seamlessly with pre-existing and widely understood narratives and broader discourses. Appeals to common sense plug into widely understood narratives of British rationality, revered by cautious and prudent Middle Englanders, opposed to the volatility of hot-headed emotion. Likewise,

---

[73] J. Holland, 'Framing the War on Terror', doctoral thesis, University of Warwick (2010).

[74] Ibid.

[75] Ibid. See, for example, J. O'Loughlin, G. Toal and V. Kolossov, 'A "risky westward turn?" Putin's 9–11 script and ordinary Russians', *Europe-Asia Studies*, 56 (2004), 3–34; J. O'Loughlin and V. Kolossov, 'Russian geopolitical culture and public opinion: the masks of Proteus revisited', *Transactions of the Institute of British Geographers*, 30 (2005), 322–35.

[76] Ibid.

[77] For an Australian context, see M. Clyne, 'The use of exclusionary language to manipulate opinion: John Howard, asylum seekers and the reemergence of political incorrectness in Australia', *Journal of Language and Politics*, 4 (2005), 173–96; K. Gleeson, 'Australia and the construction of the War on Terror', presented at the International Studies Association annual conference, San Francisco, 26–29 March 2008; K. Gleeson, *Australia's 'War on Terror' Discourse* (Abingdon/New York: Routledge, 2014); as well as Holland, *Selling the War on Terror*.

speaking of mateship feeds into and builds upon a range of interrelated and commonly understood narratives of Australian history, society and identity. To speak of common sense and mateship is to invoke national mythologies of British-ness and Australian-ness through *intertextual appeal*, whereby two or more narratives or discourses come together, mutually reinforcing each other. For the listener, the words of the speaker make sense, due to their invocation of and imbrication in pre-existing and widely accepted discourses. These pre-existing discourses have already worked to produce a cultural knowledge on which new language and new foreign policy will ideally build in the politician's quest for legitimacy.

Anglosphere leaders are storytellers. They have to be: it is part of the job description to help a nation to imagine itself as a community. Although at times implicit in UK foreign policy, it is certainly true that British leaders continue to engage in the narrative contest of compelling storytelling, not least as Britain sought to find a role in the wake of imperial decline. In the USA and Australia, as relatively new countries, such storytelling has been a clear and obvious part of their leadership.[78] In Australia, to speak of mateship is to evoke a history of comradeship of Australian males, working together to overcome the harsh Australian environment.[79] Of course, the most powerful cultural and discursively produced knowledge a political elite can invoke is that which speaks to fundamental questions of who we are, as a people. Resonance can powerfully and effectively be achieved through *appeals to and constructions of the national identity*. Political elites 'hail' their audience with these appeals to the national identity. Resonance is achieved through their 'interpellation', as they recognise themselves in these descriptions.[80] By appealing to pre-existing notions of the national identity, such as that Australians are a nation prepared to help mates out in times of hardship, just as ANZAC diggers are widely perceived to have done at Gallipoli in 1915, once the audience

---

[78] Consider, for example, the collection of seminal narrations of the national identity: R. Manne and C. Feik (eds.), *The Words that Made Australia: How a Nation Came to Know Itself* (Collingwood, Vic.: Black Inc. Agenda, 2014).

[79] On the Bushman, the Ocker and the Larrikin, see Holland and Wright, 'The double de-legitimisation of Julia Gillard'.

[80] L. Althusser, 'Ideology and the ideological state apparatus: notes towards an investigation' (1971), cited in K. M. Fierke, *Critical Approaches to International Security* (Cambridge, UK/Malden, MA: Polity Press, 2015).

recognises themselves as subjects within this narration of national identity they are more likely to support a policy calling for Australians to 'play our part' or 'stand together' with allies.[81] Inevitably, of course, as critical constructivism and post-structuralism have repeatedly shown, elite hailing and audience interpellation serve to perpetually (re-)construct and (re-)produce the national identity. Language therefore, even its most explicit appeals for support, serves to co-constitute (national) identity in the pursuit of resonant foreign policy.

Cognitive Framing

Facts cannot 'speak for themselves'; political elites and other actors necessarily make sense of 'events' by placing them within organising schema. This process of *framing* helps to determine whether political elites succeed in crafting a resonant foreign policy. Inspired by work in Cultural Studies, Michael Barnett has developed this approach within IR. Barnett has advanced a notion of framing, understood as a constant effort 'to guide political mobilisation toward a particular outcome and for a particular goal by using symbols, metaphors and cognitive cues to organise experience and fix meaning to events'.[82] His fellow 'Minnesota School' constructivists – including Alexander Wendt, Raymond Duvall, Mark Laffey, Jutta Weldes, Roxanne Doty and Ron Krebs – have furthered efforts to re-inject agency into the constructivist research agenda and acknowledge the importance of a contextually oriented strategy on the part of political elites as they craft these instrumental narratives and strategically deploy frames.[83] These frames – as overarching cognitive or organisational schemas – help to make sense of 'facts' and 'situate events' for an audience, by beginning the process of interpreting issues. In this effort to 'fashion a shared

---

[81] This latter theme was particularly prominent in John Howard's language after 9/11. It combined George H. W. Bush's call to arms in the first Gulf War with Australian calls for solidarity between mates.

[82] M. Barnett, 'Culture, strategy and foreign policy change: Israel's road to Oslo', *European Journal of International Relations*, 5 (1999), 5–36, at 8–9.

[83] See, for example, Weldes et al., 'Introduction: constructing insecurity' in J. Weldes, M. Laffey, H. Gusterson and R. Duvall (eds.), *Cultures of Insecurity: States, Communities and the Production of Danger* (Minneapolis: University of Minnesota Press, 1993); R. L. Doty, *Anti-Immigrantism in Western Democracies: Statecraft, Desire and the Politics of Exclusion* (London/New York: Routledge, 2003); Barnett, 'Culture'; see also Balzacq, 'The three faces of securitization'.

understanding', elites seek to 'mobilise and guide social action' because how events are understood has 'important consequences for mobilising action and furthering their interests'.[84]

Within a broad understanding of framing, it is possible and useful to identify and specify three specific variants, which are at times over-looked in IR and FPA literatures. To begin with, framing can connect to a growth literature in IR and Security Studies – research on the role of emotion[85] – but only if the instrumentality of the state in its strategic exploitation is acknowledged (a point that is frequently underplayed). Political elites play an important role in articulating the emotions of citizens. While an event may well inspire an affective response, its naming is usually intersubjectively arrived at and political elites are particularly well placed to guide that naming process. 'Affect is the initial component and mediation of experience by the body and the brain': 'a largely non-conscious process' and set of 'pre-conscious reactions that occur just prior to cognitive awareness'.[86] The process of articulating 'affect' – which is 'amorphous potential'[87] – takes citizens from the pre-conscious, through the subjective and self-consciously aware realm of feelings, through to the intersubjective construction of emotions. Here, we see (the largely) biological affect – the initial bodily, pre-cognitive reaction to events and the environment – become infused with the realm of the cultural, as initial impulses are labelled with emotional signifiers such as anger, sadness or fear. This process of naming helps to render these experiences far easier to understand but also potentially *and crucially* makes them politically useful. The naming of affect as emotion enables the state to create biocultural *assemblages* – the intertwining of the social and somatic[88] – and *affectively invest* an audience within particular framings and their broader foreign policy

[84] Barnett, 'Culture', p. 15.
[85] See, for example, L. Åhäll and T. Gregory, *Emotions, Politics and War* (Abingdon/New York: Routledge, 2015); and A. Ross, 'Coming in from the cold: constructivism and emotions', *European Journal of International Relations*, 12 (2006), 197–222.
[86] J. Holland and T. Solomon, 'Affect is what states make of it: articulating everyday experiences of 9/11', *Critical Studies on Security*, 2 (2014), 262–77.
[87] T. Solomon, '"I wasn't angry, because I couldn't believe it was happening": affect and discourse in responses to 9/11', *Review of International Studies*, 38 (2012), 907–28.
[88] W. Connolly, *Neuropolitics: Thinking, Culture, Speed* (Minneapolis: University of Minnesota Press, 2002).

narratives and discourses.[89] Appeals to emotion, which encourage the affective investment of an audience within a narrative or discourse, can generate a particularly powerful form of resonance. For example, an audience begins to *feel* political language, potentially curtailing the desire for greater contemplation or critical evaluation.

Affective investment is also important for the construction of political identity, especially in moments of crisis and trauma. Emma Hutchison has shown how it is necessary to update Benedict Anderson's seminal insight – that the nation is an imagined community – in order to acknowledge that political communities are, very often, affective communities. They (understand themselves to) have experienced similar affective responses to events and share a predisposition encouraging shared collective affective reactions in the future.[90] This process is at its most acute and visible in moments of narrative rupture – where long held stories and their assumptions are dramatically challenged – such as following the events of 11 September 2001.[91] Following 9/11, we can see how this process can help to constitute affective political communities, at both national and transnational scales.[92] At the national level, in his post 9/11 speeches, Bush emphasised American unity; a theme that was picked up in adverts declaring *Y pluribus unum* (out of many, one). At the Anglosphere level, political elites in the USA, UK and Australia repeatedly emphasised their mutual sadness, shock and horror at attacks that were proclaimed to target 'freedom-loving countries everywhere'. This then builds upon and goes beyond the impact of the rhetorical device of pathos, extending such appeals through the construction of emotional narratives, targeted to affectively invest audiences. In a variety of ways, therefore, social science and neuroscience researchers have shown that, in order to resonate and persuade, political elites can do far more than present logical arguments: they can invest their audience through the language of emotion and the biology of affect. In short, 'successful politicians are those who effectively combine appeals to cognition and emotion by having credible stories to tell'.[93]

[89] J. Holland, 'Constructing crises and articulating affect after 9/11' in *Emotions, Politics and War*, p. 167; also, Holland and Solomon, 'Affect'.

[90] E. Hutchison, *Affective Communities in World Politics* (Cambridge: Cambridge University Press, 2016).

[91] Holland and Solomon, 'Affect'.   [92] Hutchison, *Affective Communities*.

[93] Charteris-Black, *Politicians and Rhetoric*, p. xi.

Retaining our psychological focus, alongside appeals to emotion, political elites attempt to achieve resonance through the exploitation of audience bias. Contrary to the myths of several social science sub-disciplines, humans are not rational actors and attempts to model human behaviour on the classical theory of physics is hugely problematic.[94] Social psychology has demonstrated this effectively, revealing some of the impulses that can lead people to make less than rationally optimal decisions.[95] One infamous example is in the greater desire humans possess to avoid loss than achieve gain. This is an apparently innate human quality that can be ruthlessly exploited – or missed and lamented – by political elites framing foreign policy. Goldman and Berman, for example, argue that Bill Clinton's failure to sell his over-arching twin concepts guiding American grand strategy in the 1990s boiled down to this social psychological preference on the part of the electorate.[96] Accustomed to averting impending nuclear annihilation at the hands of the Soviet Union, Americans struggled to invest in a vision for the expansion of the number of market democracies to the extent that the policy was largely abandoned by 1997.[97] Clinton struggled to frame a resonant foreign policy as he had inadequately accounted for an inherent *psychological bias* in his audience.

Infamous examples of psychological bias are not in short supply. Consider, for instance, the propensity for an audience to bandwagon in a process of groupthink (e.g. predicting Hillary Clinton's electoral victory), a reluctance to accept new ideas that disprove long held beliefs (e.g. bafflement therefore rejection of quantum theory),[98] a preference for recent information (e.g. pre-2008 stock market optimism), availability heuristics leading to the privileging of anecdotal evidence (e.g. doubting climate change after experiencing a cold winter), or the focalism of anchoring a debate around a given point (e.g. pitching first in a salary negotiation in order to establish the debate's parameters). One salient example of the power of framing

---

[94] And one of the reasons some social scientists have explored quantum theory. See A. Wendt, *The Quantum Mind and Social Science* (Cambridge: Cambridge University Press, 2016).

[95] D. Western, *Political Brain: The Role of Emotion in Deciding the Fate of the Nation* (New York: Public Affairs, 2008).

[96] E. Goldman and L. Berman, 'Engaging the world: first impressions of a Clinton foreign policy legacy' in C. Campbell and B. Rockman (eds.), *The Clinton Legacy* (New York: Chatham House, 2000), pp. 238–39.

[97] Ibid.   [98] Wendt, *The Quantum Mind*.

and the difficulties of overcoming both affective investment and psychological bias pertains to the intractability of the abortion debate in the USA. Proponents on both sides of this debate have framed their arguments effectively to exploit affective and psychological biases. Most obviously, perhaps, a 'pro-life' frame is hard to argue against. Who does not support the right to life? While a 'pro-choice' framing taps into the promise of American freedom, and the narrative of a 'woman's right to choose' emphasises that this is an emancipatory issue for modern, enlightened liberals to support. What American wants to limit freedom? Who wants to appear misogynist? Supporters of both sides could have opted for 'anti-choice' and 'pro-death' frames respectively, but they have not for obvious but important reasons: resonance matters and it is achieved through the strategic exploitation of an audience within a specific political and cultural context. As we will see later in this chapter and in Chapter 5, that fact, remarkably, is equally true when it comes to the strategic exploitation of apparently consensual and universally good norms.[99]

Silencing Opponents

The recognition of agency, instrumentality and strategic exploitation helps us to bridge the gap between two important analytical moments in the politician's quest to control debate, dominate meaning-making and achieve hegemonic foreign policy discourse. Strategic motivations and actions inform the crafting of dominant as well as resonant foreign policy. As we progress from the consideration of resonance to questions of dominance, we move from a constructivist to an increasingly 'post-constructivist' terrain, in which soft power no longer appears so soft.[100] Rather, language and the discourses it gives rise to can *coerce* as well as *persuade*. Representational force is a crucial part of a politician's arsenal in influencing and making possible particular foreign policies.[101] Such martial language is not accidental. Representational force is 'a nonphysical but nevertheless coercive form of power that is exercised through language'; it 'should not be understood in

---

[99] M. Bentley, *Syria and the Chemical Weapons Taboo: Exploiting the Forbidden* (Manchester: Manchester University Press, 2016).

[100] Mattern, 'Why "soft power" isn't so soft'.

[101] J. B. Mattern, *Ordering International Politics: Identity, Crisis and Representational Force* (New York/Abingdon: Routledge, 2005).

juxtaposition to hard power but as a continuation of it by different means'.[102] While excellent research exists,[103] the representational force of foreign policy, as well as the importance of this force, remains chronically under-explored and under-theorised in IR. Here, I develop a three-part conceptualisation of representational force by bringing together and developing complementary insights on: (i) strategic narrative and electoral exploitation; (ii) rhetorical entrapment and coercion; and (iii) rhetorical balancing.

Political elites possess considerable agency, strategically exploiting electoral dynamics for instrumental political gain. As Bentley notes, 'few would dispute that agents at least attempt to employ language in ways explicitly designed to draw support from a specific audience, or shape debate as to best serve their interests'; 'emotive appeals', 'oratorical tricks' and an emphasis on certain words and themes are all geared, *instrumentally*, towards realising specific 'political aims'.[104] And, yet, as Bentley argues, despite 'and possibly because of this assumption of self-evidence, this is a woefully under-theorised area of study'.[105] One area of significant growth in recent years has been the 'strategic narratives' paradigm, explored below,[106] 'which asserts that actors deliberately apply specific narratives in order to promote their political ambitions'.[107] In keeping with this paradigm, Bentley argues that 'narrative creation is a... manipulative and manipulated process'.

'Strategic narratives are a means for political actors to construct a shared meaning of the past, present and future of international politics', they employ these narratives 'to shape the behaviour of domestic and international actors', in order to 'extend their influence, manage expectations and [ultimately] change the discursive environment in which they operate'.[108] 'The point of strategic narratives is to

---

[102] Mattern, 'Why "soft power" isn't so soft'.

[103] As well as Mattern, *Ordering International Politics*, see, for example, Krebs and Jackson, 'Twisting tongues'; R. Krebs and J. Lobasz, 'Fixing the meaning of 9/11: hegemony, coercion, and the road to war in Iraq', *Security Studies*, 16 (2007), 409–51; Krebs, *Narrative*; R. Krebs, 'Narrative and the making of US national security', 28 October 2015, University College London, London; McDonald and Merefield, 'How was Howard's war possible?'

[104] Bentley, *Syria and the Chemical Weapons Taboo*.   [105] Ibid.

[106] See, for example, Miskimmon et al., *Strategic Narratives*.

[107] Bentley, *Syria and the Chemical Weapons Taboo*.

[108] Miskimmon et al., *Strategic Narratives*, p. 2; see also Bentley, *Syria and the Chemical Weapons Taboo*.

influence the behaviour of others.'[109] It is more than this, however: strategic narratives cut to the heart of debates on the philosophy of social science and what it is to be human. Strategic narratives enable political elites – as intelligent and instrumental agents – to shape the structures in which they operate. It is what helps to distinguish people from plants and particles. It is a remarkably powerful ability. But it is not easy. Once achieved, however, the payoff is significant. As Bentley notes, 'actors use narratives to create a description of the world – an understanding of what politics looks like and entails – whereby they "force" their audience into adopting certain interpretations and pathways of logic that complement the aims of the constructing actor(s)'.[110] This is about far more 'than mere spin or framing', 'the control of political comprehension', or the use of language to make policy 'popular';[111] it is about stamping out the possibility of thinking and speaking otherwise.

Strategic narratives are designed to maximise resonance and coercion *within a specific context*. Political and electoral strategy, therefore, is crucial – as we have seen, even in the realm of foreign policy and even outside of election campaigns.[112] In IR and Critical Geopolitics, persuasive analyses have been undertaken that demonstrate the specificity – spatial and demographic – of foreign policy's target groups.[113] Much more rare are arguments and analyses pertaining to the manner in which the electoral landscape serves as the context in which political elites act in the pursuit of policy *dominance*. The *strategic silencing of oppositional voices* is often crucial to the creation of foreign policy discourse, which will go on to underpin policy. Just as we saw that electoral dynamics influence the targeting of key groups in the construction of resonant discourse, they are also central to the process of identifying competing alternative narratives and potential resistance. Political and electoral instrumentality motivates political elites in their pursuit of resonant *and coercive* foreign policy.[114]

---

[109] Miskimmon et al., *Strategic Narratives*, p. 2.
[110] Bentley, *Syria and the Chemical Weapons Taboo*.   [111] Ibid.
[112] Holland, *Selling the War on Terror*.   [113] O'Loughlin et al., 'Masks'.
[114] Jackson discusses the relationship between elections and counter-terrorism, for example. R. Jackson, 'An analysis of EU counterterrorism discourse post-September 11', *Cambridge Review of International Affairs*, 20 (2007), 233–47, 245.

Rhetorical coercion, very often, follows an electoral logic, as political elites both target select constituencies and attempt to silence others,
in pursuit of political gain. Again, this remains relatively under-
explored.[115] It can take place in a variety of ways, but centres on
efforts to remove the cultural and discursive materials that opponents
might otherwise have access to in order to formulate a socially sustainable rebuttal.[116] If done effectively, opponents can be left 'to contest
minor, procedural matters rather than the fundamental direction of
policy'.[117] Reluctant support – acquiescence – on the part of potential
opponents occurs where those opponents feel or believe that alternative discourses are not socially and electorally viable options. At this
moment, in this way, political language can go beyond resonance to
achieve dominance, through not only its regulation of prevalent meaning production but also its control of the debate, on both sides. Ron
Krebs, for example, has shown how this situation came to bear in the
USA during the run up to the 2003 war in Iraq.[118] For Krebs, Congressional Democrats opted to swallow their lingering and persistent
doubts about intervention – adopting a position of reluctant but vol-
untary support – due to the political landscape of, and dominant
security discourses evident within, post 9/11 America. By 2002–03,
the deck remained heavily stacked in favour of the Bush Administration. And Democrats knew that.[119]

There are, of course, a number of ways in which rhetorical coercion
can be achieved. Successful and exclusionary constructions of the
national identity, for example, can make speaking out against a policy
extremely difficult when policy is seen to be part and parcel of fulfilling
the obligations of that identity. Consider the difficulty of arguing
against the renewal of a British nuclear deterrent when facing narratives invoking the UK's identity as a long-standing world-leading state.
This coercive narrative serves to render such counter-arguments as
appearing to condemn Britain to a relegated middle-power status, a
position apparently belying – or worse, ashamed of – its history and

---

[115] For exceptions, see Mattern, 'Why "soft power" isn't so soft' and *Ordering*; the
recent work of Ron Krebs; and Holland, 'Foreign policy'.
[116] Holland, 'Foreign policy'; Krebs and Jackson, 'Twisting tongues'; and Krebs,
Narrative.
[117] Holland, 'Foreign policy'; Krebs, *Narrative*.
[118] For example, Krebs and Lobasz, 'Fixing'.
[119] Ibid.; see also Holland, 'Foreign policy'.

identity. Likewise, successful appeals to emotion and the affective investment of an audience can lead opponents to opt for silence rather than contest the tricky domain of an audience's biocultural impulses, which might involve attempting to encourage them to feel differently about an issue (rather than win an argument on the basis of logic alone). Consider, for example, the difficulty of arguing for UK National Health Service (NHS) reform or privatisation, given the overwhelming affective investment of the British public in its cause, fused at the intersection of political language and personal experience. What is clear, then, is that resonance alone tells only part of the story. Very often, resonance and dominance work hand in hand. By framing a resonant foreign policy, targeted at specific and relatively narrow audiences, political elites, very often, are also attempting to silence those groups that might otherwise voice alternatives. Such a position, if successfully achieved, is incredibly powerful, as politicians move from appealing to voters and regulating prevalent meaning production to silencing opponents and controlling debate.

Representational force can be achieved through rhetorical coercion – comprising appeals to identity, affect or norms – rhetorical entrapment, or rhetorical balancing.[120] It is crucial to the establishment of discursive dominance and is often at the heart of the establishment of era-defining hegemonic foreign and security policy paradigms. These three identified variants – coercion, entrapment and balancing – interlink and often mutually support each other. First, rhetorical coercion can leave opponents discursively disarmed through the removal of the necessary linguistic materials and devices required to formulate socially sustainable rebuttals. Rhetorical coercion can therefore manoeuvre would-be opponents into a position of reluctant acquiescence. Second, in this situation, political elites can become victims of *rhetorical entrapment*:[121] the process whereby discourses can encourage actors to behave in particular ways, narrowing down the scope for alternatives, even where perhaps these alternatives might be welcomed

---

[120] And more. This is not an exhaustive list.
[121] See, originally, F. Schimmelfennig, 'The community trap: liberal norms, rhetorical action, and the Eastern enlargement of the European Union', *International Organization*, 55 (2001), 47–80; also, more recently on Syria, J. Busby, 'Rhetorical entrapment and Syria', *Duck of Minerva*, 2 October 2015, http://duckofminerva.com/2015/10/rhetorical-entrapment-and-syria-lets-not-do-dumb-stuff.html

as preferential. This entrapment is usually the result of the interactions
of two or more actors, even where such an eventuality appears to be
the outcome of personal missteps. Consider, for example, the apparent rhetorical entrapment of Barack Obama in 2012 and 2013, as he
appeared reluctantly compelled to act by his own 'red line' on chemical weapons usage (see Chapter 5). This story veils the role of key
actors in both houses of Congress.[122] Third, political elites often
pursue a strategy of *rhetorical balancing*, emphasising secondary
foreign policy rationales.

An understanding and analysis of rhetorical balancing enables
consideration of the 'shape' of elite tactics of justification, as elites
strategically balance rhetorical arguments through the deliberate
highlighting of secondary justifications. This rhetorical balancing –
the strategic emphasis of secondary foreign policy justifications,
through the deployment of specific 'tactics of justification' – enables
political elites to outmanoeuvre and pre-empt other voices who
might develop alternative counter-arguments.[123] Discursive dominance and control of the policy debate can be achieved through the
coercive effects of emphasising secondary foreign policy rationales,
such that they narrow the discursive space from which alternative
voices might develop counter-arguments.[124] In the absence of this
strategic rhetorical balancing, opponents would be left free to
develop counter-arguments that could feasibly 'engage the primary
justifications of elites, undermining them from an entirely alternative
angle'.[125] Through rhetorical balancing, political elites 'seize the
rhetorical frames of potential opponents, folding them into their
own case for war as secondary justifications'.[126] Holland and
Aaronson have shown that this has frequently been the case in
Anglosphere wars – recently, for example, in Afghanistan and Libya.
This amounts to a linguistic out-flanking in an ongoing discursive
'war of position',[127] the outcome of which informs the possibility
for war or peace.

[122] See, for example, Krebs, *Narrative*.
[123] Holland and Aaronson, 'Dominance through coercion'; R. Cox, 'Gramsci,
hegemony and International Relations: an essay on method', *Millennium*, 12
(1983), 162–75; A. Gramsci, *Selections from the Prison Notebooks* (New
York: International Publishers, 1971); McDonald and Merefield, 'How was
Howard's war won?'
[124] Holland and Aaronson, 'Dominance'.   [125] Ibid.   [126] Ibid.   [127] Ibid.

Winning Arguments

Political elites understand that blunting the rhetorical charges of political foes is as important as crafting a resonant narrative. This pursuit is about the manoeuvring of opponents into positions where they are more likely to opt (of their own volition) for silence, acquiescence or the negotiation of procedure – such as the terms and type of intervention – rather than contest the general thrust of policy in the first place. In short, representational force, along with the crafting of resonant foreign policy, can help political elites to achieve policy dominance. This process of rhetorically pre-empting and outmanoeuvring opponents amounts to a discursive 'war of position'.[128] This term is Gramsci's.[129] He argues that political elites, in and out of power, seek popular support in order to retain or challenge institutional power.[130] Political elites attempt to maintain their primacy in a war of position by retaining the consent of the population, which requires a combination of support (through the pursuit of resonance) and acquiescence (through the coercive pursuit of dominance).

In the *Prison Notebooks*, Gramsci drew an important distinction between political elites and the general population, noting the specific 'coupled' nature of state–society relations in Anglosphere nations. This 'coupling', Gramsci argued, prevented revolution through a 'war of movement' – as was experienced with the Bolshevik Revolution in Russia, where state–society relations remained relatively de-coupled. Clearly, Gramsci's arguments retain relevance today; were this a study of the UNSC P2 – Russia and China – it is possible that an alternative theoretical framework would be required. But, the old Anglosphere coalition possesses arguably the most developed civil society in the world and highly coupled state–society relations, ensuring a war of position takes place over foreign policy. The greater connection of people to their representatives in Western states, Gramsci argued, ensures political opponents are required to achieve the support of civil society if they are to mount a successful challenge to those in power.[131] 'Such a strategy entails a "war of position", whereby opponents must build up social capital by crafting competing narratives, into which the general population buy'.[132] This process helps to shape a people's

---

[128] Ibid.   [129] Gramsci, *Selections*.
[130] Holland and Aaronson, 'Dominance'.   [131] Ibid.   [132] Ibid.

ability to imagine the proposed alternative, including popular perceptions of authority, desirability and feasibility, related to (rhetorical)
ethos, pathos and logos, as well as broader narrative appeals.

On the other side to such challenges, political elites attempt to
maintain primacy within this war of position. They do so in significant
part by 'retaining the consent of the population', which, in addition to
resonance, 'requires the acquiescence of those who might, given a more
favourable discursive terrain, attempt to craft alternative policy plat-
forms'.[133] Gramsci's war of position therefore provides us with an
overarching theoretical framework, conceptualising the relationship of
governed and government in Anglosphere democracies. This framework incorporates his 'notion of hegemony – as domination through
a combination of consent *and* coercion' and 'usefully indicates the twin
dynamics at the heart of relations between political elites and the
general population on matters of interventionist foreign policy'.[134]
Here, clearly, consent and coercion are brought into each other,
appealing to Mattern's argument that soft power really is not so soft
after all; even consent can be coerced.[135] This insight pushes into a post-
constructivist terrain, moving beyond questions of how an issue was
rendered conceivable and how it was framed to appeal to an audience
to additionally explore how potential doubters and opponents were
won over or discursively bullied into submission. Such a state of affairs
is relatively common and reflective of the often hegemonic nature of
meaning production in the realm of foreign and security policy.

Gramsci's concept is an excellent point of departure, but requires
infusing with a more specific (if overarching) view of change and
temporality. Gramsci's notion of a war of position can help us to
envisage that change is possible and how it might be realised, but it
fails to give a sense of why it is that the majority of efforts to alter the
status quo meet defeat. Why is change so difficult?[136] Perhaps more
than any other to date, Ron Krebs has extended his research on
rhetorical coercion to wrestle with this question, attempting a theorisa-
tion of how and why foreign policy (and national security) discourses
clash and resolve.[137] Key to Krebs' argument is an understanding that
political time is not linear, but progresses in a punctuated fashion,
between prolonged periods of relative stasis, followed and begun by

[133] Ibid.   [134] Ibid.   [135] Ibid.   [136] Holland, 'Why is change so hard?'
[137] Krebs, *Narrative*.

accelerated moments of discursive turbulence and change.[138] Periods of relative stasis are marked by the settled discursive nature, whereby apparently agreed-upon narrative settlements ensure regularity in meaning production, which drowns out and disqualifies challengers. Presidents and political elites who have attempted narrative overhaul – rather than minor alterations through the adoption of a rhetorical mode – in the midst of these settled and stable periods have often come unstuck.[139] Narrative overhaul – and wholesale narrative victory in a war of position – is rarely possible outside of moments of turbulence and narrative contestation. When successful in these moments, the result is a new story and foreign policy change.

The two most stable periods of American national security in recent history are the Cold War and the War on Terror. Both relied upon political elites seizing upon a moment of narrative turbulence to strategically write a new era. Following the attacks of Pearl Harbor and 9/11, political elites successfully articulated powerful – resonant and coercive – overarching national security narratives that not only appealed to key segments of the population but also made it exceptionally difficult for opponents to speak out. Ronald Reagan's popularity – at the height of the Cold War as its narratives reached an apogee of 'peace through strength' – reflects this resonance, as does George W. Bush's attainment of approval ratings in excess of 90 per cent in the weeks after 9/11. Accusations of being a communist sympathiser or a terrorist sympathiser made speaking out in opposition to the dominant security narratives of both eras problematic. During both periods, the relative stability and regularity of meaning production through narrative dominance meant that official foreign policy was hegemonic. One consequence of this was that debate occurred only at the margins, contesting details rather than the general direction and aims of American strategy. For Krebs, once a narrative has achieved this degree of sedimentation, it is very difficult to proffer an alternative overarching

---

[138] J. Holland, 'From September 11th 2001 to 9-11: from void to crisis', *International Political Sociology*, 3 (2009), 275–92; Holland, *Selling the War on Terror*; D. Nabers, 'Filling the void of meaning: identity construction in U.S. foreign policy after September 11, 2001', *Foreign Policy Analysis*, 5 (2009), 191–214; S. Croft, *Culture, Crisis and America's War on Terror* (Cambridge: Cambridge University Press, 2006); and C. Hay, *Political Analysis: A Critical Introduction* (Houndmills: Palgrave Macmillan, 2002).
[139] See Ron Krebs' body of work.

narrative in the absence of a new and unsettled narrative condition – 9/11 remains the best example of such a moment.

My previous research has traced how it is that 9/11 induced a discursive void in the United States – what Krebs would identify as a period of narrative turbulence and contestation.[140] This means that existing narratives and discourses were challenged by the prevalent interpretation of the events of 9/11. Ordinary Americans immediately perceived that something fundamental and rupturing had occurred.[141] This was an affective experience, created by years of conditioning to the apparent normality of American security culture in the 1990s (invulnerable supremacy) and/but felt at a biological level.[142] However, it was a largely personalised and fragmented experience, as language appeared to fail to articulate what was being witnessed on America's television screens. This void was not immediately filled; it took days and, for some, weeks, before the words of the Bush administration took shape and resonated.[143] Slowly, though, ordinary Americans brought their experiences of 9/11 into line with the gradually solidifying language of the Bush administration. Five weeks later, as intervention in Afghanistan loomed, this language had become dominant. Eighteen months later, it was hegemonic, as the Bush administration controlled the debate on foreign policy, having redefined American national security through the narratives that gave the War on Terror meaning.[144]

For this book and for Syria, a pertinent question became the extent to which the Anglosphere remained within that era, regulated by the hegemonic production of meaning through a dominant foreign policy discourse and national security narrative. Correspondingly, to what extent was change possible? Could Anglosphere leaders, between 2011 and 2019, aspire to new narratives or were they left to contest minor, peripheral and procedural issues – tactics not strategy, means not ends? The era of Bush's narrative hegemony extended beyond his presidency, arguably leaving Obama to pursue rhetorical plaudits rather than a more wholesale redefinition of Anglosphere foreign policy discourse. This fact would become especially salient in 2014, with the rise of ISIL, and is explored in the following chapters, but

---

[140] Holland, 'From void to crisis'.   [141] Ibid.; see also Croft, *Culture*.
[142] Holland and Jarvis, 'Night fell on a different world'; and Holland and Solomon, 'Affect'.
[143] Holland, 'From void to crisis'.   [144] Krebs, *Narrative*.

Bush's perceived linguistic failures – especially his perceived deception in Iraq – would also shape Obama and the Anglosphere's approach to tackling Assad.

Conclusion

We live in a world that is at once material and discursive. Such a claim is in no way oxymoronic. Foreign policy is both material and discursive; its bombs have material consequences, but whether they are dropped in the name of freedom or imperialism depends on how language fills those acts with meaning.[145] Foreign policy is particularly consequential in its writing of the world for three reasons. First, foreign policy's impact is significant, especially in analyses of the Anglosphere. Second, to paraphrase Anais Nin, through foreign policy we write the world in a manner that says far more about 'us' than it does about 'them'. The consequences of this can be devastating, as the work of Edward Said makes clear.[146] Third, this process feeds back into the Self, (perpetually re-)creating the national identity and how it is that a political community understands itself and its relation with the world. It is therefore vitally important to study the language of foreign policy.

In order to do so, this chapter has made a series of linked arguments, establishing a theoretical framework for the analysis in the second half of the book. First, the argument was made that the world is socially and discursively constructed. That process occurs through a combination of rhetoric, narrative and discourse, which must all be considered for a full and nuanced picture of foreign policy to emerge. Second, the chapter has repeatedly made the case that political elites act strategically in their framing of foreign policy. This entails a sophisticated reading and exploitation of the domestic political and cultural context. Third, in their formulation of strategic narratives and deployment of rhetorical devices, political elites pursue legitimacy through both resonance and coercion. Fourth, tactics of justification – rhetorical coercion, balancing, entrapment and the like – are designed to enable an actor to win out in a war of position. Victory in this enterprise enables discursive dominance to be achieved and hegemony of meaning production to

---

[145] Jackson, *Writing*. Consider also that messages were written on bombs destined for ISIL targets in the wake of the Manchester terror attack, e.g. 'Love from Manchester'.

[146] Said, *Orientalism*.

consolidate. It is an incredibly powerful and consequential position to be in. Finally, the chapter considered the temporality of wars of position, suggesting that narrative contestation, with a genuine possibility of change, relies upon moments of narrative turbulence that are few and far between. Otherwise, political elites are left to fight wars of position within overarching narrative and discursive hegemonies, relying more frequently on lower-level rhetorical devices. At its core then, the chapter has explored political possibility and ways in which foreign policy discourse is embedded within the Anglosphere, played out through a competitive and dynamic transnational war of position. In the following four chapters, this framework is used to frame and guide an analysis of Anglosphere foreign policy in Syria.

In combination, the first three chapters have set out the rationale for the book's methodological approach. In the next four chapters, the book adopts a discourse analytic method, in order to analyse the discursive war of position that has taken place – and shaped policy – for the world's most consequential military coalition since the onset of the world's foremost contemporary crisis. This analysis is divided broadly chronologically, across the Syrian Civil War's four principal phases. Within the USA, UK and Australia, foreign policy texts are analysed in line with Lene Hansen's 'Model 2' approach to discourse analysis.[147] This means that data are collected from a range of official and unofficial sources and actors, in order to explore discursive contestation in pursuit of discursive hegemony. As well as key government policy documents and speeches (including from state leaders and those with remits for foreign and defence policies), I also include for analysis the language of elected and appointed political opponents (including party leaders, shadow ministers and other elected representatives), as well as significant media outlets. While an inclusive approach to media is taken – with no outlet excluded a priori – the discourse analysis focuses on reputable mainstream media organisations (such as CNN, the BBC, ABC, *The New York Times*, *The Washington Post*, *The Guardian*, *The Telegraph*, *The Sydney Morning Herald* and *The Australian*, amongst many others). This two-step, inclusive but focused approach is important in a post-truth political and media age. It ensures, for example, that *The Daily Mail* and *Breitbart* can be included, as large and influential outlets, whilst prioritising more reputable news organisations. This approach

---

[147] Hansen, *Security as Practice*.

was enabled by making use of, first, Google's news search engine capabilities (narrowing through phase-specific keywords and time-frames), before, second, focusing in on major key and reputable outlets through LexisNexis.

Unlike Hansen, this work is informed by a critical constructivist (rather than post-structural) approach, closer to the likes of Richard Jackson and Stuart Croft. Adopting a critical approach to the analysis of discourse enables (and demands) that language is connected to broader operations of power within politics and society. By considering the strategic agency and instrumentality of politicians, as they seek to win out within national and international policy debates, this approach enables analysis to focus on the resonance and coercion of language: the often quite hard nature of soft power. Texts were read and analysed longhand, using both inductive and deductive approaches. While analysis began primarily inductively, the process became increasingly deductive, once key themes, frames, narratives, discourses and phases were identified and relatively few new nodes emerged. More than 1,000 texts from a range of significant political and media elites were read and analysed, roughly equally split between phases (approximately 250 texts in each phase), of which the most representative and high profile have been quoted and cited (approximately one quarter of texts). Texts were read and analysed for three principal discursive features: framings of the Syrian crisis and its key actors; prominent appeals to and articulations of national and Anglosphere identity; and promotion of intervention or its avoidance. In each instance, in line with Hansen's discourse analytic model, texts were connected intertextually to each other and more broadly to operations of power within the Anglosphere's war of position. In particular, analysis focused on the rhetorical, narrative and discursive features of texts that helped or hindered the development of resonant and coercive foreign policy positions. Finally, this approach asked where these discourses came from and how they were embedded within (the politics of) national and Anglosphere cultural landscapes. Together, this approach focused upon how discourses formed, evolved, clashed and resolved to shape the parameters of political possibility for the Anglosphere in Syria.

4 | *Democracy and Human Rights*

The United States strongly condemns the Syrian government's brutal repression of demonstrations.

White House Press Secretary Jay Carney[1]

Introduction

The year 2011 was significant for American foreign policy and the Middle East. In the space of six months, the United States was directly militarily involved in the deaths of two long-standing, high-profile political enemies. On 2 May, from the White House's East Room, Obama declared, 'I can report to the American people and to the world that the United States has conducted an operation that killed Osama bin Laden'.[2] This declaration followed a tense operation in which one of two American stealth helicopters crash landed, before a US Navy SEAL team successfully stormed bin Laden's Abbottabad compound, shooting the Al Qaeda leader twice in the face. By the time Pakistan was made aware of what was happening, American forces were 'burying' bin Laden's body in the North Arabian Sea. On 20 October, Obama again spoke to the nation, this time from the White House's Rose Garden, concerning the demise of another international foe: 'One of the world's longest-serving dictators is no more... the dark shadow of tyranny has been lifted'.[3] A Reaper drone, flown from Nevada, had initiated the first of two NATO airstrikes on a convoy of vehicles in Libya, spotted by British forces. These airstrikes caused Muammar Gaddafi to abandon his vehicle and seek refuge in an irrigation drain,

[1] J. Carney, 'Statement by the Press Secretary on violence in Syria', 24 May 2011.

[2] B. Obama, 'Remarks by the President on Osama bin Laden', 2 May 2011, www.whitehouse.gov/blog/2011/05/02/osama-bin-laden-dead

[3] E. MacAskill, 'Obama hails death of Muammar Gaddafi as foreign policy success', *The Guardian*, 20 October 2011, www.theguardian.com/world/2011/oct/20/obama-hails-death-gaddafi

before a grisly and confused demise at the hands of opposition forces on the ground. Unlike the move to limit the visibility of bin Laden's death, Gaddafi's body was placed in an industrial freezer near Misrata, so that Libyans could know for sure that he was dead (see Chapter 1). In six months, the USA had twice demonstrated the imperial reach of its armed forces, as *deus ex machina*, helping to rid the world of two of its highest profile villains.

Both of these deaths raised the question of who would be next. They appeared to demonstrate the efficacy of Obama's chosen model of military intervention: limited and multilateral aerial force, in support of local troops on the ground aided by a small number of American Special Forces. It had been possible to find and kill bin Laden and Gaddafi. Who else? Such questions clearly were not lost on Obama, who appeared to 'warn other Middle Eastern dictators, particularly Syrian president Bashar al-Assad, that they could be next'.[4] Although implicit, it was clear that Obama was referring to Assad when he commented that 'the rule of the iron fist in the Middle East is inevitably coming to an end'.[5] Alongside Obama, 'Vice President Joe Biden described the military model as a "prescription" for the future' and White House Press Secretary Jay Carney continued to insist that 'Assad had lost his legitimacy to rule'.[6] In these statements, we can see the first basic Anglosphere discourse that enabled and shaped policy during the first phase of the Syrian crisis – a broadly Wilsonian support for democracy amidst the context of the Arab Uprisings. However, in the warnings of former NATO commander Wesley Clark we can see the second, competing Anglosphere discourse: while 'NATO is capable of a sustained effort... Syria is going to be different from Libya'.[7] The risk, here, was that if Syria was not Libya, maybe it would be like Iraq. In the opening phases of the Syrian crisis, these two discourses structured the debate on military intervention and its avoidance: democracy promotion in the context of the Arab Spring competed against the warning that, since Syria is not Libya, the Anglosphere would do well to remember the lessons of the quagmire in Iraq.[8] Together, the interaction of these discourses and the narratives that helped to comprise them enabled and justified a policy of democracy promotion at a

[4] Ibid.   [5] Ibid.   [6] Ibid.   [7] Ibid.
[8] J. Ralph, J. Holland and K. Zhekova, 'Before the vote: UK policy discourse on Syria 2011–13', *Review of International Studies*, 43 (2017), 875–97.

distance, whereby the USA and UK led calls for regime change without committing to the military intervention that such an outcome required.

In order to explore this policy of democracy promotion at a distance – how it came about, developed and was contested, as well as its implications – this chapter is structured in three sections. In the first section, the chapter explores the Anglosphere response to the Arab Uprisings at the start of 2011, in particular in Libya. Intervention in Libya was hugely significant for the Anglosphere response to Syria, as onlookers asked whether the ongoing war to halt Gaddafi's advances would be a template to limit Assad's as well. In its second section, the chapter explores how Anglosphere foreign policy evolved as the crisis developed and Assad's use of force against civilians intensified. In the third and final section, the chapter assesses the paradoxical Anglosphere outcome arrived at in the spring and summer of 2012, as calls for regime change went unsupported, given that the military intervention Assad's downfall would require was explicitly and repeatedly ruled out. This chapter therefore explores Anglosphere foreign policy from March 2011 to July 2012, during the first phase of the Syrian crisis. Throughout this period, the chapter shows how the United States and Barack Obama led an intimately interconnected old Anglosphere coalition, even where government ministers, opposition politicians and voices in the media weighed in on unfolding policy debates, as they competed within a transnational discursive war of position. This chapter thus sets the ground for an analysis of shifting Anglosphere apprehensions, from August 2012, as chemical weapons concerns supplemented, before ultimately supplanting, calls for democracy.

Libya and the Region

The Arab Uprisings ignited by Mohamed Bouazizi's self-immolation marked the onset of a new era for the Middle East, as well as Anglosphere foreign policy. However, this new era would be heavily contingent on distant and recent Anglosphere policy in the region. In contrast to David Cameron's assertions of a British foreign policy premised upon a more muscular liberalism, Barack Obama had come to power promising change and, to an extent, international retrenchment. As Trevor McCrisken has highlighted, the hope that Obama's election promise of change engendered was always overly optimistic and, in some cases, simply misplaced.[9] While Obama had promised significant changes in domestic policy, as well as bringing the 'dumb war' in Iraq to an end, he had always stated his commitment to the prosecution of the 'War on Terror', including the war in Afghanistan, albeit in smarter and more effective ways. Obama's promise of change, at the international level, was more nuanced than was often assumed.[10]

Two years into office, Obama had already demonstrated his commitment to the war in Afghanistan, agreeing to a temporary but significant troop surge, following protracted discussions with senior advisers and military personnel.[11] It was bin Laden's killing, as the United States edged closer to a decade of conflict in Afghanistan, that helped to enable the Commander in Chief to announce a timeline for troop withdrawal. In Iraq, the Arab Spring coincided with the ongoing drawdown of American troops, already reduced to some 40,000 and due to fully withdraw by the end of 2011. In both conflicts, the USA had been committed to an explicit policy of regime change through military intervention. However, Obama only shared a belief in the validity of this 'coupled' policy – of democratisation through force – in one of these wars. That reality was the immediate policy context for the USA as the Arab Uprisings spread across the region at the start of 2011; America was involved in two wars designed to achieve new governments through hard power, but the president only vouched for the necessity and logic of one of them. Two contradictory impulses were evident: first, an American and Anglosphere propensity to fight wars in the name of security buoyed by universal belief in freedom achieved through democratisation; countered, second, by the new leader of the free world's insistence that context matters and selectivity in policy application is imperative. Bush's regionally applied Freedom Agenda was replaced by a presidential approach more akin to case-by-case issue management, which prioritised the minimisation of costs and risks,[12]

---

[9] T. McCrisken, 'Ten years on: Obama's war on terrorism in rhetoric and practice', *International Affairs*, 87 (2011), 781–801.

[10] Ibid.

[11] See P. Baker, 'How Obama came to plan for "surge" in Afghanistan', *New York Times*, 5 November 2009, www.nytimes.com/2009/12/06/world/asia/06reconstruct.html?_r=0

[12] A. Quinn, 'The art of declining politely: Obama's prudent presidency and the waning of American power', *International Affairs*, 87 (2011), 803–24.

set against a much longer and slower vision of the march of history.[13] For Obama, then, three beliefs marked him out from his predecessor: the conviction that context matters and it should inform the pursuit of universal ideals; a recognition that the arc of history bends towards justice, but it does so slowly; and, therefore, a realisation that America cannot, should not and must not attempt to do everything, everywhere, all of the time.[14]

After Bouazizi's death and following the early falls of Ben Ali in Tunisia and Mubarak in Egypt, protests reached Libya, sandwiched between the two, in late February 2011. Within a week, protests reached Tripoli. Benghazi became the de facto capital for rebel and opposition fighters, with an interim government formed. Initial opposition advances were repelled, however, as Gaddafi's loyalist and hired forces recaptured lost territory. UNSCR1973, proposed by the UK, France and Lebanon, was passed on 17 March, with Russia and China (as well as Germany, India and Brazil) abstaining from the vote. The resolution authorised the establishment of a no-fly zone, as well as permitting 'all necessary means' to be used to protect civilians from Gaddafi's forces.[15] As David Cameron put it, the resolution was about showing Gaddafi, the region and the world that 'the international community intends to back its words with action'.[16] US, UK and French airstrikes commenced two days later, in an effort to avoid a potential massacre of civilians in Benghazi, which Gaddafi had promised and western leaders believed was a viable threat. The intervention was decisive in turning the tide of the conflict and, what was by now, civil war.

As in Afghanistan, air power, local fighters and limited Special Forces had combined. Unlike Afghanistan, Obama had chosen to assist, rather than lead, as part of a policy of burden sharing with allies. By August, opposition fighters were in Tripoli. Gaddafi was killed two months later. Crucially, however, this ultimate outcome,

---

[13] J. Goldberg, 'The Obama doctrine', *The Atlantic*, April 2016, www.theatlantic.com/magazine/archive/2016/04/the-obama-doctrine/471525

[14] In fairness to George W. Bush, several of these lessons were learned in his second term and, arguably, had even informed his foreign policy in his first eight months in office. It was after 9/11, between 2001 and 2004, that hard Wilsonian hubris most dominated US foreign policy.

[15] And, interestingly, not the protection of civilians from opposition forces; a point later noted by Anne-Marie Slaughter.

[16] BBC News, 'Libya UN Resolution 1973: text analysed', 18 March 2011, www.bbc.co.uk/news/world-africa-12782972

whilst welcomed, was never explicitly stated as coalition policy. Libya was a case of military intervention without the stated intention of US-precipitated regime change. For Obama, Libyans alone, not Americans, could decide the question of Libyan governance. In Libya, therefore, the world again saw that Obama was not averse to fighting all wars, but that in policy and style he differed from his predecessor. Obama was reluctant to put boots on the ground – such a scenario was explicitly prohibited by UNSCR1973 – and did not believe that US policy should be to achieve regime change through war; that must be locally owned if it was to be seen as legitimate, even if civilians were protected and assisted by American air power.

In justifying America's intervention in Libya, Obama spoke of Wilsonian and Jeffersonian themes,[17] as well as invoking notions of American identity and exceptionalism. In a Wilsonian vein, the American president spoke of the long history of tyranny finally and inevitably ending, as Libya's forty-year nightmare came to an end and the 'grip of fear' gave way to the 'promise of freedom'.[18] Obama was clear that it was Gaddafi's actions which had made American and coalition intervention inevitable. He spoke of Gaddafi's forces bearing down on 700,000 Libyan civilians: 'Confronted by this brutal repression and a looming humanitarian crisis, I ordered warships into the Mediterranean'.[19] The result was the prevention of 'a massacre that would have reverberated across the region and stained the conscience of the world'.[20] Aware of criticisms of his protracted decision-making in Afghanistan two years earlier, Obama drew a direct parallel to Bosnia, where he noted that 'it took the international community more than a year to intervene with air power to protect civilians'. In contrast, in Libya, America and NATO had taken action in 'just' thirty-one days. And that, Obama argued, was testament to his presiding over a nation that is qualitatively different – unique and superior in its leadership of all people, everywhere:

---

[17] On Jeffersonian themes, he spoke of minimising the costs and risks to America on six separate occasions. B. Obama, 'Remarks by the President in address to the nation on Libya', 28 March 2011, www.whitehouse.gov/the-press-office/2011/03/28/remarks-president-address-nation-libya

[18] Ibid.   [19] Ibid.

[20] Ibid. See also B. Obama, 'Remarks by the President on Libya', 19 March 2011, https://obamawhitehouse.archives.gov/the-press-office/2011/03/19/remarks-president-libya; and B. Obama, 'Speech on Libya', 24 February 2011, www.nytimes.com/2011/02/24/us/politics/24obama-statement-libya.html?_r=0

To brush aside America's responsibility as a leader and – more profoundly –
our responsibilities to our fellow human beings under such circumstances
would have been a betrayal of who we are. Some nations may be able to turn
a blind eye to atrocities in other countries. The United States of America is
different. And as President, I refused to wait for the images of slaughter and
mass graves before taking action...

Born, as we are, out of a revolution by those who longed to be free, we
welcome the fact that history is on the move in the Middle East and North
Africa and that young people are leading the way. Because wherever people
long to be free, they will find a friend in the United States. Ultimately, it is
that faith – those ideals – that are the true measure of American leadership.[21]

Despite the apparent success[22] of the Libyan (and Afghan) model,
despite the similarly strategic locations of Libya and Syria at the
crossroads of their respective regions,[23] despite equally disturbing
violations of human rights and despite Obama's acknowledgement of
America's unique role in the defence and spread of freedom, there
would be no decisive or rapid response when the Arab Uprisings
spread to Syria. The response of the USA and the Anglosphere to the
emerging crisis is encapsulated in the quote at the start of this chapter:
'The United States strongly condemns the Syrian government's brutal
repression of demonstrations'.[24] This 'strong condemnation' was
repeated, amplified and endlessly reworded throughout the first few
months of the crisis in 2011. The leaders of the USA, the UK and,
slightly less frequently, Australia, all mined this theme. In April,
Obama was coupling condemnation of 'abhorrent violence' by the
Assad government with simultaneous denunciations of 'violence by
protestors'.[25] By the end of the month, however, a range of sanctions
was passed, designed to cripple the financial resources of the Syrian
regime.[26] For Obama, however, this action did not automatically

---

[21] Ibid.

[22] Obama later admitted that the lack of post-conflict planning was his
administration's greatest failure. See A. Malloy, 'Obama admits worst mistake
of his presidency', *CNN Politics*, 11 April 2016, http://edition.cnn.com/2016/
04/10/politics/obama-libya-biggest-mistake

[23] A point that those arguing against the 'Syria is not Libya' discourse would later
emphasise.

[24] J. Carney, 'Statement by the Press Secretary on violence in Syria', 24 May 2011.

[25] B. Obama, 'Statement from the President on the Violence in Syria', 8 April 2011.

[26] Executive Orders 13338, 13399 and 13460 were passed on 29 April 2011,
following a UN resolution passed in Geneva.

imply that Assad had lost the right to govern. In May, he insisted that, while Assad had chosen the 'path of murder' for now, he had to make a choice and could opt to 'lead that transition' to a democratic Syria.[27]

On the one hand, then, during the early phases of the Syrian crisis, Obama was keen to condemn violence on both sides of the emerging civil war and prepared to offer Assad the chance to choose a role in the country's transition. On the other hand, it was clear that America condemned one side in far harsher terms and that Assad's was really no choice at all. The President of the United States noted that Syria's struggle, like that of the entire region, was one with which America was intimately familiar, having itself undergone numerous calls for freedom, in a variety of forms and senses. Obama drew direct parallels between the actions of protestors in Syria and the region, including Bouazizi's initial dramatic act of resistance, with American protests, such as those of the Boston Tea Party and the actions of Rosa Parks.[28] Given the state of American politics and Obama's own occupation of the White House, these were powerful analogies to draw; they served to make indifference difficult and inaction problematic.

First, analogies such as these serve to enmesh Syria's crisis with America's story. This story is well understood. Its invocation helps to craft a resonant American – and Anglosphere – foreign policy. Talk of freedom and America's own struggle for independence and democracy helps, inevitably, to spark an effective, affective response in an American audience, familiar with this popular narrative. In addition, Obama's invocation of Rosa Parks' – and by extension, his own – story, tied as it is to the long American struggle for equal rights, helped to render this an intimately personal story. Second and relatedly, the coercive impact of this analogy was therefore stark: to deny the Syrian opposition support was, by extension, to deny the legitimacy of the historical struggle that had enabled the election of America's first black president; potential opponents were being implicitly reminded that America was founded on the principle that all men are created equal – human rights are universal. In making the pursuit of freedom in Syria an inherently American phenomenon, this framing of the crisis helped to render indifference difficult to sustain. Obama's linking of Syria's

---

[27] B. Obama, 'Remarks of President Barack Obama—as prepared for delivery—"A moment of opportunity"', State Department, 19 May 2011.

[28] B. Obama, 'Remarks by the President on the Middle East and North Africa', 19 May 2011.

plight to his personal story and the US nation's broader battle for civil
rights made opposing support for the Syrian people politically problematic; framed as an inherently liberal revolution, to ignore Syrians'
quest for freedom was to delegitimise America's struggle for universal
suffrage and denounce Obama's own ascendancy to the presidency.
This, then, was a sufficiently unpalatable outcome to dissuade many
potential doubters from speaking out.

Here, already at this early stage, we see the hard nature of soft
power, as America's coercive foreign policy helped to remove the
discursive ground from beneath the feet of neo-isolationists, still
reeling from the quagmire in Iraq. This was noticeable in the arguments that neo-isolationists resorted to making, which focused on
future wars that would snowball from potential intervention in Syria,
rather than contesting the legitimacy of action in Syria itself.[29] And
yet, both sides of this debate were forming at a time when the USA
was *not* committed to taking action in Syria. The Anglosphere, led by
Obama, was pursuing democracy promotion at a distance. Calls for
freedom, fired up by the hubris derived from Gaddafi's demise, were
tempered by the second basic discourse of the Syrian conflict's
opening phase: Syria is not Libya, remember Iraq. Over the summer
and into the autumn of 2011, these two discourses existed uneasily
together. Even as the pressure on Assad grew, resistance to intervention remained, on the basis of a greater understanding of the myriad
complexities of Syria and the difficulty of intervening militarily in the
country. The awkward and seemingly paradoxical outcome was a soft
Wilsonian language that at times sounded more like imperial condes-
cension. This language enabled and supported a policy of democracy
promotion at a distance, rendering greater involvement off limits. In
the foreign policy speeches of Anglosphere leaders, Syrians were told
that America, Britain and Australia would be 'on their side' but not
(yet) on their battlefields.

Obama's speech on 19 May 2011 was the fullest articulation of
America and the Anglosphere's early position on Syria. First, he noted
that American involvement and interest was inevitable: 'though these
countries may be a great distance from our shores, we know that our
own future is bound to this region by the forces of economics and

---

[29] Ron Paul, for example, focused his arguments on future conflict with Russia and
Iran, rather than argue against the need for action in Syria.

security, by history and by faith'.[30] Second, he spoke of the efficacy of military force, in Afghanistan and in killing bin Laden; this was not a pacifist Commander in Chief – far from it. This was a Commander in Chief who recognised the necessity of American military force and the possibilities it engendered, whilst acknowledging its limitations and potential for the generation of unforeseen consequences. Third, he spoke of self-determination in the context of continued 'humiliation' in the face of 'relentless tyranny'.[31] Revolution was about: the bringing of the light and ending the darkness; breathing again, after the suffocation of dictatorship; feeling dignity, by resisting oppression. America, he assured his audience, 'values the dignity of the street vendor in Tunisia more than the raw power of the dictator'.[32] But, fourth, came the crunch – he was not yet prepared to put US troops in the firing line: 'There must be no doubt that the United States of America welcomes change that advances self-determination and opportunity'.[33] Such a position, he argued, allowed the US to proceed not with colonial ambition but with an appropriate 'humility'.[34] Opposition to violence and support for universal human rights meant that the US seized the moral high ground without committing to the active intervention that such pronouncements needed, if violence were to end and rights be restored.

The response of Anglosphere partners to the onset of the crisis was broadly in line with that of the 'leader of the free world'. At times, however, British Prime Minister David Cameron and, in particular, Australian Foreign Secretary Kevin Rudd spoke in more belligerent terms, mirroring the greater urgency of Secretary of State Hillary Clinton. In Australia, this was neither the first nor last time that Kevin Rudd and Julia Gillard would diverge on foreign policy, with the prime minister consistently more measured and less bellicose in her statements. A similar situation had previously arisen in the early stages of discussions regarding the Libyan no-fly zone, when Rudd – seemingly more advanced in his discussions with Hillary Clinton – appeared to get out ahead of the Australian prime minister in his calls for action. For instance, Rudd had authored an assertive opinion editorial for *The Australian* championing Australia's 'long-term approach to supporting democracy'.[35]

---

[30] Obama, 'Remarks on the Middle East and North Africa'.   [31] Ibid.
[32] Ibid.   [33] Ibid.   [34] Ibid.
[35] J. Rudd, 'Keep the faith with the Arab Spring', *The Australian*, 2 May 2011, www.theaustralian.com.au/national-affairs/opinion/keep-the-faith-with-the-arab-spring/story-e6frgd0x-1226059172816

This time, with the Syrian crisis unfolding, intra-governmental disputes and power plays were similarly distracting, as the Foreign Secretary remained a 'thorn in the side' of the prime minister.[36] Leading the charge, 'Kevin Rudd was the first to call for the UN Security Council to refer Assad to the International Criminal Court'.[37]

Rudd's activism dovetailed with ongoing efforts he had initiated as far back as 2008 to secure Australia a place on the UN Security Council as a non-permanent member. In addition to this significant and expensive diplomatic push, Gillard moved to strengthen Anglosphere ties during 2011, with announcements on the expansion of American forces in Australia. These two moves split the Opposition and help to shed light on Australian discursive divisions at the start of the Syrian crisis. While welcoming the strengthening and deepening of Anglosphere ties, Leader of the Opposition (and future prime minister) Tony Abbott was scathing of Gillard and Rudd in their efforts to further Australia's UN presence. His pithy denouncement of these activities succinctly summarises Australia's principal competing discourse on Syria in 2011. Alongside denouncements of Assad's brutality and calls for democracy, a contrasting narrative emphasised Australia's own regional issues, which should be prioritised due to their geographical proximity and immediacy. In 2012, as efforts to secure an Australian UNSC seat intensified, Abbott summarised this position bluntly, condemning the Australian leadership for 'swanning around in New York talking to Africans', when they should be focused on stopping the boats of illegal immigrants coming to Australian shores back home.[38] As so often, Australia's foreign policy appeared torn between its geography and its history. Aspirations of global relevance and deeper ties to leading Anglosphere nations had to be offset against Australia's Asia-Pacific location. Tony Abbott, like the nation he would go on to lead, appeared at times to embody and articulate both positions simultaneously.

---

[36] S. Maiden, 'Rudd still a thorn in Gillard's side', *The Advertiser*, 18 June 2011, www.adelaidenow.com.au/news/rudd-still-a-thorn-in-gillards-side/story-e6frea6u-1226077790126

[37] P. Hartcher, 'Spotlight is on Assad if Gaddafi falls', *Sydney Morning Herald*, 23 August 2011, www.smh.com.au/federal-politics/political-opinion/spotlight-is-on-assad-if-gaddafi-falls-20110822-1j6oj.html

[38] R. Willingham, 'Focus on boats, not UN, Abbott tells PM', *Sydney Morning Herald*, 24 September 2012, www.smh.com.au/federal-politics/political-news/focus-on-boats-not-un-abbott-tells-pm-20120924-26gfg.html

The UK's response to the unfolding civil war was marked by several contrasts, combined with quintessential British understatement. Cameron warned that he was 'appalled' by the violence and 'stood with' the Syrian people.[39] In April 2011, as the world watched, the government moved to withdraw an invitation for the Syrian ambassador to attend the royal wedding (of Prince William and Kate Middleton). However, as late as June, the Foreign Office gave the green light to a 'personal' visit by new Member of Parliament Brooks Newmark to the Syrian leader, Bashar al-Assad. US Congressman Dennis Kucinich accompanied him. The message, seemingly approved by the US and UK leadership, was that Assad needed to give way. By August 2011, this message was articulated loud and clear across the Anglosphere. This synchronised statement came at a time of maximum British distraction, however, as riots broke out across London. Obama would later complain that 'other things' had 'distracted' the British prime minister from the conflict in Libya.[40] As looting and unrest spread across the UK capital and other major cities over five nights, Bashar al-Assad's father-in-law drew a direct comparison between the actions of British police in London and his son-in-law's directives in Homs. Fortunately for David Cameron, the British weather turned and heavy rain helped to dampen the spirits and quash the numbers of rioters. Despite the violence on British streets, August 2011 nonetheless marked a decisive turning point in Anglosphere foreign policy, as Cameron, like Obama and numerous allies, roundly and loudly turned on Assad.

Assad and the People

The Anglosphere's initial condemnation of violence generally and Assad specifically was tempered by an optimism that he might choose to reform Syria, rather than see it torn apart. Within six months, however, that optimism had ebbed away. In June, Jay Carney was still advancing general and non-committal statements urging support for human rights and democracy: 'There must be no doubt that the United States of America welcomes change that advances self-determination and opportunity'.[41] By July, these sentiments were coupled to far more

---

[39] D. Cameron, 'PM interview at the G8 summit', 27 May 2011; D. Cameron, 'European Council press conference', 24 June 2011.
[40] Goldberg, 'The Obama doctrine'.
[41] J. Carney, 'Statement by the Press Secretary on Syria', 11 June 2011.

specific warnings, as Obama insisted that, through 'his own actions, Bashar al-Assad is ensuring that he and his regime will be left in the past'.[42] The following month, Obama's patience finally ran out and, in August 2011, Anglosphere calls for Assad to go became explicit:

We have consistently said that President Assad must lead a democratic transition or get out of the way. He has not led. For the sake of the Syrian people, the time has come for President Assad to step aside.[43]

Despite ruling out the possibility of Assad's continued leadership, Obama (in contradistinction to his predecessor's style and policies) reminded the world that it 'is up to the Syrian people to choose their own leaders and we have heard their strong desire that there not be foreign intervention in their movement'.[44] The upshot of that was a policy of 'pressuring President Assad to get out of the way of this transition' to a 'Syria that is democratic, just and inclusive for all Syrians'.[45] Despite renewed and ramped up sanctions, designed to apply pressure to the regime, it was therefore clear, once again, that the 'Syrian people' would 'determine their own destiny', with America continuing 'to stand firmly on their side'.[46] In short, it was a policy of regime change, without the requisite military intervention to make it happen – or, more evocatively, a 'humanitarian crisis', short of a policy based on the responsibility to protect.[47] This, then, was far less than a 'belated hard line': for Assad, it was continued condemnation made irrelevant through reassurance that Syria was not Libya and the Anglosphere's haunting memory of Iraq.[48] Assad retained volition and chose not to go.

In late 2011, alongside Gaddafi's death, there were two significant external developments for Syria and the Anglosphere. First, Russia and China thwarted P3 efforts at achieving a UNSC resolution denouncing the actions of the Assad regime. The month before, Cameron had addressed the UN for the first time. Syria was mentioned surprisingly infrequently and only in passing, but the message was clear: it was time

---

[42] B. Obama, 'Statement by the President on the Violence in Syria', 31 July 2011.
[43] B. Obama, 'Statement by President Obama on the Situation in Syria',
    18 August 2011.
[44] Ibid.   [45] Ibid.   [46] Ibid.
[47] J. Carney, 'Statement by the Press Secretary on Syria', 11 June 2011.
[48] M. Indyk, 'Obama's belated Syria hard line', *The Daily Beast*, 19 August 2011,
    www.thedailybeast.com/articles/2011/08/18/obama-s-belated-call-for-bashar-
    al-assad-ouster-pushes-syria-closer-to-freedom.html

for the UN to act.[49] The P3 were defeated in their efforts by two vetoes, preventing the passing of a resolution which would have 'demanded that Syrian authorities immediately stop using force against civilians and allow the exercise of freedom of expression, peaceful assembly and other fundamental rights'.[50] In response, China and Russia had reiterated their opposition to sanctions, preference for open channels for dialogue and belief 'in the importance of the principle of non-intervention in domestic affairs and respect for the sovereignty and territorial integrity of Syria'.[51] As Samantha Power noted, the UN had failed to take even the 'minimum steps' necessary to protect civilians. Russian justifications centred on the need to avoid a second Libya, while diplomats calculated that China had allied with Russia due to long-standing loyalty, over and above a deeply held principle of non-interference.[52]

Second, the Arab League seized the mantle, where the UN had failed.[53] This was welcomed by the USA, UK and Australia, with a US State Department spokesman describing the Arab League's plan as the 'best opportunity' for peace in Syria currently on the table.[54] The plan commenced in two phases, with both efforts successfully securing the apparent cooperation of Assad, who committed to ceasing attacks on civilians and allowing Arab League monitors into Syria. It did not

---

[49] D. Cameron, 'Prime Minister's first speech to the UN General Assembly', 20 September 2011, www.gov.uk/government/speeches/prime-ministers-first-speech-to-the-un-general-assembly

[50] UNSC, 'Security Council fails to adopt draft resolution condemning Syria's crackdown on anti-government protestors, owing to veto by Russian Federation, China', 4 October 2011, www.un.org/press/en/2011/sc10403.doc.htm

[51] Ibid.

[52] See S. Adams, 'Failure to protect: Syria and the UN Security Council', Global Centre for the Responsibility to Protect, Occasional Paper Series no. 5, March 2015; for discussion, see S. Charap, 'Russia, Syria and the doctrine of intervention', *Survival*, 55 (2013), 35–41. For Charap, it is Russian fear that a policy of removing current governments might one day impact Moscow that motivated veto decisions. See also R. Allison, 'Russia and Syria: explaining alignment with a regime in crisis', *International Affairs*, 89 (2013), 795–823.

[53] See, for example, B. Rhodes, 'Press gaggle by Press Secretary Jay Carney and Deputy National Security Advisor for Strategic Communications Ben Rhodes', 15 November 2011.

[54] A. Quinn, 'U.S. calls Arab League Syria plan "best opportunity"', *Reuters*, 20 December 2011, www.reuters.com/article/us-syria-usa-idUSTRE7BJ28W20111220

take long, however, in both instances, for this apparent concession to be shown to be hollow, as violent crackdowns not only continued but actually intensified. By January 2012, both Arab League peace plans had come off the rails, as Assad continued to inflict revenge on the Syrian people, in an ever-bloodier civil conflict, despite having notionally committed to the process. In failure, Arab League officials, sent into Syria to monitor the violence, left the country, as the situation deteriorated from protests with sectarian undercurrents into full-blown civil war.

Indefatigable, the Arab League tried again. The third effort, at the start of 2012, was coupled to calls for UN action. Once again, however, these calls fell on unsympathetic Russian and Chinese ears. This plan would have seen joint Arab League and United Nations peacekeepers on the ground in Syria. Moscow, however, insisted that peacekeepers could only enter the fray once there was peace.[55] British Foreign Secretary William Hague, in particular, was quick to express his frustrations with Russian obstinacy;[56] the result in his eyes was that the UN had failed in its responsibilities to the Syrian people.[57] Meeting Barack Obama, David Cameron reiterated that Britain's policy – like that of the wider Anglosphere – was to 'stop the killing'; a task for which he was prepared to work with the Russians by appealing to their interests and values.[58] However, the paradox of a policy of stopping bloodshed by insisting on a transition in leadership was made abundantly clear when the prime minister had to resort to insisting on the importance of 'holding people responsible' in the future, by sending 'monitors to the Turkish border and elsewhere to make sure we document these crimes' today.[59] Rather than sending warplanes, as

---

[55] BBC News, 'Syria rejects new Arab League peace mission proposal', 13 February 2012, www.bbc.co.uk/news/world-middle-east-17008597

[56] R. Spencer, 'William Hague accuses Russia and China as Syria heads toward "civil war"', *The Telegraph*, 5 February 2012, www.telegraph.co.uk/news/worldnews/middleeast/syria/9062794/William-Hague-accuses-Russia-and-China-as-Syria-heads-toward-civil-war.html

[57] The Telegraph, 'UN has "failed" in duties to protect Syrian people, says William Hague', 12 March 2012, www.telegraph.co.uk/news/worldnews/middleeast/syria/9138600/UN-has-failed-in-duties-to-protect-Syrian-people-says-William-Hague.html

[58] D. Cameron, 'Press conference by David Cameron and Barack Obama', Cabinet Office, 15 March 2012.

[59] Ibid.

in Libya, the Anglosphere was going to continue to 'write down what has been done' in Syria.[60]

In six short months, Syria had become the world's principal crisis. Attempts at its resolution attracted the minds and efforts of some of the world's foremost dignitaries. At a summit in Baghdad in March 2012, the Arab League signed off on UN Peace Envoy Kofi Annan's six-point peace plan.[61] The former UN Secretary-General sought and obtained support from Russia and Assad; UN observers were allowed back into Syria. Once again, however, the plan was not enacted. The following month, in Houla, government forces killed 100 civilians, including fifty children.[62] A month after that, with no progress being made, UN observers withdrew. Annan's resignation followed later in the year.

The UNSC deadlock and repeated failure of the Arab League inspired the emergence of a new, alternative forum for the discussion of solutions to the Syrian crisis, temporarily side-stepping the impasse caused by Russian intransigence. The Friends of Syria Group met in late February, in Tunisia,[63] and comprised several key states, minus those that had most obstructed efforts towards a resolution. The Group officially recognised the Syrian National Council as the legitimate opposition, securing the agreement of the USA to supply $100 million of non-lethal aid. In addition, over the summer, the USA, UK, Australia and others closed ranks on Syria's diplomatic ties, expelling ambassadors around the world. The message was clear: it was not only Assad but all those involved in his maintenance of power that were now seen to be illegitimate and beyond the potential for a negotiated resolution.

Debate, Division and Cautious Support

In July 2012, opposition forces detonated a remote bomb in Damascus at a meeting of leading regime figures. Amongst the casualties were

---

[60] Ibid.
[61] K. Annan, 'Annan's peace plan for Syria', *Council on Foreign Relations*, March 2012, www.cfr.org/syria/annans-peace-plan-syria/p28380
[62] R. Spencer, 'Massacred Syrian children were "bound before being shot"', *The Telegraph*, 28 May 2012, www.telegraph.co.uk/news/worldnews/middleeast/syria/9295268/Massacred-Syrian-children-were-bound-before-being-shot.html
[63] The Group would go on to convene seven times in a range of countries, until only eleven remained in London, at the end of 2013.

Assad's brother-in-law and the defence minister, with Assad's own brother reported to be amongst the injured. Despite the potent strike, which came on the fourth day of fighting in Damascus, the bombing did not transpire to be the decisive turning point some commentators hoped it might be.[64] The events raised hopes and fears – hopes that the regime might collapse and fears that there was now no rolling back from the brink of all-out civil war. It also put yet more strain on UNSC relationships and deliberations, as Annan was attempting to shepherd a new resolution to the table.[65] The initial optimism that Assad might fall or step aside ebbed away, as the regime dug in and faced down the rebellion.[66] The vicious backlash to the bombings was a microcosm of the conflict's development during its first phase.[67]

Anglosphere foreign policy from the start of the Syrian crisis in 2011 to the summer of 2012 was marked by relative timidity and caution, even when language was strident.[68] The existence of a weighty, military-backed basic discourse, highlighting the difficulty of intervening militarily in Syria, was sufficient to curtail most official calls for action. However, in the USA, UK and Australia, liberal internationalist language, supported by long-standing and long-developed democratic identities, helped to ensure that, while war was off limits for now, Assad was widely condemned. This was, then, apparently contradictory; a policy of democracy promotion at a distance, or, if you are cynical, a policy of rhetorical lip service, given the decreasing likelihood that regime change without intervention would occur. Ironically, however, this paradoxical stance placed Obama, Cameron and Gillard at the heart of their electorates and in the middle of the increasingly vociferous debates regarding Syrian war and peace.

In the United States, Obama faced stronger calls for action from a range of political allies and opponents. In both Houses, the likes of John McCain, Lindsey Graham and Joe Liebermann led calls for the USA to do more, whether arming rebels or bombing Assad's forces.

---

[64] N. MacFarquhar, 'Syrian rebels land deadly blow to Assad's inner circle', *New York Times*, 18 July 2012, www.nytimes.com/2012/07/19/world/middleeast/suicide-attack-reported-in-damascus-as-more-generals-flee.html?_r=0
[65] Ibid.
[66] BBC News, 'Syrian President Bashar al-Assad: facing down rebellion', 21 October 2015, www.bbc.co.uk/news/10338256
[67] MacFarquhar, 'Syrian rebels'.
[68] For example, on Obama's foreign policy generally, see Quinn, 'Declining politely'.

In academia, the likes of Anne-Marie Slaughter, who had recently served under Hillary Clinton in the State Department, called for US military intervention to end the bloodshed through well-placed articles in American news outlets. And, in the media, the likes of Michael Hirsch were pushing for stronger action – and an end to Assad's 'appeasement' – in Syria. Even Obama's own Secretary of State was far more hawkish than he on the question of what to do to end the bloodshed. The discursive war of position over Syria, therefore, clearly cut across party political lines; at this stage, it was, in some respects, deeply political although non-partisan.

Together, Slaughter, McCain, Graham and Liebermann offered sustained opposition to official American and Anglosphere foreign policy. For McCain, Graham and Liebermann, the principal aim of their intervention in the debate was to pressure the US government into arming the Syrian rebels and the Syrian National Council.[69] As Liebermann argued, unveiling a House resolution, 'We in the United States have both a moral and strategic reason to support their efforts by at least giving them the means with which to defend themselves'.[70] But McCain quickly went further, arguing for the use of American airpower in Syria.[71] For McCain, the parallels between Syria and Libya were clear and the lessons of that war's success readily apparent: 'The kinds of mass atrocities that NATO intervened in Libya to prevent in Benghazi are now a reality in Homs'.[72] He noted, not inaccurately, that, due to conditions on the ground in Syria, Obama's policy of regime change without intervention was 'starting to look more like a hope than a strategy'.[73] The inevitability of neighbouring states and others intervening, McCain argued, meant that America's choice was whether to be able to shape the outcome of the crisis or wait it out on the sidelines.[74] As the Obama administration stuck to its (lack of) guns, McCain's language ramped up. Having originally praised the

---

[69] For example, A. Rubin, 'Two senators say U.S. should arm Syrian rebels', *New York Times*, 19 February 2012.

[70] A. Gharib, 'McCain, Graham, Lieberman unveil resolution calling for U.S. help in arming Syria rebels', *Think Progress*, 18 March 2012.

[71] J. McCain, 'It's time to use American airpower in Syria', *New Republic*, 5 March 2012. He would go further still, arguing, in the conflict's later phases, for 20,000 American ground troops.

[72] Ibid.   [73] Ibid.

[74] Ibid.; see also *The Telegraph*, 'US Senator John McCain calls for air strikes on Syria', 6 March 2012.

administration for its diplomatic efforts, by the summer he declared American inaction to be 'disgraceful' and 'shameful'.[75] The choice he presented was between looking back 'as we did with Bosnia and Kosovo with pride or... as we did in Rwanda'.[76] This was a potentially powerful narrative, with the latter analogy offering an affecting and widely understood anchoring frame that centred on the avoidance of loss. This was, after all, a failure to act infamously described by Tony Blair as a scar on the conscience of the world. McCain was attempting to mobilise a particularly coercive foreign policy discourse in order to acquiesce reticent opponents.

On the other side of the aisle, Princeton academic and former Clinton aide Anne-Marie Slaughter hardened her stance and counter-narrative from doubting whether the western world should 'stand by' and urging leaders to think seriously about intervening (in January 2012),[77] to the full espousal of a 'just' and 'justifiable' war (by June).[78] Military intervention, she argued, was necessary to 'halt the butchery'.[79] In an opinion editorial in the *New York Times*, Slaughter directly confronted the naysayers, whose motto of 'Syria is not Libya' she directly refuted.[80] More 'strategically located' and 'more dangerous to' American interests, Slaughter argued that 'foreign military intervention in Syria offer[ed] the best hope for curtailing a long, bloody and destabilizing civil war'.[81] With some foresight, Slaughter urged that failure to do so and opting to merely arm the opposition threatened to bring 'about exactly the scenario the world should fear most: a proxy war that [... will] fracture Syria along sectarian lines [... and] allow Al Qaeda and other terrorist groups to gain a foothold in Syria and perhaps gain access to chemical and biological weapons'.[82] Addressing Obama's concerns to avoid US-sponsored regime change

---

[75] C. McGreal, 'John McCain says US should be "ashamed" of inaction over Syria conflict', *The Guardian*, 6 June 2012.

[76] Ibid.

[77] A. Slaughter, 'How the world could – and maybe should – intervene in Syria', *The Atlantic*, 23 January 2012.

[78] A. Slaughter, 'Syrian intervention is justifiable, and just', *Washington Post*, 8 June 2012.

[79] A. Slaughter, 'How to halt the butchery in Syria', *New York Times*, 23 February 2012.

[80] Ibid. This line was repeatedly uttered by Russian Foreign Minister Sergei Lavrov.

[81] Ibid.   [82] Ibid.

directly, Slaughter argued that the 'point of an intervention in Syria would be to stop the killing', not to 'bring about regime change'.[83] This, she noted, could be achieved by protecting *all* civilians, on both sides, unlike in Libya.[84] Here, Slaughter's language spoke directly to the concerns generated by the toxic legacy of Iraq. In combination with McCain and Graham, this formed a resonant and powerful narrative, but it was insufficient to move either the president or the public.[85]

In contrast, on the other side of the debate, Ron Paul warned of American hypocrisy in the pursuit of 'empire', with lines such as, 'How would we tolerate Russia in Mexico demanding a humanitarian solution to the violence on the U.S.-Mexican border?'[86] In opposition to the US use of force, Paul was joined by Henry Kissinger, who argued against a war that would threaten global order.[87] Lamenting the fact that intervention had been discussed in terms of 'global democracy', Kissinger presented a realist and pluralist argument that international order had to be prioritised over and above international justice; solidarity with fellow humans in the cause of democracy meant nothing, he argued, if sovereignty and the system of states broke down as a result.[88] In short, for Kissinger, the Arab Spring threatened the principles of the Westphalian peace; calls for humanitarian war must be resisted in favour of calculations premised on the national interest and balance of power.[89] Obama was certainly not deaf to these arguments. He was a cautious president, aware of the twin constraints of accounting for international perception and ensuring a sustained international order.[90] He had consistently argued for a massively reduced role for the United States in pursuing regime change abroad whilst campaigning for, and on coming to, office. His 2010 National Security Strategy reassured the world that, in contrast to his predecessor, 'America will not impose any system of government on another country'.[91] There

---

[83] Slaughter, 'Syrian intervention'.   [84] Ibid.

[85] At this stage, nearly three quarters of Americans saw no obligation for the USA to intervene in Syria. CNN/ORC Poll, *CNN*, 14 February 2012, http://i2.cdn.turner.com/cnn/2012/images/02/14/rel2d.pdf

[86] R. Paul, 'Ron Paul to warmongers: leave Syria alone!', *ronpaul.com*, 19 June 2012.

[87] H. Kissinger, 'Syrian intervention risks upsetting global order', *Washington Post*, 1 June 2012.

[88] Ibid.   [89] Ibid.   [90] Holland, 'Obama as modern Jeffersonian'.

[91] B. Obama, *National Security Strategy of the United States (2010)* (Darby, PA: DIANE Publishing, 2010); see also Bouchet, 'The democracy tradition'.

was an important corollary, though: 'our long-term security and prosperity depends on our steady support for universal values'.[92] This was
where Obama promised the USA was heading in 2010 and it was
exactly where the USA was in 2012.

Within the old Anglosphere coalition, Obama and Gillard were
similarly positioned. Like Obama, Gillard had a foreign minister who
was ruthlessly ambitious, had greater foreign policy experience and
was relatively pro-interventionist. Like Obama, Gillard had politically
usurped her Foreign Secretary. Unlike Obama, Gillard had more
immediate reason to be worried, given that she had ousted Rudd in
an internal political coup, which could be reversed; it was clear to even
disinterested observers that Rudd was seeking and plotting revenge.
This would eventually be attempted in February 2012, ending months
of tension and ultimately resulting in Rudd's defeat, as well as the loss
of his ministerial brief. Bob Carr became Australia's new foreign
secretary. While Gillard and Obama both faced calls for continued
inaction in Syria, whatever the developments on the ground, these were
a relative minority, voiced by ardent anti-war campaigners and hyper-
realists. Obama and Gillard were already positioned on the non-
intervention side of the debate, which was where most of the public
resided, without ruling out the possibility of action in the future. They
were, arguably, a necessary handbrake on the establishment orthodoxy, following the heady heights and frequent wars of the Bush and
Howard administrations. Both had to learn fast: Obama's experience
was heavily skewed to domestic politics and Gillard had admitted on
coming to power that, unlike the Mandarin-speaking prime minister
she replaced, she was no foreign policy expert. A shaky first half of
2011 for her government, however, gave way to a far more assured
second half, which, once the leadership spill was successfully negoti-
ated, appeared likely to continue in 2012.[93]

After Rudd's defeat in the leadership spill and removal as foreign
secretary, Bob Carr took on the considerable portfolio that had been
vacated.[94] Following the Russian (and Chinese) veto, Canberra, like

---

[92] Ibid.
[93] M. Curley and D. Moores, 'Issues in Australian foreign policy: January to June
2011', *Australian Journal of Politics & History*, 57 (2011), 597–613; N. Bisley,
'Issues in Australian foreign policy: July to December 2011', *Australian Journal
of Politics & History*, 58 (2011), 268–82.
[94] And at times struggled with the considerable workload.

London and other cities around the world, had witnessed the trashing of the Syrian embassy, as well as protests in Sydney and Melbourne. Carr's contributions on Syria furthered both dominant discourses. First, he spoke of the fact that Syria was not Libya, due to Assad's far more significant military capability, with unusual candour: 'They have an army hugely more powerful than that of Libya.'[95] Second, he went further still, highlighting the lack of unity in the United Nations and Syria's opposition as a potential obstacle to greater action.[96] This, he admitted, meant there were obvious 'contradictions' in foreign policy when compared with the swift and decisive intervention taken in Libya.[97] He repeatedly reminded listeners that Australians were just as appalled as the rest of the Anglosphere by the violence of the Assad regime: 'Appalled that a regime could connive in or organise the execution, the killing, of men, women and children'.[98] Like Obama and Cameron, therefore, Carr had placed all options, including military intervention, on the table, with or without Russian support.[99]

In the UK, David Cameron adopted what Daddow and Schnapper have termed a 'bounded liberal posture', close to the establishment orthodoxy and the first (pre-9/11) term of Tony Blair.[100] In reality, this meant that 'cautious pragmatism has tended to win out over the proclamation of grand strategic ambition'.[101] Therefore, even while coming to power insisting, as William Hague did, 'It is not in our character to have a foreign policy without a conscience: to be idle or uninterested while others starve or murder each other in their millions is not for us', the 'Syria is not Libya' argument remained strong.[102]

---

[95] D. Flitton and J. Ireland, 'Military intervention in Syria an option: Carr', *Sydney Morning Herald*, 30 May 2012, www.smh.com.au/federal-politics/political-news/military-intervention-in-syria-an-option-carr-20120529-1zhgw.html
[96] Ibid.   [97] Ibid.   [98] Ibid.   [99] Ibid.
[100] O. Daddow and P. Schnapper, 'Liberal intervention in the foreign policy thinking of Tony Blair and David Cameron', *Cambridge Review of International Affairs*, 26 (2013), 330–49.
[101] O. Daddow, 'The use of force in British foreign policy: from New Labour to the coalition', *The Political Quarterly*, 84 (2013), 110–18.
[102] W. Hague, 'The future of British foreign policy', speech to the International Institute for Strategic Studies, 21 July 2009, www.conservatives.com/News/Speeches, cited in Daddow and Schnapper, 'Liberal intervention'. Beech and Oliver have argued that 'the global worldview of David Cameron, William Hague and their liberal Conservative colleagues can be understood as solidarist'. See M. Beech and T. Oliver, 'Humanitarian intervention and foreign policy in the Conservative-led coalition', *Parliamentary Affairs*, 67 (2013), 102–18.

Despite this, Hague deliberately contested the analogy in the summer of 2012, as he sought to apply pressure to Russia and others unwilling to back UNSC resolutions. In June 2012, Hague was quoted in the *New York Times* and elsewhere, arguing that Syria was on the brink of descending into chaos, akin not to Libya in 2011, but Bosnia in the 1990s.[103] While the likes of former High Representative Paddy Ashdown contested this claim, its strategic usefulness was widely acknowledged for a government seeking international unity and attempting to pressure others into action.[104] It was an effort to render more difficult opposition to unified condemnation at the level of the international community, by pointing to a widely understood historical comparison. When these efforts ran aground in the summer of 2012, having failed to achieve UNSC resolutions on anything other than military observers,[105] Hague moved to suggest that Anglosphere or P3 action might press ahead, without Russia.[106]

Alternatives were voiced in the UK, with debates in parliament giving MPs the chance to press home the potentially stifling complexity of the situation.[107] In the press, particularly in the right-wing tabloid *The Daily Mail*, the case was made that, despite the appalling human rights abuses, 'it would be madness for Britain to intervene'.[108] The realist premise for the argument was clear: 'Hague is quite simply deluded if he thinks that we have anything to gain from intervention

---

[103] See, for example, *The Telegraph*, 'William Hague compares Syria to Bosnia in 1990s', 10 June 2012, www.telegraph.co.uk/news/worldnews/middleeast/syria/9322600/William-Hague-compares-Syria-to-Bosnia-in-1990s.html. This argument had been put forward in the media already. See I. Black, 'Syria is looking like Bosnia 20 years ago', *The Guardian*, 28 May 2012, www.theguardian.com/world/2012/may/28/syria-looking-more-like-bosnia

[104] BBC News, 'Ashdown: "Many differences" between Syria and Bosnia', 11 June 2012, www.bbc.co.uk/news/uk-politics-18397773

[105] UNSCR2240, 2043 and 2059 were passed. Three far more impactful resolutions were vetoed between October 2011 and July 2012.

[106] R. Prince, 'William Hague: action on Syria possible without support of Russia and China', *The Telegraph*, 5 July 2012, www.telegraph.co.uk/news/worldnews/9378241/William-Hague-action-on-Syria-possible-without-support-of-Russia-and-China.html

[107] For example, see Douglas Alexander and other's comments, 'Syria', *Hansard*, House of Commons, 19 June 2012, www.publications.parliament.uk/pa/cm201213/cmhansrd/cm120619/debtext/120619-0001.htm

[108] J. Bradley, 'Yes, Syria is a tragedy but it would be madness for Britain to intervene', *Daily Mail*, 30 May 2012, www.dailymail.co.uk/debate/article-2151866/Houla-massacre-Syria-tragedy-madness-Britain-intervene.html

in the country'. Therefore, 'It would be outrageous to sacrifice the lives of any British soldiers in this conflict in which we have no national interests.'[109] As the Royal United Services Institute (RUSI) Director Michael Clarke warned that a 'hands-off approach' would be 'increasingly difficult to maintain', parts of the press feared Britain would be 'dragged into' the Syria conflict.[110] Of course, such warnings missed one of the most fundamental points: Britain, as a core member of the old Anglosphere coalition, was one of the most actively assertive states in calling for increased measures in Syria. While the 'Syria is not Libya' sub-discourse prevented intervention for now, the UK, alongside the USA and Australia, was continuing to apply the pressure and ramp up the discursive bases for intervention in the future.[111]

Conclusion

During the first seventeen months of the conflict, between January 2011 and July 2012, the crisis in Syria took shape, with key domestic and international players becoming involved and taking sides. For the Anglosphere, peace and democracy alone were no longer enough; policy shifted to the promotion of a particular type of peace and a democracy that did not feature Bashar al-Assad. While divisions were apparent in the domestic political landscapes of the USA, UK and Australia, Obama, Cameron and Gillard occupied apparently restrained positions, at the heart of their electorates and, arguably, notably more cautious than some of the calls from their respective foreign policy establishments. In each case, the Foreign Secretaries and Secretary of State were significant political figures – former or future party or state leaders – and, in each instance, they were relatively advanced in their calls for action. These positions were, however, strongest and the most bipartisan in the United States, where

---

[109] Ibid.

[110] I. Drury, 'Britain could be dragged into Syria conflict to prevent bloodshed spreading to neighbouring countries, says former Army commander', *Daily Mail*, 25 July 2012, www.dailymail.co.uk/news/article-2178526/Britain-dragged-Syria-conflict-prevent-bloodshed-spreading-neighbouring-countries-says-Army-commander.html#ixzz4APzGh8Ys

[111] However, this still, clearly, amounted to a 'strategy gap' for the UK, as it failed to align language, values and identity with actions. See J. Gaskarth, 'Strategizing Britain's role in the world', *International Affairs*, 90 (2014), 559–81.

politicians on both sides of the aisle were joined by academics and voices in the media in calling for American intervention to end the suffering in Syria. Barack Obama, at times, cut a relatively isolated figure in his insistence that regime change must be locally owned and that meant limiting American action to the countenance of voice.

The rest of the old Anglosphere coalition reached the same conclusion, amidst unique domestic contexts. In Britain, the scars of the Iraq War and Tony Blair's toxic foreign policy legacy continued to haunt the political debate. While intervention in Libya had been successfully sold as impossible to avoid and possible to do, military warnings that Syria would be considerably more difficult were resonant in a country that widely shared a perception of having been duped in 2003. 'Iraq syndrome' would be difficult to shake, meaning that there was relatively little public appetite for a new war, even where some foreign policy elites saw Britain's participation in a military intervention as a moral necessity and political inevitably. In Australia, calls for war's avoidance centred on the distance of Syria from the nation's interests, at a time where more proximal regional concerns should be prioritised. However, the call to intervention was stronger here, as represented in Rudd's activism. Iraq had not quelled Australia's humanitarian impulse to the same extent as Britain's, where a greater scepticism and cynicism of elite justifications for war had taken hold.[112]

During the first phase of the Syrian Civil War, a number of crucial features were established that would shape the development of the conflict on the ground, as well as Anglosphere foreign policy. First, and most significantly, the first stage of the war saw the development of the discursive war of position that would structure Anglosphere policy debates from 2011 through to the conflict's conclusion. Of particular importance was the early emergence of two structuring basic discourses and their powerful associated and supporting sub-discourses. The liberal optimism of the Arab Spring was tempered by the conservative timidity that followed the urge to remember Iraq. The hope, therefore, was that teleology circumvented the need for troops; Assad's

---

[112] The decision not to intervene would decrease the apparent legitimacy of future calls for humanitarian intervention, however. See A. Sarvarian, 'Humanitarian intervention after Syria', *Legal Studies*, 36 (2016), 20–47; it would also, of course, have ramifications for America's standing in the region, see F. A. Gerges, 'The Obama approach to the Middle East: the end of America's moment?', *International Affairs*, 89 (2013), 299–323.

fall would follow, regardless of direct Anglosphere participation in the conflict. Syria's differences to Libya trumped concerns to protect civilians. These basic and sub-discourses inevitably tapped into shared Anglosphere cultural dispositions (such as towards universal liberal values and regarding the mutual lessons of Iraq), as well as national-level political contexts (such as Obama's invocation of America's progression on civil rights). Within these discourses, rhetoric, oratory and narrative were all important as part of the quest to establish resonant and coercive policy positions, aimed at winning out in the ongoing war of position. Specifically, metaphor and analogy were particularly important in the conflict's opening stage, as the Anglosphere sought to frame unfolding events and storify a conflict centred on the known and familiar protagonist of the liberal revolutionary – the frequently cast and supported character of liberal, progressive history.[113]

On the ground, even at this early stage of the conflict, a number of the future directions of the civil war were already becoming apparent. First, supplies of funding and non-lethal aid to opposition forces, along with the explicit recognition of the SNC, contrasted Russia's supply of lethal munitions to Syria.[114] The fissures running through the heart of the UNSC – the international divide between the P3 and P2 – was evident in the first few weeks and months of the Syrian crisis and had solidified by the summer of 2012. It would go on to structure and shape the more explicit proxy war to come. Second, as displaced Syrians fled the country, the first refugee camps were set up in neighbouring states, such as Jordan and Lebanon, where tens of thousands of Syrian men, women and children sought refuge from the intensifying conflict.[115] Third, from January 2012, Abu Mohammed al-Jawlani began building the al-Nusra Front into a formidable opposition group, having been sent by al-Baghdadi from Iraq to Syria. Jawlani stayed loyal to Al Qaeda, causing a split with ISIL, which set the ground for

---

[113] X. Mathieu and J. Holland, 'Liberal storytelling and its illiberal consequences in Syria', Working paper.

[114] For example, R. Sherlock, 'US enlists Britain's help to stop ship "carrying Russian attack helicopters" to Syria', *The Telegraph*, 16 June 2012, www.telegraph.co.uk/news/worldnews/middleeast/syria/9336170/US-enlists-Britains-help-to-stop-ship-carrying-Russian-attack-helicopters-to-Syria.html

[115] By 2017, nearly five million Syrian refugees were spread across just five countries: Jordan, Lebanon, Egypt, Turkey and Iraq.

the fractured landscape of Islamist opposition forces that would fill the
vacuum left as the FSA declined (see Chapter 6).[116] What is clear, then,
is that the first phase of the Syrian crisis was crucial in several respects
and it never really ended. But, from August 2012, the leader of the free
world and the Anglosphere changed the nature of the crisis, for the
watching world at least.

[116] A. Zelin, 'Al-Qaeda in Syria: a closer look at ISIS', *Washington Institute*,
10 September 2013, www.washingtoninstitute.org/policy-analysis/view/al-
qaeda-in-syria-a-closer-look-at-isis-part-i

5 | Chemical Weapons

...a red line for us is we start seeing a whole bunch of chemical weapons moving around or being utilized.

President Obama[1]

Introduction

To see the names of all the children killed in Syria since 2011 would take you over nineteen hours.[2] Civilian casualties peaked in the conflict's second phase, from the summer of 2012 and into 2013. And the spectre of child fatalities was significant for Anglosphere foreign policy. The civilian death toll in this period was derived from three principal direct sources – guns, mortar fire and airstrikes – as well as the indirect consequences of conflict and displacement. Casualties from guns and mortars peaked in late summer 2012, with airstrikes also commencing at that time, as the Assad regime struggled to retain a semblance of control amidst the conflict. At the end of 2012, a fourth cause of death was added to the lethal mix: chemical weapons. Obama had explicitly warned against such developments. Through the spring, Assad repeatedly pushed against Obama's red line, until, in August 2013, one year after Obama's warning, videos emerged from Ghouta showing the deaths of more than 1,000 Syrian civilians, of all ages, choked by the effects of sarin gas. The videos were widely covered in the international media and condemned by world leaders.

Why, 'among all the ominous technologies of weaponry throughout the history of warfare', do 'chemical weapons carry a special moral stigma'?[3] The twentieth century saw the 'standardisation' of a range of

[1] B. Obama, 'Remarks by the President to the White House press corps', 20 August 2012.
[2] BBC News, 'Life and death in Syria', 15 March 2016, www.bbc.co.uk/news/resources/idt-841ebc3a-1be9-493b-8800-2c04890e8fc9
[3] R. Price, *The Chemical Weapons Taboo* (Ithaca: Cornell University Press, 1997).

terrible and lethal weaponry – the tank, strategic bombing, submarines – and yet chemical weapons have come to be understood as somehow *beyond humanity*.[4] Their use is widely seen as more than morally reprehensible: resorting to chemical weapons is frequently spoken of as being utterly contemptible. The prohibition on the use of chemical weapons in warfare has become viewed as a marker of humanity's common commitment to remaining human, even in the most troubled of times, such that their use has been rendered an act of uncivilised barbarism and, therefore, off limits.[5] By mutually agreed international norms, standards and laws, killing in warfare is understood as both permissible and necessary. But *how* you kill your enemies matters. As Price argues, there is no natural or chromosomal aversion to chemical weapons, compared with nuclear weapons or cutting steel; rather, the world's animosity towards the use of chemical weapons is political and constructed. Following repeated efforts to prevent their use, Price argues that the norm of such weapons being beyond the pale has become increasingly normalised and strongly held – what he terms, the 'increasing robustness of the taboo'. The result has been the development of a particularly coercive discourse: 'no longer is it acceptable to openly question the interpretation of chemical as abominable weapons'.[6]

This chapter explores the force of this norm, and its associated rhetoric, narratives and discourse, as the Anglosphere teetered on the brink of militarily confronting Assad in the summer of 2013. In particular, the chapter examines the strategic invocation, manipulation and avoidance of the chemical weapons norm – what Bentley has termed 'the exploitation of the forbidden'.[7] To do so, the chapter is structured in three parts. First, the chapter retraces the surprising language used by Barack Obama in August 2012, which shifted the world's focus and the nature of the Syrian crisis away from democracy promotion and towards chemical weapons use. Second, the chapter explores the dynamics of rhetorical entrapment and rhetorical coercion that Obama's infamous 'red line' initiated. Third, the chapter analyses the discursive war of position, which took place across the

[4] Ibid.
[5] R. Price, 'A genealogy of the chemical weapons taboo', *International Organization*, 49 (1995), 73–103.
[6] Price, *The Chemical Weapons Taboo*, p. 13.
[7] M. Bentley, *Syria and the Chemical Weapons Taboo: Exploiting the Forbidden* (Manchester: Manchester University Press, 2016).

transnational space of the Anglosphere during this second phase, from August 2012 to the end of 2013. This builds on the preceding chapter's analysis of calls for democracy and provides the context for Chapter 6, which explores the Anglosphere's shocked response to the rise of Islamic State – a new game-changing development in the Syrian crisis and civil war.

Red Lines and Rhetorical Entrapment

In July 2012, Obama warned that the Assad regime would 'be held accountable by the international community and the US, should they make the tragic mistake of using those weapons'.[8] The statement followed Syria's first public admission of the possession of chemical weapons, by the foreign minister, Jihad Makdissi. He warned that the stockpile would potentially see use 'in case of external aggression'.[9] In short, Assad was warning the international community against military involvement. Syria's chemical weapons had initially been procured as a deterrent against Israel (see Chapter 1); now, they were being used to deter the international community and, in particular, the United States and the Anglosphere. Israel and Jordan had already raised concerns that these weapons might be used in the event of Syria's further deterioration. And the defecting former Syrian ambassador to Iraq Nawaf Fares confirmed that the regime would have no hesitation in turning to chemical weapons in an effort to secure its survival.[10]

The following month, President Obama built significantly upon his July statements, explicitly giving voice to world and American fears with a turn of phrase that would initiate the reframing of the Syrian Civil War. When asked by a journalist at a White House press conference, the US President made a clear and explicit commitment to keeping the use of chemical weapons out of bounds, even for an authoritarian government engaged in a protracted and existential civil war.

---

[8] BBC News, 'Syria chemical weapons: Obama says world is watching', 23 July 2012, www.bbc.co.uk/news/world-middle-east-18963720
[9] Ibid.
[10] BBC News, 'Syria: Assad regime "ready to use chemical weapons"', 17 July 2012, www.bbc.co.uk/news/world-middle-east-18864629

I have, at this point, not ordered military engagement in the situation. But the point that you made about chemical and biological weapons is critical. That's an issue that doesn't just concern Syria; it concerns our close allies in the region, including Israel. It concerns us. We cannot have a situation where chemical or biological weapons are falling into the hands of the wrong people.

We have been very clear to the Assad regime, but also to other players on the ground, that a red line for us is we start seeing a whole bunch of chemical weapons moving around or being utilized. That would change my calculus. That would change my equation.[11]

The strong, unscripted language came 'to the surprise of some of the advisers' who had attended weekend meetings devising a strategy for the tough but flexible rhetorical coercion of Assad.[12] The administration had been focused on dissuading Assad from using chemical weapons, via a series of intermediaries, following intelligence reports that this was an increasing possibility.[13] Key advisers were therefore wondering where exactly the 'red line' had come from.[14] It was certainly a resonant and 'evocative phrase', which 'embedded in people's prefrontal cortex'.[15] And the media seized upon it.

For some, it was clear 'the president had defined his policy', through uncharacteristically ill-prepared remarks, 'in a way some advisers wish [ed] they could take back'.[16] The phrase moved the USA closer to Obama's least-favoured course of action: another military intervention in the Middle East. Others, however, moved to back up the Commander in Chief. The following day, White House Spokesperson Josh Earnest clarified the president's remarks:

As the President said yesterday in terms of Syria, we're watching very closely the stockpile of Syrian chemical weapons; that any use or proliferation of efforts related to those chemical weapons is something that would be very serious and it would be a grave mistake.

[11] B. Obama, 'Remarks by the President to the White House press corps', 20 August 2012.
[12] G. Kessler, 'President Obama and the "red line" on Syria's chemical weapons', 6 September 2013, www.washingtonpost.com/news/fact-checker/wp/2013/09/06/president-obama-and-the-red-line-on-syrias-chemical-weapons; see also Baker et al., 'Off-the-cuff Obama'.
[13] Baker et al., 'Off-the-cuff Obama'.
[14] Kessler, 'President Obama and the "red line"'; Baker et al., 'Off-the-cuff Obama'.
[15] Ibid.   [16] Kessler, 'President Obama and the "red line"'.

There are important international obligations that the Syrian regime must live up to in terms of the handling of their chemical weapons. And the officials who have that responsibility will be held accountable for their actions and will be held accountable for living up to those international obligations.[17]

For 'better or worse', *The Washington Post* noted that the 'red line' 'was in place'[18] and it was clear, according to *The New York Times*, that the phrase placed the administration in a 'bind'.[19] Once uttered, the red line was hard to roll back. All the Obama administration could do was wait for its potential and likely transgression.

As detailed in Chapter 1, over the coming months, Obama's red line was crossed repeatedly; chemical weapons use continued, just as it had in the months leading up to Obama's announcement.[20] In October 2012, the French raised concerns that chemical weapons had been used in Idlib province, but upon later investigation, insufficient evidence was retrieved for United Nations verification. In December, however, a number of sources confirmed the use of Agent 15 in Homs. It was clear to the US administration that Obama's red line was being tested.[21] As a test, it was successful. The Obama administration played down the reports and the Chairman of the Joint Chiefs of Staff General Martin Dempsey noted that Obama's red line, like America's foreign policy position, was one of deterrence rather than forcible preventative action.[22] But, if it was supposed to be a deterrent, it was clearly not working.

Pontificating to Peace

In March, April and May of 2013, a series of chemical weapons attacks forced the US president to reiterate his red line and the

---

[17] Ibid.   [18] Ibid.   [19] Baker et al., 'Off-the-cuff Obama'.

[20] Bentley, *Syria and the Chemical Weapons Taboo*.

[21] Rogin, 'Exclusive: secret State Department cable'.

[22] He argued that, 'The president was very clear when he said that if the Assad regime makes the tragic mistake of using chemical weapons, or fails to meet its obligation to secure them, the regime will be held accountable... Syria must understand by now that the use of chemical weapons is unacceptable. And to that extent, it provides a deterrent value.' See M. Gordon, 'Consulate supported claim of Syria gas attack, report says', *New York Times*, 15 January 2013, www.nytimes.com/2013/01/16/world/middleeast/consulate-said-to-support-claim-of-syrian-gas-attack.html?_r=1

consequences of its crossing. In Aleppo, Damascus and Sanaqueb (east of Idlib), amongst numerous other towns, reports emerged of chlorine and sarin gas being used.[23] These incidents reignited US presidential and congressional concerns, with Senators McCain and Levin pushing the Obama administration to confirm and address the issue of Assad's use of chemical weapons. Again, McCain and Graham argued for stronger US action, insisting that 'U.S. credibility is on the line... Now is not the time to merely take the next incremental step. Now is the time for more decisive actions'.[24] The Obama administration investigated the allegations of Assad's use of chemical weapons and, true to form, the president reached a 'gradual' decision as the evidence came in.[25] As CNN reported, the Syrian regime had crossed Obama's red line.[26] Ben Rhodes confirmed that 'following a deliberative review' of 'multiple, independent streams of information', the US 'intelligence community' has assessed 'that the Assad regime has used chemical weapons, including the nerve agent sarin, on a small scale against the opposition multiple times in the last year'.[27] He stressed, the 'president has said that the use of chemical weapons would change his calculus and it has'. The 'scale and scope' of support to opposition forces was to alter as a result: the US was about to arm the rebels, providing lethal rather than non-lethal aid.

From late 2012, the CIA had been training Syrian rebels to use anti-tank and anti-aircraft weapons in Jordan and Turkey. This effort was significantly expanded at the start of 2013. Actionable intelligence was now being supplied to select rebels in Syria, alongside lethal and non-lethal 'targeting packages'; a significant step up from the 'Meals Ready to Eat' that had previously been supplied.[28] However, the war of

---

[23] See Chapter 1 for details.

[24] K. DeYoung and A. Gearing, 'U.S., citing use of chemical weapons by Syria, to provide direct military support to rebels', *Washington Post*, 13 June 2013, www.washingtonpost.com/world/national-security/us-concludes-syrian-forces-used-chemical-weapons/2013/06/13/59b03c66-d46d-11e2-a73e-826d299ff459_story.html

[25] Ibid.

[26] B. Starr, J. Yellin and C. Carter, 'White House: Syria crosses "red line" with use of chemical weapons on its people', *CNN*, 14 June 2013, http://edition.cnn.com/2013/06/13/politics/syria-us-chemical-weapons

[27] DeYoung and Gearing, 'U.S., citing use of chemical weapons by Syria'.

[28] Harvard-Belfer on Syria, Belfer Center, Harvard University, http://belfercenter.ksg.harvard.edu/syria/infographics/syria_timeline.html

position continued to rage inside the Obama White House.[29] The principal division was over the nature of aid. On one side, Ambassador Rob Ford led the charge for the supply of Stinger missiles and rocket-propelled grenades. He was vociferously supported by the likes of CIA Director David Petraeus, Secretary of State Hillary Clinton and Director of the Defence Intelligence Agency Michael Flynn. For Flynn, the 'mother-may-I' process of acquiring 'fifteen bullets a month' reflected the 'completely choked' nature of the DC decision-making bureaucracy.[30] On the other side of the debate, Obama held firm, with little regard for the morality of either position, asking only, 'Will it work?'[31] If Obama already cut a relatively isolated figure, in the face of bipartisan calls for the USA to do more, it was only a pale foreshadowing of the situation that was about to unfold. Jeff Goldberg has noted that 'Obama's caution on Syria has vexed those in the administration who have seen opportunities, at different moments over the past four years, to tilt the battlefield against Assad'.[32] This moment, in the Syrian Civil War's second phase, was perhaps *the* clearest window for greater US action targeted at the conflict's true epicentre: the forces of the beleaguered and embattled Syrian government.

Following repeated evidence of chemical weapons attacks, the UN dispatched a team to Syria in order to investigate one of the spring incidents, in a suburb of Aleppo. They ended up far closer to the war's new focal point than anticipated. In an ironic twist of fate, while they were on the ground in Damascus, Syria's use of chemical weapons was about to ramp up significantly and to such an extent that it would attract the world's focus. As has been detailed in Chapter 1, in August 2013, in Ghouta, eastern Damascus, a series of sarin gas attacks took place, killing more than 1,000 civilians. The attacks were a chilling and graphic reminder of exactly why it is that chemical weapons remain a taboo. Faced with YouTube footage of asphyxiated children, *The Economist* asked, 'If this isn't a red line, what is?' The Obama administration, it seemed, agreed.[33] John Kerry joined more hawkish voices, arguing strongly for intervention:

---

[29] T. McKelvey, 'Arming Syrian rebels: where the US went wrong', *BBC News*, 10 October 2015, www.bbc.co.uk/news/magazine-33997408
[30] Ibid. [31] Ibid. [32] Ibid.
[33] Only Denis McDonough 'cautioned explicitly about the perils' of US military action. Goldberg, 'The Obama doctrine'.

As previous storms in history have gathered, when unspeakable crimes were within our power to stop them, we have been warned against the temptations of looking the other way. . . History is full of leaders who have warned against inaction, indifference and especially against silence when it mattered most.[34]

In opposition to Kerry and Samantha Power, Obama repeated the closest thing the administration had to an organising principle for foreign policy: don't do stupid shit. To the president, the potential for the USA to get bogged down in Syria looked every bit as real as it had been for his predecessor in Iraq. Mission creep, for Obama, was a likely consequence of any military solution. Certainty, or something broadly approximating it, was therefore a prerequisite for action. It is thus quite possible to suggest that it was in fact Obama's bright red line that stood out as an aberration, not his continued recalcitrance after Ghouta. Fortunately for the US President, the Anglosphere was giving him pause for thought amidst the headlong rush to war.

On a Friday evening in late August 2013, Obama took a stroll on the South Lawn of the White House with his most like-minded, anti-interventionist adviser, Chief of Staff Denis McDonough.[35] It was an important moment for the president, for the USA, for the Anglosphere and for Syria. Since the chemical weapons assault on Ghouta a week earlier, Obama had considered and entertained the likelihood of direct military intervention in Syria in the form of US-led coalition airstrikes. He had, however, just seen former British Prime Minister David Cameron lose a vote in the House of Commons that would have authorised UK participation in coalition action. Obama defaulted to his instinctive foreign policy position: a scepticism of the legitimacy, necessity and efficacy of US military action abroad,[36] as well as a deep concern regarding its implications for the domestic political landscape.[37] In this moment, the US foreign policy process witnessed

---

[34] Kerry cited in Goldberg, 'The Obama doctrine'.

[35] C. Todd, 'The White House walk-and-talk that changed Obama's mind on Syria', *NBC News*, 31 August 2013, www.nbcnews.com/news/other/white-house-walk-talk-changed-obamas-mind-syria-f8C11051182

[36] A. Quinn, 'US decline and systemic constraint' in *Obama's Foreign Policy: Ending the War on Terror* , p. 45; Quinn, 'Restraint and constraint: a cautious president in a time of limits' in *The Obama Doctrine: A Foreign Policy Legacy of Continuity?*, p. 26.

[37] Holland, 'Obama as modern Jeffersonian', pp. 40–53.

an acute concentration of agency in the hands of the president, as his thinking reverted to a position opposed to, what he termed, 'the blob' of Washington DC 'Beltway' consensus.[38]

As 'American destroyers armed with Tomahawk missiles waited in the Mediterranean Sea', Obama told reporters gathered in the White House Rose Garden that he was prepared to give the order, authorising airstrikes against Assad's forces.[39] 'But', he added, 'having made my decision as Commander in Chief based on what I am convinced is our national security interests, I'm also mindful that I'm the president of the world's oldest constitutional democracy.'[40] Obama would seek approval for airstrikes from a sceptical Republican-majority Congress. As the *New York Times* noted, he was effectively daring 'lawmakers to either stand by him or, as he put it, allow President Bashar al-Assad of Syria to get away with murdering children with unconventional weapons'.[41] However, the lack of a UN mandate – given Russia and China's position – and recent events in Westminster had given the president pause for thought. Putting the case for airstrikes to parliament, Cameron suffered a narrow shock defeat in the House of Commons, failing to secure a mandate for military intervention. As in the USA, the British domestic political landscape was fractured, with significant opposition to airstrikes across and within parties. The net effect for Obama was one of further isolation, as his red line appeared to move him into a vulnerable and apparently lonely position from which he was forced to act unilaterally and reluctantly, in a manner at odds with many of his previous foreign policy pronouncements and positions.[42] The decision to seek Congressional approval should therefore be read as an attempt, first, at strategic delay and, second, to seek political cover.[43]

---

[38] Goldberg, 'The Obama doctrine'.

[39] Baker and Weisman, 'Obama seeks approval by Congress for strike in Syria'.

[40] Ibid.   [41] Ibid.

[42] I have made this argument in two edited books, although most explicitly in the chapter, Holland, 'Obama as modern Jeffersonian'; see also Holland, 'Obama's War on Terror: why is change so hard?'; and Holland and Bentley, 'Conceptualising change and continuity in US foreign policy'. See also the many other excellent contributions to *The Obama Doctrine* and *Obama's Foreign Policy: Ending the War on Terror*.

[43] For a competing explanation focused on the debilitating role played by having competing voices and opinions in Obama's inner circle, see A. Mintz and C. Wayne, *The Polythink Syndrome: U.S. Foreign Policy Decisions on 9/11, Afghanistan, Iraq, Iran, Syria, and ISIS* (Stanford: Stanford University Press, 2016).

Although the congressional debate took place, the vote was postponed long enough for an unlikely, uncoordinated and unintentional double act to reframe the debate and offer a way out of the controversial policy, thus avoiding the potential for an unprecedented congressional rejection of a president's decision to use military force. The first half of that double act was US Foreign Secretary John Kerry, who was visiting the UK to rally international support for military intervention. When asked by a reporter if there was any way that Assad could avert airstrikes, an apparently exasperated Kerry replied, 'Sure, he could turn over every single bit of his chemical weapons to the international community in the next week – turn it over, all of it without delay and allow the full and total accounting (of it).'[44] The second half of the double act was Russian Foreign Secretary Sergei Lavrov, who seized upon the comments, responding that such an outcome was possible and would have international backing whilst avoiding further conflict. Obama's weak domestic position and reluctance to act encouraged the US administration to back the Russian plan, giving all sides breathing space, including Assad.[45] With Moscow and Damascus holding the 'diplomatic whip-hand', Obama had willingly folded, reneging on his red line in favour of a 'diplomatic game of cat and mouse' that avoided committing the US military to action in Syria.[46]

The US administration moved quickly to confirm the validity of Moscow's plan and hailed it as a significant breakthrough.[47] When American additions were made, the Russian-initiated plan comprised four principal components: full disclosure of chemical weapons capabilities; the destruction of all chemical weapons facilities; the removal of all chemical weapons from Syria; and signing up to the CWC. This would be enforced through a UN Security Council Resolution and the Organisation for the Prohibition of Chemical Weapons. The inspection

---

[44] Kerry, 'Remarks with UK Foreign Secretary William Hague'; see also Alexander, 'Syria: if Bashar al-Assad hands over chemical weapons we will not attack, says John Kerry'.

[45] P. Foster, 'Syria crisis: Obama entertaining Russian-led peace-for-weapons plan reflects weak domestic position', *The Telegraph*, 10 September 2013, www.telegraph.co.uk/news/worldnews/barackobama/10297820/Syria-crisis-Obama-entertaining-Russian-led-peace-for-weapons-plan-reflects-weak-domestic-position.html

[46] Ibid.

[47] Gordon and Myers, 'Obama calls Russia offer on Syria possible "breakthrough"'.

and destruction programme commenced in October 2013. And, although likely partial and incomplete, these efforts were sufficient to avert US and UK airstrikes. The Anglosphere, thanks to Kerry's meandering thought process, had pontificated to peace. But it had done so as one, with arguments on war and peace crossing national borders as the debate ebbed and flowed through a monolingual, transnational space.

Notwithstanding the importance of Kerry's answer and Russia's instrumental seizing of it, in America, Britain and Australia, war's avoidance relied primarily upon the discursive contestations that took place within a war of position which operated domestically and transnationally. In each instance, opposition parties and politicians were important as part of a fierce national debate on foreign policy. In the USA, Obama narrowly avoided a reluctant intervention when faced with near-unanimous calls for action from Beltway experts that he himself had helped to generate in an act of rhetorical self-entrapment. Ensnared in his own red line, the 'blob' of Beltway consensus had descended upon the president, concentrating the agency of consensus opposition in his hands, as he wrestled with his personal concerns regarding war's efficacy. In the UK, Cameron suffered an unexpected defeat in the Commons, which had been discursively spearheaded by Labour's opposition. Backbench fears of mission creep, in the shadow of Iraq, outweighed ministerial calls to do *something*. And, in Australia, Kevin Rudd lost the prime ministership to Tony Abbott, who warned that there were simply no good options to promote in Syria, meaning that it might be better to do nothing at all. In each instance, these arguments did not remain exclusively national. Abbott's line was picked up in the UK parliament, where it helped to sustain opposition to intervention, which would ultimately colour Obama's thinking as he stepped back from the brink of war. The formulation of Anglosphere foreign policy was intimately connected across the USA, UK and Australia.

Debate, Division and Diplomacy

Depending upon your retrospective position, August 2013 was either the closest the Anglosphere came to another Middle Eastern folly, or the closest the coalition came to taking action that could have shortened the suffering of the Syrian Civil War. Either way, that month serves as a clear and useful example of the instrumentality that under-pinned decision-making regarding the use of political rhetoric intended to impact broader competing discourses. After Ghouta, Obama's use of emotional and emotive language indicated his initial resolve that US military action was likely, probably necessary and potentially inevitable. In contrast to his relative strategic silence on the issue of chemical weapons in 2011 and 2012, after witnessing the atrocities of Ghouta, Obama spoke explicitly and persuasively about the devastating costs of chemical warfare. Now, he opted to repeatedly 'draw attention to the horrific physical and psychological consequences associated with chemical weapons and specifically the "appalling violence being inflicted on the Syrian people"'.[48] To mobilise support for his (temporary) cause, Obama spoke frequently and deliberately of child fatalities: 'This kind of attack is a challenge to the world. We cannot accept a world where women and children and innocent civilians are gassed on a terrible scale.'[49]

The images from this massacre are sickening: men, women, children, lying in rows, killed by poison gas; others foaming at the mouth, gasping for breath; a father clutching his dead children, imploring them to get up and walk.[50]

And, even when buying time, he asked of Congress:

Here's my question for every Member of Congress and every member of the global community: what message will we send if a dictator can gas hundreds of children to death in plain sight and pay no price?[51]

It was a theme he reiterated when seeking further political cover, in the form of a UN Security Council resolution:

And if we end up using the UN Security Council not as a means of enforcing international norms and international law, but rather as a barrier to acting

---

[48] B. Obama, 'The President's news conference with Prime Minister John Fredrik Reinfedlt of Sweden in Stockholm, Sweden: September 4', CPD (2013), www.gpo.gov/fdsys/pkg/DCPD-201300599/pdf/DCPD-201300599.pdf

[49] B. Obama, 'Remarks prior to a meeting with President Toomas H. Ilves of Estonia, President Andris Berzins of Latvia, and President Dalia Grybauskaite of Lithuania and an exchange with reporters', CPD (2013), www.gpo.gov/fdsys/pkg/DCPD-201300583/pdf/DCPD-201300583.pdf

[50] B. Obama, 'Address to the nation on the situation on Syria: September 10', CPD (2013), www.gpo.gov/fdsys/pkg/DCPD-201300615/pdf/DCPD-201300615.pdf

[51] B. Obama, 'Remarks on the situation in Syria: August 31', CPD (2013), www.gpo.gov/fdsys/pkg/DCPD-201300596/pdf/DCPD-201300596.pdf

on behalf of international norms and international law, then I think people, rightly, are going to be pretty sceptical about the system and whether it can work to protect those children that we saw in those videos.[52]

As one Russian news outlet noted, in August 2013, it appeared that the usually risk and war-averse Obama had trapped himself on a path which led unavoidably towards Syrian combat.[53] Indeed, inspired by the president's red line, the cacophony of voices inside the United States calling for action had reached something of a crescendo – as *USA Today* noted in calling for war, with the astute observation that, on the back of the president's rhetorical entrapment and the force of the chemical taboo, 'doing nothing isn't an option'.[54] Likewise, in the Senate, Lindsey Graham could no longer imagine Obama *not* launching military strikes.[55] While opponents to military action were increasingly few and far between, some remained. For instance, Senate Majority Leader Mitch McConnell was the first congressional leader to oppose the administration's plan for air strikes.[56] And, ultimately, despite the forcefulness and emotive nature of his rhetoric, Obama doubted the efficacy of intervention. His instincts were far from hawkish on Syria, and his doubts had been significantly reinforced by the war of position taking place across the Anglo-sphere. As unlikely as it sounds, UK Leader of the Opposition Ed Miliband – a politician renowned for struggling to eat a bacon sandwich – had helped to clip the wings of the greatest military force the world has ever known.

[52] B. Obama, 'The President's news conference in St. Petersburg, Russia: September 6', CPD (2013), www.gpo.gov/fdsys/pkg/DCPD-201300606/pdf/DCPD-201300606.pdf

[53] P. Escobar, '"War on chemical weapons": Obama traps himself into Syrian combat', *Russia Today*, 28 August 2015, www.rt.com/op-edge/war-chemical-weapons-obama-syria-120

[54] Editorial Board, 'Syrian chemical attack demands precise strike: our view', *USA Today*, 26 August 2013, www.usatoday.com/story/opinion/2013/08/26/syria-chemical-attack-obama-red-line-editorials-debates/2704003

[55] L. Graham @LindseyGrahamSC (11 September 2013). 'After this impassioned plea I cannot imagine Pres Obama not launching military strike if diplomacy fails, regardless of what Congress does.' He then added, 'You cannot make moral case as the leader of the Free World and then refuse to act if diplomacy fails.'

[56] R. Sanchez, 'As it happened: Barack Obama speech on Syria', *The Telegraph*, 11 September 2013, www.telegraph.co.uk/news/worldnews/middleeast/syria/10288193/As-it-happened-Barack-Obama-speech-on-Syria.html

On 29 August, the British parliament took the unusual decision to reject the prime minister's and the government's call for military intervention in response to Ghouta.[57] The vote in the House of Commons was 285 against versus 272 in support of military action, indicating how finely balanced the march to war had become in the UK and across the Anglosphere. The government's surprise and anger at the defeat was reflected in the words of one source, who accused the Leader of the Opposition of 'buggering about' and 'playing politics'.[58] The debate laid bare the discursive war of position undergirding UK – and broader Anglosphere – policies of war and peace. While Ed Miliband's case for (at the very least) delaying the rush to war was nuanced (and potentially contradictory), it hinged first and foremost on the complexity of the conflict, the inevitable drawing in of UK forces into that complexity, and the immediate legacy of recent intractable conflict in Iraq.[59] As one MP interrupted him to note, Blair's legacy and the quagmire of Iraq loomed large over the debate in the House: 'I very much welcome the Right Honourable Gentleman's doctrine that evidence should precede decision; that is a stark change from at least one of his predecessors.'[60] When pushed, Miliband confirmed that his position was arrived at, in part, due to Iraq's twin lessons: the importance of evidence and international law.

If people are asking me today to say, 'Yes, now, let us take military action,' I am not going to say that, but neither am I going to rule out military action, because we have to proceed on the basis of evidence and the consensus and support that can be built...

---

[57] For a good analysis of how this is unusual and the political pressures such a process subjects foreign policy to, see J. Strong, 'Interpreting the Syria vote: parliament and British foreign policy', *International Affairs*, 91 (2015), 1123–39; and J. Strong, 'Why parliament now decides on war: tracing the growth of the parliamentary prerogative through Syria, Libya and Iraq', *British Journal of Politics and International Relations*, 17 (2015), 604–22. The latter in particular highlights Cameron's misplaced certainty of success for the vote.

[58] T. Helm, 'No 10 launches bitter assault on Ed Miliband over Syria vote', *The Guardian*, 31 August 2013, www.theguardian.com/politics/2013/aug/31/syria-commons-vote-cameron-miliband

[59] See, for example, on the legacy of Iraq for the UK debate in particular (as well as discussion of the importance of historical analogy), J. Kaarbo and D. Kenealy, 'Precedents, parliaments and foreign policy: historical analogy in the House of Commons vote on Syria', *West European Politics*, 40 (2016), 62–79.

[60] M. Horwood, *Hansard*, 29 August 2013, www.publications.parliament.uk/pa/cm201314/cmhansrd/cm130829/debtext/130829-0001.htm

we have to assess in a calm and measured way – not in a knee-jerk way and not on a political timetable – the advantages of potential action, whether such action can be taken on the basis of legitimacy and international law and what the consequences would be.[61]

Despite the presentational nuances designed to avert criticism, the consequences for the parliamentary vote were clear: the Leader of the Opposition was 'effectively making a strong case against military action'.[62] Support for Labour's position was generally informed by Iraq's legacy. Paul Flynn and Richard Bacon, for example, emphasised the *political* as well as intelligence failure that led to the 2003 intervention.[63] And former Foreign Secretary Jack Straw and Tessa Jowell noted their own roles in helping to achieve a significant parliamentary victory in the vote authorising the 2003 war in Iraq, which had done so much to undermine public faith in the political process.[64] Ultimately, as John McDonnell noted, 'We have all been left scarred by Iraq.'[65]

Once again, these two discourses acted as 'the main convectors of discussion', or 'the key points of structuring disagreement within' the debate and its lead up.[66] On one side of the debate, a tradition of liberal internationalism continued from the 2011–12 period in which calls for democracy were applauded and its realisation assumed inevitable.[67] In this view, the chemical weapons case stood in isolation and could be cleaved off from the broader complexities of the Syrian Civil War: while Assad would inevitably fall without UK intervention, limited airstrikes were paramount to sustain the chemical weapons taboo. On the other side of the debate, the broad concern surrounding Iraq's lessons and legacy structured a narrower fear that since 'Syria is not Libya' it could potentially be another quagmire in the Middle East.

[61] E. Miliband, *Hansard*, 29 August 2013, www.publications.parliament.uk/pa/cm201314/cmhansrd/cm130829/debtext/130829-0001.htm

[62] C. Blunt, *Hansard*, 29 August 2013, www.publications.parliament.uk/pa/cm201314/cmhansrd/cm130829/debtext/130829-0001.htm

[63] P. Flynn; R. Bacon, *Hansard*, 29 August 2013, www.publications.parliament.uk/pa/cm201314/cmhansrd/cm130829/debtext/130829-0001.htm

[64] J. Straw; T. Jowell, *Hansard*, 29 August 2013, www.publications.parliament.uk/pa/cm201314/cmhansrd/cm130829/debtext/130829-0001.htm

[65] J. McDonnell, *Hansard*, 29 August 2013, www.publications.parliament.uk/pa/cm201314/cmhansrd/cm130829/debtext/130829-0001.htm

[66] Ralph et al., 'Before the vote'; Hansen, *Security as Practice*, pp. 52, 95.

[67] Ibid.

As David Davis put it, the 'clear moral imperative... to take military action in Libya [... because] if we had not acted, tens of thousands of lives would quickly have been lost... does not stand in the action we are countenancing [in Syria]'.[68] This discourse was sustained by a tradition of conservative realism, emphasising and prioritising prudence over rapid responses to morally outrageous events.[69] In the end, the spectre of Iraq ensured that conservative realism won out; the desire to avoid repeating an illegal and immoral war tempered the optimism of a broader Arab Spring discourse that had already begun to run aground, given the unexpected resilience of the Assad regime and the increasing fragmentation of rebel forces.

These discursive positions were replicated in Australia, where foreign policy towards Syria was significantly overshadowed by domestic political turmoil, as Julia Gillard was ousted by Kevin Rudd at the third attempt in June, before he lost the September 2013 general election to Tony Abbott. Rudd's second tenure at the top may have lasted less than three months, but it included the period in which the terrible events of Ghouta unfolded and the Anglosphere appeared, momentarily, to be heading for war. The election was primarily fought on economic and immigration issues, and was marked by voter fatigue with the return of Rudd and continued Labor infighting. Where foreign policy featured, it was usually focused on the Asia-Pacific, economic relations and the perennial topic of 'boat people'. However, Rudd went out of his way to express solidarity with the US position, leaning towards airstrikes, confident that sufficient evidence placed guilt at Assad's door.[70] His preferred narratives continued his predecessor Julia Gillard's robust language over the previous twelve months, which emphasised Australia's international activism and the need for a strong response in Syria.[71]

---

[68] D. Davis, *Hansard*, 29 August 2013, www.publications.parliament.uk/pa/cm201314/cmhansrd/cm130829/debtext/130829-0001.htm

[69] Ibid.

[70] L. Taylor. 'Syria: Kevin Rudd backs "robust response" over chemical weapons', *The Guardian*, 29 August 2013, www.theguardian.com/world/2013/aug/29/syria-rudd-un-security-council-australian-election

[71] See, for example, Gillard's UN address: S. Benson, 'PM Julia Gillard's tough action call wins United Nations support', *The Australian*, 27 September 2012, www.theaustralian.com.au/news/julia-gillard-arrives-for-un-address/story-e6frg6n6-1226482215413; ABC News, 'Gillard addresses UN General Assembly', 27 September 2012, www.abc.net.au/news/2012-09-27/gillard-addresses-un-general-assembly/4282652?pfmredir=sm

In contrast and direct discursive competition, Tony Abbott picked up on a growing sub-discourse that had emerged in the USA and UK: the notion that, with the decline of moderate rebel forces, there were no longer any good options in Syria. Abbott's preferred phrasing of this position, however, attracted ridicule amidst the context of partisan electoral advantage. Abbott opted to describe Syria, in colloquial terms, as 'baddies versus baddies':[72]

It's not goodies versus baddies, it's baddies versus baddies and that's why it's very important that we don't make a very difficult situation worse.[73]

In response, the prime minister, Kevin Rudd, 'a Mandarin-speaking former diplomat' noted that he had not used such terms since he was a child, and likened Abbott's foreign policy language to the John Wayne School of International Relations.[74] In case anybody had not realised, he pointed out that 'International relations is more complex than a 1950s John Wayne western.'[75]

Although simplistic, Abbott's position mirrored that of more hard-line UK conservatives, such as former Defence Secretary Liam Fox, who noted that 'there is no national interest for the United Kingdom in taking a side in that civil war. To exchange an Iran-friendly and Hezbollah-friendly Assad regime for an anti-west, anti-Christian and anti-Israel Al Qaeda regime does not seem to offer us any advantage'.[76] And, it was not even so far removed from the British and American leaders who were now pushing for airstrikes. One opposition MP, George Brandis, made the point that while 'Abbott did use vernacular speech, it's the same sort of vernacular speech, by the way, that was used by Mr Cameron and President Obama in describing the Syrian

---

[72] It is worth noting that Abbott's framings were attuned to the will of the general public, despite appearing simplistic. As McDonald has noted, Abbott's foreign policy was very much about domestic politics, in a manner reminiscent, at times, of Bill Clinton. M. McDonald, 'Australian foreign policy under the Abbott government: foreign policy as domestic politics?', *Australian Journal of International Affairs*, 69 (2015), 651–69.

[73] J. Pearlman, 'Tony Abbott ridiculed after describing Syrian conflict as "baddies versus baddies"', *The Telegraph*, 2 September 2013, www.telegraph.co.uk/news/worldnews/australiaandthepacific/australia/10279817/Tony-Abbott-ridiculed-after-describing-Syrian-conflict-as-baddies-versus-baddies.html

[74] Ibid.   [75] Ibid.

[76] L. Fox, *Hansard*, 29 August 2013, www.publications.parliament.uk/pa/cm201314/cmhansrd/cm130829/debtext/130829-0001.htm

civil conflict at various times'.[77] Indeed, Cameron had argued as recently as July 2013 that 'you've got a lot of bad guys in Syria' and Obama had stressed that 'we know who the bad guys are'.[78] Shadow Foreign Affairs Minister Julie Bishop emphasised the point: 'What Tony Abbott was articulating is what many foreign policy analysts are saying: the situation in Syria is far more nuanced than the... world view of good versus evil; on both sides of this conflict are the bad guys.'[79] The more significant point was that, with reports of increasingly radical rebel fighters, Obama's certainty in knowing who the bad guys were was not shared on the other side of the Anglosphere debate. And this growing doubt had become a fully-fledged and supporting sub-discourse of the conservative realist case against intervention. The critics of official Anglosphere policy suggested that war should be avoided, even after Ghouta. And, ultimately, their concerns won out.

Conclusion

In the Syrian Civil War's second phase, from August 2012 to September 2013, the Anglosphere war of position continued a number of important themes established in the preceding eighteen months. First, the optimism of the Arab Spring discourse remained, with hope and belief that Assad would inevitably fall. Although this optimism was tempered by every instance of brutal regime violence, there remained a widespread notion that Syria's future could not and would not feature the dictator. Second, concerns grew that Syria was distinct from Libya, given the changing and protracted nature of the crisis and, in particular, the increasingly fragmented and radical nature of the rebel forces. This sub-discourse developed to become an important counterpoint to the optimism of the Arab Spring. It was bolstered by a number of other, broadly complementary sub-discourses. Principal among these was that if Syria was not Libya, it might just be another Iraq. This

---

[77] G. Brandis, *Hansard*, 29 August 2013, www.publications.parliament.uk/pa/cm201314/cmhansrd/cm130829/debtext/130829-0001.htm

[78] Ibid.

[79] B. Jabour, 'Kevin Rudd denounces Tony Abbott's "John Wayne" views on Syria', *The Guardian*, 2 September 2013, www.theguardian.com/world/2013/sep/02/kevin-rudd-tony-abbott-syria-australia-baddies. For a detailed analysis of these groups, their beliefs and their evolution, see C. R. Lister, *The Syrian Jihad: Al-Qaeda, the Islamic State and the Evolution of an Insurgency* (New York: Oxford University Press, 2016).

specific sub-discourse, within the broader overarching call to 'remember Iraq', was vital to the UK parliamentary decision to avoid conflict. Supporting sub-discourses also included the concern, most clearly expressed by Tony Abbott, that *all* sides of the Syrian Civil War were now bad options for the Anglosphere. And, finally, these were bolstered by a concern that Assad's strength and the conflict's complexity would make intervention very difficult, with mission creep a near certainty and military failure a distinct possibility. These (sub)discourses ebbed and flowed as they competed across the transnational space of the Anglosphere, helping to inform the outcome of the Australian general election, the UK government's unexpected parliamentary defeat and Obama's ultimate decision to delay intervention by referring to Congress.

That decision, like the discourses that underpinned it, was far-reaching. It not only averted intervention in the short term, but moreover made intervention more difficult in the long term. As Tierney, writing in *The Atlantic*, argued, the problem with focusing on chemical weapons was the potential for the preoccupation to make solving the Syrian Civil War even more challenging.[80] As he put it, 'If Assad agrees to forsake sarin, how can we intervene if he continues to slaughter civilians while technically playing by our rules?'[81] This amounted to a missed opportunity, never to be repeated. While there was 'no question that Obama escaped a seemingly impossible situation', via an unexpected diplomatic solution that offered 'a face-saving way to claim some success', it was nonetheless an outcome that left Syrians 'very much in the line of fire'.[82] As this chapter began by recounting, in Syria, in 2013, chemical weapons were a fourth direct cause of death.

The real weapons of mass destruction in Syria are conventional arms like artillery, guns and mortars... Guns and bombs are no less barbaric than gas... It's like telling Al Capone he can't murder people with a baseball bat – disappointing perhaps, but he does have other options.[83]

Tierney's prescient fear was that 'enforcing the chemical weapons taboo could have the perverse effect of encouraging brutality against

---

[80] D. Tierney, 'Syria's 99 percent: the problem with focusing on chemical weapons', *The Atlantic*, 12 September 2013, www.theatlantic.com/international/archive/2013/09/syrias-99-percent-the-problem-with-focusing-on-chemical-weapons/279622
[81] Ibid.   [82] Ibid.   [83] Ibid.

Syrian civilians – so long as it happens in a conventional way'. Acting on the chemical weapons taboo was less about Syrian civilians than it was 'about protecting a norm that Washington thinks is valuable for wider U.S. foreign policy'; it is 'about defending America's reputation' and, crucially, 'Obama's credibility'.[84]

Solving the issue without intervention enabled Obama to claim his diplomatic route was vindicated. Furthermore, it also helped to reaffirm the positive identity markers and affective binds of the Anglosphere's liberal western identity, despite ostensibly making it harder to achieve the coalition's original objective of ousting Assad. In short, it made future military assistance for the 99 per cent facing death through non-chemical means more difficult to render politically possible. Ironically and tragically, the claims available to Anglosphere leaders – centred on the apparent victory of a diplomatic solution – served both to reinforce the old coalition's shared identity whilst further resigning Syrians to brutal annihilation. Syria, reimagined as a battle to prohibit the use of chemical weapons, appeared solved, in lieu of further bloodshed. This appearance, made possible through the conflict's framing, was devastating in that it disavowed the coalition most capable of tipping the scales in the Syrian people's favour from any apparent duty to do so decisively, whilst further disassociating Assad from legitimate rule or the possibility of diplomatic negotiations.

In this vein, Bentley argues that Obama strategically manipulated the chemical weapons taboo to suggest that American foreign policy was focused on solving Syria's principal crisis.[85] To an important extent, this is certainly true, but it risks veiling the process through which Obama actively lost control of American foreign policy discourse in the lead up to the situation's resolution. Obama had enacted rhetorical self-entrapment, whereby an inadvertently ad libbed red line later came to ensnare him, tethering him to a position he had hoped to never occupy. This red line took on a discursive force all of its own, helping to wholly reframe Syria and reimagine the Anglosphere's relationship to the Civil War. It was ironic that doubters of intervention's usefulness, across the Anglosphere, struggled to oppose a discourse premised upon the rendering off-limits of an abhorrent weapon, even though the Leader of the Free World remained unconvinced by the logical policy outcome that had been unleashed by the power of his

[84] Ibid.   [85] Bentley, *Syria and the Chemical Weapons Taboo*.

own words on the topic. The result of this farcical situation was particularly tragic.

Obama's strategic focusing on this particular norm enabled 'more violence and more deaths than would have happened in the absence of the taboo as the cornerstone of US foreign policy', whilst simultaneously veiling American inaction in other domains, such as pushing for regime change, promoting democracy or protecting human rights, clearly violated by the use of other abhorrent – but not forbidden – weapons. Suggesting that Syria's main concern was, for example, the use of sarin gas, averted attention from barrel bombs and sieges that the USA had done little to address. The strategic emphasis of this particular norm therefore served the useful purpose of eviscerating American responsibility in dealing with the wider crisis; it also, however, *coerced* listeners into siding with policy arguments. Who does not think that gassing civilians is bad? This strategic emphasis, therefore, is 'not merely a general appeal to the basic emotive construct of the taboo; that is, the idea these weapons are abhorrent to the point of prohibition and prescription'; rather, it is a 'calculated strategy... to draw on the most compelling aspects of' particular norms 'in order to achieve strategic aims' by *forcing* an audience to comply with policy preferences. This enables political elites to go beyond winning support by limiting the possibility of opposing dominant discourses.[86] Far more than inspiring resonance through their intertextual enmeshing with 'pre-existing frames of understanding', this strategy can help to enable a 'control' of policy debates and thus policy.[87] In this instance, then, the discursive war of position was won not through the question of intervention or its avoidance, but rather through the reframing of the Syrian crisis as *about* chemical weapons, when, in reality, this was only one small but abhorrent component of a crisis of myriad complexities and which was about to become even more intractable.

[86] Ibid.   [87] Ibid.

6 | *Islamic State*

Our objective is clear: we will degrade and ultimately destroy ISIL.

President Barack Obama[1]

Introduction

Islamic State[2] rose to prominence and global infamy during the first half of 2014, as they retreated from rebel- and government-held areas in western, southern and northern Syria, but consolidated and extended their control across significant swathes of the east, before pushing into western Iraq. At this stage, Anglosphere pronouncements on ISIL were limited, as the extent and speed of the group's military and geographical gains took nearly all onlookers by surprise. This relative silence was reinforced by the diversion of the West's attention to Ukraine, where, in March 2014, Russian Special Forces and Russian-backed separatists seized control of Crimea. Obama's foreign policy, during the period in which ISIL went from an apparent 'JV team' to proclaimed Islamic caliphate, was preoccupied with the question of how to respond to Russian aggression in Eastern Europe, rather than terrorist gains in eastern Syria. Addressing the annexation of Crimea and the question of Ukraine's territorial integrity, Obama drew on his preferred competing traditions of US foreign policy, reasserting the importance of sovereignty and self-determination,[3] but ensuring the world knew that

[1] B. Obama, 'President Obama: "We will degrade and ultimately destroy ISIL"', White House, 10 September 2014, www.whitehouse.gov/blog/2014/09/10/president-obama-we-will-degrade-and-ultimately-destroy-isil

[2] For discussion of the political issues surrounding the group's naming, see A. Siniver and S. Lucas, 'The Islamic State lexical battleground: US foreign policy and the abstraction of threat', *International Affairs*, 92 (2016), 63–79. In particular, it is important that they note Obama's preferred name for the group helped to absolve the USA of a responsibility to act.

[3] B. Obama, 'Statement by the President on Ukraine', White House, 17 March 2014.

America's actions were limited to sanctions and the countenance of voice: war, once again, was off limits.[4] It was, then, a response that was in line with that of the US position on Syria and, indeed, the undergirding philosophical foundations of an Obama Doctrine.[5]

That position underwent a significant recalculation in August 2014, as the Syrian crisis and civil war entered a new third phase, characterised by ISIL's dramatic and unexpected rise, ahead of the self-proclaimed realisation of an 'Islamic State'. As detailed in Chapter 1, from a position of significant but bit-part player, ISIL's acquisition of territory, personnel and military capability accelerated dramatically into the summer of 2014, whilst, at the same time, their command over Raqqa was consolidated. In August 2014, one year on from the Ghouta attack and two years on from Obama's red line, the world's attention was suddenly drawn away from Crimea and back to Syria and Iraq. As part of its western Iraq offensive,[6] ISIL drove Iraqi government forces out of a series of key towns, seizing US weaponry and taking control of large population centres. At the start of June, ISIL seized control of Mosul, in northern Iraq. By the end of the month, al-Baghdadi was proclaiming himself as Caliph of a new Islamic Caliphate. In early August, ISIL captured Wana, Sumar and Sinjar in northern Iraq. As detailed in Chapter 1, the latter is a Yazidi city and its capture precipitated an impending genocide which, finally, prompted the White House into (reluctant) action. As in Libya, Obama's hand had once again been forced by the prospect of a massacre; the emergent pattern was indicative of a president reluctant to respond militarily short of a looming crisis in the form of potentially genocidal slaughter.[7]

In order to explore Anglosphere foreign policy towards Syria during the civil war's third phase, this chapter is structured in three parts. First, the chapter considers the evolving, growing and solidifying Anglosphere discourse on Islamic State during the first half of 2014,

---

[4] 'We are not going to be getting into a military excursion in Ukraine', Obama told San Diego's KNSD TV. See Russia Today, 'Obama rules out US military involvement in Ukraine', 19 March 2014, www.rt.com/news/ukraine-diplomacy-obama-russia-949

[5] See, for example, Bentley and Holland, *The Obama Doctrine*; C. Dueck, *The Obama Doctrine: American Grand Strategy Today* (New York: Oxford University Press, 2015).

[6] See the start of section three of Chapter 1 on the Anbar Campaign.

[7] Of course, for many, including the 5,000 Yazidis killed in the Sinjar massacre, the crisis certainly was not averted as the response came too late.

as the group gained ground and prominence in the Syrian crisis. Obama is shown to have been predictably slow to respond to the rise of ISIL, before lurching into action as catastrophe neared. An initial position of relative under-reaction is contrasted with later efforts to justify Anglosphere intervention, marking the return of the old Anglosphere coalition to Iraq, as well as to Syria. Second, the chapter considers how this new discourse mined the still active themes of the War on Terror, now in its thirteenth year. Surprisingly, perhaps, the new interventionist policy is shown to have been enabled by rearticulating several of the War on Terror's dominant tropes. This cultural context and intertextuality was significant, despite the popular predisposition to oppose the '9/11 wars'.[8] Third, the chapter considers opposition voices, mapping the discursive war of position that structured Anglosphere debates and policy regarding the appropriate and necessary response to the rise of ISIL. In particular, in the UK, a second parliamentary vote on military action in Syria provided a useful window through which to view the discourses structuring the Anglosphere's ability to respond militarily to the new threat. Unlike in 2013, the successful passing of the parliamentary motion enabled the old Anglosphere coalition to once again unite on the battlefield, as it has been doing for the past century. And, once again, Australia was there, as an eager participant, continuing the heritage of Gallipoli's Aussie Diggers in the Anglosphere's latest 'foxholes'.[9]

The Rise of Islamic State

Following ISIL's capture of Mosul and ten days ahead of the proclamation of the Caliphate, concerns grew within the Obama administration that the group's advance might not end in Baghdad's suburbs; now there were fears for the Iraqi state, as well as for Americans living and working in the country. Obama addressed the nation, to outline the US response to the fact that, as it transpired, ISIL were no longer an amateur operation. The relocation of some US military

---

[8] J. Burke, *The 9/11 Wars* (London: Penguin UK, 2011).

[9] 'Aussies know how to fight and I like having them in a foxhole if we're in trouble'. Obama, cited in N. O'Malley, 'Obama will "not rule anything out" in Iraq, saying US can always count on Australia', *Sydney Morning Herald*, 13 June 2014, www.smh.com.au/world/obama-will-not-rule-anything-out-in-iraq-saying-us-can-always-count-on-australia-20140612-zs694.html

personnel and embassy staff was the president's first response and reassurance. His second was to increase US intelligence, such that America might be able to base policy on an improved knowledge of ISIL's activities, which, at this stage, was dramatically deficient. Third, Obama pledged up to 300 additional US military advisers to 'train, advise and support' Iraqi security forces, which were being overrun.[10] Fourth, however, came a forewarning: US military assets were being pre-positioned in the region, and once they had the requisite intelligence and knew where to strike, it seemed likely that US airpower would be used to target ISIL positions. And, fifth, Obama continued a long-standing theme of his foreign policy, talking of the regional importance of burden sharing, based on the mutual benefits of a functioning Iraqi state. He ended, however, by reiterating his scepticism of military action's efficacy, as the troubling legacy of the 2003 war in Iraq continued to loom large:

In closing, recent days have reminded us of the deep scars left by America's war in Iraq. Alongside the loss of nearly 4,500 American patriots, many veterans carry the wounds of that war and will for the rest of their lives. Here at home, Iraq sparked vigorous debates and intense emotions in the past and we've seen some of those debates resurface.

But what's clear from the last decade is the need for the United States to ask hard questions before we take action abroad, particularly military action. The most important question we should all be asking, the issue that we have to keep front and center – the issue that I keep front and center – is what is in the national security interests of the United States of America. As Commander in Chief, that's what I stay focused on. As Americans, that's what all of us should be focused on.[11]

Facing press questions immediately afterwards, Obama explicitly reiterated that potential airstrikes and the use of American military personnel in intelligence and support capacities would not lead the US back down the path of another quagmire in Iraq:

...we always have to guard against mission creep, so let me repeat what I've said in the past: American combat troops are not going to be fighting in Iraq again.

[10] B. Obama, 'Remarks by the President on the Situation in Iraq', White House, 19 June 2014, www.whitehouse.gov/the-press-office/2014/06/19/remarks-president-situation-iraq
[11] Ibid.

We do not have the ability to simply solve this problem by sending in tens of thousands of troops and committing the kinds of blood and treasure that has already been expended in Iraq. Ultimately, this is something that is going to have to be solved by the Iraqis.[12]

While, therefore, Obama identified the US as having 'humanitarian interests in preventing bloodshed', 'strategic interests in stability in the region' and 'counterterrorism interests' in targeting ISIL, all of which 'have to be addressed', that process would begin with a hardened Baghdad perimeter, rather than taking the fight to ISIL.[13] Three days later, the US president went on CBS to communicate the US position to a broader audience. He argued that 'what we can't do is think that we're just going to play whack-a-mole and send US troops occupying various countries wherever these organizations pop up'. And, confronting the arguments of more hawkish voices from within the US war of position, he denied that more aggressive support of moderate rebels might have prevented the establishment of a security vacuum that ISIL could exploit. Reiterating a key conservative realist sub-discourse, the notion that there was a moderate opposition capable of defeating Assad and confronting ISIL, he insisted, was pure fantasy.[14] However, while the discourses of the conservative realist position would continue to hold sway on the issue of tackling Assad, it would not take long for the balance on ISIL to tip decisively to a liberal internationalist, pro-interventionist stance. The deciding factor, as in Libya, would be an impending massacre.

Throughout July, ISIL continued to make gains across the region, but Obama held firm as the US gathered more information on the group's positions and capabilities. For Republican Speaker of the House John Boehner the situation was quintessential Democrat dithering: 'It's not like we haven't seen this problem coming for over a year. They're

---

[12] Ibid.
[13] Ibid. Obama also spoke about the situation inside Syria, noting the continued US assistance to the opposition, but the 'challenge' of having 'former farmers or teachers or pharmacists who now are taking up opposition against a battle-hardened regime, with support from external actors that have a lot at stake' – 'is there the capacity of moderate opposition on the ground to absorb and counteract extremists that might have been pouring in, as well as an Assad regime supported by Iran and Russia that outmanned them and was ruthless'.
[14] R. Kaplan, 'Obama: U.S. can't "play whack-a-mole" with militant groups', *CBS*, 22 June 2014, www.cbsnews.com/news/obama-america-cant-play-whack-a-mole-with-militant-groups

100 miles from Baghdad and what's the president doing? Taking a nap.' Likewise, in contrast to policy options, news coverage at this stage had often been preoccupied with Obama's choice of name for the group, occasionally at the expense of impending security and/or human rights concerns.[15] By early August, however, Obama's prolonged caution, along with the global media's inattention, had become untenable.[16] The ISIL assault on Sinjar began on 3 August and, within two days, tens of thousands of its inhabitants had fled to the mountains, where they risked dehydration (see Chapter 1). Two days later, on 7 August, in a policy that echoed George W. Bush's words at the outset of Operation Enduring Freedom in Afghanistan,[17] President Obama authorised airstrikes against ISIL positions, as well as aid drops to the fleeing Yazidis.[18] Obama explained, bluntly:

When we face a situation like we do on that mountain – with innocent people facing the prospect of violence on a horrific scale, when we have a mandate to help – in this case, a request from the Iraqi government – and when we have the unique capabilities to help avert a massacre, then I believe the United States of America cannot turn a blind eye. We can act, carefully and responsibly, to prevent a potential act of genocide. That's what we're doing on that mountain.[19]

Reassuring doubters, he argued that many Americans would quite rightly be 'concerned about any American military action in Iraq, even limited strikes like these', but he insisted that he 'will not allow the United States to be dragged into fighting another war in Iraq'.[20]

The following day, the US officially declared the situation as genocidal. Addressing the nation, Obama insisted that 'our attention is focused on preventing an act of genocide and helping the men and women and children on the mountain, countless Iraqis [who] have been driven or fled from their homes, including many Christians'. But, 'even as we deal with these immediate situations, we continue to

---

[15] These discussions continued through 2015, 2016 and 2017.
[16] O'Malley, 'Obama will "not rule anything out" in Iraq'.
[17] Bush famously promised that as America drops bombs, 'we will also drop food'.
[18] The UK would be involved from the outset, although initially providing non-lethal assistance.
[19] B. Obama, 'President Obama makes a statement on the crisis in Iraq', White House, 7 August 2014, www.whitehouse.gov/blog/2014/08/07/president-obama-makes-statement-iraq
[20] Ibid.

pursue a broader strategy in Iraq'.[21] That broader strategy, though, was clearly playing second fiddle to the US responsibility to protect in Sinjar. Yazidis had fled for their lives when faced with the near-unimaginable decision to either be slaughtered by advancing ISIL fighters, or take their chances in the mountains, where they risked dying of thirst:

In recent days, Yezidi women, men and children from the area of Sinjar have fled for their lives. And thousands – perhaps tens of thousands – are now hiding high up on the mountain, with little but the clothes on their backs. They're without food, they're without water. People are starving. And children are dying of thirst. Meanwhile, ISIL forces below have called for the systematic destruction of the entire Yezidi people, which would constitute genocide. So these innocent families are faced with a horrible choice: descend the mountain and be slaughtered, or stay and slowly die of thirst and hunger.[22]

Armed with the moral imperative to act, plus the explicit request of the Iraqi government to help, Obama made a convincing case for intervention. He faced criticisms on both sides – with key figures concerned at the use of 'limited airstrikes' and others fearing the very real potential for mission creep and the return to the mistakes of his predecessor. But the presidential case for war was compelling, tapping into motifs of American global leadership, human rights norms and narrative myths of American exceptionalism; this, the president told Americans, is more than just right, it is who we are and who we must be:

As Commander in Chief, I will not allow the United States to be dragged into fighting another war in Iraq... [but] My fellow Americans, the world is confronted by many challenges. And while America has never been able to right every wrong, America has made the world a more secure and prosperous place. And our leadership is necessary to underwrite the global security and prosperity that our children and our grandchildren will depend upon. We do so by adhering to a set of core principles. We do whatever is necessary to protect our people. We support our allies when they're in danger. We lead coalitions of countries to uphold international norms. And we strive to stay true to the fundamental values – the desire to live with basic freedom and

---

[21] B. Obama, 'Statement by the President on Iraq', White House, 9 August 2014, www.whitehouse.gov/the-press-office/2014/08/09/statement-president-iraq

[22] Obama, 'President Obama makes a statement on the crisis in Iraq'.

dignity – that is common to human beings wherever they are. That's why people all over the world look to the United States of America to lead. And that's why we do it... So let me close by assuring you that there is no decision that I take more seriously than the use of military force. Over the last several years, we have brought the vast majority of our troops home from Iraq and Afghanistan. And I've been careful to resist calls to turn time and again to our military... But when the lives of American citizens are at risk, we will take action. That's my responsibility as Commander in Chief. And when many thousands of innocent civilians are faced with the danger of being wiped out and we have the capacity to do something about it, we will take action. That is our responsibility as Americans. That's a hallmark of American leadership. That's who we are.[23]

Obama's oratorical and rhetorical eloquence was a powerful tool throughout his presidency. His ability to combine pathos, logos and ethos with a fluency of narrative storytelling helps him to stand out as an American leader particularly gifted when it came to the written and spoken word. Here, Obama re-told a familiar story of reluctant and benevolent American leadership, fit for a pressing new moment, when the United States would, once again, accept freedom's mantle. Obama's words constructed a coercive foreign policy, achieving dominance through the posing of a question few wish to be asked. Rather than face opposition on the merits and ethics of war, Obama's language forced opponents to confront the potential criticism of shirking American leadership, or, worse still, being un-American. Few desire a discursive battle on such terms; there is much to lose and victory is difficult. For them, even if harbouring doubts, acquiescence is often easier and more logical.

A New War on Terror

The following week, on 15 August, UNSCR2170 was passed, condemning ISIL's brutality. The resolution, tragically, came four days prior to the brutal execution of James Foley. The graphic execution contributed to the rapid escalation of fear and outrage inside of the USA. As Lindsey Graham, a member of the Senate Armed Services Committee, put it, 'Mr. President, be honest with the threat we face...

---

[23] B. Obama, 'Statement by the President', State Dining Room, The White House, 7 August 2014, https://obamawhitehouse.archives.gov/the-press-office/2014/08/07/statement-president

they are coming.'[24] His concerns and preferred method of response found supporters on both sides of the aisle, with approving voices amongst the president's own party. As California Senator Dianne Feinstein, a fellow Democrat and the chairwoman of the Senate Intelligence Committee, argued: 'It takes an army to defeat an army and I believe that we either confront [ISIL] now or we will be forced to deal with an even stronger enemy in the future... Inaction is no longer an option.'[25] These fears were far from quelled when the president admitted that, when it came to ISIL inside of Syria,[26] 'We don't have a strategy yet.'[27] In Obama's defence, however, a strategy was rapidly – if belatedly – starting to take shape.[28]

That strategy would comprise multiple complementary strands, including the composition of coalitions at four levels: (i) immediate regional partners, including moderate Syrian rebels; (ii) regional allies, such as the Iraqi government, the Peshmerga and, more recently and controversially, Iran, despite their support for Assad; (iii) a broad international coalition, brought together at summits such as the NATO meeting in Wales on 4–5 September, as well as subsequent agreements in Paris on 15 September and in Egypt in early October; and (iv) a core coalition of states committed to taking and leading significant military action, centred on the old Anglosphere coalition but extending to include states such as France.[29] In addition to efforts to strangle ISIL's funding and better support their Syrian opponents, it was American

---

[24] Fox News, 'Graham: Islamic State will attack on US soil, Obama must stop terror group's rise', 10 August 2014, www.foxnews.com/politics/2014/08/10/graham-islamic-state-will-attack-on-us-soil-obama-must-stop-terror-groups-rise.html

[25] Feinstein is also quoted in Fox News, 'Graham: Islamic State will attack on US soil'.

[26] As opposed to in Iraq.

[27] D. Boyer, 'Obama confesses: "We don't have a strategy yet" for Islamic State', *Washington Times*, 28 August 2014, www.washingtontimes.com/news/2014/aug/28/obama-admits-isil-dilemma-we-dont-have-strategy-ye

[28] Obama admitted that the USA had misjudged both the rise of ISIL and the ability of the Iraqi army. S. Payne, 'Obama: U.S. misjudged the rise of the Islamic State, ability of Iraqi army', *Washington Post*, 28 September 2014, www.washingtonpost.com/world/national-security/obama-us-underestimated-the-rise-of-the-islamic-state-ability-of-iraqi-army/2014/09/28/9417ab26-4737-11e4-891d-713f052086a0_story.html?utm_term=.39389ec513b3

[29] P. Wintour and E. MacAskil, 'Obama announces "core coalition" to confront Isis threat', *The Guardian*, 6 September 2014, www.theguardian.com/world/2014/sep/05/obama-core-coalition-10-countries-to-fight-isis

military might – in the form of airstrikes and the assistance of US Special Forces – that was by far the most significant development after Sinjar. Although initially constrained to invited action inside of Iraq, it did not take long, following the execution of James Foley, for Obama to announce the extension of these efforts into Syria, in order to take the fight to ISIL in their newly consolidated heartland. Following the commencement of airstrikes, airdrops and airlifts in Iraq at the start of August, the USA extended these efforts over the Syrian border in September. And, in November, Obama announced he would send an additional 1,500 US troops to Iraq, doubling the number there, in order to advise and train Iraqis and Kurds as they planned a counter-offensive against ISIL.[30] This military strategy was justified with recourse to a series of narratives and discourses that had been central to George W. Bush's War on Terror; they were folded within the new basic and sub-discourses of the Syrian crisis and civil war.

The invocation of this language was both intuitive and strategic. Obama had never set out to undo all of his predecessor's foreign policy, but rather, to fight better and more intelligently where the US national interest was legitimately engaged (see Chapter 2).[31] Obama had arguably been heard to promise more change than he ever specified desiring on the campaign trail. While Iraq was a 'dumb war', he had long held the view that the battle against Al Qaeda in Afghanistan and Pakistan was vital to the short-, medium- and long-term security of the USA. In this respect, the president's mining of the language of the War on Terror was predictable. While a policy of intervening against a state's leader was off limits, even where that leader was held up to be despicable, counter-terrorism efforts in other states were not only justified but imperative. For Obama, then, Assad was to Saddam Hussein in the 2003 Iraq War what ISIL were to Al Qaeda in the 2001 war in Afghanistan; regime change remained off limits, but degrading and destroying a terrorist group with global reach was necessary. And, in selling this policy to the American people, the language chosen to justify this course of action drew upon the resonant

---

[30] H. Cooper and M. Shear, 'Obama to send 1,500 more troops to assist Iraq', *New York Times*, 7 November 2014, www.nytimes.com/2014/11/08/world/middleeast/us-to-send-1500-more-troops-to-iraq.html; BBC News, 'Obama signals "new phase" against Islamic State in Iraq', 9 November 2014, www.bbc.co.uk/news/world-middle-east-29979042

[31] McCrisken, 'Ten years on'.

and embedded narratives and discourses established in the aftermath of 9/11, as George W. Bush made the case for Operation Enduring Freedom. In words that resembled those of the predecessor he had railed against on the campaign trail, Obama promised:

I have made it clear that we will hunt down terrorists who threaten our country, wherever they are... That means I will not hesitate to take action against ISIL in Syria, as well as Iraq. This is a core principle of my presidency: if you threaten America, you will find no safe haven.[32]

CNN chief political analyst Gloria Borger noted just how hard it was for a president who campaigned on the extrication of American troops from Iraq to give this speech.[33] There were no two ways about it: a broadly anti-interventionist president was opting to insert the USA 'into the middle of a Syrian civil war'.[34] But the new policy and the speech that launched it found significant bipartisan support from Graham and Feinstein, as well as Republicans such as Mike Rogers and Michael McCaul, who both noted that, in facing the reality of the threat posed by ISIL, the president had taken an encouraging step in the right direction.[35]

While outrage at ISIL's actions in Syria and Iraq was commonplace, especially in the wake of the executions of James Foley and Stephen Sotloff, it was the threat to the USA that was often foremost in the thoughts and words of American politicians. For instance, with direct reference to 9/11 and Afghanistan, former ambassador Ryan Crocker made the case for concern succinctly, when he stated:

They are more numerous, they are better armed, they are far better financed, they are better experienced [than Al Qaeda] and perhaps most critically there are several thousand of them who hold Western passports, including American passports... They don't need to get a visa; they just need to get on a plane... If we don't think we're on their target list, we are delusional.[36]

In language eerily reminiscent of thirteen years previous, Obama argued that Syria is:

ground zero for jihadists around the world... over the past couple of years, during the chaos of the Syrian civil war, where essentially you have huge

---

[32] T. Cohen, 'Obama outlines ISIS strategy: airstrikes in Syria, more U.S. forces', *CNN*, 11 September 2014, http://edition.cnn.com/2014/09/10/politics/isis-obama-speech/index.html
[33] Ibid.   [34] Ibid.   [35] Ibid.   [36] Ibid.

swaths of the country that are completely ungoverned, they were able to reconstitute themselves and take advantage of that chaos.[37]

And, using several techniques of dehumanisation that were common to the Bush presidency, Obama described ISIL as a 'cancer'[38] and 'pure evil'.[39] The logical upshot, as in the US-led battle to confront Al Qaeda, was that there 'can be no reasoning, no negotiation, with this brand of evil'; the 'only language understood by killers like this is the language of force. So the United States of America will work with a broad coalition to dismantle this network of death'.[40] He was joined by David Cameron, in promising that, as after 9/11, Anglosphere allies would not be cowed by this new threat.[41]

Obama's foreign policy, generally, was certainly constrained by the discursive limitations set by the still-resonant narratives of the War on Terror, but the president also instrumentally opted to mine several of its key features in order to sell military intervention, specifically.[42] This, then, serves as a useful example of the culturally embedded nature of Anglosphere foreign policy discourse, which is both drawn from and framed to enmesh with the political and cultural landscape.[43]

---

[37] Reuters, 'Obama: U.S. intelligence underestimated militants in Syria – CBS', 28 September 2014, www.reuters.com/article/us-mideast-crisis-syria-obama-idUSKCN0HN0QN20140928

[38] P. Sherwell, 'Barack Obama denounces Islamic State as "cancer" that must be "extracted" from Middle East', *The Telegraph*, 20 August 2014, www.telegraph.co.uk/news/worldnews/barackobama/11047264/Barack-Obama-denounces-Islamic-State-as-cancer-that-must-be-extracted-from-Middle-East.html

[39] R. Callimachi, 'Obama calls Islamic State's killing of Peter Kassig "pure evil"', *New York Times*, 16 November 2014, www.nytimes.com/2014/11/17/world/middleeast/peter-kassig-isis-video-execution.html

[40] D. McManus, 'President Obama will go out with a war cry', *Los Angeles Times*, 27 September 2014, www.latimes.com/nation/la-oe-mcmanus-column-obama-foreign-policy-20140928-column.html

[41] J. Pace, 'Obama, Cameron: we will "not be cowed" by Islamic State militants', *PBS*, 4 September 2014, www.pbs.org/newshour/rundown/obama-cameron-will-cowed-islamic-state-militants

[42] For discussion, see M. Bentley, 'Ending the unendable: the rhetorical legacy of the war on terror' in *The Obama Doctrine: A Legacy of Continuity in US Foreign Policy?*; and R. Jackson and C. Tsui, 'War on terror II: Obama and the adaptive evolution of US counterterrorism' in *The Obama Doctrine*.

[43] See Holland, *Selling the War on Terror*; and J. Holland, 'Coalition foreign policy in the "War on Terror": a framework for analysing foreign policy as culturally embedded discourse', CRIPS Working Paper Series, University of Warwick, 10 October 2007, https://warwick.ac.uk/fac/soc/pais/currentstudents/phd/

Building upon the still solid discursive foundations laid by the Bush administration enabled Obama to craft a conceivable, resonant and coercive foreign policy discourse.[44] The memory of 9/11 and the visceral desire to exact retribution on those who perpetrated the acts of that day were important for the Obama administration, as they made the case that taking the fight to ISIL would limit the possibilities of future attacks on the US homeland by a group that had evolved from Al Qaeda to become something even more fundamentally threatening to American life and global security.

Where Obama did achieve some change in his re-workings of Bush's language, this was primarily focused on two areas. First, Obama constructed a broader and more encompassing identity into which Americans and their enemies fitted.[45] Civilisation and barbarism did for Obama what American and terrorist had done for Bush. This reworking served to naturalise coalition participation, in a manner similar to Bush's calls to 'freedom-loving nations', whilst also facilitating the condemnation of a group whose atrocities went beyond tactical political violence to include wholesale abuse of populations in pursuit of a new form of social organisation. Obama's preferred signifiers helped to foster an inclusive coalition identity – bolstering an Anglosphere-level affective community, arguably in slight contrast to Bush's tendency to prioritise American identity markers. Second, Obama repeatedly stressed his desire and ability to avoid mission creep, which might lead Americans back to a full-scale intervention. This was, then, an 'adaptive evolution' of the discourses of the War on Terror, even if Obama strategically avoided the label; the 'rhetorical legacy' of his predecessor, which had been so problematic for the president when he sought to avoid military interventions overseas, was now eminently useful in framing the case for conflict in terms that were appealing to supporters and coercive of doubters. Who would not want to defend civilisation in the face of barbaric evil? Or, more to the point, who might be politically brave enough to make the counter-argument, given the costs in terms of public opinion and, perhaps, votes? Obama's foreign policy came packaged with significant

resources/crips/working_papers/2008/crips_paper_-_jack_holland_-_submitted1.pdf

[44] See Holland, 'Foreign policy and political possibility'.
[45] B. Fermor, 'Shifting binaries: the colonial legacy of Obama's war on terror' in *The Obama Doctrine*.

representational force for its detractors, in addition to its resonant appeals to its target audience.

Like the President of the United States, the British and Australian prime ministers during the Syrian Civil War's third phase – Cameron, Abbott and Turnbull – all made use of the language of the War on Terror in framing a persuasive foreign policy for their domestic populations. On 26 September 2014, Britain commenced Operation Shader: humanitarian relief efforts at Mount Sinjar transformed into invited airstrikes. It would not be until the end of 2015, however, that the UK could formally engage in the conflict in Syria, following a second and this time successful vote in the House of Commons. Between September 2014 and December 2015, Britain's role was limited to surveillance and intelligence efforts, although UK pilots did fly with American counterparts, in lieu of parliamentary approval. The British effort after December 2015 was significant, however, with more than 1,000 ISIL fighters killed in over 1,000 targeted airstrikes (although these were heavily weighted towards strikes in Iraq).[46] This contribution and the vote that enabled it were triggered by a request in September 2015 for allies fighting in Iraq to join the USA in extending their efforts into Syria. Australia was one of the first states to agree to the request, commencing airstrikes inside Syria in September 2015, along with Canada and France.[47] The Australian contribution came despite the domestic turmoil of another leadership spill and change of prime minister, as Tony Abbott was ousted by Malcolm Turnbull. Both prime ministers, however, were adamant that Australia would play its full part in the battle against ISIL through Operation Okra. Tony Abbott had previously been reported to ask key advisers how Australia might do more to confront ISIL, while Malcom Turnbull opted to extend Australia's remit to strike support facilities as well as frontline combatants.[48] Once again, up until November 2015, Australia

---

[46] B. Stevenson, 'UK air strike data shows scale of involvement in Iraq and Syria', *Flight Global*, 31 May 2016, www.flightglobal.com/news/articles/uk-air-strike-data-shows-scale-of-involvement-in-ira-425822

[47] BBC News, 'Australia launches first air strikes inside Syria', 16 September 2016, www.bbc.co.uk/news/world-australia-34265118

[48] R. Taylor, 'Australia to step up airstrikes on Islamic State', *Wall Street Journal*, 31 August 2016, www.wsj.com/articles/australia-to-step-up-airstrikes-on-islamic-state-1472696172. It is difficult to measure an overall military contribution, but the claim made by both Turnbull and Foreign Secretary Julie Bishop held up, in particular regarding boots on the ground. This situation

was the 'second largest international contributor' to an Anglosphere-led military campaign, this time 'in Iraq and Syria'.[49] Across the Anglosphere, political leaders – and frequently their opponents – reworked the language of the War on Terror in selling a policy of military intervention to their domestic populations.

In all three members of the old Anglosphere coalition, debates ensued as to what the new group should be called, following Baghdadi's declaration of a caliphate under the name of Islamic State. In the USA, Obama stuck rigidly to ISIL. In the UK, Cameron also urged the media to use ISIL, rather than Islamic State, or at least prefix descriptions with 'so-called'.[50] Some MPs and journalists opted to use 'Daesh', following its increased popularity in France. Cameron's descriptions of the group evolved and solidified quickly, following the 'appalling development of ISIL taking so much ground in the middle of Iraq' in the first half of 2014.[51] In Canberra, watched on by his 'own Australian auntie', Cameron outlined his Anglosphere affections at length, as well as the ISIL threat and the importance of the old coalition once again taking the fight to mutual enemies.[52] The root cause of this evil, he told Australians, was 'not poverty', 'exclusion', or 'foreign policy', but 'the extremist narrative'.[53] Cameron

altered, first, following the Paris Attacks and the French decision to send the Charles de Gaulle aircraft carrier to the region and, second, the successful British parliamentary vote. ABC News, 'Fact check: is Australia's military contribution to the fight against Islamic State the second largest?', 3 March 2016, www.abc .net.au/news/2015-12-22/fact-check-australias-contribution-against-islamic-state/6977668

[49] M. Kenny, 'Malcolm Turnbull slaps down the military option in Syria, calls for compromise', *Sydney Morning Herald*, 19 November 2015, www.smh.com.au/ federal-politics/political-news/malcolm-turnbull-slams-russian-contradictions-while-admitting-australian-bombs-in-syria-20160918-grj532.html

[50] For example, M. Weaver, 'Syria debate: the linguistic battle over what to call Islamic State', *The Guardian*, 2 December 2015, www.theguardian.com/world/ 2015/dec/02/syria-debate-the-linguistic-battle-over-what-to-call-islamic-state

[51] D. Cameron, 'David Cameron and NATO Secretary General press conference', 19 June 2014, www.gov.uk/government/speeches/david-cameron-and-nato-secretary-general-press-conference

[52] 'It is right that once again… British and Australian forces are operating alongside each other; supporting all those in Iraq and Syria who want a future for their countries where all their people are represented and where there is no place for extremism and terror'. D. Cameron, 'Australian Parliament: David Cameron's speech', 14 November 2014, www.gov.uk/government/speeches/ australian-parliament-david-camerons-speech

[53] Ibid.

made tackling extremism a high priority, outlining, the following summer, his desire to combat, not Islam, but 'ideology' and the 'extreme doctrine of Islamist extremism'.[54] In opposition to Britain, as a 'beacon to the world', he set out ISIL's 'despicable', 'sick', 'poisonous' worldview.[55] This worldview – and the extremist ideology that sustained it – Cameron argued, was the problem. Extremism was framed as the first step to terrorism: 'the extremist world view is the gateway and violence is the ultimate destination'.[56]

This portrayal of the process of radicalisation had significant implications for British counter-terrorism strategy, as the government framed 'extremist' views as a precursor to violent extremist actions. The challenge, of course, was to identify and classify 'extremism', in much the same way as its supposed opposite, 'British values'.[57] But, in outlining ISIL's cause in an effort to 'de-glamourise' it, Cameron reminded an audience of British school children that ISIL:

is a group that throws people off buildings, that burns them alive... its men rape underage girls and stone innocent women to death. This isn't a pioneering movement – it is vicious, brutal and a fundamentally abhorrent existence.[58]

He reminded those tempted to join ISIL:

You won't be some valued member of a movement. You are cannon fodder for them. They will use you. If you are a boy, they will brainwash you, strap bombs to your body and blow you up. If you are a girl, they will enslave and abuse you. That is the sick and brutal reality of ISIL.[59]

And these themes were furthered as Cameron addressed the United Nations in September 2014, one day prior to the commencement of Operation Shader.[60]

---

[54] D. Cameron, 'Extremism: PM speech', 20 July 2015, www.gov.uk/government/speeches/extremism-pm-speech
[55] Ibid.   [56] Ibid.
[57] For discussion, see L. Jarvis and E. Atakav, 'British (Muslim) values', PaCCS Blog, 2016, www.paccsresearch.org.uk/blog/british-muslim-values
[58] Ibid.   [59] Ibid.
[60] D. Cameron, 'PM speech at the UN General Assembly 2014', 15 September 2016, www.gov.uk/government/speeches/pm-speech-at-the-un-general-assembly-2014. See also D. Cameron, 'Prime Minister on ISIL at UN General Assembly', 19 September 2015, www.gov.uk/government/speeches/prime-minister-on-isil-at-un-general-assembly, where he made the point about doing more to counter extremism, as well as violent extremism. For instance, the

The root cause of this terrorist threat is a poisonous ideology of Islamist extremism. This is nothing to do with Islam, which is a peaceful religion which inspires countless acts of generosity every day. Islamist extremism on the other hand believes in using the most brutal forms of terrorism to force people to accept a warped world view and to live in a quasi-mediaeval state.[61]

After setting out the need to curtail free speech in the cause of defeating (violent) extremism, Cameron turned to Syria. He drew a clear demarcating line between Assad and ISIL in order to address growing critique of Anglosphere foreign policy and military intervention – was it not counter-productive to target ISIL, given the group were fighting Assad, potentially contributing to his downfall, as explicitly desired and demanded throughout the civil war to date? 'Doing a deal with Assad', Cameron argued, 'will not defeat ISIL'. Cameron ruled out 'Western ground troops directly trying to pacify or reconstruct' the Middle East, but argued for 'an intelligent and comprehensive approach', which 'should include a place for our military', even if that action would, at the outset, be limited to Iraq.[62]

In Australia, Prime Minister Tony Abbott was quick to mimic the language of John Howard and George W. Bush.[63] Justifying Australia's military deployment to Iraq, Abbott framed his decision as a response to the 'murderous rage of the ISIL death cult'.[64] His comments built on earlier rhetoric, noting that ISIL were an 'apocalyptic death cult', aiming 'to have heads on stakes'.[65] The phrase 'death cult'

---

line: 'courage and selflessness stand in stark contrast to the empty callousness of their murderers'.

[61] Cameron, 'PM speech at the UN General Assembly'.   [62] Ibid.

[63] Even if he was keen to make his own significant linguistic decision, including opting to call ISIL Daesh and avoid the term 'war' in describing Australia's contribution to coalition combat operation. See, for example, A. Sharwood, 'Tony Abbott almost says Australia is at war with ISIS. Sort of', *ABC News*, 19 September 2014, www.news.com.au/national/tony-abbott-almost-says-australia-is-at-war-with-isis-sort-of/news-story/ff846451234537a86c25c069f64cd4dd. See also Holland, 'Howard's war on terror'.

[64] AP, 'Australian war planes to join airstrikes on Isil in Iraq', *The Telegraph*, 3 October 2014, www.telegraph.co.uk/news/worldnews/islamic-state/11137690/Australian-war-planes-to-join-airstrikes-on-Isil-in-Iraq.html

[65] D. Hurst, 'Tony Abbott intensifies rhetoric about Isis, calling it an "apocalyptic death cult"', *The Guardian*, 30 September 2014, www.theguardian.com/world/2014/sep/30/tony-abbott-intensifies-rhetoric-about-isis-calling-it-an-apocalyptic-death-cult

was repeated frequently by the Australian prime minister and foreign secretary, as they sought, once again, to ensure public support for significant Australian military action overseas. In December 2014, following the 'Sydney siege', in which eighteen Australians were taken hostage and three people died, Abbott described the perpetrator, Man Haron Monis, as having cloaked 'his actions with the symbolism of the ISIL death cult'.[66] At times, for instance, following the publication of a photo of an Australian boy holding a severed head in Raqqa (see Chapter 1), Abbott also spoke of barbarism, promising that, given these 'atrocities', 'we are ready to assist in any way we can should we be asked to assist by the Americans'.[67]

This resolve to stand with the Americans in combatting ISIL was shared by both junior members of the old Anglosphere coalition. In Britain, this was reinforced for David Cameron following the Souse attack in Tunisia, in which thirty Britons were amongst those killed. For the British prime minister, it was further evidence of the need to 'be stronger at standing up for our values – of peace, democracy, tolerance, freedom'.[68] Once again framed through the lens of ideology and values, Cameron insisted that Britain and the world 'must be more intolerant of intolerance – rejecting anyone whose views condone the Islamist extremist narrative and create the conditions for it to flourish'.[69] He contrasted terrorist cowardice with Great British spirit, insisting, in language reminiscent of the War on Terror, that Britain:

---

[66] C. Sheets, 'ISIS-Sydney connection: Australian PM says Man Haron Monis identified with terrorist group', *International Business Times*, 15 December 2014, www.ibtimes.com/isis-sydney-connection-australian-pm-says-man-haron-monis-identified-terrorist-group-1758983

[67] L. Bourke and M. Levy, '"Barbaric" nature of ISIL on display with photos of boy holding decapitated head, says Prime Minister Tony Abbott', *Sydney Morning Herald*, 11 August 2014, www.smh.com.au/federal-politics/political-news/barbaric-nature-of-isil-on-display-with-photos-of-boy-holding-decapitated-head-says-prime-minister-tony-abbott-20140810-3dh8q.html. For discussion of the implications of foreign fighters from Australia, see A. Zammit, 'Australian foreign fighters: risks and responses', *Lowy Institute*, 16 April 2015, www.lowyinstitute.org/publications/australian-foreign-fighters-risks-and-responses

[68] P. Dominiczak, 'Tunisia attack: David Cameron calls for fightback against intolerance as 30 Britons confirmed dead', *The Telegraph*, 29 June 2015, www.telegraph.co.uk/news/worldnews/africaandindianocean/tunisia/11704972/Tunisia-attack-David-Cameron-calls-for-fightback-against-intolerance-as-30-Britons-confirmed-dead.html

[69] Ibid.

will not be cowed... To our shock and grief we must add another word: resolve. Unshakeable resolve. We will stand up for our way of life. So ours must be a full-spectrum response – a response at home and abroad; in the immediate aftermath and far into the future.[70]

In the wake of the attack, Cameron promised a 'full spectrum response' to defend 'our way of life'[71] in what he termed 'the struggle of our generation'.[72] While the attack received less attention in the USA and Australia, both Obama and Abbott called for a united, multilateral response to confront ISIL, with the American President again noting that, in lieu of international support, US efforts would be akin to playing 'whack-a-mole' with the terrorist group.[73] Reassuring Anglosphere allies that they would not be fighting alone, Tony Abbott made the stark warning that opting out was no longer possible: Tunisia 'illustrates, yet again, that as far as the Daesh death cult is concerned, it is coming after us... We may not always feel that we are at war with them, but they certainly think that they are at war with us'[74] – a sentiment that was seemingly confirmed by the Friday 13th Paris attacks at the end of the year. Following the attacks, in the French parliament, Le Marseillaise rang out. The country's anthem, sung now by its politicians, is a revolutionary war song, rallying citizens to fight.[75]

Ten thousand miles away, despite his ousting as prime minister, Tony Abbott concurred as he continued to peddle a strong interventionist

[70] Ibid.
[71] Russia Today, 'Cameron vows "full spectrum" British response to ISIS Tunisia shooting', 29 June 2015, www.rt.com/uk/270331-cameron-response-tunisia-attack
[72] BBC News, 'Tunisia attack: Cameron says IS fight "struggle of our generation"', 29 June 2015, www.bbc.co.uk/news/uk-33307279; also M. Chorley, 'National minute's silence for victims of Tunisia atrocity to be held at noon on Friday as Cameron vows: "We will not cower"', *Daily Mail*, 29 June 2015, www.daily mail.co.uk/news/article-3142884/David-Cameron-says-beat-ISIS-terrorists-threaten-way-life-Sousse-terror-attack.html
[73] Fox News, 'Obama's "whack-a-mole" warning on ISIS', 6 July 2015, www.foxnews.com/politics/2015/07/06/obama-concedes-isis-has-gone-global-but-vows-will-ultimately-prevail.html?refresh=true
[74] O. Chang, 'Tony Abbott says the death cult is "coming after us" after global terror attacks', *Business Insider Australia*, 28 June 2015, www.business insider.com.au/tony-abbott-says-the-death-cult-is-coming-after-us-after-global-terror-attacks-2015-6
[75] The rendition came three days after the attacks. Lyrics include a promise to cut the throats of enemies – sons and mothers likewise – as well as to soak French lands with impure blood.

line, assuring Australians that there was no alternative to military victory: 'The point I make is that this ISIL caliphate – it can't be contained. It has to be defeated and it's not going to go away just by wishing it to go away.'[76] In contrast to Abbott's call to arms, his successor Malcolm Turnbull reiterated the need for a comprehensive strategy that included a political solution.[77] The Australian prime minister dampened Abbott's warnings, arguing, in his maiden national security address to parliament, that Australia needed a 'calm, clinical, professional, effective' foreign policy, not 'gestures and machismo'.[78] But, as well as re-invoking George W. Bush's phrase, 'freedom-loving nations', Turnbull contrasted Australian values with those of the 'thugs and tyrants' of ISIL.[79] And, in case there was any doubt, he labelled the Paris attacks as 'the work of the devil'.[80] Even where calls for measured and varied responses were being made, these calls came from within the assumptions and narratives of a hegemonic War on Terror discourse, reworked from the post-9/11 era for that of the Syrian Civil War.[81] Turnbull's discursive strategy therefore replicated Obama's: accept the constraints of an overarching, hegemonic discursive inheritance, but promise to enact policy *better* and more intelligently. Turnbull acknowledged that national security priorities were not about to be overhauled: he had to work within enduring discursive structures that only permitted more minor rhetorical and tactical innovations.

The response to the Paris attacks from all three Anglosphere leaders was an extension of earlier discursive efforts to fix the meaning of ISIL[82]

---

[76] S. McKeith, 'ISIS must be defeated in wake of Paris attacks: Abbott', 15 November 2015, www.huffingtonpost.com.au/2015/11/14/isis-must-be-defeated-in-wake-of-paris-attacks-abbott

[77] M. Kenny, 'Malcolm Turnbull slaps down the military option in Syria'.

[78] J. Owens, 'Response to terror threat must be calm, clinical: Turnbull', *The Australian*, 24 November 2015, www.theaustralian.com.au/national-affairs/response-to-terror-threat-must-be-calm-clinical-turnbull/news-story/c0d93da3ae920cbcb1fe5f6c0bae8bba

[79] M. Turnbull, 'National security statement Parliament House, Canberra', 24 November 2015.

[80] J. McCurry and K. Rawlinson, 'Paris terror attacks: world leaders condemn "the work of the devil"', *The Guardian*, 14 November 2015, www.theguardian.com/world/2015/nov/14/paris-terror-attacks-world-leaders-condemn-the-work-of-the-devil

[81] See Krebs, *National Security*.

[82] For example, D. Cameron, 'PM press statement following Paris talks', 23 November 2015, www.gov.uk/government/speeches/pm-press-statement-following-paris-talks

with reference to widely understood and accepted discourses on global terrorism. Obama, in particular, led efforts to universalise the nature of the attacks, which he argued struck a blow against 'all of humanity' and 'universal values'.[83] For US Secretary of State John Kerry, as well as being 'an assault on our common humanity', the attacks were 'heinous, evil' and 'vile'.[84] For Britain's David Cameron, with Paris only a two-and-a-half-hour train ride from London, the security implications were immediate. In addition to an increased British security presence on London's streets, Cameron responded to the Paris attacks by arguing that the UK *must* now join the United States in taking military action against ISIL in Syria.[85] In view of the 'direct and growing threat to the country', Cameron urged that the UK had to take action, targeting the 'head of the snake'.[86] Amidst these descriptions of evil and arguments for UK airstrikes in Syria, journalists and political pundits began to speculate that parliament could vote on military action 'as early as Christmas'. In the end, this would prove to be wrong; capitalising on the outpouring of public concern after the Paris attacks and internal disarray amongst opposition ranks, the Conservative government published a dossier of evidence for airstrikes ahead of a vote on 2 December 2015. In Westminster, 2015 looked a lot like 2003, with a government returned to office publishing legalistic dossiers making the case for war, ahead of military action in the Middle East. Blair's ghost, unsurprisingly, loomed large.

Debate, Division and War

In the UK, the second parliamentary vote on Syria provided a useful window through which to observe the discursive war of position, as competing arguments clashed and ultimately resolved in favour of the government's official position. It was also the key moment in which the old Anglosphere coalition reverted to its default position, with all three members participating fully in military intervention, against an enemy defined as the antithesis of the English-speaking nations, as the

---

[83]   Ibid.   [84]   Ibid.
[85]   S. Swinford, 'David Cameron prepared to hold Syria vote as early as Christmas', *The Telegraph*, 17 November 2015, www.telegraph.co.uk/news/uknews/terrorism-in-the-uk/12001899/david-cameron-syria-air-strikes-vote-christmas.html
[86]   Ibid.

pinnacle of civilisation. The government's case for extending UK military intervention into Syria began with Defence Minister Michael Fallon pitch rolling for a full spectrum response as early as July, following the attack in Sirte, Tunisia.[87] Fallon and the prime minister knew that this ground-setting exercise was crucial to winning the vital war of position in the UK, ahead of a necessary second vote on Syria. Backing the defence secretary in the summer, as he set the ground for the forthcoming debate, Cameron argued: 'I want Britain to do more. I'll always have to take my parliament with me. We're talking and discussing at the moment, including with the opposition parties in Britain, what more we can do. But be in no doubt, we're committed to working with you to destroy the caliphate in both countries.'[88]

The opposition towards which Cameron's focus had turned was led by Labour Party leader Jeremy Corbyn, who had surprisingly risen to power following his nomination, which had been intended primarily only to widen the policy debates surrounding the leadership election. His victory came on the back of a staunch left-wing agenda, which included vocal opposition to the folly of Iraq in 2003 and any potential for repeating it in the future. Throughout his leadership, Corbyn addressed concerns that British foreign and counter-terrorism policy placed too much emphasis on military solutions and not enough on diplomatic ones.[89] However, at the start of December 2015, the discursive foundations of the case against extending British airstrikes into Syria were far shakier than those supporting the government's case for war, which had benefitted from the recent Paris attacks and the public's memory of 7/7. Indeed, the issue divided the Labour Party all the way to the top. In the days leading up to the 2 December parliamentary vote, Corbyn was accused of aiding and abetting the intimidation of MPs considering

---

[87] BBC News, 'Consider Syria IS strikes, defence secretary urges MPs', 3 July 2015, www.bbc.co.uk/news/uk-33358267

[88] BBC News, 'UK will help destroy Islamic State, David Cameron tells US', *BBC News*, 19 July 2015, www.bbc.co.uk/news/uk-33584548

[89] For example, Corbyn had drawn previous criticism for comparing ISIL and Israel, as well as questioning Britain's shoot-to-kill policy in the case of a terror attack in the UK. By 2016, he was still urging that diplomatic back-channels were opened to ISIL to enable political discussions that might end the conflict sooner. See, for instance, J. Stone, 'Jeremy Corbyn says there could be benefits to opening diplomatic back-channels with Isis', *The Independent*, 17 January 2016, www.independent.co.uk/news/uk/politics/jeremy-corbyn-says-there-could-be-benefits-to-opening-diplomatic-back-channels-with-isis-a6817181.html

supporting the government's motion.[90] And, several party members openly questioned the electoral impact of the internal party 'debacle' on the issue, as Corbyn failed to achieve the collective party position he had promised, ultimately authorising a free vote.[91]

In the chamber, Corbyn summarised his position thus: the prime minister's case 'doesn't stack up';[92] it's 'bomb first, talk later'.[93] The rebuttal from the prime minster could not have been made in stronger – or less fair – terms. Facing a partisan challenge in the discursive war of position, Cameron opted to play the strongest of rhetorical cards in his possession: he labelled the Leader of the Opposition a 'terrorist sympathiser'.[94] The impact of such a claim is hugely significant, rendering political opponents as more than just policy foes, but rather potential enemies of the state. The representational force of such a move is considerable, as wavering politicians are flushed from their cover, opting to acquiesce and support a government motion that, had the political and electoral stakes been lower, they may have opted to oppose, for practical and ethical reasons.[95] This *hard* soft power was combined by the prime minister with: an Anglospheric challenge that Britain must 'answer the call from our allies';[96] alliterative rhetorical appeals to deeply resonant discourses of the War on Terror and

---

[90] P. Dominiczak, 'Jeremy Corbyn faces humiliation as more than 100 Labour MPs plan to defy leader over Syria air strikes', *The Telegraph*, 27 November 2015, www.telegraph.co.uk/news/politics/Jeremy_Corbyn/12021973/Jeremy-Corbyn-faces-humiliation-as-more-than-100-Labour-MPs-plan-to-defy-leader-over-Syria-air-strikes.html

[91] Ibid.

[92] BBC News, 'Syria vote: Cameron and Corbyn clash over air strikes', 2 December 2015, www.bbc.co.uk/news/uk-politics-34980504

[93] N. Watt, 'David Cameron accuses Jeremy Corbyn of being "terrorist sympathiser"', *The Guardian*, 2 December 2015, www.theguardian.com/politics/2015/dec/01/cameron-accuses-corbyn-of-being-terrorist-sympathiser. Cameron was, arguably, extreme in his denunciation of opponents of airstrikes as 'terrorist sympathisers', a term which drew criticism but was successful in helping to coerce support for war. When challenged, he opted not to apologise for this description but did concede that there was honour in voting either for or against airstrikes.

[94] BBC, 'Syria vote'.

[95] See Holland, 'Foreign policy'; Krebs, *National Security*; Mattern, *Ordering International Politics*.

[96] See also Defence Secretary Fallon noting 'We can't leave it to French, Australian and American aircraft to keep our own British streets safe': BBC News, 'David Cameron condemns Russia's strikes in Syria', 3 October 2015, www.bbc.co.uk/news/uk-34432440

broader Orientalist barbarism, as he spoke of ISIL as 'woman-raping, Muslim-murdering, mediaeval monsters'; and an exploitation of the fear that the Paris attacks marked the UK out as next, as ISIL continued 'plotting to kill us and to radicalise our children right now'.[97] He also borrowed from Tony Abbott in suggesting that 'this evil death cult is neither a true representation of Islam nor is it a state'.[98] This was an accomplished rhetorical, discursive and political performance by the prime minister, but, such was the force of the discursive position from which the policy was promoted, he was ultimately out-done by a Labour politician who opted to cross the aisle.

The second UK vote on Syria was ultimately won by and will be remembered for the performance of Labour's Shadow Foreign Secretary Hilary Benn. His speech received rave reviews from fellow parliamentarians, political pundits and journalists. It mined a Gladstonian liberal tradition, albeit a particularly muscular variant, supported by realist self-interest. And it was flourished with the rhetorical and discursive themes that were familiar under Tony Blair. Its rhetorical delivery, at times whispered in hushed tones, helped it to stand out as *the* bipartisan articulation of the median point of Britain's discursive war of position at the time of the second vote on Syria. Making use of many of the same appeals Cameron had articulated and tapping into a long British history of confronting evil, Benn reminded the chamber, bluntly, that ISIL are 'fascists and fascists must be defeated'.[99] The speech received 'rapturous applause' from Conservative benches both because members agreed with it and it supported the prime minister's cause, while moving Corbyn still further from the centre of British electoral politics.[100] Albeit in less high-profile positions, Benn also received support from Alan Johnson, Dame Margaret Beckett and Yvette Cooper – all former Labour ministers – as well as former party leader Ed Miliband, orchestrator of the government's previous defeat.

The strength of the growing discursive hegemony was observable in the fact that, where disputation arose, it was often the contention of specific facts and claims *within* the overarching official discourse, pushed by the government's benches. As Cameron noted, 'I respect

[97] BBC, 'Syria vote'; Watt, 'David Cameron'.
[98] D. Cameron, 'PM's opening statement to Commons debate on military action in Syria', 2 December 2015, www.gov.uk/government/speeches/pms-opening-statement-to-commons-debate-on-military-action-in-syria
[99] BBC, 'Syria vote'.   [100] Ibid.

the fact that we are all discussing how to fight terrorism, not whether to fight terrorism'; it was, quite simply, understood, this time, to be 'Britain's duty' to do something.[101] For example, drawing on an alternative sub-discourse that Tony Abbott had previously summarised as 'baddies versus baddies', numerous members of the House challenged the notion that there was a moderate rebel army – perhaps comprising 70,000 ready, willing and capable fighters – simply awaiting UK aerial assistance. The challenge, though, was one of figures not fundamentals. And while the latter was attempted – for example, Angus Robertson urged MPs to 'remember Iraq' – the government had successfully divided the Syrian crisis into two components: the contentious issue of Assad's forces and the need for regime change; and the battle to confront the new 'death cult' of ISIL, before it was too late. The division enabled the government to rely on the support of several Liberal Democrats, despite their previous and long-standing opposition to the 2003 Iraq War. For Liberal Democrat Leader Tim Farron, it was important not to learn the wrong lessons from the 'illegal, counterproductive war in Iraq'; in this instance, 'it is right to take military action to degrade and defeat this evil death cult'.[102] Such support was sufficient for the government's motion to pass 397 to 223. Just hours later, four Tornado jets took off from a British base in Cyprus, heading for Syria.[103] The old Anglosphere coalition was once again united on a new battlefield, against a new enemy, but it was arguably just the latest Anglo-Saxon war against what was perceived and constructed to be a stark and dangerous alterity: violent, evil and barbaric savages.

The discursive war of position was fought across the Anglosphere, but nowhere with the clarity or significance of the British context, which resulted directly from the unexpected government defeat in the 2013 chemical weapons vote. In Australia, Malcom Turnbull continued Abbott's policy, albeit adopting a different rhetorical and discursive strategy, marked by greater caution. He noted, for example,

---

[101] D. Cameron, *Hansard*, 2 December 2015, www.publications.parliament.uk/pa/cm201516/cmhansrd/cm151202/debtext/151202-0001.htm
[102] BBC, 'Syria vote'.
[103] P. Wintour, 'Britain carries out first Syria airstrikes after MPs approve action against Isis', *The Guardian*, 3 December 2015, www.theguardian.com/world/2015/dec/02/syria-airstrikes-mps-approve-uk-action-against-isis-after-marathon-debate

the need to ensure that the 'right [non-Australian] boots on the ground' were in place, ahead of achieving a crucial 'political settlement'.[104] His language, however, had come a long way from his warnings, whilst still gunning to become prime minister, that Australia's narrative on ISIL risked turning the counter-terrorism debate into a 'caricature':[105]

Now, just as it's important not to underestimate or be complacent about the national security threat from Daesh, it is equally important not to overestimate that threat.

Daesh is not Hitler's Germany, Tojo's Japan or Stalin's Russia.

Its leaders dream that they, like the Arab armies of the seventh and eighth centuries, will sweep across the Middle East into Europe itself. They predict that before long they will be stabling their horses in the Vatican.

Well, Idi Amin wasn't the king of Scotland either. We should be careful not to say or do things which can be seen to add credibility to these delusions.[106]

On the other side of the political divide, the ALP's Bill Shorten promised to put the national interest over and above partisan politicking.[107] For the Green's Christine Milne, however, the memory of Afghanistan loomed large, since many Australians would 'remember young people dying in that conflict... They will be asking themselves as we stand here today: why are we going to another war in the Middle East?'[108] The position was dismissed (unfairly) by critics as posturing, given that the executive (not parliament) retained the power (by custom and convention) to authorise the military deployment. Even after the Paris attacks, Turnbull's language, in contrast to his predecessor's, was noteworthy for its caution: 'We must not let grief or anger cloud our judgement. Our response must be as clear-eyed and strategic as it is determined... Calm, clinical, professional, effective. That's how we defeat this menace.'[109]

[104] Z. Daniel, 'Islamic State: Prime Minister Malcolm Turnbull calls for "right boots on the ground" in Iraq and Syria', *ABC News*, 14 January 2015, www.abc.net.au/news/2016-01-19/prime-minister-malcolm-turnbull-washington-speech-barack-obama/7097166

[105] T. Iggulden, 'Malcolm Turnbull warns against overstating threat of Islamic State, denies comments directed at PM', *ABC News*, 8 July 2015, www.abc.net.au/news/2015-07-07/turnball-warns-against-overstating-threat-of-islamic-state/6602638

[106] Ibid.   [107] Hurst, 'Tony Abbott intensifies rhetoric about Isis'.   [108] Ibid.

[109] M. Grattan, 'Turnbull warns of increased threat of terrorism in the region after recent attacks', *The Conversation*, 24 November 2015, https://the conversation.com/turnbull-warns-of-increased-threat-of-terrorism-in-the-region-after-recent-attacks-51187

In the United States, like Australia and Britain, the discursive war of position significantly narrowed in response to the atrocities carried out by ISIL and the threat they posed to neighbouring countries. The vast majority of Republicans sided with the president's decision to take the fight to ISIL in Syria and, initially, to protect Yazidis in Iraq. While some pushed for greater action still – such as a greater American troop presence on the ground – those voices remained relatively marginalised by the toxic legacy and memory of the Iraq War.[110] Perhaps most significantly, in the push for US-led coalition warfare, Americans were now overwhelmingly supportive of a US role in combatting ISIL, as long as coalition partners were with them.[111]

Conclusion

In the Syrian Civil War's third phase, beginning in December 2013, but really taking off from the start of 2014, the Anglosphere war of position continued a number of important themes established in the war's preceding two phases, but was dramatically reframed in line with a new, game-changing development. First, for the Anglosphere and others, Syria was now two conflicts, not one. These revolved around Assad and ISIL respectively. Second, across the old Anglosphere coalition, reworked and updated discourses of the War on Terror helped to make it possible to prosecute a military campaign in which over 50,000 ISIL fighters were killed in two years at a cost of $10 billion.[112]

[110] Some academics have raised this point, though, such as, S. M. Saideman, 'The ambivalent coalition: doing the least one can do against the Islamic state', *Contemporary Security Policy*, 37 (2016), 289–305; and, for a larger-scale analysis, see R. J. Lieber, *Retreat and Its Consequences: American Foreign Policy and the Problem of World Order* (New York: Cambridge University Press, 2016).

[111] Only 4 per cent of Americans, in the wake of the Paris attacks, thought the USA should leave the fight to others. Rasmussen Reports, '49% Want to Declare War on ISIS', 23 November 2015, www.rasmussenreports.com/public_content/ politics/current_events/israel_the_middle_east/49_want_to_declare_war_on_isis. A considerable majority of Britons also favoured UK airstrikes, alongside the USA. A. Taylor and R. Noack, 'What the world thinks of Obama's plan to fight the Islamic State', *Washington Post*, 11 September 2014, www.washingtonpost .com/news/worldviews/wp/2014/09/11/what-the-world-thinks-of-obamas-plan- to-fight-the-islamic-state/?utm_term=.71e62d98dd3f

[112] BBC News, 'Islamic State "has lost 50,000 fighters" over two years', 9 December 2016, www.bbc.co.uk/news/world-middle-east-38252092; US Department of Defense, 'Operation Inherent Resolve', 26 September 2016, www.defense.gov/News/Special-Reports/0814_Inherent-Resolve

The resonance and rhetorical force of this discourse once again helped to justify and naturalise Britain and Australia fighting side-by-side with Anglosphere allies. And, moreover, it helped to enable the notion to take hold that this was an imperative war, despite the concerns that lingered, supported by a Syria is not Libya sub-discourse and the toxic legacy of Iraq. Despite this, discursive coercion – the hard nature of soft power – in all three coalition states saw the ongoing war of position become heavily lopsided, with debate, ultimately, coming to focus on the details of deployment and contestation limited to facts on the ground. The fundamental direction and necessity of this latest Anglosphere war effort enjoyed broad support, with the notable absence of bipartisanship at the very top levels of the British Labour Party. Where disagreement did arise, it was usually an urging for leaders to do more and not less in confronting the 'death cult' of ISIL.

Moreover, this narrowed war of position was also evident in debates concerning Anglosphere foreign policy towards Assad. Obama remained adamant that victory against ISIL would ultimately require the removal of Assad from power.[113] In a continuation of the discursive stalemate reached in 2013, these calls were shared across the Anglosphere. In Australia, the Labor Party toed a bipartisan line, stressing that, while Assad's 'ongoing presence would only serve as a spur to armed resistance and provide a rallying call for extremists', the 'history of success of western-led armies in this region, is poor to say the least'. Quite simply, Bill Shorten noted the 'very real risk of a protracted ground war, involving Australian personnel in danger with limited potential for it to contribute to the long-term solution we should be seeing'.[114] The underlying discourses of the Syrian Civil War – broad support for the promise of democracy ignited by the Arab Spring and deep concern at western interventionism underpinned by the legacy of Iraq – remained very much intact, despite the significant Anglosphere consensus that action against ISIL was necessary and, indeed, imperative.[115]

---

[113] BBC News, 'Syria war: "Assad must go" to ensure IS defeat – Obama', 29 September 2015, www.bbc.co.uk/news/world-middle-east-34393523

[114] Grattan, 'Turnbull warns'.

[115] Sadly and tragically, a less consensual response was reached on what by now was an unprecedented refugee crisis. See C. Hope, 'American states turn against Syrian refugees after Paris attacks', 17 November 2015, www.telegraph.co.uk/news/worldnews/northamerica/usa/11999130/American-states-turn-against-Syrian-refugees-after-Paris-attacks.html

In the Syrian Civil War's third phase, the ascendency of ISIL gave rise to a number of important developments in the Anglosphere discursive war of position. First, this stage of the conflict made clear the enduring significance of the discourses of the 'War on Terror'. No Anglosphere leader was able to shake off the discursive stranglehold their predecessors' language had on contemporary conflict and policy. Second, in particular, this hold centred on the continued affective and emotional resonance of a specific understanding of 9/11. ISIL were understood with direct reference to Al Qaeda and the events of 11 September 2001. Third, the language of 'terror' remained just as coercive regarding Syria as it had with respect to Afghanistan and Iraq previously. The notion of a 'terror threat' compelled would-be policy detractors to bite their tongues, lest they be portrayed as a 'terrorist sympathiser' or 'appeaser'. Fourth, the (re-)new(ed) terror threat once again helped to co-constitute the Anglosphere in relational and binary terms. Understood as the antithesis of violent and fanatical hatred, the fidelity of kinship between the USA, UK and Australia was renewed in opposition to a racially and religiously proscribed Other. In light of ISIL's heinous acts in Syria and beyond, Anglosphere leaders did not have to work hard to reproduce discourses of civilisation and barbarism, which helped citizens to make sense of an increasingly complex civil war, as well as their relationship to it.

7 | *Proxy War*

They are backing the butcher Assad....

British Prime Minister David Cameron[1]

Introduction

On 27 May 2015, ISIL 'Caliphate cubs' – children and teenagers – filed into the Roman amphitheatre of Palmyra in the central Syrian desert. ISIL had seized control of the city and the ancient ruins six days previously. The children lined up behind twenty-five regime soldiers, who had been arranged in a single line, on their knees.[2] In front of a large crowd and against the backdrop of a huge ISIL flag, the child soldiers drew their pistols and, on command, executed Assad's troops with simultaneous gunshots. Video of the incident surfaced the following month, alongside images of the strung-up and beheaded body of Khaled al-Asaad, an archaeologist who had served as the keeper of Palymra's ruins for over half a century.[3] He was reported to have refused to reveal the location of key artefacts,[4] given ISIL's repeated destruction of objects, statues and buildings that they believed to be

---

[1] '...*which is a terrible mistake for them and for the world*'. David Cameron cited in W. James, 'Cameron says Russian military action in Syria a "terrible mistake"', *Reuters*, 4 October 2015, http://uk.reuters.com/article/uk-mideast-crisis-syria-britain-idUKKCN0RY08520151004

[2] I. Calderwood, 'Slaughter in the Roman amphitheatre', *MailOnline*, 4 July 2015, www.dailymail.co.uk/news/article-3149469/Slaughter-amphitheatre-ISIS-executioners-brutally-shoot-dead-25-Syrian-regime-soldiers-bloodthirsty-crowds-ancient-Palmyra-ruin.html

[3] B. Schatz, 'ISIS beheaded an 82-year-old archaeologist who refused to reveal the location of ancient artifacts', *Mother Jones*, 19 August 2015, www.motherjones.com/politics/2015/08/isis-beheads-syrian-archaeologist-palmyra

[4] K. Shaheen and I. Black, 'Beheaded Syrian scholar refused to lead Isis to hidden Palmyra antiquities', *The Guardian*, 19 August 2015, www.theguardian.com/world/2015/aug/18/isis-beheads-archaeologist-syria

heresy.[5] The sign placed in front of his mutilated body listed his crimes, including links to the regime and management of Palmyra's 'idols'.[6]

One year on, on 5 May 2016, renowned Russian conductor Valery Gergiev – formerly of the London Symphony Orchestra and 'the Kremlin's favourite'[7] – stood looking towards the stage upon which those captors had been shot by their child executioners, underneath ISIL's variant of the Black Standard. In stark contrast to the previous atrocities, Gergiev's eyes focused on St Petersburg's Mariinsky Orchestra, as he led them through pieces by Johann Bach and Sergei Prokofiev, in front of a crowd comprising Russian journalists, soldiers and even government ministers.[8] The apparent serenity of the classical concert would have been difficult to imagine in the summer of 2015 and marked a clear and deliberate counterpoint to ISIL's savagery. To ensure that this strategic juxtaposition was emphasised, Russian President Vladimir Putin unexpectedly appeared via video link. His intention was to portray Russia as 'a force for good', benefitting the world by confronting international terrorism.[9] And what better could illustrate Russia's actions on behalf of the civilised world than a concert at the site where, only one year earlier, Syrian children had been forced to murder their fellow countrymen?[10]

The historic city of Palmyra is described by UNESCO as 'an oasis in the Syrian desert': 'the monumental ruins of a great city that was one of the most important cultural centres of the ancient world'.[11] Tragically, during the Syrian Civil War's fourth phase, the city became a significant prize in a military tug-of-war. Palmyra was seized by ISIL in May 2015, as part of a broader offensive. In the coming months, numerous

---

[5] Asaad was not the only one. See R. Spencer, 'Islamic State begins beheading regime fighters in Palmyra', *The Telegraph*, 21 May 2015, www.telegraph .co.uk/news/worldnews/middleeast/syria/11621055/Islamic-State-begins-beheading-regime-fighters-in-Palmyra.html

[6] Shaheen and Black, 'Beheaded Syria scholar'.

[7] L. Harding, 'Palmyra hosts Russian concert after recapture by Syrian forces', *The Guardian*, 5 May 2016, www.theguardian.com/world/2016/may/05/palmyra-amphitheatre-hosts-russian-concert-after-recapture-by-syrian-forces

[8] He had done likewise in South Ossetia in August 2008 (following Russia's invasion of Georgia).

[9] BBC News, 'Russia's Valery Gergiev conducts concert in Palmyra ruins', 5 May 2016, www.bbc.co.uk/news/world-middle-east-36211449

[10] Of course, many onlookers would have preferred to have seen Putin speak of respecting international borders and protecting civilians.

[11] UNESCO, 'Site of Palmyra', http://whc.unesco.org/en/list/23

sites of significant historical interest were destroyed and hundreds of locals killed or displaced, as residents were 'trapped between the Syrian army's bombs and the Islamic State's brutality'.[12] Several Syrians complained that the international community harboured greater concerns for the city's ruins than neighbouring Tadmur's 50,000 inhabitants.[13] In September 2015, however, the tide turned decisively in favour of Assad's forces, as Russia unexpectedly entered the fray in Syria at his behest.[14]

Russia's intervention was hugely significant for the outcome of the Syrian Civil War. Despite lip-service being paid to the battle against ISIL, Russia's intervention came in support of, and following a request from, Assad.[15] Moreover, the majority of Russia's efforts were directed against increasingly fractured opposition groups other than ISIL. As the first Russian military intervention outside of the territory of the former Soviet Union since the end of the Cold War, this was a significant decision and gamble for Vladimir Putin, who pitched the intervention as cost-neutral, since it amounted to a live-fire training exercise for Russian forces. However, before the end of the year, two major incidents would test the Russian President's resolve. First, in response to the downing of Metrojet 9268 by an apparent IED[16] at the end of October, Putin opted to increase Russia's efforts in Syria, 'so as to make it clear to the criminals that vengeance is inevitable'.[17] Second, in November, came the shooting down of a Russian attack aircraft jet by a Turkish F-16, following its crossing of the Turkish border. In the fallout following the shooting, the ejected Russian pilot was shot by

[12] B. Alshami, 'Between bombs and beheadings: Palmyra after the ISIS takeover', *News Deeply*, 21 July 2015, www.newsdeeply.com/syria/articles/2015/07/21/between-bombs-and-beheadings-palmyra-after-the-isis-takeover

[13] Ibid.

[14] Although, in December 2016 and into January 2017, ISIL once again made advances into Palmyra, meeting fierce government and Russian resistance. And, once again, beheadings and destruction soon followed. See BBC News, 'Syria: IS destroys part of Palmyra amphitheatre', 20 June 2017, www.bbc.co.uk/news/world-middle-east-38689131

[15] See, for explanation, R. Allison, 'Russia and Syria'.

[16] The Russian investigation later concurred with western assessments, suggesting the plane was brought down by an apparent explosion caused by up to one kilogram of TNT.

[17] S. Calder, 'Russian plane crash Q&A: why has Russia now confirmed Metrojet flight 9268 was bombed?', *The Independent*, 17 November 2015, www.independent.co.uk/news/world/europe/russian-plane-crash-qa-why-has-russia-now-confirmed-metrojet-flight-9268-was-bombed-a6737701.html

rebel forces as he descended by parachute.[18] Putin's response was furious and Russia's military intervention in Syria was, once again, further escalated.

Following these incidents, Putin moved to further widen the apparent divide between Russian efforts and those of NATO members, including what he – alongside several observers in the west – saw as Turkey's de facto support for ISIL.[19] Russian ground troops were deployed to Syria at the end of 2015, with Russian airstrikes reaching a crescendo at the start of 2016.[20] The intensity of the airstrikes overwhelmed rebel and opposition fighters, enabling Assad's forces to make significant advances on the ground. These territorial advances provided a notable position of strength for Assad, from which negotiations and ceasefires could be pursued. The importance of Russian airstrikes was made most apparent by their selective engagement and resulting absence from specific theatres. For example, when absent in battles led by Iranian-backed pro-government militias, Assad's progress was almost impossible.[21] Where Russian-assisted progress was perhaps slowest and most deadly was Aleppo. But, gradually and painfully, by December 2016, sustained attrition meant that even the rebel-held swath of Eastern Aleppo was re-taken, with large-scale evacuations of civilians coordinated by the ICRC (see Chapter 1). In the fourth phase of the Civil War, the addition of Russia's military weight to the previously finely balanced conflict decisively (if not conclusively) tilted the scales in Assad's favour.

In order to analyse Anglosphere foreign policy during the Syrian Civil War's fourth phase, this chapter is structured in three parts. In its first section, the chapter considers the Anglosphere's dominant and official discursive response to Russia's shock intervention in the conflict, noting that, while unity was retained, some small fractures began to emerge amongst the authorised elite voices of the old Anglosphere coalition. Second, the chapter explores the impact of the new landscape

---

[18] An attempted rescue was launched, in which a second Russian was also killed.

[19] Not least, given Turkey's decision not to draw a distinction between the YPG (crucial to coalition efforts on the ground) and the PKK.

[20] S. Sheller, 'Russia is in charge in Syria: how Moscow took control of the battlefield and negotiating table', *War on the Rocks*, 28 June 2016, https://warontherocks.com/2016/06/russia-is-in-charge-in-syria-how-moscow-took-control-of-the-battlefield-and-negotiating-table

[21] For instance, in the countryside, south of Aleppo. Ibid.

of the Syrian Civil War on the extant discourses that gave it meaning, as they once again clashed and developed in response to Putin's intervention. Here, the chapter notes that, in the fourth phase, the Anglosphere's transnational discursive war of position evolved and shifted, in particular due to the growth of the notion that it was now imperative to end the conflict, even if that meant abandoning the core liberal principles that had underpinned the Anglosphere's response to the crisis since its outset. Third, the chapter considers another unforeseen shock and game-changing event, replete with complex ties to Putin's Russia: the election of Donald Trump as the 45th President of the United States. Trump's particular brand of populist Jacksonian foreign policy, along with his complex and controversial relationship with Russia, made his unlikely victory particularly consequential for the discourses and policies of war and peace in Syria, now at the centre of increasingly explicit Great Power proxy conflict.

Russia, Assad and Proxy War

At the start of September 2015, 'Russia quietly sent military personnel and tanks into Syria', alarming onlookers in the USA, UK, Australia and France.[22] At the end of that month, for the first time in a decade, Russian President Vladimir Putin took the opportunity to address the United Nations. He followed on from Barack Obama and, although speaking for less than half of the time of his American counterpart, dramatically stole the show. Russia's intervention in Syria, he suggested, was part of the same struggle that America and its allies were fighting. Now, he suggested, as at the start of the 1940s, the Anglosphere could and should opt to unite with Russia, in facing down a common enemy in Islamic State.

We should finally acknowledge that no one but President Assad's armed forces and Kurd militia are truly fighting the Islamic State and other terrorist organizations in Syria... We think it is an enormous mistake to refuse to cooperate with the Syrian government and its armed forces, who are valiantly fighting terrorism face to face.[23]

[22] M. Korin, 'Putin's Syria gambit', *The Atlantic*, 28 September 2015, www .theatlantic.com/international/archive/2015/09/putin-russia-syria-united-nations/407716
[23] Ibid.

As *The Observer's* John Schindler put it: 'there's a new sheriff in town'.[24]

On the one hand, Russia's intervention in Syria changed everything. And, on the other hand, it changed absolutely nothing at all. The Anglosphere's mutual foreign policy position had long previously been hamstrung, torn between the liberal call for Assad's inevitable and necessary removal from power and tempered realist desire to avoid paying the costs that would be required to ensure such an aspiration was realised. Putin's intervention clearly if not decisively strengthened Assad's hand, but this only served to exacerbate the gap at the heart of Anglosphere foreign policy in Syria, rather than create it. Now, however, it was clear to Obama, Cameron and Turnbull that any change in Syria's governance would require a period of political transition. And official Anglosphere foreign policy discourse largely acknowledged the newly apparent starkness of that reality.

In September 2015, for example, in his speech at the UN, Obama took aim at Putin, insisting that Assad must go, but a period of transition would be inevitable. He 'rejected the notion of partnering with "tyrants like Assad who drop barrel bombs on innocent children"'.[25] Obama noted 'that while the U.S. is willing to "work with any nation including Russia and Iran" to end the conflict in Syria', he remained torn between the liberal cry that 'there cannot be after so much bloodshed, so much carnage, a return to the status quo' and his instinctive realist pragmatism: 'Realism dictates that compromise will be required... realism also requires a managed transition away from Assad and to a new leader'.[26] The following month, the president moved to de-centre America's own story and desires from the equation, while continuing to lament Russian intervention: 'This is not some superpower chessboard contest', but Putin 'doesn't distinguish between ISIL and a moderate Sunni opposition that wants to see Mr Assad go. From their perspective, they're all terrorists. And that's a recipe for disaster'.[27]

[24] Ibid.
[25] J. Keating, 'Obama counters Putin on Syria', *Slate*, 28 September 2015, www.slate.com/blogs/the_slatest/2015/09/28/obama_general_assembly_speech_president_says_assad_must_go_rejects_russia.html
[26] Ibid.
[27] S. Walker et al., 'Obama says Russian strategy in Syria is "recipe for disaster"', *The Guardian*, 2 October 2015, www.theguardian.com/world/2015/oct/02/us-coalition-warns-russia-putin-extremism-syria-isis

In short, he urged that Russia heed America's own experience in the region: a 'military solution alone – an attempt by Russia and Iran to prop up Assad and try to pacify the population – is just going to get them stuck in a quagmire and it won't work'.[28] This nuanced position, balanced between traditions and extremes, found support amongst some of the Anglosphere commentariat, even where it was further tempered. As Thomas Freidman put it, Obama may well have been right, but he appeared to be a 'leader who lacks the courage of his own ambivalence'.[29] Nonetheless, Secretary of State John Kerry gave voice to a position amounting to 'Assad must go, just not straight way': 'Assad must go... [but] it doesn't have to be on Day One or Month One'.[30]

In November, following the Paris terrorist attacks, Obama was asked explicitly about the twin competing foci of US foreign policy – defeating ISIL and removing Assad – in light of Russia's intervention into the fray. His response was robust:

[We are] destroying ISIL... with every aspect of American power and with all the coalition partners that we've assembled. It's going to get done. It will be helpful if Russia directs its focus on ISIL and I do think that as a consequence of ISIL claiming responsibility for bringing down their plane, there is an increasing awareness on the part of President Putin that ISIL poses a greater threat to them than anything else in the region.[31]

The president, therefore, remained hopeful, asking whether Russia could 'make the strategic adjustment that allows them to be effective partners with us and the other 65 countries who are already part of the counter-ISIL campaign'.[32] The world, Obama noted, simply did not 'know that yet'.[33] But, given that 'their principal targets have been the moderate opposition that they felt threatened Assad', it was clear to

---

[28] Ibid.; also, K. Liptak, 'Obama: Russia heading for "quagmire" in Syria', *CNN*, 2 October 2015, http://edition.cnn.com/2015/10/02/politics/president-obama-syria-russia-assad

[29] T. Friedman, 'Syria, Obama and Putin', *New York Times*, 30 September 2015, www.nytimes.com/2015/09/30/opinion/thomas-friedman-syria-obama-and-putin.html?_r=0

[30] P. McDonnell, 'Analysis: with Syria policy in tatters, Obama may relax stance on Assad', *LA Times*, 27 September 2015, www.latimes.com/world/middleeast/la-fg-analysis-syria-policy-assad-20150927-story.html

[31] B. Obama, 'Press conference by President Obama', *White House*, Kuala Lumpur, 22 November 2015, https://obamawhitehouse.archives.gov/the-press-office/2015/11/22/remarks-president-obama-press-conference

[32] Ibid.   [33] Ibid.

most onlookers that the US president was attempting to inspire a change of Russian policy, rather than offer an accurate portrayal of the current state of play.[34] As Obama acknowledged:

[Russia's] principal goal appeared to be – if you follow the strikes that they took – to fortify the position of the Assad regime. And that does not add to our efforts against ISIL. In some ways, it strengthens it because ISIL is also fighting many of those groups that the Russians were hitting... So they're going to have to make an adjustment in terms of what they're prioritizing.[35]

He chose to remain, however, hopeful on both fronts, noting that 'Russia has not officially committed to a transition of Assad moving out, but they did agree to the political transition process.' He placed emphasis on the potential for mutually beneficial policy aspirations to be adopted, suggesting that he thought America might soon 'find out... whether or not we can bring about that change of perspective with the Russians'. He reiterated the US position, however, that compromise would need to come from the Russians because Assad's position was untenable and intolerable:

The issue with Assad is not simply the way that he has treated his people. It's not just a human rights issue. It's not just a question of supporting somebody who has been ruthlessly dropping bombs on his own civilian populations. As a practical matter, it is not conceivable that Mr. Assad can regain legitimacy in a country in which a large majority of that country despises Assad and will not stop fighting so long as he's in power, which means that the civil war perpetuates itself... [the message, crafted for Putin's ears, was clearly that] this is a practical issue, not just a matter of conscience.[36]

For his critics, this optimism would appear misplaced at best and naïve at worst.

Following the further escalation of Russian military activity inside of Syria, by the spring of 2016 Obama's strategy shifted. While he continued to downplay the centrality of Great Power proxy warfare to Syria's Civil War – 'This is not a contest between me and Putin'[37] – the president retained a keen focus on the Russian president, even if his message had been refocused in line with the new reality that impacted

[34] Ibid.   [35] Ibid.   [36] Ibid.
[37] N. Toosi, 'Obama on Syria: 'This is not a contest between me and Putin', *Politico*, 16 February 2016, www.politico.com/story/2016/02/syria-russia-cease-fire-219328

on the Anglosphere's accumulated triptych military objectives. First, Obama continued, with limited success, to pressure Putin to 'work together on the problems we all face [in the form of ISIL]'.[38] Having failed to get Russia to focus primarily on ISIL, the US president was by now effectively reduced to lobbying Putin on America and the Anglosphere's second and third priority areas: the end of the civil war in Syria and the removal of Assad from power. On the latter, however, he was quite clearly failing to find any sympathy from Russia. One of the initial aims of the Anglosphere – the removal of Assad – was now rendered increasingly unlikely due directly to Russia's influence and new centrality within the conflict. Struggling to achieve any headway with the Russians on the twin threats the Anglosphere identified – ISIL and Assad – Obama opted to instead focus on a more modest objective, calling on Putin to apply pressure on Assad to comply with a cessation of hostilities.[39] Even here though, progress was tortuous. As Obama was forced to admit, as late as September 2016 (one year on from Putin's intervention): 'Given the gaps of trust that exist' calls for any cessation of hostilities represented 'a tough negotiation',[40] even if Putin remained outwardly confident that such a development was possible.[41]

Through the Syrian Civil War's fourth phase, the Anglosphere remained largely united, despite the emergence of minor cracks and divergences, not least within the domestic landscape of its most junior partner, with Tony Abbott reluctantly making way as Malcolm Turnbull seized the leadership. To begin with, the key question was whether the patrician Turnbull would continue Abbott's 'gung-ho' Syria policy,[42] following his 'ouster'. American counterparts were keenly aware that 'Washington ha[d] lost its biggest booster for

[38] J. Borger, 'Putin says he can work with Obama despite trading barbs on Syria and Isis', *The Guardian*, 29 September 2015, www.theguardian.com/world/2015/sep/27/putin-russia-syria-assad-propaganda-gangster

[39] M. Shear and N. Cumming-Bruce, 'Obama calls on Putin to help reduce violence in Syria after peace talks stall', *New York Times*, 18 April 2016, www.nytimes.com/2016/04/19/world/middleeast/syria-talks-stall-as-opposition-negotiators-withdraw.html

[40] M. Landler, '"Gaps of trust" with Russia bar a Syrian truce, Obama says', *New York Times*, 5 September 2016, www.nytimes.com/2016/09/06/world/europe/g20-obama-syria.html?_r=0

[41] Ibid.

[42] H. Clark, 'Australia begins flights over Syria', *The Diplomat*, 14 September 2015, http://thediplomat.com/2015/09/australia-begins-flights-over-syria

Australian action against ISIS'.[43] And this view appeared vindicated as one of Turnbull's first calls was to temporarily suspend Australian airstrikes, following Putin's intervention. His justification centred on a newly emergent theme of Australian foreign policy discourse that would become important in the following weeks and months – the notion that Syria's complexity was part of the problem and a preventer of any resolution.[44] Chief of Joint Operations David Johnston, for example, 'conceded that Russia's involvement in the region has added a level of complexity to the deadly conflict': 'It is increasingly a complex area in Syria and I think the entry of Russian forces increases that complexity further.'

Extending this theme, Foreign Minister Julie Bishop continued to invoke memories of Abbott's 'baddies versus baddies' statement, arguing that, 'if the Assad regime were to be removed or collapse, it would create a vacuum that could be filled by an even more diabolical presence'.[45]

Nevertheless, Australia remained a stalwart and steadfast Anglosphere ally, contributing a significant share of military operations. Australia even changed the law in order to enable the extension of their airstrikes to target ISIL support personnel.[46] And they were a key player in a series of airstrikes that accidentally killed a moderate number of Assad's forces.[47] The US–Australian joint response to that incident, but particularly the stance taken in Canberra, was one of apology accompanied by vocal criticism of Russia for politicising the mistake.[48] In this instance and throughout, complexity remained a

[43] Ibid.

[44] S. Medhora, 'Australian jets diverted from Syria as Russia's entry complicates mission', *The Guardian*, 7 October 2015, www.theguardian.com/australia-news/2015/oct/07/australian-airstrikes-in-syria-on-hold-as-russias-entry-complicates-mission

[45] A. Lockyer, 'Australia's possible strategy shift on Syria is a nod to Russia's influence', *The Conversation*, 1 October 2015, http://theconversation.com/australias-possible-strategy-shift-on-syria-is-a-nod-to-russias-influence-48380

[46] P. Karp, 'Australia to change law to allow strikes on more Isis combatants', *The Guardian*, 1 September 2016, www.theguardian.com/australia-news/2016/sep/01/australia-to-change-law-to-allow-strikes-on-more-isis-combatants

[47] P. Karp, 'Malcolm Turnbull says Australia involved in mistaken bombing of Syrian troops', *The Guardian*, 19 September 2016, www.theguardian.com/australia-news/2016/sep/19/malcolm-turnbull-says-australia-bombed-syrian-troops-by-mistake

[48] M. Kenny, 'Malcolm Turnbull slams Russian "contradictions" while admitting Australian bombs in Syria', *Sydney Morning Herald*, 19 September 2016,

recurrent Australian narrative theme. It was a narrative that emphasised warnings against 'proxy war'[49] but noted the ways in which the
involved parties were now so 'intractably opposed' that it was inevitably difficult to make any headway.[50]

In this context and from the outset of the new Australian leadership,
Julie Bishop and Malcolm Turnbull were relatively quick to note the
need for Assad to stay on during a transition towards power sharing.[51]
The language of Australian foreign policy in this period was, at times,
more nuanced than in the USA and UK, with Prime Minister Turnbull
noting that, 'Plainly, when you look at Daesh, the basis [of the extremist
movement] is the Sunni population that has felt disenfranchised in Syria
with very good reason and has also felt left out of the new government
in Iraq.'[52] Such a statement was out of step with the official language of
the old Anglosphere coalition's senior partners, acknowledging as it did
the social bases that helped to underpin the Islamist terrorist and
insurgent group. However, on Assad at least, Turnbull and Australia
remained in line with their coalition allies, expressing adamantly that
Assad would inevitably have to make way following a transition period
and as part of a political solution to the crisis:

As far as Assad is concerned, I think it is clear that there can be no solution in
Syria other than a political solution. There is no military solution... a key
element of any political solution must be a transition from Mr Assad and from
his leadership to other leadership; that is clear and that is a factor that is driven
by the depth of the antagonisms against the Assad regime within Syria.[53]

www.smh.com.au/federal-politics/political-news/malcolm-turnbull-slams-
russian-contradictions-while-admitting-australian-bombs-in-syria-20160918-
grj532.html

[49] Ibid.

[50] D. Shanahan, 'Malcolm Turnbull warns of Russia-US proxy war in Syria', *The
Australian*, 22 September 2016, www.theaustralian.com.au/national-affairs/
foreign-affairs/malcolm-turnbull-warns-of-russiaus-proxy-war-in-syria/news-
story/907fc9264751b65e8db2a69e7f7919fa

[51] K. Murphy, 'Apec summit: Malcolm Turnbull says Syria solution hinges on
power sharing', *The Guardian*, 18 November 2015, www.theguardian.com/
world/2015/nov/18/apec-summit-malcolm-turnbull-says-syria-solution-hinges-
on-power-sharing

[52] Ibid.

[53] D. Hurst, 'Malcolm Turnbull says transition from Assad is the only option for
Syria', *The Guardian*, 5 October 2015, www.theguardian.com/australia-news/
2015/oct/05/malcolm-turnbull-says-transition-from-assad-is-the-only-option-
for-syria

While the Australian government was careful not to overstep the mark with Anglosphere partners, Turnbull and Bishop's language did mark a disjuncture with US and UK counterparts in two senses: Australia's calls for Assad to be a part of the solution in Syria were far clearer and made far earlier than British and American acknowledgements that political transition would be necessary. Two sub-discourses – complexity and the tainted plethora of opposition groups – fed into this position, sustaining the new notion that there was 'an emerging consensus that the Assad regime would likely be pivotal in fortifying the Syrian state and preventing further gains by the Islamic State group'.[54] Bishop argued that it was clear 'there must be a political as well as a military solution to the conflict in Syria' and, moreover, there was 'an emerging view in some quarters that the only conceivable option would be a national unity government involving President Assad'.[55]

After meeting Putin, Turnbull's calls for transition and compromise were noted in the Australian media, with academic contributors emphasising the initial impossibility of free and fair elections in the absence of so many displaced Syrians.[56] However, in lock step with the USA and UK, Turnbull remained wedded explicitly to the tension at the heart of Anglosphere foreign policy in Syria: 'Clearly a political solution is required, but as far as our involvement is concerned it is focused solely on Daesh and it is part of our work to defend Iraq.'[57] In other words, Assad must go, but it is not the job of the Anglosphere to make that happen. What was seen to be Australia's job was the battle against ISIL. And, on that front, praise from Anglosphere allies was particularly high, with US officials noting that, 'On the list of people who need to step up, they [Australia] are at the bottom'.[58] Despite

---

[54] Staff and wires, 'Australia set to abandon opposition to Assad as part of Syria settlement', *The Guardian*, 26 September 2015, www.theguardian.com/australia-news/2015/sep/26/australia-set-to-abandon-opposition-to-assad-as-part-of-syria-settlement

[55] Ibid.   [56] Kenny, 'Malcolm Turnbull slaps down'.

[57] Hurst, 'Malcolm Turnbull says transition from Assad is the only option for Syria'.

[58] Colonel Steve Warren, US military spokesman, cited in S. Kimmorley, 'US military praises Australia's efforts in Iraq and Syria, Turnbull calls on Europe to "step up"', *Business Insider*, 16 January 2016, www.businessinsider.com.au/us-military-praises-australias-efforts-in-iraq-and-syria-turnbull-calls-on-europe-to-step-up-2016-1

praise such as this, Australia's calls to end the conflict, whatever the necessary compromises that might entail, continued unabated. Assad was, very much, now seen as part of the solution by Australia.[59] By the end of 2016, Bishop and Turnbull even floated language suggesting Russia *and the United States* might consider withdrawal from Syria, in lieu of a peace settlement.[60] Clearly, the old Anglosphere coalition was under strain, with its most junior partner resisting the potential for indefinite military expenditure in a conflict that appeared to have no possibility for a good outcome and every likelihood of an undesirable settlement, regardless of continued Anglosphere airstrikes.

As Obama's reign came towards its end, it was clear that Russia had out-manoeuvred the USA and the Anglosphere. The USA had been 'boxed out' by Russia's initial unexpected decision to intervene, its effective military contribution and the platform that generated for negotiations and temporary ceasefires.[61] This relative isolation of American and Anglosphere power endured through to the end of Obama's tenure.[62] Defending his foreign policy legacy, President Obama reiterated his denigration of Russia's actions and the Anglo-sphere's long-standing position on Assad:

We have seen a deliberate strategy of surrounding, besieging and starving innocent civilians... Responsibility for this brutality lies in one place alone: the Assad regime and its allies Russia and Iran... The blood for these atrocities are on their hands... The Assad regime cannot slaughter its way to legitimacy.[63]

---

[59] P. Maley, 'Assad "part of solution in Syria" – Julie Bishop signals policy change', *The Australian*, 25 September 2015, www.theaustralian.com.au/national-affairs/foreign-affairs/assad-part-of-solution-in-syria–julie-bishop-signals-policy-change/news-story/038662bcde096e87a74d1f83cb9869e9

[60] J. Owens, 'Agree to ceasefire or withdraw from Syria Julie Bishop tells US and Russia', *The Australian*, 26 September 2016, www.theaustralian.com.au/national-affairs/foreign-affairs/agree-to-ceasefire-or-withdraw-from-syria-julie-bishop-tells-us-and-russia/news-story/10822cc8a028ca4def5239262b8b005b

[61] P. Shinkman, 'Russia's cease-fire in Syria boxes out the U.S.', *US News*, 29 December 2016, www.usnews.com/news/world/articles/2016-12-29/vladimir-putins-cease-fire-in-syria-boxes-out-barack-obama

[62] P. Wintour, 'Sponsors of Syria talks in Astana strike deal to protect fragile ceasefire', *The Guardian*, 24 January 2017, www.theguardian.com/world/2017/jan/24/syria-talks-astana-russia-turkey-iran-ceasefire

[63] R. Brown and K. Liptak, 'Obama: Syrians' blood on hands of Assad and Russia', *CNN*, 16 December 2016, http://edition.cnn.com/2016/12/16/politics/obama-syria-assad-russia-aleppo

On America's inaction – the lack of direct military intervention targeted at Assad's forces – Obama was unusually candid and robust in his defence of US policy:

Unless we were all-in and willing to take over Syria, we were going to have problems... I understand the impulse to want to do something, but ultimately what I've had to do is to think about what we can sustain, what is realistic. And my first priority has to be what's the right thing to do for America... Based on hours of meetings... where we went through every option in painful detail... short of putting large numbers of US troops on the ground, uninvited, without any international law mandate, without sufficient support from Congress [it would have been impossible].[64]

This was, then, an admittance that a concern, as a modern Jeffersonian president,[65] for the high price of American blood and treasure, coupled to the risks of quagmire for a war-weary country, outweighed the potential benefits of regime change, for Americans and for Syrians. The latter's continued massacre was a price worth paying, despite the repeated normative liberal mantra and insistence that Assad must go. Quite simply and arguably quite sadly, Obama noted that the reason Assad had remained in place was, when it came to toppling the regime, America 'couldn't do it on the cheap'.[66]

What, then, of the old Anglosphere coalition's second member, the United Kingdom? Sadly for the war effort, this was not the first time that Prime Minister David Cameron would become distracted. Just as riots on the streets of London had detracted from British efforts in Libya, as the PM's head was turned to the consequences of domestic civil unrest, so once again was the UK establishment unexpectedly preoccupied with an uprising at home. This time, however, collective displeasure was expressed through the ballot box. Having been relatively unaffected by the 2015 General Election, British foreign policy was set for a potentially fundamental realignment the following year. In the months leading up to 23 June, British politics was increasingly dominated by the UK's referendum on membership of the European Union. The outcome was neither expected nor desired by the majority of the country's elected representatives, policy makers and practitioners. 'Brexit' would become the word of the year, as the decision to leave

---

[64] Ibid.   [65] Holland, 'Obama as modern Jeffersonian'.
[66] Brown and Liptak, 'Obama'.

the EU threatened to envelope all who stood in its way – including the prime minister, who stepped down to be replaced by Theresa May – and extend its tentacles into each and every aspect of British political life. The UK, once again, had more pressing concerns, far closer to home, with which to contend.

Following Putin's intervention, Britain's position was initially in lock step with Obama, as Cameron, buoyed by his electoral victory and freed from the constraints of coalition government, denounced him as 'backing the butcher Assad'.[67] He decried Russia's new war as a 'terrible mistake'.[68] But his urging for Putin to 'change direction' and join Anglosphere efforts targeting ISIL fell on deaf ears.[69] Like Obama and Turnbull, Cameron altered the UK's stance on Assad's imminent removal from power, admitting that the Syrian leader would be retained through a transition phase.[70] Anglosphere foreign policy remained united even in its evolution in line with the new geopolitical reality in Syria. That reality served only to increase the refugee flow out of Syria, as the number of displaced persons ballooned and Syrians fled from Russian air power. Throughout the fourth phase of the Syrian Civil War, as Europe accommodated a growing number of Syrian refugees, the UK's focus remained on addressing the issue at source through increased aid.[71] In the wake of a Brexit outcome fuelled in significant part by migration concerns, new prime minister Theresa May made little effort to alter Cameron's position on refugees, or indeed modify British foreign policy towards Syria at all. The UK, like the USA and Australia, remained a key player in the battle against ISIL but uncommitted to the action necessary to topple the regime responsible for the deaths of seven times as many Syrians. The Anglosphere remained united in opposition to ISIL and Assad, but on the latter, the coalition responded broadly as one to the commencement of proxy

---

[67] James, 'Cameron says Russian military action in Syria a "terrible mistake"'.
[68] Ibid.   [69] Ibid.
[70] B. Riley-Smith, 'Cameron drops demand for Assad to go, as he targets Isil', *The Telegraph*, 26 September 2015, www.telegraph.co.uk/news/worldnews/middleeast/syria/11894052/Cameron-drops-demand-for-Assad-to-go-as-he-targets-Isil.html
[71] J. Stone, 'Increasing humanitarian aid to Syria will stop refugees travelling to Europe, David Cameron says', *The Independent*, 4 February 2016, www.independent.co.uk/news/uk/politics/increasing-humanitarian-aid-to-syria-will-stop-refugees-travelling-to-europe-david-cameron-says-a6852941.html

war, noting the necessity of a compromise: a period of transition, leading to a political solution. Now, though, as before, there was a lack of commitment to the military solution required to ensure that preferred outcome would be realised.

Debate, Division and Political Transition

Throughout the Syrian Civil War's fourth phase, the Anglosphere war of position continued to rage. Critics remained spread along a spectrum of interventionist positions, critiquing the official coalition's policy from a range of vantage points, with calls for more and less intervention pivoting around the twin enemies of ISIL and Assad. On the former, calls from some to end the war against ISIL remained a relative minority, faced with greater demands to do more to end the atrocities the group continued to carry out. On ISIL, support was generally broad, as the coalition appeared to strike a measured balance, defending allies and containing the threat posed, without committing wholesale to boots on the ground in Syria. On Assad, debate raged, with calls to confront the regime militarily ebbing in light of the new reality that Putin's actions had engendered. Now, official Anglosphere policy was increasingly faced with arguments that it was time to abandon liberal calls for Assad to go, bringing coalition policy into line with the new era of realpolitik that had engulfed Syria. In the fourth phase of the crisis, in the midst of Great Power proxy warfare, critical voices primarily coalesced around the need to compromise on liberal values and their associated calls for regime change, in order to achieve a greater good: the end of the conflict in Syria, even if that came at the price of Assad's ultimate victory.

Democrats such as Samantha Power continued to apply interventionist pressures through appeals to human rights; she argued, accurately enough, that there had been 'a meltdown of humanity' in Aleppo, asking, of Putin as well as Washington's policy makers, 'is there nothing that will shame you?' On the other side of the aisle and therefore continuing to contribute to a bipartisan interventionist counterpoint to the Obama administration, the usual suspect Republicans – foremost Lindsay and McCain – persevered in making the case for greater US action to end Syria's suffering. In a joint statement, for example, the senators noted that Putin's entry into the fray was 'the inevitable result of hollow words and inaction' on the part of President

Obama.[72] However, notwithstanding these continued calls to do more, the war of position's centre of gravity was shifting away from liberal interventionism and its associated discourses. Thomas Friedman, amongst others, succinctly articulated this renewed suspicion of more hawkish voices in the wake of Russia's intervention.

Obama's Republican critics... blithely advocate 'fire, ready, aim' in Syria without any reason to believe their approach will work there any better than it did for us in Iraq or Libya [by now seen as a failure, following the country's descent into chaos]. People who don't know how to fix inner-city Baltimore think they know how to rescue downtown Aleppo – from the air![73]

For Friedman, these were, quite simply, 'critics who lack the wisdom of their own experience'.[74]

The memory of Iraq continued to loom large, haunting the corridors of the White House and colouring discussions of US options in Syria. Russia's intervention had only served to bolster the concerns that had arisen as a result of the 'dumb war's' toxic legacy. For his critics, however, this was now a fundamental and disabling problem: Obama's 'errors of understanding and judgment' were 'driven by' his 'commitment to avoid his predecessor's mistakes'.[75]

The Obama presidency's relentless focus on avoiding entanglements came alongside a failure to reckon with risks – especially those risks that grow from inaction.[76]

Iraq's legacy went much of the way to explaining the fact that Obama's foreign policy was built upon the mantra of 'don't do stupid shit'.[77] For critics of his administration's interventionist timidity, this mantra led, ironically, to ill-advised dithering and avoidance of confrontation at key moments where and when American military might could have effectively been deployed to US and global advantage. With Obama, though, as always, such an approach was viewed as imperative caution, married to pragmatist ethics – it amounted to a balanced,

---

[72] Brown and Liptak, 'Obama: Syrians' blood on hands of Assad and Russia'.
[73] Friedman, 'Syria, Obama and Putin'.   [74] Ibid.
[75] T. Cofman Wittes, 'The slipperiest slope of them all', *The Atlantic*, 12 March 2016, www.theatlantic.com/international/archive/2016/03/obama-doctrine-goldberg-inaction/473520
[76] Ibid.
[77] For discussion, see Bentley and Holland, *The Obama Doctrine* and Bentley and Holland, *Obama's Foreign Policy*.

reasoned and rational stance. As Jeff Goldberg astutely summarised, 'Obama has bet and seems prepared to continue betting, that the price of direct U.S. action would be higher than the price of inaction... And he is sanguine enough to live with the perilous ambiguities of his decisions',[78] including the denouncement of his political adversaries within America's war of position.

Despite the apparent lack of good options at this stage of the crisis, Obama came in for significant criticism in the face of Putin's apparently superior geostrategic manoeuvring. Prominent neoconservative Max Boot gave clear and explicit voice to the growing notion that there was a clash between Obama's broadly liberal worldview (and the call for Assad to go) and Putin's decidedly more nineteenth century philosophy of realpolitik. For Boot, in line with many other onlookers and commentators at the time, in 'the clash between these two incompatible visions of the world, there is no doubt which one is winning'; he painted a picture of Putin 'rewriting the rules of the international game in his favor', from Crimea to Syria.[79]

Seen through a lens of morality, what Putin has done is monstrous – he is helping to prop up a bloodthirsty regime that has been responsible for killing hundreds of thousands of people and turning millions more into refugees. But from the narrow vantage point of Russian self-interest, Putin has pulled off another coup and shown that he is a more adept international poker player than his counterpart in Washington.[80]

The narrative here was clear: in 'the Syria chess game', Putin had outwitted Obama[81] and Russia – not America – was the 'big winner' of any temporary Syrian truce, including in February 2016[82] and January 2017.

[78] Goldberg, 'Obama'.
[79] M. Boot, 'How a monstrous Putin beat the U.S. in Syria', *LA Times*, 15 March 2016, www.latimes.com/opinion/op-ed/la-oe-boot-putin-removes-troops-from-syria-20160316-story.html
[80] Ibid.
[81] I. Tharoor, 'In the Syria chess game, did Putin outwit Obama?', *Washington Post*, 16 March 2016, www.washingtonpost.com/news/worldviews/wp/2016/03/16/in-the-syria-chessgame-did-putin-outwit-obama/?utm_term=.35831ca0192b
[82] S. Joshi, 'Russia is the big winner in Syria's flawed "truce"', *The Guardian*, 12 February 2016, www.theguardian.com/commentisfree/2016/feb/12/russia-big-winner-syria-flawed-truce-assad-europe-us

The strength of this narrative was sufficient for it to undergird a more wholesale discursive challenge to the official (liberal) Anglosphere mantra of Assad must go. Given Putin's effective realpolitik, renewed calls for the Anglosphere to adapt were commonplace. Amongst these calls was the urging for coalition leaders to acknowledge that Assad's removal should – both ethically and pragmatically – be a secondary concern to the principal aim of a liberal foreign policy posture: ending the war in Syria and the suffering of the Syrian people. Recurrent protagonist and *Guardian* journalist Simon Jenkins argued as much: 'the only way to stop the slaughter in Syria is for the US and its allies to work with President Assad – and to stop worrying about what looks good'.[83]

Within this resurgent discourse, the caution of a realist-premised avoidance of intervention, on the basis of the claim that 'Syria is not Libya (it might be Iraq)' had now led, perhaps inevitably, to the need to extend that realist logic to relations with the Assad regime, in order to achieve an outcome that satisfied conservative realist and liberal normative aims. While this outcome might admittedly be sub-optimal, the proponents of this cause pointed to the far worse consequences of remaining prisoner to the original liberal discourse of Assad must go. In their admittance that Assad would ultimately have to stay for a while, Anglosphere leaders were influenced by and partially sympathetic to this argument, but unable or unwilling to abandon their calls for a post-Assad Syria. They were, effectively, trapped on a sub-optimal policy course by the strength of their own liberal arguments regarding Assad's position, which had proven so resonant.

In the UK, Labour leader Jeremy Corbyn attempted to build grass-roots support for his opposition both to airstrikes against ISIL and the possibility of any military confrontation with Assad. While the latter had elite and popular appeal, the former was readily framed, by politicians and the media, as akin to terrorist sympathising. Despite the domestic turbulence of the Brexit vote, the Leader of the Opposition did repeatedly return to the issue of Syria's resolution, pressing the prime minister to act in the wake of Aleppo's 'meltdown of humanity'. That pressure, however, was to encourage the prime minister to seek an end to the suffering, through means short of British military

---

[83] S. Jenkins, 'Why the west should listen to Putin on Syria', *The Guardian*, 29 September 2015, www.theguardian.com/commentisfree/2015/sep/29/west-vladmir-putin-syria-us-assad

intervention. The calls to end what some had described as a 'modern-day Guernica' centred on humanitarian corridors, peace talks and UN aid.[84] On the other side of the House of Commons Andrew Mitchell warned of Britain's 'complicity' in the atrocities by not having taken action.[85] Mitchell, a former Conservative minister, spoke in impassioned terms, reminding parliamentarians that Britain had a decade-old commitment to the responsibility to protect, as well as denouncing the hypocrisy of confronting terrorism while tolerating 'state terror'.[86] Former Chancellor of the Exchequer George Osborne went further still, noting that the UK and the broader Anglosphere was partially responsible for the crisis in Aleppo:

I think we are deceiving ourselves in this Parliament if we believe that we have no responsibility for what has happened in Syria.

The tragedy in Aleppo did not come out of a vacuum, it was created by a vacuum, a vacuum of western leadership, of American leadership, British leadership.

Corbyn loyalists, however, remained limited in their criticism of the UK's position, insisting – in line with the zeitgeist – that Assad would '*one day* be brought to account'.[87] The apparent futility of such a position was, perhaps, best illustrated by the interruption of the former Head of the Stop the War Coalition's speech by peace activists demanding Labour do more to end Syria's suffering.[88]

   With a government trapped in its own ends-means gap and an opposition led by a particularly anti-interventionist democratic social-ist, it was left to the media to ask why and how it was that Britain had 'abandoned Syrian moderates to the bombs of Putin and Assad'?[89]

---

[84] J. Elgot, 'Jeremy Corbyn: Theresa May needs to press for Syria crisis resolution', *The Guardian*, 13 December 2016, www.theguardian.com/uk-news/2016/dec/13/corbyn-may-to-press-for-syria-crisis-aleppo-theresa-may

[85] M. Wilkinson, 'Syria's "meltdown of humanity": emergency Commons debate as Aleppo civilians executed, children trapped under bombardment', *The Telegraph*, 13 December 2016, www.telegraph.co.uk/news/2016/12/13/syria-aleppo-mps-emergency-debate-live

[86] Ibid.   [87] Ibid. Emphasis added. The line was Emily Thornberry's.

[88] C. Johnston, 'Peter Tatchell disrupts Jeremy Corbyn speech with Syria protest', *The Guardian*, 10 December 2016, www.theguardian.com/uk-news/2016/dec/10/peter-tatchell-disrupts-jeremy-corbyn-speech-with-syria-protest

[89] C. Coughlin, 'Why has Britain abandoned Syrian moderates to the bombs of Putin and Assad?', 10 February 2016, www.telegraph.co.uk/news/worldnews/middleeast/syria/12149161/Why-has-Britain-abandoned-Syrian-moderates-to-the-bombs-of-Putin-and-Assad.html

Cameron, unsurprisingly, did have an answer to this, just not the one that most people would have expected. He essentially agreed with the Australian critiques developed by Abbott and Turnbull, of there being no good options amidst increasing complexity; there were no longer sufficient moderate opposition fighters on the ground to support. He quipped, 'there aren't enough opposition ground troops', 'they're not all in the right places' and 'they're not all the sort of people you bump into at a Liberal Democrat party conference'.[90] This amounted to a significant problem for the Anglosphere: progress against Assad was impossible without ground support and there were few groups that the coalition could stomach supporting. Putin reminded Malcolm Turnbull of as much when they met, as he retorted by asking the Australian prime minster, 'I'm fighting for the legitimate Government of Syria... Who are you fighting for?'[91]

For Australian Leader of the Opposition Bill Shorten, it was clear that Syria's long-term solution had to be owned by Syrians. Despite praising the efforts of Anglosphere combat troops, Shorten reiterated Obama's argument that a military solution alone was impossible and that indefinite warfare was not an option.[92] Perhaps Australia's most significant moment of uncertainty arose following the botched airstrikes of September 2016, which accidentally targeted regime forces. Scepticism about Australia's role, however, was still muted, despite condemnation of the errant airstrikes. Where denouncements did come, these were usually from smaller parties such as the Greens: their Defence spokesman Senator Scott Ludlam argued against Australia's role in the conflict in the first place. His was a reminder of the urgent need to de-escalate and de-militarise the conflict; sentiments which, by now, were finding increasing consensus across Australia

---

[90] M. Dathan, 'Syria air strikes: David Cameron admits "there aren't enough" moderate fighters on the ground and some are "hardline"', *The Independent*, 12 January 2016, www.independent.co.uk/news/uk/politics/syria-air-strikes-david-cameron-admits-there-aren-t-enough-moderate-fighters-on-the-ground-and-some-a6808021.html

[91] C. Uhlmann, '"Who are you fighting for?" Malcolm Turnbull, Vladimir Putin and the new geopolitical reality', *ABC News*, 7 September 2016, www.abc.net.au/news/2016-09-07/g20-malcolm-turnbull-vladimir-putin-syria-war-exchange/7822542

[92] J. Owens, 'Middle East must own Iraq, Syria violence: Bill Shorten', *The Australian*, 30 November 2015, www.theaustralian.com.au/national-affairs/middle-east-must-own-iraq-syria-violence-bill-shorten/news-story/c03f05d0827d2c7ddc33c7335b86c53f

and the old Anglosphere coalition.[93] It was former US president Jimmy Carter, however, who perhaps best articulated the growing consensus on Syria, amidst the desperation inspired by Russia's intervention on behalf of Assad. Now, all that was left was to end the conflict, since it was unlikely to end well and certainly not on the terms Anglosphere states had hoped. For Carter, a good first step would be to put aside the demand that had so motivated Anglosphere foreign policy: insisting, at the outset, that Assad must go was now to insist that the Syrian Civil War – the world's foremost crisis and the cause of near-unspeakable suffering – continue indefinitely. Before consideration of anything else, it was necessary to simply 'stop the killing'.[94]

Enter Donald Trump

If Brexit had been a fundamental shock and distraction within the old Anglosphere coalition, few predicted the scale of 2016's second political earthquake. On 9 November 2016, despite gaining nearly three million fewer votes than Democratic nominee Hillary Clinton, Donald J. Trump won 306 Electoral College votes in what was, undoubtedly, an impressive presidential election victory, reminiscent of Ronald Reagan and George H. W. Bush. The implications of his win for both US foreign policy generally and policies towards Syria specifically were not immediately clear, not least because of the president's (partly habitual and partly deliberate) tendency towards self-contradiction, in combination with the unexpected and unpredicted nature of his victory.[95] Likewise, Trump's impact on the Anglosphere was also not immediately self-evident, given the co-existence of frequent denigrations of free-riding allies, a mantra of 'America first' and a tendency towards a racialised view of domestic and international politics, more reminiscent of the Anglosphere's foundational eras than contemporary world politics.

If the implications of Trump's ascendency for the broader Anglosphere alliance were not immediately clear, analysts, like policy makers,

---

[93] A. Henderson, 'Syria crisis: Defence Minister says air strikes will continue despite botched operation', *ABC News*, 19 September 2016, www.abc.net.au/news/ 2016-09-19/syria-air-strikes-will-continue-despite-botched-operation/7858694

[94] J. Carter, 'A first step for Syria? Stop the killing', *New York Times*, 20 September 2016, www.nytimes.com/2016/09/21/opinion/jimmy-carter-a-first-step-for-syria-stop-the-killing.html?_r=0

[95] W. Gallo, 'Trump embraces unpredictability as foreign policy strategy', *Voice of America* (2016).

nonetheless scrambled to find clues as to what was in store. One anecdotal early shift came in the return of Winston Churchill's bust to the Oval Office. Obama had infamously removed the effigy of a man who had fought colonial wars against his Kenyan ancestors. Trump had no such qualms. As Stephen Bannon confirmed at the Conservative Political Action Conference, the administration's raison d'etre could be found in the belief of a positive core culture of American-ness which should be celebrated and defended in the context of globalisation's onslaught against it. This, then, was an administration that was geared up to fight and win a cultural – as well as religious and racial – battle, designed to Make America Great Again. It was a culturally and racially informed understanding of the world that would not have been lost on the Anglosphere's founding figures, enthused with notions of Anglo-Saxon racial superiority. Such assumptions of common cultural identity were set to override any temporary disputes, such as Malcolm Turnbull's early scolding for having secured a deal on refugees that Trump would not have made. Therefore, while allies fretted about the US shift from burden-sharing, as advocated by Obama, to burden-shedding under Trump, the old Anglosphere coalition was at least inoculated by virtue of perceived cultural and civilisational affiliation.[96]

Trump's election campaign had been a whirlwind of bluster, lies[97] and assertive American nationalism.[98] Off the back of such clearly apparent ignorance, in combination with unabashed racism and misogyny, few gave the billionaire and reality television star much hope.[99] Yet, as Samuel Huntington had observed and foreseen, the growing gap between the 'thank God for America' public and the 'dead souls' of American elites was precisely the problem for the mass electorate and the reason metropolitan leaders could not fathom his success.[100] And, alongside

---

[96] D. Bandow, 'Trump and US alliances', *Foreign Affairs*, 25 January 2017.

[97] *New York Times*, 'Trump's lies: the definitive list', 23 June 2017, www.nytimes.com/interactive/2017/06/23/opinion/trumps-lies.html

[98] For a history and discussion of American nationalism's unusual features, see M. Pei, 'The paradoxes of American nationalism', *Foreign Policy*, 136 (2003), 31–7.

[99] Alongside Michael Moore's warnings, the two main forecast models that do not use popular vote – Helmut Norpoth's (econometric) primary model and Allan Lichtman's (algorithmic) 'Keys to the White House' model – both forecast Trump's victory months before the election.

[100] S. P. Huntington, 'Dead souls: the denationalization of the American elite', *The National Interest*, 75 (2004), 5–18.

economic nationalism – to address the 'rusted out factories, scattered like tombstones' across the American landscape[101] – Trump promised another policy in line with the desires of so-called ordinary Americans:

We will seek friendship and goodwill with the nations of the world, but we do so with the understanding that it is the right of all nations to put their own interests first.

We do not seek to impose our way of life on anyone, but rather to let it shine as an example. We will shine for everyone to follow.

We will reinforce old alliances and form new ones – and unite the civilized world against radical Islamic terrorism, which we will eradicate completely from the face of the Earth.

At the bedrock of our politics will be a total allegiance to the United States of America.[102]

Trump fused assertive patriotism with a Jacksonian promise to live-and-let-live right up until the point that an adversary threatened Americans' physical or economic well-being.[103] The result was that the USA was now primed for a repeated series of under-reactions on the world stage, with the very real possibility of spectacular over-reaction, in the event the nation was threatened. While it was not, however, Trump promised to work with any regime that could further the American interest, even those as apparently unpalatable as Russia and Syria. Trump's foreign policy stance towards Russia and Syria, like the rest of the world, was avowedly transactional – premised on deal-making and achieving the best possible outcome for America. Liberal values simply did not come into it.

Our goal is stability not chaos... We will partner with any nation that is willing to join us in the effort to defeat ISIS and radical Islamic terrorism.[104]

---

[101] D. Trump, 'Transcript: Donald Trump's foreign policy speech', *The New York Times*, 27 April 2016, www.nytimes.com/2016/04/28/us/politics/transcript-trump-foreign-policy.html

[102] Ibid.

[103] W. R. Mead, 'The Jacksonian revolt', *Foreign Affairs* (2017); see also T. Cha, 'The return of Jacksonianism: the international implications of the Trump phenomenon', *The Washington Quarterly*, 39 (2016), 83–97.

[104] Trump's thank you speech in Cincinnati, cited by J. M. Dorsey, 'The rise of Trump and its global implications—Trump's Middle East: back to the future', *RSIS Commentaries*, (2016), 304–16.

For Trump, then, it was clear that ISIL was a problem and a threat that needed to be eradicated. Assad, on the other hand, was not and could thus be approached like any other state leader: through the lens of realpolitik, deal-making and attempting to strike a bargain that worked best for the United States, even where that might mean relegating liberal values, or increasing the risks to allies.

The potential ramifications of this stance were hard to overstate. As Joseph Nye noted, it was now reasonable to ask the question: 'Will the liberal order survive?'[105] The most significant beneficiaries of this approach were two of America's hitherto greatest enemies. As Jeffrey Stacy, writing in *Foreign Affairs*, noted: 'World leaders have gone from being taken aback about Donald Trump's unexpected victory to being outright alarmed. The exceptions to this rule are Vladimir Putin and Bashar al-Assad.'[106] To be clear, Putin and Assad were 'the chief beneficiaries' of Trump's stated foreign policy position.[107] On Syria, as US Ambassador to the UN Nikki Haley informed reporters, 'You pick and choose your battles... our priority is no longer to sit there and focus on getting Assad out.'[108] On Putin, America's new president set the USA up to 'avoid acting contrary to Russian interests', in part by removing support for the moderate opposition fighting Assad.[109] No longer just as bad as the Syrian dictator, official US policy now viewed rebel fighters as 'worse than Assad'.[110] And American drone strikes continued Obama's targeting of the Islamist factions within their ranks.[111]

The composition of Trump's top foreign policy team indicated his intention to shake up Washington – draining the swamp and changing the foreign policy culture. One of the most alarming fell early. Michael Flynn lasted just over three weeks as National Security Advisor. The retired general had previously entertained a range of distasteful conspiracy theories, not least asking whether the chemical weapons attack at Ghouta might have been a false-flag event,

[105] J. S. Nye, 'Will the liberal order survive?', *Foreign Affairs* (2017).
[106] J. A. Stacey, 'The Trump doctrine', *Foreign Affairs* (2016).   [107] Ibid.
[108] M. Nichols, 'U.S. priority on Syria no longer focused on "getting Assad out": Haley', *Reuters*, 30 March 2017, www.reuters.com/article/us-mideast-crisis-syria-usa-haley-idUSKBN1712QL
[109] Ibid.   [110] Ibid.
[111] M. Chulov and T. McCarthy, 'US drone strike in Syria kills top al-Qaida leader, jihadis say', *The Guardian*, 27 February 2017, www.theguardian.com/world/2017/feb/27/us-drone-strike-in-syria-kills-top-al-qaida-leader-jihadis-say

designed to drag the USA into war in Syria. His downfall, however, came off the back of an even more alarming series of events, which were read within an emerging and controversial narrative of Russian collusion. Flynn's demise came following his lying about contact with Russian officials during the transition period ahead of Trump's inauguration. His replacement, Herbert McMaster, lasted just over one year and offered a far more nuanced view on relations with key states, as well as non-state actors, potentially at odds with the president's. This, however, only partially offset an administration unusually and significantly tilted towards pro-Russian statements and policies. Not least, Secretary of State Rex Tillerson was a long-standing critic of Russian sanctions, the former chief executive of Exxon Mobil, an associate of key Russian officials and the recipient of the Russian Order of Friendship medal, pinned on his chest by Vladimir Putin.[112] And Trump's own early statements on Putin and Russia were invariably positive and optimistic.

In combination, the new administration's lack of hostility to Assad, suspicion of Syrian rebels and apparent eagerness to work with Russia amounted to a situation in which it was both conceivable and likely that Assad's fate would be better than Obama's preferred political transition. Although it seemed clear that the new president was temperamentally unfit to be the Leader of the Free World, early optimism arose that Trump's crude transactional realism might be funnelled into a coherent strategy to end the war.[113] It was hoped that working with Russia and allowing Assad – guilty as he was – to stay in power might have enabled an earlier end to the world's worst crisis, alongside a unified ground effort to 'destroy and degrade' ISIL. When it came to the old Anglosphere coalition's efforts against ISIL, the new president was clear that he would continue and take further Obama's policy of destroying and degrading the group. Trump's campaign statements included the beliefs that killing the families of terrorists would act as a deterrent and that torture worked. There was, then, for President Trump, a clear divide between

---

[112] N. Farquhar and A. Kramer, 'How Rex Tillerson changed his tune on Russia and came to court its rulers', *New York Times*, 20 December 2016, www.nytimes.com/2016/12/20/world/europe/russia-rex-tillerson-donald-trump-secretary-of-state.html

[113] For discussion, see, A. J. Tabler and D. Ross, 'A Syria policy for Trump', *Foreign Affairs* (2016).

the twin foci of Syria's civil war: one was to be tolerated, the other eliminated. The ground appeared set for the partnership to enact such a policy, broadening out from the extant coalition to include and enlist Russian efforts. Putin's reward for agreeing to do so seemed straightforward: fight ISIL, keep Assad.[114] This was transactional foreign policy at its simplest, amidst the world's most complex crisis and civil war. After only three months in office, however, that position appeared on the verge of an abrupt U-turn.

In April 2017, in response to a chemical weapons attack at Khan Shaykhun in Idlib, President Trump ordered the launch of fifty-nine Tomahawk cruise missiles targeted at the Shayrat airbase near Homs. Justifying the airstrikes in an address to the nation, Trump emphasised the Syrian president's killing of innocent and 'beautiful babies'. His language, therefore, constituted a dramatic shift from that which helped to get him elected. On the campaign trail, when interviewed about chemical weapons, Trump had downplayed their significance.[115] Likewise, after Ghouta in 2013, Trump tweeted: 'President Obama, do not attack Syria. There is no upside and a tremendous downside. Save your powder for another (and more important) day!'[116] Yet, the day before airstrikes commenced, Trump spoke aboard Air Force One, hinting at what was to come: harsh condemnation of Assad, fixated on the cruel murder of infants, set the ground for military action. As Trump made clear, America's red line had been crossed and retaliation must follow.

What Assad did is terrible... one of the truly egregious crimes and it shouldn't have happened and it shouldn't be allowed to happen... a disgrace to humanity'.[117]

---

[114] A. Vatanka, 'Iran and Assad in the age of Trump', *Foreign Affairs* (2016).

[115] A. Vitali, 'Donald Trump praises Saddam Hussein's approach to terrorism – again', NBC, 6 July 2016, www.nbcnews.com/politics/2016-election/donald-trump-praises-saddam-hussein-s-approach-terrorism-again-n604411

[116] D. Trump, @realdonaldtrump (7 September 2013). 'President Obama, do not attack Syria. There is no upside and tremendous downside. Save your "powder" for another (and more important) day!', https://twitter.com/realdonaldtrump/status/376334423069032448?lang=en

[117] D. Trump, 'Remarks by President Trump to the press—aboard Air Force One en route West Palm Beach, Florida', 6 April 2017, www.whitehouse.gov/the-press-office/2017/04/06/remarks-president-trump-press-aboard-air-force-one-en-route-west-palm

[E]ven beautiful little babies. Their deaths was an affront to humanity... When you kill babies. Babies! Little babies... that crosses many, many lines.[118]

The next day, he added:

Assad launched a horrible chemical weapons attack on innocent civilians. Using a deadly nerve agent. Assad choked out the lives of helpless men, women and children. It was a slow and brutal death for so many. Even beautiful babies were cruelly murdered in this very barbaric attack. No child of God should ever suffer such horror.

I call on all civilized nations to join us in seeking to end the slaughter and bloodshed in Syria... We pray for the lives of the wounded and for the souls of those who have passed.[119]

After only seventy-seven days, the sight of a massacre at Khan Shaykhun appeared to cause an about-turn in Trump's Syria policy. And, despite the reversal, he was backed – loudly and clearly – by Anglosphere allies, even though it took them by surprise.

Once again, the reduction of the Syrian Civil War to the issue of Assad's use of chemical weapons was problematic. First, retaliatory military action gave the illusion of having solved a wider problem, when, in reality, chemical weapons were a relatively minor source of death for Syrian civilians. Second, taking action against the use of chemical weapons gave greater legitimacy to apparently more civilised acts of killing, helping, paradoxically, to enable Assad's military route to victory in Syria, assisted by Russia. Trump's intervention was conceptually enlightening, however, revealing as it did that the limits of transactional realpolitik seemed to be found at the asphyxiation of innocent children. At this point, Trump's realist foreign policy sentiments were replaced by a highly emotional language, centred on anger and disgust. Even for Trump, at this point, America had a responsibility to protect and to punish because there were some things that were beyond the pale, even for pragmatic, 'America first' presidents.

If Trump hoped that the strikes would deter Assad, he was wrong. One year later, in April 2018, the Syrian regime carried out a chemical attack at Douma. Over seventy people were killed, likely by a nerve

---

[118] J. Borger, 'Syria chemical attack has changed my view of Assad, says Trump', *The Guardian*, 6 April 2017, www.theguardian.com/us-news/2017/apr/05/syria-chemical-gas-attack-donald-trump-nikki-haley-assad

[119] D. Trump, 'Statement by President Trump on Syria', 7 April 2017, www.white house.gov/the-press-office/2017/04/06/statement-president-trump-syria

agent such as sarin. Once again and partially motivated by the possibility of generating a clear demarcation between his and his predecessor's policies, Trump decided to enforce the Anglosphere's 'red line'. Joined by the UK and France, the USA led a series of airstrikes against a range of Syrian regime sites, which amounted to twice the military force used the previous year. As before, military action was primarily symbolic, designed to preserve a norm of international behaviour, rather than alter the course of the civil war. In fact, the action made clear the limits of the Anglosphere's reach and influence, following the onset of explicit proxy conflict. Although regime abilities to shoot down incoming missiles were vastly overstated, the relative ineffectiveness of the airstrikes made clear the Anglosphere's decreased influence in the Syrian theatre. The Anglosphere had, by this stage, been wholly outmanoeuvred by Russia, which had acted consistently and then decisively in support of Assad. Following the airstrikes, however, that did not prevent Trump from echoing the ill-advised words of George W. Bush in declaring 'mission accomplished' in Syria.

At the end of 2018, Trump took Anglosphere and other military allies by surprise, announcing that, having defeated ISIL – Trump's 'only reason for being there' – the USA would begin to withdraw troops from Syria. With ISIL degraded but not yet destroyed, a finely balanced situation on the ground, in particular for Kurdish forces and myriad interested third parties such as Iran, Trump's decision was met with despair and condemnation by many partners. Lindsey Graham lamented the 'Obama-like mistake', which made it harder to achieve stabilisation in Syria.[120] Rushed withdrawal, he warned, could create a situation in Syria akin to 'Iraq on steroids'.[121] The surprise announcement led directly to the resignations of US Defense Secretary James Mattis and Washington's envoy for the war against ISIL, Brett McGurk. Trump could not have been further from the position of his principal advisers, such as Pompeo and Bolton, as well as key allies. In a small concession, his advisers did manage to secure a longer

[120] J. Borger and M. Chulov, 'Trump shocks allies and advisers with plan to pull US troops out of Syria', *The Guardian*, 20 December 2018, www.the guardian.com/us-news/2018/dec/19/us-troops-syria-withdrawal-trump

[121] Lindsey Graham cited in Reuters in Ankara, '"Iraq on steroids": senator in Syria warning as Trump receives remains', *The Guardian*, 19 January 2019, www.theguardian.com/world/2019/jan/19/syria-lindsey-graham-iraq-on-steroids-trump?CMP=Share_iOSApp_Other

timeframe for US drawdown, increased from thirty days to four months. Privately, analysts wondered if that deadline might drift indefinitely, even following ISIL's apparent last stand at Baghouz in the spring of 2019. Nonetheless, despite the concerns of fellow Republicans, personnel across government and allies such as the UK and France, America's 2,000 troops began to cross the Syrian border into Iraq at the start of 2019, contributing to the creation of a security vacuum and Kurdish fears of yet another US abandonment. Trump's warnings in support of the latter were particularly stark: the US president threatened to 'devastate' the Turkish economy should they target the Kurds.[122] The subtle, careful diplomacy of a Jeffersonian president this was not; America and the Anglosphere was now led by a fiery and unpredictable leader, moulded in the school of Andrew Jackson. For Trump, it was time for others, closer to the action, to step up and do their bit; America was done being taken for a ride.

In October 2019, Trump's abandonment of the Kurds was made explicit, as US special forces were ordered to leave the safe zone on the Turkish-Syrian border. Trump was condemned by the House and praised by Assad, as Turkish forces advanced, met by a new ad hoc and previously unthinkable alliance of convenience between the Syrian Democratic Forces and YPG. As ISIL captives were shown escaping from Kurdish-controlled camps, the USA launched a raid on al-Baghdadi's temporary hiding place, killing the terror group's leader. Trump's approach to Syria was neatly encapsulated in a few short weeks as he chose to abandon the Kurds, drawing Assad's praise and assisting Russia's interests, before revelling in the death of the ISIL leader. Anglosphere allies in Australia noted the benefits of Baghdadi's death, but also the risks to the coalition if the USA could so readily abandon those they had fought alongside.

Conclusion

Throughout the Syrian Civil War's fourth phase, Assad and Russia's reluctance to fight ISIL was relatively easy to understand: Putin and the

[122] J. Hudson and K. Fahim, 'Trump vows to "devastate" Turkish economy if U.S.-backed Kurds are attacked', *The Washington Post*, 14 January 2019, www.washingtonpost.com/world/national-security/trumps-vow-to-devastate-turkey-rattles-negotiations-over-syria-withdrawal/2019/01/14/1a61049c-17ff-11e9-88fe-f9f77a3bcb6c_story.html?noredirect=on&utm_term=.25bf889b91aa

Syrian regime calculated that, once the civil war was won and legitimacy restored, crushing ISIL, alone, would be a relatively easy task. During this phase of the conflict, however, and despite the intervention of Russia, ISIL kept the old Anglosphere coalition preoccupied. As *The Guardian* put it, ISIL were the enemy for the Anglosphere, but it was Assad that was the problem.[123] Five years on from the conflict's outset, the liberal mantra of 'Assad must go', in conjunction with the realist urging to 'remember Iraq', remained powerful constraints on Anglosphere policy options. Obama continued to hold the line, insisting, 'It would be a mistake for the United States, or Great Britain, or a combination of Western states to send in ground troops and overthrow the Assad regime.'[124] As one journalist put it, 'President Obama and his word-smithing staff may well spend the balance of their White House days dropping rhetorical barrel bombs on imaginary critics even as Bashar al-Assad's pilots roll the real things off the ramps of Russian helicopters onto children and their parents down below.'[125] Donald Trump's defeat of Hillary Clinton threatened to undermine Obama's five-year commitment to this balanced, but arguably debilitated position.

If in 2008 Barack Obama was the 'change candidate', in 2016 Hillary Clinton promised continuity and Donald Trump positioned himself as the outsider who would shake up the establishment. Throughout his campaign, the transition and the outset of his presidency, his language repeatedly seemed to shatter the previous markers of acceptability. Discursive constraints did not appear to matter to America's 45th president.[126] In reflecting on the legacy of his monograph in a new and unforeseen era, Ron Krebs has pointed out that Trump is not in actual fact contesting the established and establishment discursive landscape. Rather, he is exploiting the gap between

---

[123] *The Guardian*, 'The Guardian view on Syria policy: Isis is the enemy but Assad is the problem', 5 December 2015, www.theguardian.com/commentisfree/2015/dec/09/the-guardian-view-on-syria-policy-isis-is-the-enemy-but-assad-is-the-problem

[124] F. Hof, 'Obama drops rhetoric as Assad drops barrel bombs', *The Atlantic*, 27 April 2016.

[125] Ibid.

[126] R. Krebs, 'Author's response: International Politics Reviews Symposium on Narrative and the Making of US National Security', *International Politics Reviews*, 4 (2016), 112–16.

elite and public discourse.[127] For Krebs, then, Trump has not set about
changing elite Anglosphere foreign policy discourse by having arguments with policy makers on their own terms, but rather has won out
by speaking from an entirely different discursive foundation: that of
everyday America. The implications of such an effort are potentially
considerable. Obama remained largely trapped within his inherited
discursive era, earning plaudits for offering soaring rhetorical innovation that, nonetheless, did not contest or alter the base assumptions of
post-9/11 international security. Trump may just do that, dismantling
the shibboleths of cosmopolitanism upon which America's creed has
more recently hitherto been built. Trump's efforts to dismantle Bush's
national security narrative have the potential to bring about significant
discursive change, reworking America's image of itself into something
approximating that which early Anglosphere pioneers would have
recognised and understood.[128]

The implications of this in Syria are profound, as the conflict continues to produce refugees in the millions, no longer deemed welcome
in the United States. In Syria's fourth phase, the breakdown of humanity in Aleppo, as Russian-backed regime forces slowly inched forwards
in the Eastern rebel-held swath of Syria's largest city, was perhaps best
encapsulated, once again, in a single photograph of an innocent child.
In echoes of the emotional outpourings that had accompanied Alan
Kurdi's washing up on a Turkish beach and the disgust felt at the sight
of YouTube videos revealing asphyxiation at Ghouta, one photograph
again sparked outrage. Omran Daqneesh was pictured, sat in the back
of an ambulance, 'having just been pulled from the rubble of his home.
Looking lost, he wipes his dusty forehead, before realising his hand is
covered in blood'.[129] As one Middle East correspondent reflected, 'this
confused, hurt little boy captures the absolute horror that continues to
unfold each day in Aleppo, in full view of the world'.[130] Yet, across the
Anglosphere, the political climate and its associated discourses were

---

[127] Ibid., p. 116.
[128] P. Harris, 'George W. Bush's national security legacy is the ultimate sacred
cow – that's why Donald Trump is going after it', *USApp–American Politics
and Policy Blog* (2016).
[129] S. McNeil, 'Video of bloodied five-year-old in Aleppo shows children continue
to pay price of Syria conflict', *ABC News*, 18 August 2016, www.abc.net.au/
news/2016-08-18/children-continue-to-pay-price-of-syria-conflict/7761322
[130] Ibid.

shifting: refugees were no longer a priority and hospitality was no longer a sensible national trait. As British Shadow Home Secretary Yvette Cooper put it, David Cameron's policy on refugees was 'putting this House and this country to shame'.[131] With Donald Trump's ill-fated and ill-prepared 'Muslim Ban', the situation in the United States was worse still. And, as for the coalition's junior partner, Malcolm Turnbull insisted that Trump should honour the US deal to take Australia's fair share of those who had fled unspeakable atrocities, whether in Syria or previous Anglosphere wars. Across the Anglosphere, political leaders were failing in their 'special responsibility' to protect Syrians, whether in Aleppo, or as they desperately tried to reach New York, London or Sydney.[132]

---

[131] J. Stone, 'David Cameron "shaming" Britain's reputation by rejecting Syrian refugee children, Yvette Cooper says', *The Independent*, 27 April 2016, www.independent.co.uk/news/uk/politics/syrian-refuges-child-david-cameron-yvette-cooper-pmqs-britain-shaming-reputation-video-alf-dubs-a7003251.html

[132] Ralph and Souter, 'A special responsibility'.

Conclusion

...beautiful babies were cruelly murdered in this very barbaric attack. No child of God should ever suffer such horror.[1]

President Trump on the victims of a chemical weapons attack in Syria

I can look in their face and tell them they can't come here.[2]

President Trump on Syria's child refugees

Language

This book has argued that the reality of the Syrian Civil War has been socially constructed through the rhetoric, narratives and discourses of Anglosphere political and media elites. This is perhaps best illustrated by the changing characterisation of the crisis through its four principal phases, as the conflict went from being about the promotion of democracy, to the prohibition of chemical weapons, to the halting of ISIL, to the complexities of Great Power proxy war. Within each of these phases, a discursive war of position raged across the transnational space of the Anglosphere. In each instance, official foreign policy discourses competed with alternative framings of the conflict, pushing for different policy responses. In these discursive wars of position, war and peace have been sold to Anglosphere audiences and policy rendered a possibility. At times, so effective was this selling that its opposition became difficult and dangerous to sustain. Skilfully crafted, resonant rhetoric coupled with coercive narratives to challenge the

---

[1] D. Trump, 'Statement by the president on Syria', 6 April 2017, www.white house.gov/the-press-office/2017/04/06/statement-president-trump-syria

[2] Trump, on the campaign trail in 2016, responding to a question on Syria's child refugees. His response was met with applause. R. Revesz, 'Donald Trump: I will look Syrian kids in the face and say "go home"', *The Independent*, 9 February 2016, www.independent.co.uk/news/world/americas/us-elections/donald-trump-i-will-look-syrian-kids-in-the-face-and-say-go-home-a6863876.html

motives of would-be political adversaries. Despite being equally invested in finding 'good' outcomes, (potential) opponents were painted as terrorist sympathisers and even enemies of the state, encouraging reluctant acquiescence to hegemonic positions. It is impossible to overstate the importance of these framings: they helped to enable and sustain the world's foremost crisis in the form of the Syrian Civil War.

It is possible to imagine revisionist counter-factual histories of the Anglosphere's foreign policy towards Syria after 2011. War's avoidance was initially premised upon the notion that Syria was not like Libya: it was a difficult military intervention to carry out. And yet, Syria's forces would certainly have been no match for Anglosphere military might. In 2011 and 2012, still giddy from the apparent success of killing Osama bin Laden and flushing out Gaddafi into rebel hands, the Anglosphere could have made the case for military intervention to prevent slaughter, as they had done at Benghazi. The risks of inaction were well known, but felt to be inferior to the costs of military confrontation. In 2012, Obama set the Anglosphere on a war footing, awaiting the trigger to act. It came in 2013. Had David Cameron's case for war been more effective – more resonant and coercive – and had his opponent's concerns been framed less well, it is overwhelmingly likely that the old Anglosphere coalition would have gone to war in Syria, against Assad, in order to remove chemical weapons from the equation, long before Donald Trump had even announced he was running for president. The probable spillover of that effort – the inevitable mission creep of conflict – would likely have set the civil war on a very different trajectory, coming prior to ISIL's Anbar Campaign and Russia's entry into the fray. This book has made the case that war's avoidance, just as much as war, is reliant upon the construction and selling of foreign policy discourse. James Der Derian was correct when he argued that war is premised upon how we see, think and speak of others. So too is peace. War and peace are premised upon how well competing discourses are constructed – how they clash, combine and resolve.

Table 1 maps out, in summary and heuristic form, the evolution of the Anglosphere's discursive war of position from the onset of the Syrian Civil War in 2011, through its four subsequent overlapping phases. The table shows how the Syrian Civil War's two principal basic discourses – 'Arab Spring' and 'Remember Iraq' – tapped into and drew upon two broad and long-standing Anglosphere foreign policy traditions: liberal internationalism and conservative realism. Within

Table 1 *Anglosphere foreign policy discourses during the Syrian Civil War*

Anglosphere foreign policy traditions	Liberal internationalism		Conservative realism	
	Neoconservatism, hard Wilsonianism, liberal interventionism, Empire, imperialism, vindicationalist exceptionalism, English School solidarism	Multilateralism, soft Wilsonianism, Jeffersonianism, ethical foreign policy, internationalism, regionalism, R2P, exemplarist exceptionalism	Hobbesianism, Total War, America First, Jacksonianism, ethno-nationalism, (military) populism	English School pluralism, pragmatism, national interest, Hamiltonianism, common sense, (neo-)realism, realpolitik, caution, cost/risk-benefit
Foreign policy discourses	*'Arab Spring'*		*'Remember Iraq'*	
1. *Democracy promotion*	Assad's fall inevitable (2011–12) Right side of history/teleology (2011–15) R2P (2011–)		Syria is not Libya (2011–) Assad's military strength (2011–) International order (2011–)	
2. *Chemical weapons*	Chemical weapons taboo (2012–) Human rights atrocities/innocent children (2013–)		Mission creep (2013) No good options/'baddies vs baddies' (2013–)	
3. *Islamic State*	Humanitarian intervention, Yazidis (2014–) ISIL 'death cult' (2014–)		Iraq's integrity (2014–) New War on Terror (2014–)	ISIL 'death cult' (2014–)
4. *Proxy war*	Condemnation of Russia (2015–) Political transition (2015–) Aleppo war crime (2016–)		Avoid Great Power proxy war (2015–) Conflict's complexity (2015–) Work with Russia vs ISIL (2016–)	
Policy implication	Assad must go		War's avoidance	
	direct ← military/non-military intervention → indirect		hard to do ← military intervention → not national interest	

both traditions, important nuances and divergences are evident. Liberal internationalism, for example, varies between imperial liberal interventionism, on the one hand, embodied in neoconservative and vindicationalist calls to act and, on the other hand, the exemplarism of Jeffersonian multilateralism. Within realism, we see an increasingly stark and significant divergence between the pragmatic caution of defensive structural realists on the one hand, and the military populism of resurgent ethno-nationalists on the other. It is legitimate to ask if and where these latter Jacksonians might find common cause with harder variants of Wilsonianism, as the spectrum of foreign policy traditions is, perhaps, increasingly better represented as a circle.

Nonetheless, this table usefully maps out the evolution and distribution of dominant and competing Anglosphere foreign policy discourses as they gave meaning to Syria's war and helped to determine its outcome. Obama's occupation of a central point – balancing (relatively timid) Jeffersonian concerns for (international) liberty with realism's caution, pragmatism and cost-benefit calculation – rendered him a reluctant revolutionary in Syria. In contrast, the likes of Clinton, Rudd, Power, McCain and Graham all frequently occupied more strident liberal positions, espousing calls for the Anglosphere to do more. At the other extreme, Trump's relative indifference to human suffering at the hands of Assad contrasted with his calls to confront 'radical Islamic terrorism'.[3] At this end of the spectrum, calls to avoid war with Assad via the claim that there were no good options contrasted with the subsequent cry to crush ISIL – even to torture them and kill their families.

As Table 1 shows, during the civil war's first phase, the warning to 'remember Iraq' and cry that 'Syria is not Libya' combined with other complementary sub-discourses that noted Assad's military strength. Kissingerian defensive realist calls to prioritise international order over international justice balanced a sub-discourse of the responsibility to protect: caution and post-Iraq concerns ensured that pluralism held firm in the face of affecting solidarist narratives. The case for war's avoidance was buoyed by liberal internationalists' insistence of history's teleological unfolding: Assad, it was assumed, would fall, with or without direct military assistance for the rebels. The perception was that the Anglosphere could end up on the right side of history through

---

[3] A phrase banished by Obama but relished in the new Trump administration.

indirect support for the Free Syrian Army, who would inevitably prevail, without the risks of potentially getting bogged down in a new quagmire in the Middle East.

War's avoidance for the Anglosphere in Syria's second phase was a surprise, given the strength of the chemical weapons taboo explicitly evoked by Obama. His emphasis on the massacre of innocent children – in unusually emotional language – following the Ghouta attacks geared the Anglosphere for war, on the basis of powerfully resonant language that served to further sear images of suffering into the minds of his audience. But, in Westminster, realist concerns that Cameron's government had overplayed their hand regarding effective ground forces – as Tony Abbott put it, the 'baddies vs baddies' argument – allied with fears of inevitable mission creep. Once engaged, how would Anglosphere troops avoid the vortex of a messy and seemingly intractable conflict? The worry that prohibiting chemical weapons might, once again, evolve into a policy of Anglosphere-imposed regime change in the Middle East was enough to temper calls for war and unexpectedly defeat the UK government in parliament. The vote gave Obama pause for thought and, true to form, he chose to buy time, before backing away from a military-premised solution.

ISIL's Anbar Campaign would shift the Anglosphere war of position dramatically and create a new, potentially confrontable adversary in Syria and Iraq. The call to act, directly and militarily, was now near unanimous. Dissenters were few and far between, risking their denunciation as 'terrorist sympathisers'. Moderate realists called for Iraq's protection, followed by the logical extension of the mission – against a legitimately threatening enemy – over the Syrian border. Populists united with neoconservatives in calls to crush the 'death cult'. And, across the liberal internationalist wing of Anglosphere politics, calls to protect Yazidis from annihilation and/or brutal mediaeval repression were both loud and resonant. During the Syrian Civil War's third phase, the Anglosphere evoked the language of the War on Terror, despite realist concerns that history would repeat Iraq's mistakes. Soaring universalist moral contrasts once again helped to underpin a rush to war – a praxis and discourse that served to co-constitute the Anglosphere in opposition to a barbarian enemy. As they had at foundation, civilisational and religious imagery reproduced a collective understanding of the English-speaking peoples.

In 2015, Putin and Russian military might changed the game once more, as the Syrian Civil War entered its fourth phase. As Table 1 tracks, Australian concerns regarding the complexity of the conflict and the inevitable need to support political transition soon became shared by official authorised voices across the Anglosphere. Condemnation of Syria's brutal realpolitik and resurgent denunciations of war crimes in Aleppo were ultimately outweighed in the Anglosphere war of position by calls to not only avoid Great Power war, but, moreover, to prioritise the defeat of ISIL. It was Trump's unexpected electoral victory that gave this position its clearest boost and its clearest challenge. First, he set about transforming America's role as promoter and protector of liberal world order to an 'America First' superpower pursuing transactional benefits in the Middle East. Second, he initiated a dramatic U-turn, bombing Assad's forces – twice – when confronted with images of asphyxiated children.

Throughout the civil war's four phases, the Anglosphere war of position was fought using a combination of rhetoric, narrative and discourse. Benn's hushed tones and Trump's effective narrative of American renewal embody the rhetorical oratory and strategic storytelling essential to the building of effective discourses that compete and win out within a war of position. It is these discourses and their sustaining sub-discourses that shape and determine Anglosphere foreign policy, through their selling of war and peace. The importance of this contest cannot be overstated: its outcome determined the Anglosphere's policies on war and peace. Syria's fate hung in the balance of these transnational debates.

The Anglosphere

Trump's impact has been felt across the Anglosphere and, despite the mantra of 'America First' that helped to propel him to the presidency, it is likely that the English-speaking nations will continue to work ever-more closely together, bound, once again, by notions of racial (and religious) kinship. Rather than being something wholly new, this is the continuation of trends established since the Anglosphere's formation, supported by racialised understandings of mutual wars and religious fervour.

Alongside claims on language and a retracing of Syria's demise, one of the arguments that this book has put forward is that Anglosphere foreign policy functions increasingly as one. There has been a long historical build-up to this point, with repeated patterns of coalition warfare, but, with centuries of mutual affinities secured and registered, technology is furthering and deepening the linguistic ties that bind together this foremost global coalition of states. This trend appears set to continue. Brexit in the UK, ongoing Australian concerns about rising Asian powers and Trump's unabashed brand of ethno-nationalism all appear set to combine in a powerful reminder of the linguistic, cultural and racial basis of international relations generally and the Anglosphere specifically. These factors have long been down-played and overlooked in academia, for understandable if misplaced reasons. Recent events mean that such a situation is no longer wise or desirable. Renewed academic interest in the rejection of cosmopolitan and globalist views may help researchers better resist the risks of such approaches. Understanding the Anglosphere for what it is and is likely to remain can hopefully generate an improved basis on which to critique its foreign policies and improve its actions in the world, for the good of all. It is imperative to explore the resurgent racial and religious underpinnings of the coalition if we are to more fully under-stand it, at a time when the world risks lurching dramatically away from a globalised liberal world order.

In addition to emphasising the racial narratives at the heart of the old Anglosphere coalition, this book has also explored and conceptual-ised the group's co-constitution through warfare. While certainly haunted by the failures experienced in the quagmire of Iraq, even that war brought the Anglosphere closer together on the battlefield, helping to co-constitute the English-speaking nations as one. Such historical and contemporary experiences render this coalition far more than merely a gathering of linguistic cousins. The question of mutual par-ticipation in future wars is now no longer a question at all; rather, the issue of coalition warfare is only made unfamiliar when one of these three allies unexpectedly opts out of mutual conflict. Such a situation was evident in 2013, as Obama had to readjust to the new and unexpected situation of facing the prospect of US-led war in lieu of the participation of one of America's two foremost allies. When the old Anglosphere coalition did go to war in Syria, against ISIL, it served, once again, to help shape the identity of the group, in relational and binary terms, reinforcing the notion that these states represent and fight for the universal values of civilisation – the shared values of freedom and democracy. Make no mistake, however, that this language of liberal universalism is increasingly tied to a previously more implicit construction of Anglosphere exceptionalism, underpinned by creed and religion, in a return to the discourses evident during the Anglosphere's formation that have long since been rendered off limits as the politically incorrect sentiments they are. In these new times, a Republican Congressman can speak of 'rebuilding civilisation' by limiting migration because it depends on 'our babies' and not theirs.[4] And these tendencies extend across the Anglosphere, as the UK voted in 2016 to render itself poorer and less ethnically diverse and Australia continues to denigrate 'boat people'.

Even more so than Saddam Hussein, Osama bin Laden and Al Qaeda, ISIL represented a group that could be and have been readily constructed as the Anglosphere's antithesis. So clearly brutal in their tactics and intentionally mediaeval in their worldview, ISIL posed a useful foil to the Anglosphere in making the case for war. This was a group so wholly and totally Other, identity construction could work through simple binary juxtapositions. Bush's 'good Americans' and 'evil terrorists' was played out, once again, for Anglosphere leaders, as they framed the 'death cult' that was fit for no other policy than 'degrade and destroy'. While Obama, like other Anglosphere leaders, went out of his way to play up the un-Islamic nature of ISIL, Trump's election saw a return of the prominence of religion in how the English-speaking world would come to view and construct their enemies and themselves. On taking office, Trump has relished uttering every syllable of 'radical Islamic terrorism' and his executive orders have targeted the threat, as his administration sees it, coming from *all* citizens of key majority Muslim states. Under Trump, religion has once again become an explicit – rather than implicit – marker of otherness and a shortcut to assessing threat. And yet, despite Trump's initial fixation on ISIL and relative indifference to the plight of Assad, the terrorist group remained the lesser threat to the people of Syria. It was Assad's denial of democratic rights and series of brutal crackdowns that initiated and sustained the conflict as it descended into civil war. It was his battle tactics, aided by Russian

---

[4] S. King, @Stevekingia (12 March 2017). 'Wilders understands that culture and demographics are our destiny. We can't restore our civilisation with somebody else's babies', https://twitter.com/SteveKingIA/status/840980755236999169

military might, that instigated the majority of the conflict's war crimes. What lessons, therefore, might we draw from Syria?

Syria

In March 2017, Syrian regime and Russian fighters once again were posing for selfies amidst the ruins of Palmyra, having, for the second time in the civil war, pushed ISIL fighters a few kilometres beyond the ancient site. As local Syrians came to inspect the damage caused to the artefacts, they were greeted by yet more devastation. This time, the amphitheatre stage that had hosted brutal executions and a Russian classical concert had been significantly defiled. As well as the carved façade of the amphitheatre, ISIL had destroyed the tetrapylon,[5] to add to the earlier destruction of the Temples of Bel and Baal Shamin.[6] The jam jars that had held candles during the surreal orchestral performance were still there; now, though, they were home to several families of beetles. But, of course, the 'Palmyra ruins pale into insignificance' in comparison with the more than 400,000 killed Syrians and the 'millions displaced over the course of Syria's six-year Civil War'.[7] Two reports detailed the level of destruction – both visible and invisible – inflicted on Syria's children.

The first, UNICEF's, described the most recent phase of the civil war as Syria 'hitting rock bottom'.[8] In 2016 alone some 650 Syrian children were killed in the war, with a further 650 injured.[9] A further 850 were recruited to fight. With one in three schools out of use, nearly two million Syrian children were not currently receiving any form of education. Often, schools had been transformed into shelters and hospitals. Despite the risks, in 2016, 12,500 Syrian children had

---

[5] R. Maclean, 'Desecrated but still majestic: inside Palmyra after second Isis occupation', *The Guardian*, 9 March 2017, www.theguardian.com/world/2017/mar/09/inside-palmyra-syria-after-second-isis-islamic-state-occupation

[6] K. Shaheen, 'Isis destroys tetrapylon monument in Palmyra', *The Guardian*, 20 January 2017, www.theguardian.com/world/2017/jan/20/isis-destroys-tetrapylon-monument-palmyra-syria

[7] Maclean, 'Desecrated'.

[8] UNICEF, 'Hitting rock bottom: how 2016 became the worst year for Syria's children', *UNICEF*, March 2017, http://news.bbc.co.uk/1/shared/bsp/hi/pdfs/13_03_17_unicef_report_syria.pdf

[9] Ibid. Of course, these numbers are very likely to be low, given the difficulties of documenting the deaths and injuries of children in 'hard to reach areas'.

crossed active conflict lines in order to sit exams. UNICEF's Regional Director reported to the UN Security Council on the plight of Syrian schoolchildren and their families in this hellish situation:

A father in Aleppo lives with the trauma of letting his daughters go to school. They left their makeshift home one morning with their schoolbags on their backs. Only their lifeless bodies returned after a shell slammed into their classroom.[10]

With 85 per cent of Syrians now living below the poverty line, children had become an important part of the economic landscape, working in a variety of roles across the country. They faced increasing food insecurity, with one quarter of children in besieged and difficult-to-reach areas suffering stunted growth. A total of seven million Syrians faced food insecurities during Syria's fourth and climactic phase. And access to tap water was now no longer guaranteed for two thirds of the population, as water denial was repeatedly used as a weapon of war.[11]

The second report, Save the Children's,[12] detailed the psychological trauma inflicted upon Syria's children. The 'living nightmare' was now all that many of them knew. Over two thirds of them experienced 'toxic stress' and PTSD as a result of the conflict. As one teacher noted:

The children are psychologically crushed and tired. When we do activities like singing with them, they don't respond at all. They don't laugh like they would normally. They draw images of children being butchered in the war, or tanks, or the siege and the lack of food.[13]

One Syrian child, aged between eight and eleven, succinctly summarised her position: 'I'm afraid of going to school because a plane will bomb us'.[14] Childhood ended early during the Syrian Civil War's unfolding phases. Two thirds of children had lost a family member and checkpoints were increasingly manned by boys under the age of fifteen. A majority of Syrians knew children who had been recruited by one of the myriad warring factions. And a majority of Syria's

---

[10] C. Geert, UNICEF Regional Director, Statement to the UN Security Council, cited in UNICEF, 'Hitting rock bottom'.

[11] Ibid.

[12] Save the Children, 'Invisible wounds', 2017, https://i.stci.uk/sites/default/files/Invisible%20Wounds%20March%202017.pdf

[13] Teacher in the besieged town of Madaya to Save the Children, cited in Save the Children, 'Invisible wounds'.

[14] Ibid.

adolescents were, perhaps understandably, reported to have turned to drugs to deal with the stress of the war.[15]

Amidst the numbing barrage of tragic statistics, it is important to remember that the destruction of Syria and its people was not inevitable. That might seem obvious to many readers, but it is an imperative point to reiterate. As Lene Hansen has shown, discourses of intrinsic and endemic hatred fuelling conflict can lead to political hand-washing and apathy.[16] Ethno-religious differences in Syria are neither natural nor intractable and they certainly, alone, do not account for the intolerable bloodshed the civil war has caused. Likewise, ISIL may well appear to be almost unfathomably cruel in its treatment of minority groups and proclaimed apostates, but fathoming – understanding while retaining a staunch opposition to cruelty – is a vital part of the process of peace-making, counter-terrorism and counter-insurgency. Dissident and mainstream Antipodean voices from Richard Jackson to Julie Bishop have reminded us of as much, acknowledging the necessity of considering the sources of grievance that motivate violence and even, however difficult, remembering the importance of considering the emancipation of subjugated communities as part of a multi-faceted foreign policy, which goes beyond – inevitably futile and potentially counter-productive – aims to destroy and degrade enemies through hard power alone. *If* ISIL draws sustenance from the legitimate grievances of long-oppressed Syrian Sunnis, then their concerns and travails must be heard and addressed, alongside robust denunciations of violence and exclusively military-premised security solutions. Long-term peace and the safety of millions of people depend upon it.

While the Anglosphere's military might certainly therefore has a role to play – as it did in halting the advances of the Anbar Campaign – we must not forget that enemies are rarely bombed out of existence. Britain is the foremost Anglosphere ally to have learned that lesson, in dealing with the IRA. And, yet, even in Westminster, debate has coalesced around the gravity of the hegemonic narrative on the necessary use of force inside Syria. That hegemony, however, was achieved only when confronting ISIL, not Assad, despite the empirical reality of the latter's more significant threat to the Syrian people. What continues to matter most, across the Anglosphere, is the perceived proximity of threat to 'our own' people. The Anglosphere continues to understand

---

[15] Ibid.   [16] Hansen, *Security as Practice.*

international relations and international security through a racial lens. As even dispassionate observers understand, when terrorism or refugees spill over to western countries, the language of war and peace takes on a fierce urgency, compared with when those whose lives are risked inhabit the distant lands of the Middle East. This is not just the brute materiality of geography – the Anglosphere remains fixated on the security of its own distant lands – as culture and language trump proximity. Calls to understand the latent underlying conditions that foster violent extremism and for great powers to apply a responsibility to protect equally and evenly, regardless of race, are certainly not new, but their reiteration remains vitally important.

There is, however, an even more urgent policy lesson to draw out of the Anglosphere's failed approach to Syria. That lesson is simple: the Anglosphere must pursue 'joined-up' foreign policy, wherein ends and means are aligned, in order to serve an overarching goal of peace and prosperity. The Anglosphere's tragic choice during the civil war's opening phases – to lock Assad out of talks without taking the action necessary to remove him – helped to establish and perpetuate the conditions that encouraged the Syrian Civil War to play out as a slow and grinding massacre. Throughout the Syrian Civil War, the Anglosphere's two basic discourses remained intact, despite the fact that their interaction and co-existence served to generate an ends-means gap in foreign policy that helped to sustain eight years of conflict and a civil war that *literally* decimated the Syrian population. It would have been far better to *either* talk to Assad *or* topple him, militarily. The former would clearly have been preferential. Despite the difficulty of defending talking to a brutal dictator, such (realist) acts can and must be justified when they serve the ultimate and overriding (liberal) goal of stopping the killing. Where the Anglosphere lacks the stomach to enforce liberal ends with military might, it is better to commit the political humbug of negotiating with dictators in pursuit of the greater good of achieving peace. Realism is sometimes the most ethical option.

Beyond talking with Assad, the Anglosphere's second option, in the war's early stages, was to militarily intervene to remove the Syrian leader. This would not have been easy or without significant costs, but it too would have been preferential to contributing to the creation of an intractable civil war. Of course, retrospect makes it relatively straightforward to ascertain the crucial moment at which opportunity arose and was not seized. But it is worth contemplating how many assessments of history will continue to look back and praise Obama's caution and pragmatism in Syria, as well as his denunciations of Assad.[17] This, then, is an important lesson for the Anglosphere to learn: intervention's avoidance, for the world's foremost coalition, is just as significant as war's pursuit. The impact of Iraq's toxic legacy must now be balanced against the realisation that war's avoidance can sometimes reap similar tragedy. The deaths of hundreds of thousands of Iraqis that resulted from an illegal Anglosphere war must be balanced against the deaths of hundreds of thousands of Syrians left to battle Assad alone. In Syria, where the Anglosphere has withdrawn from the world stage, others have rushed in to fill the void and achieve outcomes that are particularly unsavoury. It is therefore imperative to balance liberal calls for democracy with realist conservative caution, but this balance cannot be allowed to generate a debilitating and sustained ends-means gap in Anglosphere foreign policy that serves, ultimately and tragically, to help sustain human suffering. The Anglosphere cannot and should not do everything, everywhere, but it also cannot afford to retrench and roll back to the extent that the ends-means gap grows to breaking point, allowing purely realist actors, such as Russia, to call the shots. While a return to the heady neoconservative days of 2003 should be avoided, so too should we resist the urge to add the human rights of Syrians to the funeral pyre of Iraq. In Syria, Anglosphere foreign policy, enabled and underpinned by a transnational discursive war of position, helped to perpetuate civil war. It would be far better to have 'joined-up' Anglosphere foreign policy than an ends-means gap resulting from good intentions but delivering the worst of outcomes.

Finally, where liberal discourses must prevail is in the as-yet-unrealised special responsibility to protect that all three of the old Anglosphere coalition states share.[18] Having, in significant part, created the political conditions for ISIL's rise and Assad's continued reign, there can be no ignoring the plight of Syria's victims. Trump's stance on refugees – captured in the conclusion's opening quotation – is, sadly, far from unique. Despite a total lack of empirical evidence, refugees have been conflated with terrorists as potential Trojan horses. This is

---

[17] M. S. Indyk, K. G. Lieberthal and M. E. O'Hanlon, 'Scoring Obama's foreign policy: a progressive pragmatist tries to bend history', *Foreign Affairs*, 91 (2012), 29–43.

[18] Ralph and Souter, 'A special responsibility'.

an immoral response to near-unimaginable human suffering. Syria's refugees have fled the worst of worlds and the Anglosphere is morally and legally compelled to help them. The USA, UK and Australia should and must provide aid, safe haven and a chance to build a new life in countries that are directly implicated in the reasons for Syrian refugees having to flee their homelands in existential fear. Anything less is not worthy of states that proclaim to have given the world freedom and democracy; states that continue to uphold a moral commitment to universal shared values.

References

ABC News, 'Fact check: Is Australia's military contribution to the fight against Islamic State the second largest?', *ABC News*, 3 March 2016, www.abc.net.au/news/2015-12-22/fact-check-australias-contribution-against-islamic-state/6977668

'Gillard addresses UN General Assembly', 27 September 2012, www.abc .net.au/news/2012-09-27/gillard-addresses-un-general-assembly/42826 52?pfmredir=sm

Ackerman, S. and Roberts, D. 'Chuck Hagel forced to step down as US defense secretary', *The Guardian*, 24 November 2014, www.theg uardian.com/us-news/2014/nov/24/chuck-hagel-step-down-us-defence-secretary

Adams, S. 'Failure to protect: Syria and the UN Security Council', Global Centre for the Responsibility to Protect, Occasional Paper Series no. 5, March 2015, www.globalr2p.org/media/files/syriapaper_final.pdf

AFP, '"More than 90%" of Russian airstrikes in Syria have not targeted Isis, US says', *The Guardian*, 7 October 2015, www.theguardian.com/ world/2015/oct/07/russia-airstrikes-syria-not-targetting-isis

Åhäll, L. and Gregory, T. (eds.), *Emotions, Politics and War* (Abingdon/New York: Routledge, 2015).

Al Jazeera, 'Gas used in Homs leaves seven people dead and scores affected, activists say', 24 December 2012, http://blogs.aljazeera.com/topic/syria/ gas-used-homs-leaves-seven-people-dead-and-scores-affected-activists-say

Alexander, D. 'Syria', *Hansard*, House of Commons, 19 June 2012, www .publications.parliament.uk/pa/cm201213/cmhansrd/cm120619/debtext/ 120619-0001.htm

Alexander, H. 'Syria: if Bashar al-Assad hands over chemical weapons we will not attack, says John Kerry', *The Telegraph*, 9 September 2013, www.telegraph.co.uk/news/worldnews/middleeast/syria/10295638/Syria-If-Bashar-al-Assad-hands-over-chemical-weapons-we-will-not-attack-says-John-Kerry.html

Allison, R. 'Russia and Syria: explaining alignment with a regime in crisis', *International Affairs*, 89 (2013), 795–823.

Almasmari, H. and Hannah, J. 'Yemen: bombs kill 137 at mosques; ISIS purportedly lays claim', *CNN*, 21 March 2015, http://edition.cnn.com/2015/03/20/middleeast/yemen-violence

Alshami, B. 'Between bombs and beheadings: Palmyra after the ISIS takeover', *News Deeply*, 21 July 2015, www.newsdeeply.com/syria/articles/2015/07/21/between-bombs-and-beheadings-palmyra-after-the-isis-takeover

Amman, M., Knaup, H., Neukirch, R. and Pfister, R. 'Quiet capitulation: Merkel slowly changes tune on refugee issue', *Der Spiegel*, 20 November 2015, www.spiegel.de/international/germany/angela-merkel-changes-her-stance-on-refugee-limits-a-1063773.html

Amnesty International, 'Syria: "Death everywhere" – war crimes and human rights abuses in Aleppo, Syria', 5 May 2015, www.amnesty.org/en/documents/mde24/1370/2015/en

Annan, K. 'Annan's peace plan for Syria', Council On Foreign Relations, March 2012, www.cfr.org/syria/annans-peace-plan-syria/p28380

AP, 'Australian war planes to join airstrikes on Isil in Iraq', *The Telegraph*, 3 October 2014, www.telegraph.co.uk/news/worldnews/islamic-state/11137690/Australian-war-planes-to-join-airstrikes-on-Isil-in-Iraq.html

Associated Press, 'Syria says it will use chemical weapons if attacked', *USA Today*, 23 July 2012, http://usatoday30.usatoday.com/news/world/story/2012-07-23/Syria-violence-rebels/56425402/1

Bacon, R. *Hansard*, 29 August 2013, www.publications.parliament.uk/pa/cm201314/cmhansrd/cm130829/debtext/130829-0001.htm

Baker, P. 'How Obama came to plan for "surge" in Afghanistan', *New York Times*, 5 November 2009, www.nytimes.com/2009/12/06/world/asia/06reconstruct.html?_r=0

Baker, P. and Weisman, J. 'Obama seeks approval by Congress for strike in Syria', *New York Times*, 31 August 2013, www.nytimes.com/2013/09/01/world/middleeast/syria.html

Baker, P., Landler, M., Sanger, D. and Barnard, A. 'Off-the-cuff Obama line put U.S. in bind on Syria', *New York Times*, 4 May 2013, www.nytimes.com/2013/05/05/world/middleeast/obamas-vow-on-chemical-weapons-puts-him-in-tough-spot.html?pagewanted=all

Bakri, N. 'Defectors claim attack that killed Syria soldiers', *New York Times*, 26 October 2011, www.nytimes.com/2011/10/27/world/middleeast/army-defectors-in-syria-take-credit-for-deadly-attack.html

Balzacq, T. 'The three faces of securitization: political agency, audience and context', *European Journal of International Relations*, 11 (2005), 171–201.

Bandow, D. 'Trump and US alliances', *Foreign Affairs*, 25 January 2017, www.foreignaffairs.com/articles/united-states/2017-01-25/trump-and-us-alliances

Barnes, T. and Duncan, J. *Writing Worlds: Discourse, Text and Metaphor in the Representation of Landscape* (Abingdon/New York: Routledge, 1991).

Barnett, M. 'Culture, strategy and foreign policy change: Israel's road to Oslo', *European Journal of International Relations*, 5 (1999), 5–36.

Bastni, H. 'Iran quietly deepens involvement in Syria's war', *BBC News*, 20 October 2015, www.bbc.co.uk/news/world-middle-east-34572756

BBC News, 'Ashdown: "Many differences" between Syria and Bosnia', 11 June 2012, www.bbc.co.uk/news/uk-politics-18397773

'Australia launches first air strikes inside Syria', 16 September 2016, www.bbc.co.uk/news/world-australia-34265118

'Consider Syria IS strikes, defence secretary urges MPs', 3 July 2015, www.bbc.co.uk/news/uk-33358267

'David Cameron condemns Russia's strikes in Syria', 3 October 2015, www.bbc.co.uk/news/uk-34432440

'Guide to the Syrian rebels', 13 December 2013, www.bbc.co.uk/news/world-middle-east-24403003

'Islamic State "has lost 50,000 fighters" over two years', 9 December 2016, www.bbc.co.uk/news/world-middle-east-38252092

'Libya UN Resolution 1973: text analysed', 18 March 2011, www.bbc.co.uk/news/world-africa-12782972

'Life and death in Syria', 15 March 2016, www.bbc.co.uk/news/resources/idt-841ebc3a-1be9-493b-8800-2c04890e8fc9

'Obama signals "new phase" against Islamic State in Iraq', 9 November 2014, www.bbc.co.uk/news/world-middle-east-29979042

'Russia's Valery Gergiev conducts concert in Palmyra ruins', 5 May 2016, www.bbc.co.uk/news/world-middle-east-36211449

'Syria: Assad regime "ready to use chemical weapons"', 17 July 2012, www.bbc.co.uk/news/world-middle-east-18864629

'Syria: IS destroys part of Palmyra amphitheatre', 20 June 2017, www.bbc.co.uk/news/world-middle-east-38689131

'Syria chemical weapons: Obama says world is watching', 23 July 2012, www.bbc.co.uk/news/world-middle-east-18963720

'Syria conflict: Aleppo civilians suffer "unthinkable atrocities"', 5 May 2015, www.bbc.co.uk/news/world-middle-east-32581007

'Syria crisis: rebels leave Homs', 9 December 2015, www.bbc.co.uk/news/world-middle-east-35048404

'Syria crisis: where key countries stand', 30 October 2015, www.bbc.co.uk/news/world-middle-east-23849587

'Syria protests: Assad to lift state of emergency', 21 April 2011, www.bbc.co.uk/news/world-middle-east-13134322

'Syria rejects new Arab League peace mission proposal', 13 February 2012, www.bbc.co.uk/news/world-middle-east-17008597

'Syria vote: Cameron and Corbyn clash over air strikes', 2 December 2015, www.bbc.co.uk/news/uk-politics-34980504

'Syria war: "Assad must go" to ensure IS defeat – Obama', 29 September 2015, www.bbc.co.uk/news/world-middle-east-34393523

'Syrian President Bashar al-Assad: facing down rebellion', 21 October 2015, www.bbc.co.uk/news/10338256

'Tunisia attack: Cameron says IS fight "struggle of our generation"', 29 June 2015, www.bbc.co.uk/news/uk-33307279

'UK troops in Afghanistan to come under US command', 21 May 2010, http://news.bbc.co.uk/1/hi/uk/8697371.stm

'UK will help destroy Islamic State, David Cameron tells US', 19 July 2015, www.bbc.co.uk/news/uk-33584548

'US says it will give military aid to Syria rebels', 14 June 2013, www.bbc.co.uk/news/world-us-canada-22899289

Beaumont, P. 'Snowden files reveal US and UK spied on feeds from Israeli drones and jets', *The Guardian*, 29 January 2016, www.theguardian.com/world/2016/jan/29/snowden-files-us-uk-spied-feeds-israeli-drones-jets

Beech, M. and Oliver, T. 'Humanitarian intervention and foreign policy in the conservative-led coalition', *Parliamentary Affairs*, 67 (2013), 102–18.

Bell, D. *The Idea of Greater Britain: Empire and the Future of World Order, 1860–1900* (Princeton: Princeton University Press, 2007).

Bennett, J. *The Anglosphere Challenge: Why the English-Speaking Nations Will Lead the Way in the Twenty-First Century* (Plymouth: Rowman & Littlefield, 2007).

'The emerging Anglosphere', *Orbis*, 46 (2002), 111–26.

Benson, S. 'PM Julia Gillard's tough action call wins United Nations support', *The Australian*, 27 September 2012, www.theaustralian.com.au/news/julia-gillard-arrives-for-un-address/story-e6frg6n6-1226482215413

Bentley, M. 'Ending the unendable: the rhetorical legacy of the war on terror' in M. Bentley and J. Holland (eds.), *The Obama Doctrine: A Legacy of Continuity in US Foreign Policy?* (Abingdon/New York: Routledge, 2016).

Bentley, M. and Holland, J. *Obama's Foreign Policy: Ending the War on Terror* (Abingdon/New York: Routledge, 2014).

The Obama Doctrine: A Legacy of Continuity in US Foreign Policy? (Abingdon/New York: Routledge, 2016).

Syria and the Chemical Weapons Taboo: Exploiting the Forbidden (Manchester: Manchester University Press, 2016).

Berger, J. and Morgan, J. 'The ISIS Twitter census', Brooking Institute, March 2015, www.brookings.edu/~/media/research/files/papers/2015/03/isis-twitter-census-berger-morgan/isis_twitter_census_berger_morgan.pdf

Berinsky, A. 'Assuming the costs of war: events, elites, and American public support for military conflict', *The Journal of Politics*, 69 (2007), 975–97.

Bisley, N. 'Issues in Australian foreign policy July to December 2011', *Australian Journal of Politics & History*, 58 (2011), 268–82.

Black, E. 'Damascus, the city where everything's for sale but no one's buying', *The Guardian*, 26 April 2013, www.theguardian.com/world/2013/apr/26/damascus-economic-dead-zone

Black, I. 'Report on Syria conflict finds 11.5% of population killed or injured', *The Guardian*, 11 February 2016, www.theguardian.com/world/2016/feb/11/report-on-syria-conflict-finds-115-of-population-killed-or-injured

'Syria is looking like Bosnia 20 years ago', *The Guardian*, 28 May 2012, www.theguardian.com/world/2012/may/28/syria-looking-more-like-bosnia

Blunt, C. *Hansard*, 29 August 2013, www.publications.parliament.uk/pa/cm201314/cmhansrd/cm130829/debtext/130829-0001.htm

Boettcher, W. and Cobb, M. 'Don't let them die in vain: casualty frames and public tolerance for escalating commitment in Iraq', *The Journal of Conflict Resolution*, 53 (2009), 677–97.

'Echoes of Vietnam? Casualty framings and public perceptions of success and failure in Iraq', *Journal of Conflict Resolution*, 50 (2006), 831–54.

Boot, M. 'How a monstrous Putin beat the U.S. in Syria', *LA Times*, 15 March 2016, www.latimes.com/opinion/op-ed/la-oe-boot-putin-removes-troops-from-syria-20160316-story.html

Borgen, J. 'Merkel spying claim: with allies like these, who needs enemies?', *The Guardian*, 23 October 2013, www.theguardian.com/world/2013/oct/23/merkel-nsa-phone-allies-enemies

Borger, J. 'Putin says he can work with Obama despite trading barbs on Syria and Isis', *The Guardian*, 29 September 2015, www.theguardian.com/world/2015/sep/27/putin-russia-syria-assad-propaganda-gangster

'Syria chemical attack has changed my view of Assad, says Trump', *The Guardian*, 6 April 2017, www.theguardian.com/us-news/2017/apr/05/syria-chemical-gas-attack-donald-trump-nikki-haley-assad

Borger, J. and Chulov, M. 'Trump shocks allies and advisers with plan to pull US troops out of Syria', *The Guardian*, 20 December 2018, www.theguardian.com/us-news/2018/dec/19/us-troops-syria-withdrawal-trump

Bouchet, N. 'The democracy tradition in US foreign policy and the Obama presidency', *International Affairs*, 89 (2013), 31–51.

Bourke, L. and Levy, M. '"Barbaric" nature of ISIL on display with photos of boy holding decapitated head, says Prime Minister Tony Abbott', *Sydney Morning Herald*, 11 August 2014, www.smh.com.au/federal-politics/political-news/barbaric-nature-of-isil-on-display-with-photos-of-boy-holding-decapitated-head-says-prime-minister-tony-abbott-20140810-3dh8q.html

Bowen, J. *The Arab Uprisings: The People Want the Fall of the Regime* (London: Simon & Schuster, 2012).

Boyer, D. 'Obama confesses: "We don't have a strategy yet" for Islamic State', *Washington Times*, 28 August 2014, www.washingtontimes .com/news/2014/aug/28/obama-admits-isil-dilemma-we-dont-have-strat egy-ye

Bradley, J. 'Yes, Syria is a tragedy but it would be madness for Britain to intervene', *Daily Mail*, 30 May 2012, www.dailymail.co.uk/debate/art icle-2151866/Houla-massacre-Syria-tragedy-madness-Britain-intervene .html

Brandis, G. *Hansard*, 29 August 2013, www.publications.parliament.uk/pa/ cm201314/cmhansrd/cm130829/debtext/130829-0001.htm

Brands, G. *What America Owes the World: The Struggle for the Soul of Foreign Policy* (New York: Cambridge University Press, 1998).

Breen-Smyth, M. 'When the past is present: the casualty, the body and its politics', inaugural lecture at the University of Surrey, 8 March 2012.

Brown, R. and Liptak, K. 'Obama: Syrians' blood on hands of Assad and Russia', *CNN*, 16 December 2016, http://edition.cnn.com/2016/12/16/ politics/obama-syria-assad-russia-aleppo

Browning, C. and Tonra, B. 'Beyond the West and towards the Anglosphere?', pp. 1–21, www.academia.edu/341929/Beyond_the_West_and_Towards_ the_Anglosphere

'Beyond the West and towards the Anglosphere?' in Browning, C. and Lehti, M. (eds.), *The Struggle for the West: A Divided and Contested Legacy* (Abingdon: Routledge, 2010).

Buck, J. 'Asma al-Assad: a rose in the desert', *Vogue*, March 2011, http:// gawker.com/asma-al-assad-a-rose-in-the-desert-1265002284

Bulley, D. 'The politics of ethical foreign policy: a responsibility to protect whom?', *European Journal of International Relations*, 16 (2010), 441–61.

Burke, J. *The 9/11 Wars* (London: Penguin UK, 2011).

Busby, J. 'Rhetorical entrapment and Syria', *Duck of Minerva*, 2 October 2015, http://duckofminerva.com/2015/10/rhetorical-entrapment-and- syria-lets-not-do-dumb-stuff.html

Calder, S. 'Russian plane crash Q&A: why has Russia now confirmed Metrojet flight 9268 was bombed?', *The Independent*, 17 November 2015, www.independent.co.uk/news/world/europe/russian-plane-crash- qa-why-has-russia-now-confirmed-metrojet-flight-9268-was-bombed- a6737701.html

Calderwood, I. 'Slaughter in the Roman amphitheatre: horrific moment ISIS child executioners brutally shoot dead 25 Syrian regime soldiers in front of bloodthirsty crowds at ancient Palmyra ruin', *MailOnline*, 4 July

2015, www.dailymail.co.uk/news/article-3149469/Slaughter-amphitheatre-ISIS-executioners-brutally-shoot-dead-25-Syrian-regime-soldiers-blood thirsty-crowds-ancient-Palmyra-ruin.html

Callimachi, R. 'Obama calls Islamic State's killing of Peter Kassig "pure evil"', *New York Times*, 16 November 2014, www.nytimes.com/2014/11/17/world/middleeast/peter-kassig-isis-video-execution.html

Cameron, D. 'Australian Parliament: David Cameron's speech', 14 November 2014, www.gov.uk/government/speeches/australian-parliament-david-camerons-speech

'David Cameron and NATO Secretary General press conference', 19 June 2014, www.gov.uk/government/speeches/david-cameron-and-nato-sec retary-general-press-conference

'European Council press conference', 24 June 2011, www.gov.uk/govern ment/speeches/european-council-press-conference-24-june-2011

'Extremism: PM speech', 20 July 2015, www.gov.uk/government/speeches/extremism-pm-speech

Hansard, 2 December 2015, www.publications.parliament.uk/pa/cm201 516/cmhansrd/cm151202/debtext/151202-0001.htm

'PM interview at the G8 summit', 27 May 2011, www.gov.uk/govern ment/speeches/pm-interview-at-the-g8-summit

'PM press statement following Paris talks', 23 November 2015, www.gov .uk/government/speeches/pm-press-statement-following-paris-talks

'PM speech at the UN General Assembly 2014', 15 September 2016, www.gov.uk/government/speeches/pm-speech-at-the-un-general-assembly-2014

'PM's opening statement to Commons debate on military action in Syria', 2 December 2015, www.gov.uk/government/speeches/pms-opening-statement-to-commons-debate-on-military-action-in-syria

'Press conference by David Cameron and Barack Obama', Cabinet Office, 15 March 2012, www.gov.uk/government/speeches/press-conference-by-david-cameron-and-barack-obama

'Prime Minister on ISIL at UN General Assembly', 19 September 2015, www.gov.uk/government/speeches/prime-minister-on-isil-at-un-general-assembly

'Prime Minister's first speech to the UN General Assembly', 20 September 2011, www.gov.uk/government/speeches/prime-ministers-first-speech-to-the-un-general-assembly

Camilleri, J. 'A Leap into the past – in the name of the national interest', *Australian Journal of International Affairs*, 57 (2003), 448–9.

Campbell, D. *Writing Security: United States Foreign Policy and the Politics of Identity*, Revised Edition (Minneapolis: University of Minnesota Press, 1998).

Carney, J. 'Statement by the Press Secretary on Syria', 11 June 2011, https://obamawhitehouse.archives.gov/the-press-office/2011/06/11/statement-press-secretary-syria

'Statement by the Press Secretary on violence in Syria', 24 May 2011, https://obamawhitehouse.archives.gov/the-press-office/2011/03/24/statement-press-secretary-violence-syria

Carter, J. 'A first step for Syria? Stop the killing', *New York Times*, 20 September 2016, www.nytimes.com/2016/09/21/opinion/jimmy-carter-a-first-step-for-syria-stop-the-killing.html?_r=0

Cha, T. 'The return of Jacksonianism: the international implications of the Trump phenomenon', *The Washington Quarterly*, 39 (2016), 83–97.

Chang, O. 'Tony Abbott says the death cult is "coming after us" after global terror attacks', *Business Insider Australia*, 28 June 2015, www.businessinsider.com.au/tony-abbott-says-the-death-cult-is-coming-after-us-after-global-terror-attacks-2015-6

Charap, S. 'Russia, Syria and the doctrine of intervention', *Survival*, 55 (2013), 35–41.

Charteris-Black, J. *Politicians and Rhetoric: The Persuasive Power of Metaphor* (Houndmills: Palgrave Macmillan, 2005).

Chastain, M. 'ISIS propaganda manual reveals social media strategy', *Breitbart*, 28 October 2015, www.breitbart.com/national-security/2015/10/28/isis-propaganda-manual-reveals-social-media-strategy

Chilton, P. *Analysing Political Discourse: Theory and Practice* (London/New York: Routledge, 2004).

Chorley, M. 'National minute's silence for victims of Tunisia atrocity to be held at noon on Friday as Cameron vows: "We will not cower"', *Daily Mail*, 29 June 2015, www.dailymail.co.uk/news/article-3142884/David-Cameron-says-beat-ISIS-terrorists-threaten-way-life-Sousse-terror-attack.html

Chulov, M. and McCarthy, T. 'US drone strike in Syria kills top al-Qaida leader, jihadis say', *The Guardian*, 27 February 2017, www.theguardian.com/world/2017/feb/27/us-drone-strike-in-syria-kills-top-al-qaida-leader-jihadis-say

Churchill, W. *A History of the English-Speaking Peoples, Volume 4: The Great Democracies* (New York: Rosetta Books, 2013).

A History of the English-Speaking Peoples: A One-Volume Abridgement (New York: Skyhorse Publishing, 2011 [1956]).

Clark, H. 'Australia begins flights over Syria', *The Diplomat*, 14 September 2015, http://thediplomat.com/2015/09/australia-begins-flights-over-syria

Clarke, I. *Legitimacy in International Society* (Oxford: Oxford University Press, 2007).

Clyne, M. 'The use of exclusionary language to manipulate opinion: John Howard, asylum seekers and the reemergence of political incorrectness in Australia', *Journal of Language and Politics*, 4 (2005), 173–96.

CNN/ORC Poll, *CNN*, 14 February 2012, http://i2.cdn.turner.com/cnn/2012/images/02/14/rel2d.pdf

Cofman Wittes, T. 'The slipperiest slope of them all', *The Atlantic*, 12 March 2016, www.theatlantic.com/international/archive/2016/03/obama-doctrine-goldberg-inaction/473520

Cohen, T. 'Obama outlines ISIS strategy: airstrikes in Syria, more U.S. forces', *CNN*, 11 September 2014, http://edition.cnn.com/2014/09/10/politics/isis-obama-speech/index.html

Coleman, P. 'Why Anglos run the world: a taste for war', *Quadrant*, 50 (2006), 88–90.

Connolly, W. *Neuropolitics: Thinking, Culture, Speed* (Minneapolis: University of Minnesota Press, 2002).

Conquest, R. *The Dragons of Expectation: Reality and Delusion in the Course of History* (London: Duckworth, 2006).

Contorno, S. 'What Obama said about Islamic State', *Politifact*, 7 September 2014, www.politifact.com/truth-o-meter/statements/2014/sep/07/barack-obama/what-obama-said-about-islamic-state-jv-team

Cooper, H. and Shear, M. 'Militants' siege on mountain in Iraq is vver, Pentagon says', *New York Times*, 13 August 2014, www.nytimes.com/2014/08/14/world/middleeast/iraq-yazidi-refugees.html?_r=1

'Obama to send 1,500 more troops to assist Iraq', *New York Times*, 7 November 2014, www.nytimes.com/2014/11/08/world/middleeast/us-to-send-1500-more-troops-to-iraq.html

Coughlin, C. 'Why has Britain abandoned Syrian moderates to the bombs of Putin and Assad?', *The Telegraph*, 10 February 2016, www.telegraph.co.uk/news/worldnews/middleeast/syria/12149161/Why-has-Britain-abandoned-Syrian-moderates-to-the-bombs-of-Putin-and-Assad.html

Cox, R. 'Gramsci, hegemony and International Relations: an essay on method', *Millennium*, 12 (1983), 162–75.

Crines, A. 'Rhetoric and the coalition: governing in the national interest?' *Representation*, 49 (2013), 207–18.

Croft, S. *Culture, Crisis and America's War on Terror* (Cambridge: Cambridge University Press, 2006).

Curley, M. and Moores, D. 'Issues in Australian foreign policy: January to June 2011', *Australian Journal of Politics & History*, 57 (2011), 597–613.

Daddow, O. 'The use of force in British foreign policy: from New Labour to the coalition', *The Political Quarterly*, 84 (2013), 110–18.

Daddow, O. and Schnapper, P. 'Liberal intervention in the foreign policy thinking of Tony Blair and David Cameron', *Cambridge Review of International Affairs*, 26 (2013), 330–49.

Daley, P. 'It is beyond time for Britain to apologise to Australia's indigenous people', *The Guardian*, 25 January 2016, www.theguardian.com/commentisfree/2016/jan/26/it-is-beyond-time-for-britain-to-apologise-to-australias-indigenous-people

Daniel, Z. 'Islamic State: Prime Minister Malcolm Turnbull calls for "right boots on the ground" in Iraq and Syria', *ABC News*, 14 January 2015, www.abc.net.au/news/2016-01-19/prime-minister-malcolm-turnbull-washington-speech-barack-obama/7097166

Danjoux, I. 'Negotiating security', presented at the International Studies Association annual conference, San Francisco, 26–29 March 2008.

Dathan, M. 'Syria air strikes: David Cameron admits "there aren't enough" moderate fighters on the ground and some are "hardline"', *The Independent*, 12 January 2016, www.independent.co.uk/news/uk/politics/syria-air-strikes-david-cameron-admits-there-aren-t-enough-moderate-fighters-on-the-ground-and-some-a6808021.html

Davey, M. 'Stan Grant's speech on racism and the Australian Dream goes viral', *The Guardian*, 24 January 2016, www.theguardian.com/australia-news/2016/jan/24/stan-grants-speech-on-racism-and-the-australian-dream-goes-viral

Davis, D. *Hansard*, 29 August 2013, www.publications.parliament.uk/pa/cm201314/cmhansrd/cm130829/debtext/130829-0001.htm

DeYoung, K. and Gearing, A. 'U.S., citing use of chemical weapons by Syria, to provide direct military support to rebels', *Washington Post*, 13 June 2013, www.washingtonpost.com/world/national-security/us-concludes-syrian-forces-used-chemical-weapons/2013/06/13/59b03c66-d46d-11e2-a73e-826d299ff459_story.html

Debats, D. A., McDonald, T. and Williams, M. 'Mr Howard goes to Washington: September 11, the Australian–American relationship and attributes of leadership', *Australian Journal of Political Science*, 42 (2007), 231–51.

Debrix, F. and Weber, C. (eds.), *Rituals of Mediation: International Politics and Social Meaning* (Minneapolis: University of Minnesota Press, 2003).

Deudney, D. 'Greater Britain or greater synthesis: Seeley, Mackinder, and Wells on Britain in the global industrial era', *Review of International Studies*, 27 (2001), 187–208.

Diab, M. 'Syria's chemical and biological weapons: assessing capabilities and motivations', *The Nonproliferation Review*, Fall 1997, http://cns.miis.edu/npr/pdfs/diab51.pdf

Dominiczak, P. 'Jeremy Corbyn faces humiliation as more than 100 Labour MPs plan to defy leader over Syria air strikes', *The Telegraph*, 27 November 2015, www.telegraph.co.uk/news/politics/Jeremy_Corbyn/ 12021973/Jeremy-Corbyn-faces-humiliation-as-more-than-100-Labour-MPs-plan-to-defy-leader-over-Syria-air-strikes.html

'Tunisia attack: David Cameron calls for fightback against intolerance as 30 Britons confirmed dead', *The Telegraph*, 29 June 2015, www.tele graph.co.uk/news/worldnews/africaandindianocean/tunisia/11704972/ Tunisia-attack-David-Cameron-calls-for-fightback-against-intolerance-as-30-Britons-confirmed-dead.html

Dorsey, J. M. 'The rise of Trump and its global implications – Trump's Middle East: back to the future', RSIS Commentaries, 15 December 2016, www .rsis.edu.sg/rsis-publication/rsis/co16304-the-rise-of-trump-and-its-global-implications-trumps-middle-east-back-to-the-future/#.XcGY2m52uM8

Doty, R. L. 'Foreign policy as social construction: a post-positivist analysis of US counterinsurgency policy in the Philippines', *International Studies Quarterly*, 37 (1993), 297–320.

Anti-Immigrantism in Western Democracies: Statecraft, Desire and the Politics of Exclusion (London/New York: Routledge, 2003).

Drury, I. 'Britain could be dragged into Syria conflict to prevent bloodshed spreading to neighbouring countries, says former Army commander', *Daily Mail*, 25 July 2012, www.dailymail.co.uk/news/article-2178526/ Britain-dragged-Syria-conflict-prevent-bloodshed-spreading-neighbouring-countries-says-Army-commander.html#ixzz4APzGh8Ys

Dueck, C. *The Obama Doctrine: American Grand Strategy Today* (New York: Oxford University Press, 2015).

Dumbrell, J. 'Working with allies: the United States, the United Kingdom, and the War on Terror', *Politics and Policy*, 34 (2006), 452–72.

Dunne, T. 'When the shooting starts: Atlanticism in British security strategy', *International Affairs*, 80 (2004), 893–909.

Dyrenfurth, N. 'Battlers, refugees and the republic: John Howard's language of citizenship', *Journal of Australian Studies*, 28 (2005), 183–96.

'John Howard's hegemony of values: the politics of "mateship" in the Howard decade', *Australian Journal of Political Science*, 42 (2007), 211–30.

Editorial Board, 'Syrian chemical attack demands precise strike: our view', *USA Today*, 26 August 2013, www.usatoday.com/story/opinion/2013/ 08/26/syria-chemical-attack-obama-red-line-editorials-debates/2704003

Elgot, J. 'Jeremy Corbyn: Theresa May needs to press for Syria crisis resolution', *The Guardian*, 13 December 2016, www.theguardian.com/uk-news/2016/ dec/13/corbyn-may-to-press-for-syria-crisis-aleppo-theresa-may

Entous, A. 'U.S., allies to boost aid to Syria rebels', *Wall Street Journal*, 4 November 2015, www.wsj.com/articles/u-s-allies-to-boost-aid-to-syria-rebels-1446682624

Escobar, P. '"War on chemical weapons": Obama traps himself into Syrian combat', *Russia Today*, 28 August 2015, www.rt.com/op-edge/war-chemical-weapons-obama-syria-120

Fahim, K. and Saad, H. 'A faceless teenage refugee who helped ignite Syria's war', *New York Times*, 8 February 2013, www.nytimes.com/2013/02/09/world/middleeast/a-faceless-teenage-refugee-who-helped-ignite-syrias-war.html?_r=1

Fairclough, N. *New Labour, New Language?* (London: Routledge, 2000).

Farquhar, N. and Kramer, A. 'How Rex Tillerson changed his tune on Russia and came to court its rulers', *New York Times*, 20 December 2016, www.nytimes.com/2016/12/20/world/europe/russia-rex-tillerson-donald-trump-secretary-of-state.html

Fermor, B. 'Shifting binaries: the colonial legacy of Obama's war on terror' in Bentley, M. and Holland, J. (eds.), *The Obama Doctrine: A Legacy of Continuity in US Foreign Policy?* (Abingdon/New York: Routledge, 2016).

Fierke, K. M. 'Multiple identities, interfacing games: the social construction of Western action in Bosnia', *European Journal of International Relations*, 2 (1996), 467–97.

    Critical Approaches to International Security (Cambridge, UK/Malden, MA: Polity Press, 2015).

Fischer, D. *Albion's Seed: Four British Folkways in America* (Oxford: Oxford University Press, 1989).

Fitzgibbon, J. 'Shaping peace and security in the Asia-Pacific region: the New Australian government's defence and security priorities', Lowy Institute for International Policy, Brookings Institute, Washington DC, 15 July 2008.

Fitzpatrick, J. 'European settler colonialism and national security ideologies in Australian history' in Leaver, R. and Cox, D. (eds.), *Middling, Meddling, Muddling: Issues in Australian Foreign Policy* (St Leonards: Allen & Unwin, 1997).

Flanagan, R. 'A decade of John Howard has left a country of timidity, fear and shame', *The Guardian*, 26 November 2007, www.theguardian.com/commentisfree/2007/nov/26/comment.australia

Flitton, D. and Ireland, J. 'Military intervention in Syria an option: Carr', *Sydney Morning Herald*, 30 May 2012, www.smh.com.au/federal-politics/political-news/military-intervention-in-syria-an-option-carr-20120529-1zhgw.html

Flock, E. 'Syria revolution: a revolt brews against Bashar al-Assad's regime', *Washington Post*, 15 March 2011, www.washingtonpost.com/blogs/ blogpost/post/syria-revolution-revolt-against-bashar-al–assads-regime/ 2011/03/15/ABrwNEX_blog.html

Flynn, P. *Hansard*, 29 August 2013, www.publications.parliament.uk/pa/ cm201314/cmhansrd/cm130829/debtext/130829-0001.htm

Foster, P. 'Syria crisis: Obama entertaining Russian-led peace-for-weapons plan reflects weak domestic position', *The Telegraph*, 10 September 2013, www.telegraph.co.uk/news/worldnews/barackobama/10297820/ Syria-crisis-Obama-entertaining-Russian-led-peace-for-weapons-plan- reflects-weak-domestic-position.html

Foucault, M. *The Order of Things: An Archaeology of the Human Sciences* (London/New York: Routledge, 2001 [1966]).

Fox News, 'Graham: Islamic State will attack on US soil, Obama must stop terror group's rise', 10 August 2014, www.foxnews.com/politics/2014/ 08/10/graham-islamic-state-will-attack-on-us-soil-obama-must-stop- terror-groups-rise.html

'Obama's "whack-a-mole" warning on ISIS', 6 July 2015, www.foxnews .com/politics/2015/07/06/obama-concedes-isis-has-gone-global-but-vows- will-ultimately-prevail.html?refresh=true

Fox, L. *Hansard*, 29 August 2013, www.publications.parliament.uk/pa/ cm201314/cmhansrd/cm130829/debtext/130829-0001.htm

Friedman, T. 'Syria, Obama and Putin', *New York Times*, 30 September 2015, www.nytimes.com/2015/09/30/opinion/thomas-friedman-syria- obama-and-putin.html?_r=0

Fukuyama. F. *The End of History and the Last Man* (London: Penguin, 2012 [1992]).

Fuller, C. 'Assassin in chief' in Bentley, M. and Holland, J. (eds.), *The Obama Doctrine: A Legacy of Continuity in US Foreign Policy?* (Abing- don/New York: Routledge, 2016).

'The eagle comes home to roost: the historical origins of the CIA's lethal drone program', *Intelligence & National Security*, 30 (2014), 769–92.

Fulton, W., Holliday, J. and Wyer, S. 'Iranian strategy in Syria', Institute for the Study of War, May 2013, www.understandingwar.org/sites/default/ files/IranianStrategyinSyria-1MAY.pdf

Gallo, W. 'Trump embraces unpredictability as foreign policy strategy', *Voice of America*, 24 November 2016, www.voanews.com/usa/trump- embraces-unpredictability-foreign-policy-strategy

Gamble, A. 'The Anglo-American hegemony: from Greater Britain to the Anglosphere', PAIS Graduate Working Papers, University of Warwick, Number 05/06 (2006), 8, www2.warwick.ac.uk/fac/soc/pais/current students/phd/resources/crips/working_papers/2006/working_paper_5_gamble.pdf

Between Europe and America: The Future of British Politics (Houndmills: Palgrave Macmillan, 2003).

Gardner, B. 'Foley murder video "may have been staged"', *The Telegraph*, 25 August 2014, www.telegraph.co.uk/news/worldnews/middleeast/iraq/11054488/Foley-murder-video-may-have-been-staged.html

Gaskarth, J. 'Strategizing Britain's role in the world', *International Affairs*, 90 (2014), 559–81.

Gelpi, C., Feaver, P. and Reifler, J. *Paying the Human Costs of War: American Public Opinion and Military Casualties in Conflicts* (Princeton: Princeton University Press, 2009).

Gerges, F. A. 'The Obama approach to the Middle East: the end of America's moment?', *International Affairs*, 89 (2013), 299–323.

Gharib, A. 'McCain, Graham, Lieberman unveil resolution calling for U.S. help in arming Syria rebels', *Think Progress*, 18 March 2012, https://thinkprogress.org/mccain-graham-lieberman-unveil-resolution-calling-for-u-s-help-in-arming-syria-rebels-aded30960af2

Gilmour, I. 'Termagant', *London Review of Books*, 22 (2000), 12–13.

Gilsinan, K. 'How ISIS territory has changed since the U.S. bombing campaign began', *The Atlantic*, 11 September 2015, www.theatlantic.com/international/archive/2015/09/isis-territory-map-us-campaign/404776

Gleeson, K. 'Australia and the construction of the War on Terror', presented at the International Studies Association annual conference, San Francisco, 26–29 March 2008.

Australia's 'War on Terror' Discourse (Abingdon/New York: Routledge, 2014).

Goldberg, J. 'The Obama doctrine', *The Atlantic*, April 2016, www.theatlantic.com/magazine/archive/2016/04/the-obama-doctrine/471525

Goldman, E. and Berman, L. 'Engaging the world: first impressions of a Clinton foreign policy legacy' in Campbell, C. and Rockman, B. (eds.), *The Clinton Legacy* (New York: Chatham House, 2000).

Gordon, M. 'Consulate supported claim of Syria gas attack, report says', *New York Times*, 15 January 2013, www.nytimes.com/2013/01/16/world/middleeast/consulate-said-to-support-claim-of-syrian-gas-attack.html?_r=1

Gordon, M. and Myers, S. 'Obama calls Russia offer on Syria possible "breakthrough"', *New York Times*, 9 September 2013, www.nytimes.com/2013/09/10/world/middleeast/kerry-says-syria-should-hand-over-all-chemical-arms.html?pagewanted=all

Graham-Harrison, E. 'Kurds fear Isis use of chemical weapon in Kobani', *The Guardian*, 24 October 2014, www.theguardian.com/world/2014/oct/24/kurds-fear-isis-chemical-weapon-kobani

Gramsci, A. *Selections from the Prison Notebooks* (New York: International Publishers, 1971).

Grattan, M. 'Turnbull warns of increased threat of terrorism in the region after recent attacks', *The Conversation*, 24 November 2015, https://theconversation.com/turnbull-warns-of-increased-threat-of-terrorism-in-the-region-after-recent-attacks-51187

Gregory, D. *The Colonial Present: Afghanistan, Palestine, Iraq* (Malden, MA/Oxford/Carlton, Vic.: Blackwell Publishing, 2004).

Gutteridge, N. and Maddox, D. 'Voice of defiance: Hilary Benn's impassioned speech shames Corbyn and moves MPs to tears', *The Express*, 3 December 2015, www.express.co.uk/news/politics/623874/Hilary-Benn-makes-impassioned-speech-convincing-Labour-to-back-strikes

Haglund, D. G. 'Canada and the Anglosphere: in, out, or different?', *Options Politiques*, 1 February 2005, https://policyoptions.irpp.org/fr/magazines/canada-in-the-world/canada-and-the-anglosphere-in-out-or-indifferent

Hague, W. 'The future of British foreign policy', speech to the International Institute for Strategic Studies, 21 July 2009, www.conservatives.com/News/Speeches

Halliday, F. *Shocked and Awed: How the War on Terror and Jihad Have Changed the English Language* (London: I.B. Tauris, 2010).

Hamblin, J. 'What does sarin do to people?', *The Atlantic*, 6 May 2013, www.theatlantic.com/health/archive/2013/05/what-does-sarin-do-to-people/275577

Hannan, D. *How We Invented Freedom & Why It Matters* (London: Head of Zeus, 2013).

Hansen, L. *Security as Practice: Discourse Analysis and the Bosnian War* (Abingdon/New York: Routledge, 2006).

Harari, Y. *Sapiens: A Brief History of Humankind* (London: Random House, 2014).

Harding, L. 'Palmyra hosts Russian concert after recapture by Syrian forces', *The Guardian*, 5 May 2016, www.theguardian.com/world/2016/may/05/palmyra-amphitheatre-hosts-russian-concert-after-recapture-by-syrian-forces

Harries, O. 'Anglo-Saxon attitudes: the making of the modern world', *Foreign Affairs*, 87 (2008), 170–4.

'Punching above our weight?' Boyer Lectures, ABC Radio National, 21 December 2003, www.abc.net.au/rn/boyerlectures/stories/2003/987633.htm

Harris, P. 'George W. Bush's national security legacy is the ultimate sacred cow – that's why Donald Trump is going after it', *USApp–American Politics and Policy Blog*, 19 February 2016, https://blogs.lse.ac.uk/

usappblog/2016/02/19/george-w-bushs-national-security-legacy-is-the-ultimate-sacred-cow-thats-why-donald-trump-is-going-after-it

Hartcher, P. 'Spotlight is on Assad if Gaddafi falls', *Sydney Morning Herald*, 23 August 2011, www.smh.com.au/federal-politics/political-opinion/spotlight-is-on-assad-if-gaddafi-falls-20110822-1j6oj.html

Harvard-Belfer on Syria, Belfer Center, Harvard University, http://belfer center.ksg.harvard.edu/syria/infographics/syria_timeline.html

Hay, C. *Political Analysis: A Critical Introduction* (Houndmills: Palgrave Macmillan, 2002).

Heer, J. 'Operation Anglosphere: today's most ardent American imperialists weren't born in the USA', *Boston Globe Ideas*, 23 March 2003, www .jeetheer.com/politics/anglosphere.htm

Helm, T. 'No 10 launches bitter assault on Ed Miliband over Syria vote', 31 August 2013, www.theguardian.com/politics/2013/aug/31/syria-com mons-vote-cameron-miliband

Henderson, A. 'Syria crisis: Defence Minister says air strikes will continue despite botched operation', *ABC News*, 19 September 2016, www.abc .net.au/news/2016-09-19/syria-air-strikes-will-continue-despite-botched-operation/7858694

Hitchens, C. *Blood, Class and Empire: The Enduring Anglo-American Relationship* (London: Atlantic Books, 2004).

Hof, F. C. 'Obama drops rhetoric as Assad drops barrel bombs', *The Atlantic*, 27 April 2016, www.theatlantic.com/international/archive/2016/04/obama-syria-policy/480030

Holland, J. 'Blair's War on Terror: selling intervention to Middle England', *British Journal of Politics and International Relations*, 14 (2012), 74–95.

'By insisting Assad must go, the West has prolonged the Syrian conflict', *The Independent*, 14 April 2017, www.independent.co.uk/news/world/politics/by-insisting-assad-must-go-the-west-has-prolonged-the-syrian-conflict-a7681671.html

'Coalition foreign policy in the "War on Terror": a framework for analysing foreign policy as culturally embedded discourse', CRIPS Working Paper Series, University of Warwick, 10 October 2007, https://warwick .ac.uk/fac/soc/pais/currentstudents/phd/resources/crips/working_papers/2008/crips_paper_-_jack_holland_-_submitted1.pdf

'Constructing crises and articulating affect after 9/11' in Åhäll, L. and Gregory, T. (eds.), *Emotions, Politics and War* (Abingdon/New York: Routledge, 2015).

'Foreign policy and political possibility', *European Journal of International Relations*, 19 (2013), 48–67.

'Framing the War on Terror', doctoral thesis, University of Warwick (2010).

'From September 11th 2001 to 9-11: from void to crisis', *International Political Sociology*, 3 (2009), 275–92.

'Howard's "War on Terror": a conceivable, communicable and coercive foreign policy discourse', *Australian Journal of Political Science*, 45 (2010), 643–61.

'Obama as modern Jeffersonian' in Bentley, M. and Holland, J. (eds.), *The Obama Doctrine: A Legacy of Continuity in US Foreign Policy?* (Abingdon/New York: Routledge, 2016).

'Obama's War on Terror: why is change so hard?' in Bentley, M. and Holland, J. (eds.), *Obama's Foreign Policy: Ending the War on Terror* (Abingdon/New York: Routledge, 2014).

'Review of Shocked and Awed: How the War on Terror and Jihad Have Changed the English Language. London: I.B. Tauris, 2010', *Critical Studies on Terrorism*, 4 (2011), 293–5.

Selling the War on Terror: Foreign Policy Discourses after 9/11 (Abingdon/New York: Routledge, 2012).

Holland, J. and Aaronson, M. 'Dominance through coercion: rhetorical balancing and the tactics of justification in Afghanistan and Libya', *Intervention and Statebuilding*, 8 (2014), 1–20.

'Strategic rhetorical balancing and the tactics of justification in Afghanistan, Libya and Beyond', *Intervention and Statebuilding*, 10 (2016), 3–24.

Holland, J. and Bentley, M. 'Conceptualising change and continuity in US foreign policy' in Bentley, M. and Holland, J. (eds.), *Obama's Foreign Policy: Ending the War on Terror* (Abingdon/New York: Routledge, 2014).

Holland, J. and Jarvis, L. '"Night fell on a different world": experiencing, constructing and remembering 9/11', *Critical Studies on Terrorism*, 7 (2014), 184–204.

Holland, J. and McDonald, M. 'Australian identity, interventionism and the "War on Terror"' in Siniver, A. (ed.), *International Terrorism Post 9/11: Comparative Dynamics and Responses* (Abingdon/New York: Routledge, 2010).

Holland, J. and Solomon, T. 'Affect is what states make of it: articulating everyday experiences of 9/11', *Critical Studies on Security*, 2 (2014), 262–77.

Holland, J. and Wright, K. 'The double delegitimisation of Julia Gillard: gender, the media and Australian political culture', *Australian Journal of Politics and History*, 63 (2018), 588–602.

Holliday, J. 'The struggle for Syria in 2011: an operational And regional analysis', Institute for the Study of War, December 2011, www.under standingwar.org/sites/default/files/Struggle_For_Syria.pdf

Hope, C. 'American states turn against Syrian refugees after Paris attacks', *The Telegraph*, 17 November 2015, www.telegraph.co.uk/news/world news/northamerica/usa/11999130/American-states-turn-against-Syrian-refugees-after-Paris-attacks.html

Horwood, M. *Hansard*, 29 August 2013, www.publications.parliament.uk/pa/cm201314/cmhansrd/cm130829/debtext/130829-0001.htm

Howard, J. 'Address to 11 September ecumenical service', St. Christopher's Cathedral, Manuka, Canberra, 11 September 2002.

'Address to the National Press Club', 11 September 2002.

'Address to troops in Iraq', 25 April 2004.

'The Anglosphere and the advance of freedom', Heritage Lectures 1176, Heritage Foundation, speech given 28 September 2010, published 3 January 2011.

Hudson, J. and Fahim, K. 'Trump vows to "devastate" Turkish economy if U.S.-backed Kurds are attacked', *The Washington Post*, 14 January 2019, www.washingtonpost.com/world/national-security/trumps-vow-to-devastate-turkey-rattles-negotiations-over-syria-withdrawal/2019/01/14/1a61049c-17ff-11e9-88fe-f9f77a3bcb6c_story.html?noredirect=on&utm_term=.25bf889b91aa

Huntington, S. *The Clash of Civilizations: and the Remaking of World Order* (New York: Simon & Schuster, 1996).

Huntington, S. P. 'Dead souls: the denationalization of the American elite', *The National Interest*, 75 (2004), 5–18.

Hurd, I. *After Anarchy: Legitimacy and Power in the United Nations Security Council* (Princeton: Princeton University Press, 2007).

Hurst, D. 'Abbott confirms Australian military deploying to Iraq to help tackle Isis threat', *The Guardian*, 14 April 2015, www.theguardian.com/australia-news/2015/apr/14/abbott-confirms-australian-military-deploying-to-iraq-to-help-tackle-isis-threat

'Malcolm Turnbull says transition from Assad is the only option for Syria', *The Guardian*, 5 October 2015, www.theguardian.com/australia-news/2015/oct/05/malcolm-turnbull-says-transition-from-assad-is-the-only-option-for-syria

'Tony Abbott intensifies rhetoric about Isis, calling it an "apocalyptic death cult"', *The Guardian*, 30 September 2014, www.theguardian.com/world/2014/sep/30/tony-abbott-intensifies-rhetoric-about-isis-calling-it-an-apocalyptic-death-cult

Hutchison, E. *Affective Communities in World Politics* (Cambridge: Cambridge University Press, 2016).

Iggulden, T. 'Malcolm Turnbull warns against overstating threat of Islamic State, denies comments directed at PM', *ABC News*, 8 July 2015, www.abc.net.au/news/2015-07-07/turnball-warns-against-overstating-threat-of-islamic-state/6602638

Indyk, M. 'Obama's belated Syria hard line', *The Daily Beast*, 19 August 2011, www.thedailybeast.com/articles/2011/08/18/obama-s-belated-call-for-bashar-al-assad-ouster-pushes-syria-closer-to-freedom.html

Indyk, M. S., Lieberthal, K. G. and O'Hanlon, M. E. 'Scoring Obama's foreign policy: a progressive pragmatist tries to bend history', *Foreign Affairs*, 91 (2012), 29–43.

Jabour, B. 'Kevin Rudd denounces Tony Abbott's "John Wayne" views on Syria', *The Guardian*, 2 September 2013, www.theguardian.com/world/2013/sep/02/kevin-rudd-tony-abbott-syria-australia-baddies

Jackson, R. 'An analysis of EU counterterrorism discourse post-September 11', *Cambridge Review of International Affairs*, 20 (2007), 233–47.

Jackson, R. and Tsui, C. 'War on terror II: Obama and the adaptive evolution of US counterterrorism' in Bentley, M. and Holland, J. (eds.), *The Obama Doctrine: A Legacy of Continuity in US Foreign Policy?* (Abingdon/New York: Routledge, 2016).

Writing the War on Terrorism (Manchester: Manchester University Press, 2005).

James, C. 'Tales of torture, mutilation and rape as Isis targets key town of Kobani', *The Guardian*, 4 October 2014, www.theguardian.com/world/2014/oct/04/turkey-troops-isis-siege-kobani-refugees-rape-and-murder

James, W. 'Cameron says Russian military action in Syria a "terrible mistake"', *Reuters*, 4 October 2015, http://uk.reuters.com/article/uk-mideast-crisis-syria-britain-idUKKCN0RY08520151004

Jarvis, L. and Atakav, E. 'British (Muslim) values', PaCCS Blog, 2016, www.paccsresearch.org.uk/blog/british-muslim-values

Jarvis, L. and Holland, J. 'We (for)got him: remembering and forgetting in the narration of bin Laden's Death', *Millennium Journal of International Studies*, 42 (2014), 425–47.

Jenkins, J. 'What The Atlantic left out about ISIS according to their own expert', *Think Progress*, 20 February 2015, http://thinkprogress.org/world/2015/02/20/3625446/atlantic-left-isis-conversation-bernard-haykel

Jenkins, S. 'Why the west should listen to Putin on Syria', *The Guardian*, 29 September 2015, www.theguardian.com/commentisfree/2015/sep/29/west-vladmir-putin-syria-us-assad

Johns, R. and Davies, G. 'The impact of military and civilian casualties on British public support for war: an experimental study', presented at the International Studies Association Annual Conference, Montreal, Canada, 16 March 2011.

Johnson, H. 'U.S. Holocaust Museum: the Islamic State's war on Yazidis is genocide', *Foreign Policy*, 12 November 2015, http://foreignpolicy.com/2015/11/12/u-s-holocaust-museum-the-islamic-states-war-on-yazidis-is-genocide

Johnston, C. 'Peter Tatchell disrupts Jeremy Corbyn speech with Syria protest', *The Guardian*, 10 December 2016, www.theguardian.com/uk-news/2016/dec/10/peter-tatchell-disrupts-jeremy-corbyn-speech-with-syria-protest

Joshi, S. 'Russia is the big winner in Syria's flawed "truce"', *The Guardian*, 12 February 2016, www.theguardian.com/commentisfree/2016/feb/12/russia-big-winner-syria-flawed-truce-assad-europe-us

Jowell, T. *Hansard*, 29 August 2013, www.publications.parliament.uk/pa/cm201314/cmhansrd/cm130829/debtext/130829-0001.htm

Kaarbo, J. and Kenealy, D. 'Precedents, parliaments, and foreign policy: historical analogy in the House of Commons vote on Syria', *West European Politics*, 40 (2016), 62–79.

Kanat, K. B. *A Tale of Four Augusts: Obama's Syria Policy* (Ankara: SETA Publications, 2015).

Kaplan, R. 'Obama: U.S. can't "play whack-a-mole" with militant groups', *CBS*, 22 June 2014, www.cbsnews.com/news/obama-america-cant-play-whack-a-mole-with-militant-groups

Karouny, M. 'Life under Isis: for residents of Raqqa is this really a caliphate worse than death?' *The Independent*, 5 September 2014, www.independent.co.uk/news/world/middle-east/life-under-isis-for-residents-of-raqqa-is-this-really-a-caliphate-worse-than-death-9715799.html

Karp, P. 'Australia to change law to allow strikes on more Isis combatants', *The Guardian*, 1 September 2016, www.theguardian.com/australia-news/2016/sep/01/australia-to-change-law-to-allow-strikes-on-more-isis-combatants

'Malcolm Turnbull says Australia involved in mistaken bombing of Syrian troops', *The Guardian*, 19 September 2016, www.theguardian.com/australia-news/2016/sep/19/malcolm-turnbull-says-australia-bombed-syrian-troops-by-mistake

Keating, J. 'Obama counters Putin on Syria', *Slate*, 28 September 2015, www.slate.com/blogs/the_slatest/2015/09/28/obama_general_assembly_speech_president_says_assad_must_go_rejects_russia.html

Keating, P. 'Redfern speech (Year for the World's Indigenous People)', ANTaR, 10 December 1992, https://antar.org.au/sites/default/files/paul_keating_speech_transcript.pdf

Kenny, M. 'Malcolm Turnbull slaps down the military option in Syria, calls for compromise', *Sydney Morning Herald*, 19 November 2015, www.smh.com.au/federal-politics/political-news/malcolm-turnbull-calls-for-practical-deal-in-syria-despite-terrorists-20151118-gl1yme.html

'Malcolm Turnbull slams Russian "contradictions" while admitting Australian bombs in Syria', *Sydney Morning Herald*, 19 September 2016, www.smh.com.au/federal-politics/political-news/malcolm-turn bull-slams-russian-contradictions-while-admitting-australian-bombs-in-syria-20160918-grj532.html

Kerry, J. 'Remarks at the United Nations Security Council Meeting', 18 December 2015, www.state.gov/secretary/remarks/2015/12/250800.htm

'Remarks on the US Strategy in Syria', The White House, 12 November 2015, www.state.gov/secretary/remarks/2015/11/249454.htm

'Remarks with UK Foreign Secretary William Hague', at the Foreign and Commonwealth Office, London, 9 September 2013, US Department of State, www.state.gov/secretary/remarks/2013/09/213956.htm

Kessler, G. 'President Obama and the "red line" on Syria's chemical weapons', 6 September 2013, www.washingtonpost.com/news/fact-checker/wp/2013/09/06/president-obama-and-the-red-line-on-syrias-chemical-weapons

Kimmorley, S. 'US military praises Australia's efforts in Iraq and Syria, Turnbull calls on Europe to "step up"', *Business Insider*, 16 January 2016, www.businessinsider.com.au/us-military-praises-australias-efforts-in-iraq-and-syria-turnbull-calls-on-europe-to-step-up-2016-1

King, S. @stevekingia (12 March 2017). 'Wilders understands that culture and demographics are our destiny. We can't restore our civilization with somebody else's babies...', Twitter Page, 12 March 2017, https://twitter.com/SteveKingIA/status/840980755236999169

Kissane, D. 'Anglosphere united? Examining and explaining 20th century war time alliances in the English speaking world', Centre d'Etudes Franco-Americain de Management, 2010, http://ssrn.com/abstract=1688272

Kissinger, H. 'Syrian intervention risks upsetting global order', *Washington Post*, 1 June 2012, www.washingtonpost.com/opinions/syrian-interven tion-risks-upsetting-global-order/2012/06/01/gJQA9fGr7U_story.html

Korin, M. 'Putin's Syria gambit', *The Atlantic*, 28 September 2015, www.theatlantic.com/international/archive/2015/09/putin-russia-syria-united-nations/407716

Krebs, R. 'Narrative and the making of US national security', 28 October 2015, University College London, London.

Narrative and the Making of U.S. National Security (Cambridge: Cambridge University Press, 2015).

Krebs, R. and Jackson, P. 'Twisting tongues and twisting arms: the power of political rhetoric', *European Journal of International Relations*, 13 (2007), 35–66.

Krebs, R. and Lobasz, J. 'Fixing the meaning of 9/11: hegemony, coercion, and the road to war in Iraq', *Security Studies*, 16 (2007), 409–51.

Krebs, R. R. 'Author's response: International Politics Reviews symposium on Narrative and the Making of US National Security', *International Politics Reviews*, 4 (2016), 112–16.

Kumar, N. 'ISIS claims suicide bombing in Afghanistan that killed 35', *Time*, 18 April 2015, http://time.com/3827434/isis-suicide-bombing-afghanistan

LA Times, 'San Bernadino shooting updates', 9 December 2015, www .latimes.com/local/lanow/la-me-ln-san-bernardino-shooting-live-updates-htmlstory.html

LaCanna, X. 'NT political figure Matthew Gardiner breaks silence on Kurdish groups', *ABC News*, 28 April 2015, www.abc.net.au/news/2015-04-28/nt-political-figure-matthew-gardiner-breaks-silence/6428608

Landler, M. '"Gaps of trust" with Russia bar a Syrian truce, Obama says', *New York Times*, 5 September 2016, www.nytimes.com/2016/09/06/world/europe/g20-obama-syria.html?_r=0

Le Drian, Y. 'Britain, France needs you in this fight against ISIL', *The Guardian*, 26 November 2015, www.theguardian.com/commentisfree/2015/nov/26/britain-france-fight-isis

Lederman, J. 'War with Isis: US investigating chemical weapons attacks against Kurds in Iraq', *The Independent*, 15 August 2015, www .independent.co.uk/news/world/middle-east/war-with-isis-us-investigating-chemical-weapons-attacks-against-kurds-in-iraq-10456619.html

Legrand, T. 'Learning mandarins: elite policy transfer networks in the Anglosphere', paper presented at the IPSA World Congress, Montreal, July 2014. 'Transgovernmental policy networks in the Anglosphere', *Policy Administration*, 93 (2015), 973–91.

Library of Congress, 'Have you been to the polar bear's garden?', www.loc .gov/wiseguide/mar05/bear.html

Lieber, R. J. *Retreat and Its Consequences: American Foreign Policy and the Problem of World Order* (New York: Cambridge University Press, 2016)

Liptak, K. 'Obama: Russia heading for "quagmire" in Syria', *CNN*, 2 October 2015, http://edition.cnn.com/2015/10/02/politics/president-obama-syria-russia-assad

Lister, C. R. *The Syrian Jihad: Al-Qaeda, the Islamic State and the Evolution of an Insurgency* (New York: Oxford University Press, 2016).

Lloyd, J. 'The Anglosphere project', *The New Statesman*, 13 March 2000, www.newstatesman.com/node/193400

Lockyer, A. 'Australia's possible strategy shift on Syria is a nod to Russia's influence', *The Conversation*, 1 October 2015, http://theconversation .com/australias-possible-strategy-shift-on-syria-is-a-nod-to-russias-influ ence-48380

Lucas, A. 'Syrians make emotional return to Homs', *The Star*, 9 May 2014, www.thestar.com/news/world/2014/05/09/syrians_make_emotional_ return_to_homs.html

Lund, A. 'Assessing the Russian intervention in Syria', *Carnegie*, 7 December 2015, http://carnegieendowment.org/syriaincrisis/?fa=62207

'Say hello to the Islamic Front', *Carnegie*, 22 November 2013, http:// carnegieendowment.org/syriaincrisis/?fa=53679

'Syria's Kurds at the center of America's anti-jihadi strategy', Carnegie Center, 2 December 2015, http://carnegieendowment.org/syriaincrisis/? fa=62158

'Ten most important developments in Syria in 2015', *Syria Comment*, 3 January 2016, www.joshualandis.com/blog/ten-most-important-devel opments-syria-2015

'The non-state militant landscape in Syria', Combatting Terrorism Center, West Point, 27 August 2013, https://ctc.usma.edu/posts/the-non-state-militant-landscape-in-syria

Lynch, T. 'Presentation on Australia–US relations', BISA US Foreign Policy Working Group, annual conference, London School of Economics, September 2014.

Lyon, R. 'Editors' picks for 2016: "An introverted Anglosphere?"', *The Strategist*, Australian Strategic Policy Institute, 29 December 2016, www.aspistrategist.org.au/editors-picks-2016-introverted-anglosphere

Lyon, R. and Tow, W. 'The future of the Australian–US security relationship', paper presented at Strategic Studies Institute, December 2003, www.strategicstudiesinstitute.army.mil/pdffiles/00047.pdf

MacAskill, E. 'Obama hails death of Muammar Gaddafi as foreign policy success', *The Guardian*, 20 October 2011, www.theguardian.com/ world/2011/oct/20/obama-hails-death-gaddafi

MacFarquhar, N. 'Syrian rebels land deadly blow to Assad's inner circle', *New York Times*, 18 July 2012, www.nytimes.com/2012/07/19/world/middle east/suicide-attack-reported-in-damascus-as-more-generals-flee.html?_r=0

Maclean, R. 'Desecrated but still majestic: inside Palmyra after second Isis occupation', *The Guardian*, 9 March 2017, www.theguardian.com/ world/2017/mar/09/inside-palmyra-syria-after-second-isis-islamic-state-occupation

Maiden, S. 'Rudd still a thorn in Gillard's side', *The Advertiser*, 18 June 2011, www.adelaidenow.com.au/news/rudd-still-a-thorn-in-gillards-side/ story-e6frea6u-1226077790126

Maley, P. 'Assad "part of solution in Syria" – Julie Bishop signals policy change', *The Australian*, 25 September 2015, www.theaustralian.com .au/national-affairs/foreign-affairs/assad-part-of-solution-in-syria–julie-bishop-signals-policy-change/news-story/038662bcde096e87a74d1f83 cb9869e9

Malloy, A. 'Obama admits worst mistake of his presidency', *CNN Politics*, 11 April 2016, http://edition.cnn.com/2016/04/10/politics/obama-libya-biggest-mistake

Malsin, J. 'Russian airstrikes in Syria seem to be hurting civilians more than ISIS', *Time*, 30 November 2015, http://time.com/4129222/russia-air strikes-syria-civilian-casualties-isis

Manne, R. and Feik, C. (eds.), *The Words that Made Australia: How a Nation Came to Know Itself* (Collingwood, Vic.: Black Inc. Agenda, 2014).

Marsden, L. *For God's Sake: the Christian Right and US Foreign Policy* (London: Zed Books Ltd, 2013).

Marszal, A. 'Isil "broadcast video of pilot burning on giant public screen to young children"', *The Telegraph*, 4 February 2015, www.telegraph.co .uk/news/worldnews/islamic-state/11390609/Isil-broadcast-video-of-pilot-burning-on-giant-public-screen-to-young-children.html

'Jordanian pilot "burned alive" in new Isil video', *The Telegraph*, 3 February 2015, www.telegraph.co.uk/news/worldnews/islamic-state/11387756/Jor danian-pilot-burned-alive-in-new-Isil-video.html

Mathieu, X. and Holland, J. 'Liberal storytelling and its illiberal consequences in Syria', Working paper.

Mattern, J. 'Why "soft power" isn't so soft: representational force and the sociolinguistic construction of attraction in world politics', *Millennium Journal of International Studies*, 33 (2005), 583–612.

Mattern, J. B. *Ordering International Politics: Identity, Crisis, and Representational Force* (New York/Abingdon: Routledge, 2005).

McCain, J. 'It's time to use American airpower in Syria', *New Republic*, 5 March 2012, https://newrepublic.com/article/101405/mccain-speech-america-airpower-syria

McCrisken, T. 'Justifying sacrifice: Barack Obama and the selling of the war in Afghanistan', presented at the British International Studies Association annual conference of the US Foreign Policy Working Group, University of Leeds, 14 September 2010.

'Ten years on: Obama's war on terrorism in rhetoric and practice', *International Affairs*, 87 (2011), 781–801.

American Exceptionalism and the Legacy of Vietnam (Houndmills: Palgrave Macmillan, 2003).

McCurry, J. and Rawlinson, K. 'Paris terror attacks: world leaders condemn "the work of the devil"', *The Guardian*, 14 November 2015, www.theguardian.com/world/2015/nov/14/paris-terror-attacks-world-leaders-condemn-the-work-of-the-devil

McDonald, M. 'Australian foreign policy under the Abbott government: foreign policy as domestic politics?', *Australian Journal of International Affairs*, 69 (2015), 651–69.

McDonald, M. and Jackson, R. 'Selling war: the coalition of the willing and the "War on Terror"', paper presented at International Studies Association Conference, San Francisco, 26–29 March 2008.

McDonald, M. and Merefield M. 'How was Howard's war possible? Winning the war of position over Iraq', *Australian Journal of International Affairs*, 64 (2010), 186–204.

'"Lest we forget": the politics of memory and Australian military intervention', *International Political Sociology*, 4 (2010), 287–302.

McDonnell, J. *Hansard*, 29 August 2013, www.publications.parliament.uk/pa/cm201314/cmhansrd/cm130829/debtext/130829-0001.htm

McDonnell, P. 'Analysis: with Syria policy in tatters, Obama may relax stance on Assad', *LA Times*, 27 September 2015, www.latimes.com/world/middleeast/la-fg-analysis-syria-policy-assad-20150927-story.html

McGreal, C. 'John McCain says US should be "ashamed" of inaction over Syria conflict', *The Guardian*, 6 June 2012, www.theguardian.com/world/2012/jun/06/john-mccain-us-inaction-syria

McKeith, S. 'ISIS must be defeated in wake of Paris attacks: Abbott', 15 November 2015, www.huffingtonpost.com.au/2015/11/14/isis-must-be-defeated-in-wake-of-paris-attacks-abbott

McKelvey, T. 'Arming Syrian rebels: where the US went wrong', *BBC News*, 10 October 2015, www.bbc.co.uk/news/magazine-33997408

McManus, D. 'President Obama will go out with a war cry', *Los Angeles Times*, 27 September 2014, www.latimes.com/nation/la-oe-mcmanus-column-obama-foreign-policy-20140928-column.html

McNeil, S. 'Video of bloodied five-year-old in Aleppo shows children continue to pay price of Syria conflict', *ABC News*, 18 August 2016, www.abc.net.au/news/2016-08-18/children-continue-to-pay-price-of-syria-conflict/7761322

Mead, L. M. 'Why Anglos lead', *The National Interest*, 82 (2006), 1–8.

Mead, W. *Power, Terror, Peace, and War: America's Grand Strategy in a World at Risk* (New York/Toronto: Random House, 2005).

Mead, W. R. 'The Jacksonian revolt', *Foreign Affairs*, March/April 2017, www.foreignaffairs.com/articles/united-states/2017-01-20/jacksonian-revolt

God and Gold: Britain, America, and the Making of the Modern World (New York: Alfred Knopf, 2007).

Special Providence: American Foreign Policy and How It Changed the World (New York/London: Routledge, 2002).

'Review: The United States; The Anglosphere challenge: why the English-speaking nations will lead the way in the twenty-first century', *Foreign Affairs*, 84 (2005).

Medhora, S. 'Australian jets diverted from Syria as Russia's entry complicates mission', *The Guardian*, 7 October 2015, www.theguardian.com/australia-news/2015/oct/07/australian-airstrikes-in-syria-on-hold-as-russias-entry-complicates-mission

Miliband, E. *Hansard*, 29 August 2013, www.publications.parliament.uk/pa/cm201314/cmhansrd/cm130829/debtext/130829-0001.htm

Mintz, A. and Wayne, C. *The Polythink Syndrome: U.S. Foreign Policy Decisions on 9/11, Afghanistan, Iraq, Iran, Syria, and ISIS* (Stanford: Stanford University Press, 2016).

Miskimmon, A., O'Loughlin, B. and Roselle, L. *Strategic Narratives: Communication Power and the New World Order* (New York/Abingdon: Routledge, 2013).

Mitzen, J. 'Ontological security in world politics: state identity and the security dilemma', *European Journal of International Relations*, 12 (2006), 341–70.

Mueller, J. *War, Presidents and Public Opinion* (New York: Wiley, 1973).

Muir, J. 'Analysis' in 'Syria vows "decisive" response in Jisr al-Shughour', *BBC News*, 7 June 2011, www.bbc.co.uk/news/world-middle-east-13677200

Murphy, K. 'Apec summit: Malcolm Turnbull says Syria solution hinges on power sharing', *The Guardian*, 18 November 2015, www.theguardian.com/world/2015/nov/18/apec-summit-malcolm-turnbull-says-syria-solution-hinges-on-power-sharing

Nabers, D. 'Filling the void of meaning: identity construction in U.S. foreign policy after September 11, 2001', *Foreign Policy Analysis*, 5 (2009), 191–214.

Nalapat, M. D. 'India & the Anglosphere', *New Criterion*, 29 (2011).

Naylor, H. 'Islamic State has killed many Syrians, but Assad's forces have killed more', *Washington Post*, 5 September 2015, www.washingtonpost.com/world/islamic-state-has-killed-many-syrians-but-assads-forces-have-killed-even-more/2015/09/05/b8150d0c-4d85-11e5-80c2-106ea7fb80d4_story.html

New York Times, 'Trump's lies: the definitive list', *New York Times*, 23 June 2017, www.nytimes.com/interactive/2017/06/23/opinion/trumps-lies.html

Nichols, M. 'U.S. priority on Syria no longer focused on "getting Assad out": Haley', *Reuters*, 30 March 2017, www.reuters.com/article/us-mideast-crisis-syria-usa-haley-idUSKBN1712QL

Nietzsche, F. *Beyond Good and Evil* (New York: Vintage Books, 1966).

NPR [National Public Radio] staff and wires, 'Syria "Great Friday" protest turns bloody', 22 April 2011, www.npr.org/2011/04/22/135628118/syrian-forces-protesters-face-off-on-great-friday

Nye, J. S., Jr. *Soft Power: The Means to Success in World Politics* (New York: Public Affairs, 2005).

'Will the liberal order survive?' *Foreign Affairs*, January/February 2017, www.foreignaffairs.com/articles/2016-12-12/will-liberal-order-survive

O'Bagy, E. 'The Free Syrian Army', Institute for the Study of War, March 2013, www.understandingwar.org/sites/default/files/The-Free-Syrian-Army-24MAR.pdf

O'Hagan, J. *Conceptions of the West in International Relations Thought: From Oswald Spengler to Edward Said* (Basingstoke: Macmillan, 2002).

O'Loughlin, J. and Kolossov V. 'Russian geopolitical culture and public opinion: the masks of Proteus revisited', *Transactions of the Institute of British Geographers*, 30 (2005), 322–35.

O'Loughlin, J., Tuathail, G. Ó. and Kolossov V. 'A "risky westward turn"? Putin's 9–11 script and ordinary Russians', *Europe-Asia Studies*, 56 (2004), 3–34.

O'Malley, N. 'Obama will "not rule anything out" in Iraq, saying US can always count on Australia', *Sydney Morning Herald*, 13 June 2014, www.smh.com.au/world/obama-will-not-rule-anything-out-in-iraq-saying-us-can-always-count-on-australia-20140612-zs694.html

O'Sullivan, J. 'A British-led Anglosphere in world politics?' *The Telegraph*, 29 December 2007, www.telegraph.co.uk/comment/3645011/A-British-led-Anglosphere-in-world-politics.html

Obama, B. 'Address to the nation on the situation on Syria: September 10', CPD (2013), www.gpo.gov/fdsys/pkg/DCPD-201300615/pdf/DCPD-201300615.pdf

'President Obama makes a statement on the crisis in Iraq', The White House, 7 August 2014, www.whitehouse.gov/blog/2014/08/07/president-obama-makes-statement-iraq

'President Obama: "We will degrade and ultimately destroy ISIL"', The White House, 10 September 2014, www.whitehouse.gov/blog/2014/09/10/president-obama-we-will-degrade-and-ultimately-destroy-isil

'Press conference by President Obama', The White House, Kuala Lumpur, 22 November 2015, https://obamawhitehouse.archives.gov/the-press-office/2015/11/22/remarks-president-obama-press-conference

'Remarks by the President in address to the nation on Libya', The White House, 28 March 2011, www.whitehouse.gov/the-press-office/2011/03/28/remarks-president-address-nation-libya

'Remarks by the President on Libya', The White House, 19 March 2011, https://obamawhitehouse.archives.gov/the-press-office/2011/03/19/remarks-president-libya

'Remarks by the President on Osama bin Laden', The White House, 2 May 2011, www.whitehouse.gov/blog/2011/05/02/osama-bin-laden-dead

'Remarks by the President on the Middle East and North Africa', The White House, 19 May 2011, https://obamawhitehouse.archives.gov/the-press-office/2011/05/19/remarks-president-middle-east-and-north-africa

'Remarks by the President on the situation in Iraq', The White House, 19 June 2014, www.whitehouse.gov/the-press-office/2014/06/19/remarks-president-situation-iraq

'Remarks by the President to the White House press corps', James S. Brady Press Briefing Room, The White House, 20 August 2012, www.whitehouse.gov/the-press-office/2012/08/20/remarks-president-white-house-press-corps

'Remarks of President Barack Obama—as prepared for delivery—"A moment of opportunity"', State Department, 19 May 2011, https://obamawhitehouse.archives.gov/the-press-office/2011/05/19/remarks-president-barack-obama-prepared-delivery-moment-opportunity

'Remarks on the situation in Syria: August 31', CPD (2013), www.gpo.gov/fdsys/pkg/DCPD-201300596/pdf/DCPD-201300596.pdf

'Remarks prior to a meeting with President Toomas H. Ilves of Estonia, President Andris Berzins of Latvia, and President Dalia Grybauskaite of Lithuania and an exchange with reporters', CPD (2013), www.gpo.gov/fdsys/pkg/DCPD-201300583/pdf/DCPD-201300583.pdf

'Speech on Libya', *The New York Times*, 24 February 2011, www.nytimes.com/2011/02/24/us/politics/24obama-statement-libya.html?_r=0

'Statement by President Obama on the situation in Syria', The White House, 18 August 2011, https://obamawhitehouse.archives.gov/the-press-office/2011/08/18/statement-president-obama-situation-syria

'Statement by the President', State Dining Room, The White House, 7 August 2014, https://obamawhitehouse.archives.gov/the-press-office/2014/08/07/statement-president

'Statement by the President on Iraq', The White House, 9 August 2014, www.whitehouse.gov/the-press-office/2014/08/09/statement-president-iraq

'Statement by the President on ISIL', The White House, 10 September 2014, www.whitehouse.gov/the-press-office/2014/09/10/statement-president-isil-1

'Statement by the President on the violence in Syria', The White House, 31 July 2011, https://obamawhitehouse.archives.gov/the-press-office/2011/07/31/statement-president-violence-syria

'Statement by the President on Ukraine', The White House, 17 March 2014, https://obamawhitehouse.archives.gov/the-press-office/2014/03/17/statement-president-ukraine

'Statement from the President on the violence in Syria', The White House, 8 April 2011, https://obamawhitehouse.archives.gov/the-press-office/2011/04/08/statement-president-violence-syria

'The President's news conference in St. Petersburg, Russia: September 6', CPD (2013), www.gpo.gov/fdsys/pkg/DCPD-201300606/pdf/DCPD-201300606.pdf

'The President's news conference with Prime Minister John Fredrik Reinfedlt of Sweden in Stockholm, Sweden: September 4', CPD (2013), www.gpo.gov/fdsys/pkg/DCPD-201300599/pdf/DCPD-201300599.pdf

National Security Strategy of the United States (2010) (Darby, PA: DIANE Publishing, 2010).

Orwell, G. *Nineteen Eighty-Four* (London: Penguin, 2004 [1949]).

Politics and the English Language (London: Penguin, 2013 [1946]).

Owens, J. 'Agree to ceasefire or withdraw from Syria Julie Bishop tells US and Russia', *The Australian*, 26 September 2016, www.theaustralian.com.au/national-affairs/foreign-affairs/agree-to-ceasefire-or-withdraw-from-syria-julie-bishop-tells-us-and-russia/news-story/10822cc8a028ca4def5239262b8b005b

'Middle East must own Iraq, Syria violence: Bill Shorten', *The Australian*, 30 November 2015, www.theaustralian.com.au/national-affairs/middle-east-must-own-iraq-syria-violence-bill-shorten/news-story/c03f05d0827d2c7ddc33c7335b86c53f

'Response to terror threat must be calm, clinical: Turnbull', *The Australian*, 24 November 2015, www.theaustralian.com.au/national-affairs/response-to-terror-threat-must-be-calm-clinical-turnbull/news-story/c0d93da3ae920cbcb1fe5f6c0bae8bba

Oxford English Dictionary, 'Anglosphere', www.oxforddictionaries.com/definition/english/anglosphere (accessed 3 November 2019)

'Language', www.oxforddictionaries.com/definition/english/language (accessed 4 November 2019)

Pace, J. 'Obama, Cameron: we will "not be cowed" by Islamic State militants', *PBS*, 4 September 2014, www.pbs.org/newshour/rundown/obama-cameron-will-cowed-islamic-state-militants

Parmar, I. '"I'm proud of the British Empire": why Tony Blair backs George W. Bush', *The Political Quarterly*, 76 (2005), 218–31.

'Anglo-American elites in the interwar years: idealism and power in the intellectual roots of Chatham House and the Council on Foreign Relations', *International Relations*, 16 (2002), 53–75.

Paul, R. 'Ron Paul to warmongers: leave Syria alone!', *ronpaul.com*, 19 June 2012, www.youtube.com/watch?v=l8EWN3fKilw

Payne, S. 'Obama: U.S. misjudged the rise of the Islamic State, ability of Iraqi army', *Washington Post*, 28 September 2014, www.washingtonpost .com/world/national-security/obama-us-underestimated-the-rise-of-the-islamic-state-ability-of-iraqi-army/2014/09/28/9417ab26-4737-11e4-891d-713f052086a0_story.html?utm_term=.39389ec513b3

Pearlman, J. 'Tony Abbott ridiculed after describing Syrian conflict as "baddies versus baddies"', *The Telegraph*, 2 September 2013, www .telegraph.co.uk/news/worldnews/australiaandthepacific/australia/1027 9817/Tony-Abbott-ridiculed-after-describing-Syrian-conflict-as-baddies-versus-baddies.html

Pei, M. 'The paradoxes of American nationalism', *Foreign Policy*, 136 (2003), 31–7.

Phillips, C. 'Into the quagmire: Turkey's frustrated Syria policy', *Chatham House*, December 2012, www.chathamhouse.org/sites/files/chatham house/public/Research/Middle%20East/1212bp_phillips.pdf

Ponnuru, R. 'The empire of freedom: where the United States belongs: the Anglosphere', *National Review*, 55 (2003), 4–6.

Porter, L. 'Destruction of Middle East's heritage is "cultural genocide"', *The Telegraph*, 23 July 2015, www.telegraph.co.uk/travel/destinations/ middleeast/11756540/Destruction-of-Middle-Easts-heritage-is-cultural-genocide.html

Power, S. @AmbassadorPower (24 August 2015). 'Before today, the #UNSC had never had a meeting on #LGBT rights. This was long overdue—a small but important step that must not be our last', Twitter Page, https:// twitter.com/AmbassadorPower/status/635873001913851904?ref_src= twsrc%5Etfw

Price, R. 'A genealogy of the chemical weapons taboo', *International Organization*, 49 (1995), 73–103.

The Chemical Weapons Taboo (Ithaca: Cornell University Press, 1997).

'William Hague: action on Syria possible without support of Russia and China', *The Telegraph*, 5 July 2012, www.telegraph.co.uk/news/world news/9378241/William-Hague-action-on-Syria-possible-without-support-of-Russia-and-China.html

Quinn, A. 'Restraint and constraint: a cautious president in a time of limits' in Bentley, M. and Holland, J. (eds.), *The Obama Doctrine: A Legacy of Continuity in US Foreign Policy?* (Abingdon/New York: Routledge, 2016).

'The art of declining politely: Obama's prudent presidency and the waning of American power', *International Affairs*, 87 (2011), 803–24.

'US decline and systemic constraint' in Bentley, M. and Holland J. (eds.), *Obama's Foreign Policy: Ending the War on Terror* (Abingdon/New York: Routledge, 2013).

'U.S. calls Arab League Syria plan "best opportunity"', *Reuters*, 20 December 2011, www.reuters.com/article/us-syria-usa-idUSTRE7BJ28W201 11220

Ralph, J. and Souter, J. 'A special responsibility to protect: the UK, Australia and the rise of Islamic State', *International Affairs*, 91 (2015), 709–23.

Ralph, J., Holland, J. and Zhekova, K. 'Before the vote: UK policy discourse on Syria 2011–13', *Review of International Studies*, 43 (2017), 875–97.

Ralph, J. G. 'What should be done? Pragmatic constructivist ethics and the responsibility to protect', *International Organization*, 72 (2018), 173–203.

Rasmussen Reports, '49% want to declare war on ISIS', 23 November 2015, www.rasmussenreports.com/public_content/politics/current_events/israel_the_middle_east/49_want_to_declare_war_on_isis

Reus-Smit, C. 'International crises of legitimacy', *International Politics*, 44 (2007), 157–74.

Reuters, 'Obama: U.S. intelligence underestimated militants in Syria – CBS', 28 September 2014, www.reuters.com/article/us-mideast-crisis-syria-obama-idUSKCN0HN0QN20140928

Reuters in Ankara, '"Iraq on steroids": senator in Syria warning as Trump receives remains', *The Guardian*, 19 January 2019, www.theguardian.com/world/2019/jan/19/syria-lindsey-graham-iraq-on-steroids-trump?CMP=Share_iOSApp_Other

Revesz, R. 'Donald Trump: I will look Syrian kids in the face and say "go home"', *The Independent*, 9 February 2016, www.independent.co.uk/news/world/americas/us-elections/donald-trump-i-will-look-syrian-kids-in-the-face-and-say-go-home-a6863876.html

Rhodes, B. 'Press gaggle by Press Secretary Jay Carney and Deputy National Security Advisor for Strategic Communications Ben Rhodes', The White House, 15 November 2011, https://obamawhitehouse.archives.gov/the-press-office/2011/11/15/press-gaggle-press-secretary-jay-carney-and-deputy-national-security-adv

Riley-Smith, B. 'Cameron drops demand for Assad to go, as he targets Isil', *The Telegraph*, 26 September 2015, www.telegraph.co.uk/news/world news/middleeast/syria/11894052/Cameron-drops-demand-for-Assad-to-go-as-he-targets-Isil.html

Roe, P. 'Actor, audience(s) and emergency measures: securitization and the UK's decision to invade Iraq', *Security Dialogue*, 39 (2008), 615–33.

Rogerway, T. 'Meet the hell cannon, the Free Syrian Army's homemade howitzer', *Foxtrot Alpha*, 29 August 2014, http://foxtrotalpha.jalopnik

.com/meet-the-hell-cannon-the-free-syrian-armys-homemade-ho-16281 14916

Rogin, J. 'Exclusive: secret State Department cable: chemical weapons used in Syria', *Foreign Policy*, 15 January 2013, https://foreignpolicy.com/ 2013/01/15/exclusive-secret-state-department-cable-chemical-weapons-used-in-syria

Romero, D. 'ISIS timeline: a year under the so-called Islamic State', *The Independent*, 28 June 2015, www.independent.co.uk/news/world/ middle-east/isis-timeline-a-year-under-the-so-called-islamic-state-10342 197.html

Ross, A. 'Coming in from the cold: constructivism and emotions', *European Journal of International Relations*, 12 (2006), 197–222.

Rubin, A. J. 'Two senators say U.S. should arm Syrian rebels', *New York Times*, 19 February 2012, www.nytimes.com/2012/02/20/world/mid dleeast/mccain-and-graham-suggest-helping-syrian-rebels.html

Rudd, J. 'Keep the faith with the Arab spring', *The Australian*, 2 May 2011, www.theaustralian.com.au/national-affairs/opinion/keep-the-faith-with-the-arab-spring/story-e6frgd0x-1226059172816

Russia Today, 'Cameron vows "full spectrum" British response to ISIS Tunisia shooting', *Russia Today*, 29 June 2015, www.rt.com/uk/270331-cameron-response-tunisia-attack

'Obama rules out US military involvement in Ukraine', 19 March 2014, www.rt.com/news/ukraine-diplomacy-obama-russia-949

S. B. 'If this isn't a red line, what is?', *The Economist*, 21 August 2013, www.economist.com/blogs/pomegranate/2013/08/syria-s-war

Said, E. *Orientalism* (New York: Vintage, 1994 [1979]).

Saideman, S. M. 'The ambivalent coalition: doing the least one can do against the Islamic state', *Contemporary Security Policy*, 37 (2016), 289–305.

Salloum, R. 'From jail to jihad: former prisoners fight in Syrian insurgency', *Der Spiegel*, 10 October 2013, www.spiegel.de/international/world/ former-prisoners-fight-in-syrian-insurgency-a-927158.html

Sanchez, R. 'As it happened: Barack Obama speech on Syria', *The Telegraph*, 11 September 2013, www.telegraph.co.uk/news/worldnews/mid dleeast/syria/10288193/As-it-happened-Barack-Obama-speech-on-Syria .html

Sarvarian, A. 'Humanitarian intervention after Syria', *Legal Studies*, 36 (2016), 20–47.

Saul, J. 'Syria air strike: Twitter user Abdulkader Hariri live tweets US Islamic State attack "before Pentagon breaks news"', *The Independent*, 23 September 2014, www.independent.co.uk/news/world/middle-east/ twitter-user-live-tweets-attack-before-pentagon-breaks-news-9749973 .html

Save the Children, 'Invisible wounds', 2017, https://i.stci.uk/sites/default/files/Invisible%20Wounds%20March%202017.pdf

Schatz, B. 'ISIS beheaded an 82-year-old archaeologist who refused to reveal the location of ancient artifacts', *Mother Jones*, 19 August 2015, www.motherjones.com/politics/2015/08/isis-beheads-syrian-archaeologist-palmyra

Schimmelfennig, F. 'The community trap: liberal norms, rhetorical action, and the Eastern enlargement of the European Union', *International Organization*, 55 (2001), 47–80.

Shaheen, K. 'Isis destroys tetrapylon monument in Palmyra', *The Guardian*, 20 January 2017, www.theguardian.com/world/2017/jan/20/isis-destroys-tetrapylon-monument-palmyra-syria

'Syria war: "unthinkable atrocities" documented in report on Aleppo', *The Guardian*, 5 May 2015, www.theguardian.com/world/2015/may/05/syria-forces-war-crime-barrel-bombs-aleppo-amnesty-report

Shaheen, K. and Black, I. 'Beheaded Syrian scholar refused to lead Isis to hidden Palmyra antiquities', *The Guardian*, 19 August 2015, www.theguardian.com/world/2015/aug/18/isis-beheads-archaeologist-syria

Shanahan, D. 'Malcolm Turnbull warns of Russia-US proxy war in Syria', *The Australian*, 22 September 2016, www.theaustralian.com.au/national-affairs/foreign-affairs/malcolm-turnbull-warns-of-russiaus-proxy-war-in-syria/news-story/907fc9264751b65e8db2a69e7f7919fa

Sharma, S. 'What made Turkey change its Syria policy?', *Middle East Eye*, 1 October 2015, www.middleeasteye.net/news/what-made-turkey-change-its-syria-policy-519642437

Sharwood, A. 'Tony Abbott almost says Australia is at war with ISIS. Sort of', *ABC News*, 19 September 2014, www.news.com.au/national/tony-abbott-almost-says-australia-is-at-war-with-isis-sort-of/news-story/ff846451234537a86c25c069f64cd4dd

Shear, M. and Cumming-Bruce, N. 'Obama calls on Putin to help reduce violence in Syria after peace talks stall', *New York Times*, 18 April 2016, www.nytimes.com/2016/04/19/world/middleeast/syria-talks-stall-as-opposition-negotiators-withdraw.html

Sheets, C. 'ISIS–Sydney connection: Australian PM says Man Haron Monis identified with terrorist group', *International Business Times*, 15 December 2014, www.ibtimes.com/isis-sydney-connection-australian-pm-says-man-haron-monis-identified-terrorist-group-1758983

Sheller, S. 'Russia is in charge in Syria: how Moscow took control of the battlefield and the negotiating table', *War on the Rocks*, 28 June 2016, https://warontherocks.com/2016/06/russia-is-in-charge-in-syria-how-moscow-took-control-of-the-battlefield-and-negotiating-table

Sherlock, R. 'US enlists Britain's help to stop ship "carrying Russian attack helicopters" to Syria', *The Telegraph*, 16 June 2012, www.telegraph .co.uk/news/worldnews/middleeast/syria/9336170/US-enlists-Britains-help-to-stop-ship-carrying-Russian-attack-helicopters-to-Syria.html

Sherwell, P. 'Barack Obama denounces Islamic State as "cancer" that must be "extracted" from Middle East', *The Telegraph*, 20 August 2014, www.telegraph.co.uk/news/worldnews/barackobama/11047264/Barack-Obama-denounces-Islamic-State-as-cancer-that-must-be-extracted-from-Middle-East.html

Shinkman, P. 'Russia's cease-fire in Syria boxes out the U.S.', *US News*, 29 December 2016, www.usnews.com/news/world/articles/2016-12-29/vladimir-putins-cease-fire-in-syria-boxes-out-barack-obama

Siniver, A. and Lucas, S. 'The Islamic State lexical battleground: US foreign policy and the abstraction of threat', *International Affairs*, 92 (2016), 63–79.

Sinjab, L. 'Middle East unrest: silence broken in Syria', *BBC News*, 19 March 2011, www.bbc.co.uk/news/world-middle-east-12794882

Slaughter, A. 'How the world could – and maybe should – intervene in Syria', *The Atlantic*, 23 January 2012, www.theatlantic.com/international/arch ive/2012/01/how-the-world-could-and-maybe-should-intervene-in-syria/ 251776

'How to halt the butchery in Syria', *New York Times*, 23 February 2012, www.nytimes.com/2012/02/24/opinion/how-to-halt-the-butchery-in-syria.html

'Syrian intervention is justifiable, and just', *Washington Post*, 8 June 2012, www.washingtonpost.com/opinions/syrian-intervention-is-justifiable-and-just/2012/06/08/gJQARHGjOV_story.html

Solomon, E. 'Isis Inc: how oil fuels the jihadi terrorists', *Financial Times*, 14 October 2015, www.ft.com/cms/s/2/b8234932-719b-11e5-ad6d-f4ed76f0900a.html#axzz3uPxjJcxg

Solomon, T. '"I wasn't angry, because I couldn't believe it was happening": affect and discourse in responses to 9/11', *Review of International Studies*, 38 (2012), 907–28.

Spencer, R. 'Isil carried out massacres and mass sexual enslavement of Yazidis, UN confirms', *The Telegraph*, 14 October 2014, www.tele graph.co.uk/news/worldnews/islamic-state/11160906/Isil-carried-out-massacres-and-mass-sexual-enslavement-of-Yazidis-UN-confirms.html

'Islamic State begins beheading regime fighters in Palmyra', *The Telegraph*, 21 May 2015, www.telegraph.co.uk/news/worldnews/middleeast/syria/ 11621055/Islamic-State-begins-beheading-regime-fighters-in-Palmyra .html

'Massacred Syrian children were "bound before being shot"', *The Tele-graph*, 28 May 2012, www.telegraph.co.uk/news/worldnews/middleeast/syria/9295268/Massacred-Syrian-children-were-bound-before-being-shot.html

'William Hague accuses Russia and China as Syria heads toward "civil war"', *The Telegraph*, 5 February 2012, www.telegraph.co.uk/news/worldnews/middleeast/syria/9062794/William-Hague-accuses-Russia-and-China-as-Syria-heads-toward-civil-war.html

Squires, N. 'More than 2,500 refugees and migrants have died trying to cross the Mediterranean to Europe so far this year, UN reveals', *The Tele-graph*, 31 May 2016, www.telegraph.co.uk/news/2016/05/31/more-than-2500-refugees-and-migrants-have-died-trying-to-cross-t

Stacey, J. A. 'The Trump doctrine', *Foreign Affairs*, 14 November 2016, www.foreignaffairs.com/articles/middle-east/2016-11-14/trump-doctrine

Staff and wires, 'Australia set to abandon opposition to Assad as part of Syria settlement', *The Guardian*, 26 September 2015, www.theguardia.com/australia-news/2015/sep/26/australia-set-to-abandon-opposition-to-assad-as-part-of-syria-settlement

Starr, B., Yellin, J. and Carter, C. 'White House: Syria crosses "red line" with use of chemical weapons on its people', *CNN*, 14 June 2013, http://edition.cnn.com/2013/06/13/politics/syria-us-chemical-weapons

Steafel, E. 'Paris terror attack: everything we know on Saturday afternoon', *The Telegraph*, 21 November 2015, www.telegraph.co.uk/news/world news/europe/france/11995246/Paris-shooting-What-we-know-so-far.html

Stephenson, N. *The Diamond Age: Or, A Young Lady's Illustrated Primer* (New York: Random House, 1995).

Stevenson, B. 'UK air strike data shows scale of involvement in Iraq and Syria', *Flight Global*, 31 May 2016, www.flightglobal.com/news/art icles/uk-air-strike-data-shows-scale-of-involvement-in-ira-425822

Stone, J. 'David Cameron "shaming" Britain's reputation by rejecting Syrian refugee children, Yvette Cooper says', *The Independent*, 27 April 2016, www.independent.co.uk/news/uk/politics/syrian-refuges-child-david-cameron-yvette-cooper-pmqs-britain-shaming-reputation-video-alf-dubs-a7003251.html

'Increasing humanitarian aid to Syria will stop refugees travelling to Europe, David Cameron says', *The Independent*, 4 February 2016, www.independent.co.uk/news/uk/politics/increasing-humanitarian-aid-to-syria-will-stop-refugees-travelling-to-europe-david-cameron-says-a6 852941.html

'Jeremy Corbyn says there could be benefits to opening diplomatic back-channels with Isis', *The Independent*, 17 January 2016, www.inde

pendent.co.uk/news/uk/politics/jeremy-corbyn-says-there-could-be-bene
fits-to-opening-diplomatic-back-channels-with-isis-a6817181.html

Stoter, B. 'After mass rape by the Islamic State, Yazidi women still struggle to break the silence', *Al-Monitor*, 9 September 2015, www.al-monitor.com/pulse/originals/2015/09/yazidi-women-rape-slave-islamic-state.html

Straw, J. *Hansard*, 29 August 2013, www.publications.parliament.uk/pa/cm201314/cmhansrd/cm130829/debtext/130829-0001.htm

Strong, J. 'Interpreting the Syria vote: parliament and British foreign policy', *International Affairs*, 91 (2015), 1123–39.

'Why parliament now decides on war: tracing the growth of the parliamentary prerogative through Syria, Libya and Iraq', *British Journal of Politics and International Relations*, 17 (2015), 604–22.

Suchman, M. 'Managing legitimacy: strategic and institutional approaches', *Academy of Management Review*, 20 (2005), 571–610.

Sullivan, P. 'Sustaining the fight: a cross-sectional time series analysis of public support for ongoing military interventions', *Conflict Management and Peace Science*, 25 (2008), 112–35.

Swinford, S. 'David Cameron prepared to hold Syria vote as early as Christmas', *The Telegraph*, 17 November 2015, www.telegraph.co.uk/news/uknews/terrorism-in-the-uk/12001899/david-cameron-syria-air-strikes-vote-christmas.html

Tabler, A. J. and Ross, D. 'A Syria policy for Trump', *Foreign Affairs*, 28 November 2016, www.foreignaffairs.com/articles/syria/2016-11-28/syria-policy-trump

Taylor, A. and Noack, R. 'What the world thinks of Obama's plan to fight the Islamic State', *Washington Post*, 11 September 2014, www.washingtonpost.com/news/worldviews/wp/2014/09/11/what-the-world-thinks-of-obamas-plan-to-fight-the-islamic-state/?utm_term=.71e62d98dd3f

Taylor, L. 'Syria: Kevin Rudd backs "robust response" over chemical weapons', *The Guardian*, 29 August 2013, www.theguardian.com/world/2013/aug/29/syria-rudd-un-security-council-australian-election

Taylor, R. 'Australia to step up airstrikes on Islamic State', *Wall Street Journal*, 31 August 2016, www.wsj.com/articles/australia-to-step-up-air strikes-on-islamic-state-1472696172

Team Observers, 'Who is the Free Syrian Army?', *France 24*, 8 October 2012, http://observers.france24.com/en/20120810-syria-free-syrian-army-structure-funding-ideology-methods-fight-against-assad-regime

Tharoor, I. 'In the Syria chess game, did Putin outwit Obama?', *Washington Post*, 16 March 2016, www.washingtonpost.com/news/worldviews/wp/2016/03/16/in-the-syria-chessgame-did-putin-outwit-obama/?utm_term=.35831ca0192b

The Economist, 'The Assad family: where are they now?', 21 February 2013, www.economist.com/blogs/pomegranate/2013/02/assad-family

The Guardian, 'UN: Islamic State may have committed genocide against Yazidis in Iraq', 19 March 2015, www.theguardian.com/world/2015/mar/19/un-islamic-state-genocide-yazidis-iraq-human-rights-war-crimes

'The Guardian view on Syria policy: ISIS is the enemy but Assad is the problem', 5 December 2015, www.theguardian.com/commentisfree/2015/dec/09/the-guardian-view-on-syria-policy-isis-is-the-enemy-but-assad-is-the-problem

The Telegraph, 'UN has "failed" in duties to protect Syrian people, says William Hague', *The Telegraph*, 12 March 2012, www.telegraph.co.uk/news/worldnews/middleeast/syria/9138600/UN-has-failed-in-duties-to-protect-Syrian-people-says-William-Hague.html

'US Senator John McCain calls for air strikes on Syria', *The Telegraph*, 6 March 2012, www.telegraph.co.uk/news/worldnews/middleeast/syria/9125238/US-Senator-John-McCain-calls-for-air-strikes-on-Syria.html

'William Hague compares Syria to Bosnia in 1990s', *The Telegraph*, 10 June 2012, www.telegraph.co.uk/news/worldnews/middleeast/syria/9322600/William-Hague-compares-Syria-to-Bosnia-in-1990s.html

The Week, 'Syria gas attack: death toll at 1,400 worst since Halabja', *The Week*, 22 August 2013, www.theweek.co.uk/world-news/syria-uprising/54759/syria-gas-attack-death-toll-1400-worst-halabja

Tierney, D. 'Syria's 99 percent: the problem with focusing on chemical weapons', *The Atlantic*, 12 September 2013, www.theatlantic.com/international/archive/2013/09/syrias-99-percent-the-problem-with-focusing-on-chemical-weapons/279622

Toal, G. [Gearóid Ó. Tuathail] *Critical Geopolitics: The Politics of Writing Global Space* (Minneapolis: University of Minnesota Press, 1996).

Todd, C. 'The White House walk-and-talk that changed Obama's mind on Syria', *NBC News*, 31 August 2013, www.nbcnews.com/news/other/white-house-walk-talk-changed-obamas-mind-syria-f8C11051182

Toosi, N. 'Obama on Syria: "This is not a contest between me and Putin"', *Politico*, 16 February 2016, www.politico.com/story/2016/02/syria-russia-cease-fire-219328

Trump, D. 'Statement by President Trump on Syria', 7 April 2017, www.whitehouse.gov/the-press-office/2017/04/06/statement-president-trump-syria

'Statement by the president on Syria', 6 April 2017, www.whitehouse.gov/the-press-office/2017/04/06/statement-president-trump-syria

'Transcript: Donald Trump's Foreign Policy Speech', *The New York Times*, 27 April 2016, www.nytimes.com/2016/04/28/us/politics/transcript-trump-foreign-policy.html

Trump, T. 'Remarks by President Trump to the Press—Aboard Air Force One En Route West Palm Beach, Florida', 6 April 2017, www.white house.gov/the-press-office/2017/04/06/remarks-president-trump-press-aboard-air-force-one-en-route-west-palm

@realdonaldtrump (7 September 2013). 'President Obama, do not attack Syria. There is no upside and tremendous downside. Save your "powder" for another (and more important) day!', Twitter Page, https://twitter.com/realdonaldtrump/status/376334423069032448?lang=en

Turnbull, M. 'National security statement Parliament House, Canberra', 24 November 2015, www.malcolmturnbull.com.au/media/national-security-statement

Turner, C. 'David Cameron "knew British pilots were bombing Syria" – as it happened, July 17, 2015', *The Telegraph*, 17 July 2015, www.tele graph.co.uk/news/uknews/defence/11745689/British-pilots-in-air-strikes-against-Isil-in-Syria-live.html

Turner, J. 'Strategic differences: Al Qaeda's split with the Islamic State of Iraq and al-Sham', *Small Wars & Insurgencies*, 26 (2015), 208–25.

Uhlmann, C. '"Who are you fighting for?" Malcolm Turnbull, Vladimir Putin and the new geopolitical reality', *ABC News*, 7 September 2016, www.abc.net.au/news/2016-09-07/g20-malcolm-turnbull-vladimir-putin-syria-war-exchange/7822542

UNESCO, 'Site of Palmyra', http://whc.unesco.org/en/list/23

UNHCR, 'Syria regional refugee response', Inter-agency information sharing portal, http://data.unhcr.org/syrianrefugees/regional.php

UNICEF, 'Hitting rock bottom: how 2016 became the worst year for Syria's children', March 2017, http://news.bbc.co.uk/1/shared/bsp/hi/pdfs/13_03_17_unicef_report_syria.pdf

United Nations Mission to Investigate Allegations of the Use of Chemical Weapons in the Syrian Arab Republic, 'Final report', December 2013, https://unoda-web.s3.amazonaws.com/wp-content/uploads/2013/12/report.pdf

United Nations, 'In ISIL-controlled territory, 8 million civilians living in "state of fear" – UN expert', 31 July 2015, www.un.org/apps/news/story.asp?NewsID=51542#.VmwwM4SwEbA

UNSC, 'Security Council fails to adopt draft resolution condemning Syria's crackdown on anti-government protestors, owing to veto by Russian Federation, China', 4 October 2011, www.un.org/press/en/2011/sc10403.doc.htm

US Department of Defense, 'Operation Inherent Resolve', 26 September 2016, www.defense.gov/News/Special-Reports/0814_Inherent-Resolve

Vatanka, A. 'Iran and Assad in the age of Trump', *Foreign Affairs*, 29 November 2016, www.foreignaffairs.com/articles/syria/2016-11-29/iran-and-assad-age-trump

Vick, K. 'Chancellor of the free world', *Time*, December 2015, http://time.com/time-person-of-the-year-2015-angela-merkel

Vitali, A. 'Donald Trump praises Saddam Hussein's approach to terrorism – again', *NBC*, 6 July 2016, www.nbcnews.com/politics/2016-election/donald-trump-praises-saddam-hussein-s-approach-terrorism-again-n604411

Vucetic, S. 'A racialized peace? How Britain and the US made their relationship special', *Foreign Policy Analysis*, 7 (2011), 403–21.

'Bound to follow? The Anglosphere and US-led coalitions of the willing, 1950–2001', *European Journal of International Relations*, 17 (2011), 27–49.

'The logics of culture in the Anglosphere' in Batora, J. and Mokra, A. (eds.), *Culture and External Relations: Europe and Beyond* (Farnham: Ashgate, 2011).

'Why did Canada sit out of the Iraq war? One constructivist analysis', *Canadian Foreign Policy Journal*, 13 (2006), 133–53.

The Anglosphere: A Genealogy of a Racialized Identity in International Relations (Stanford: Stanford University Press, 2011).

Walker, S., Gambino, L., Black, I. and Shaheen, K. 'Obama says Russian strategy in Syria is "recipe for disaster"', *The Guardian*, 2 October 2015, www.theguardian.com/world/2015/oct/02/us-coalition-warns-russia-putin-extremism-syria-isis

Watt, N. 'David Cameron accuses Jeremy Corbyn of being "terrorist sympathiser"', *The Guardian*, 2 December 2015, www.theguardian.com/politics/2015/dec/01/cameron-accuses-corbyn-of-being-terrorist-sympathiser

Weaver, M. 'Syria debate: the linguistic battle over what to call Islamic State', *The Guardian*, 2 December 2015, www.theguardian.com/world/2015/dec/02/syria-debate-the-linguistic-battle-over-what-to-call-islamic-state

'Syria, Libya and Middle East unrest – Monday 9 May 2011', *The Guardian*, 9 May 2011, www.theguardian.com/world/middle-east-live/2011/may/09/syria-libya-middle-east-unrest-live

Weldes, J. 'Making state action possible: the United States and the discursive construction of "the Cuban problem", 1960–1994', *Millennium: Journal of International Studies*, 25 (1996), 361–98.

Weldes, J., Laffey, M., Gusterson, H. and Duvall, R. 'Introduction: Constructing insecurity' in Weldes, J., Laffey, M., Gusterson, H. and Duvall, R. (eds.), *Cultures of Insecurity: States, Communities, and the Production of Danger* (Minneapolis: University of Minnesota Press, 1993).

Wendt, A. 'Anarchy is what states make of it: the social construction of power politics', *International Organisation*, 46 (1992), 391–425.

Social Theory of International Politics (Cambridge: Cambridge University Press, 1999).

The Quantum Mind and Social Science (Cambridge: Cambridge University Press, 2016).

Wesley, M. and Warren, T. 'Wild colonial ploys: currents of thought in Australian foreign policy making', *Australian Journal of Political Science*, 35 (2000), 9–26.

Western, D. *Political Brain: The Role of Emotion in Deciding the Fate of the Nation* (New York: Public Affairs, 2008).

Western, J. 'The war over Iraq: selling war to the American public', *Security Studies*, 14 (2005), 106–39.

Selling Intervention and War: The Presidency, the Media, and the General Public (Baltimore: Johns Hopkins University Press, 2005).

Whitaker, B. 'Syria will change – with or without Assad', *The Guardian*, 9 May 2011, www.theguardian.com/commentisfree/2011/may/09/syria-assad-uprising

Whyte, L. 'Caliphate cubs of Isis: "The children with armpit hair were killed. I became a boy soldier"', *International Business Times*, 15 December 2015, www.ibtimes.co.uk/caliphate-cubs-isis-children-armpit-hair-were-killed-i-became-boy-soldier-1533264

Wibben, A. 'How stories matter: thoughts on contextuality, temporality, reflexivity & certainty', *Duck of Minerva*, 29 December 2015, http://duckofminerva.com/2015/12/how-stories-matter.html#more-28374

Wilkinson, M. 'Syria's "meltdown of humanity": emergency Commons debate as Aleppo civilians executed, children trapped under bombardment', *The Telegraph*, 13 December 2016, www.telegraph.co.uk/news/2016/12/13/syria-aleppo-mps-emergency-debate-live

Willingham, R. 'Focus on boats, not UN, Abbott tells PM', *Sydney Morning Herald*, 24 September 2012, www.smh.com.au/federal-politics/political-news/focus-on-boats-not-un-abbott-tells-pm-20120924-26gfg.html

Winter, A. 'Race, empire and the British-American "special relationship" in the Obama era' in Scott-Smith, G. (ed.), *Obama, US Politics, and Transatlantic Relations: Change or Continuity?* (Brussels: Peter Lang, 2012).

Wintour, P. 'Britain carries out first Syria airstrikes after MPs approve action against Isis', *The Guardian*, 3 December 2015, www.theguardian.com/world/2015/dec/02/syria-airstrikes-mps-approve-uk-action-against-isis-after-marathon-debate

'Sponsors of Syria talks in Astana strike deal to protect fragile ceasefire', *The Guardian*, 24 January 2017, www.theguardian.com/world/2017/jan/24/syria-talks-astana-russia-turkey-iran-ceasefire

Wintour, P. and MacAskil, E. 'Obama announces "core coalition" to confront Isis threat', *The Guardian*, 6 September 2014, www.theguardian .com/world/2014/sep/05/obama-core-coalition-10-countries-to-fight-isis

Withnall, A. 'Aylan Kurdi's story', *The Independent*, 22 September 2015, www.independent.co.uk/news/world/europe/aylan-kurdi-s-story-how-a-small-syrian-child-came-to-be-washed-up-on-a-beach-in-turkey-10484588.html

Wood, G. 'What ISIS really wants, *The Atlantic*, March 2015, www.theatlantic .com/magazine/archive/2015/03/what-isis-really-wants/384980

Wood, P. 'Islamic State: Yazidi women tell of sex-slavery trauma', *BBC News*, 22 December 2014, www.bbc.co.uk/news/world-middle-east-30573385

Wright, T. 'Last Australian soldiers leave Iraq, ending 11-year campaign', *Sydney Morning Herald*, 26 November 2013, www.smh.com.au/fed eral-politics/political-news/last-australian-soldiers-leave-iraq-ending-11 year-campaign-20131126-2y7bz.html

Zammit, A. 'Australian foreign fighters: risks and responses', Lowy Institute, 16 April 2015, www.lowyinstitute.org/publications/australian-foreign-fighters-risks-and-responses

Zelin, A. 'Al-Qaeda in Syria: a closer look at ISIS, Washington Institute, 10 September 2013, www.washingtoninstitute.org/policy-analysis/view/ al-qaeda-in-syria-a-closer-look-at-isis-part-i

Index

285